GOVERNING THE GLOBAL ECONOMY

Governing the Global Economy explores the dynamic interaction between politics and economics, between states and markets, and between international and domestic politics. The contributors study how the governance of the global economy is shaped by interaction between international institutions, domestic politics, and multinational enterprises, from a wide range of theoretical perspectives and methods.

Presenting a fresh approach to the study of international political economy, this volume covers:

- the systemic characteristics of the liberal world order;
- the role of international institutions;
- domestic economic politics and policies;
- the strategies and behavior of multinational enterprises.

The volume also includes topical discussions of the challenges to the global economy from the recent financial crisis and analysis of economic politics, in particular the regions of Africa and Europe as well as the countries of Japan and South Korea.

With contributions from prominent scholars in political science, economics, and business studies, who have all contributed greatly to advancing the study of political economy over the last decade, *Governing the Global Economy* aims to bridge the gap between undergraduate textbooks and advanced theory. It is essential reading for all students and scholars of international political economy and globalization.

Dag Harald Claes is Professor at the Department of Political Science, University of Oslo, Norway.

Carl Henrik Knutsen is PhD fellow at the Department of Political Science, University of Oslo, Norway.

Routledge/Warwick Studies in Globalisation

Edited by Shaun Breslin and published in association with the Centre for the Study of Globalisation and Regionalisation, University of Warwick.

Editorial Board: Jason Sharman, Griffith University, Australia; Diane Stone, University of Warwick, UK; and Catherine E. Weaver, University of Texas at Austin.

What is globalisation and does it matter? How can we measure it? What are its policy implications? The Centre for the Study of Globalisation and Regionalisation at the University of Warwick is an international site for the study of key questions such as these in the theory and practice of globalisation and regionalisation. Its agenda is avowedly interdisciplinary. The work of the Centre will be showcased in this series.

This series comprises two strands:

Warwick Studies in Globalisation addresses the needs of students and teachers, and the titles will be published in hardback and paperback. Titles include:

Globalisation and the Asia-Pacific
Contested territories
Edited by Kris Olds, Peter Dicken, Philip F. Kelly, Lily Kong and Henry Wai-chung Yeung

Regulating the Global Information Society
Edited by Christopher Marsden

Banking on Knowledge
The genesis of the global development network
Edited by Diane Stone

Historical Materialism and Globalisation
Edited by Hazel Smith and Mark Rupert

Civil Society and Global Finance
Edited by Jan Aart Scholte with Albrecht Schnabel

Towards a Global Polity
Edited by Morten Ougaard and Richard Higgott

New Regionalisms in the Global Political Economy
Theories and cases
Edited by Shaun Breslin, Christopher W. Hughes, Nicola Phillips and Ben Rosamond

Development Issues in Global Governance
Public–private partnerships and market multilateralism
Benedicte Bull and Desmond McNeill

Globalizing Democracy
Political parties in emerging democracies
Edited by Peter Burnell

The Globalization of Political Violence
Globalization's shadow
Edited by Richard Devetak and Christopher W. Hughes

Regionalisation and Global Governance
The taming of globalisation?
Edited by Andrew F. Cooper, Christopher W. Hughes and Philippe De Lombaerde

Global Finance in Crisis
The politics of international regulatory change
Edited by Eric Helleiner, Stefano Pagliari and Hubert Zimmermann

Business and Global Governance
Edited by Morten Ougaard and Anna Leander

Governing the Global Economy
Politics, institutions and economic development
Edited by Dag Harald Claes and Carl Henrik Knutsen

Routledge/Warwick Studies in Globalisation is a forum for innovative new research intended for a high-level specialist readership, and the titles will be available in hardback only. Titles include:

1. Non-State Actors and Authority in the Global System
Edited by Richard Higgott, Geoffrey Underhill and Andreas Bieler

2. Globalisation and Enlargement of the European Union
Austrian and Swedish social forces in the struggle over membership
Andreas Bieler

CENTRE FOR THE
STUDY OF
GLOBALISATION AND
REGIONALISATION

GOVERNING THE GLOBAL ECONOMY

Politics, institutions, and economic development

Edited by Dag Harald Claes and Carl Henrik Knutsen

Routledge
Taylor & Francis Group

LONDON AND NEW YORK

First published 2011
by Routledge
2 Park Square, Milton Park, Abingdon, Oxon OX14 4RN

Simultaneously published in the USA and Canada
by Routledge
270 Madison Avenue, New York, NY 10016

Routledge is an imprint of the Taylor & Francis Group, an informa business

British Library Cataloguing in Publication Data
A catalogue record for this book is available from the British Library

Library of Congress Cataloging in Publication Data
Governing the global economy : politics, institutions, and economic development / edited by Dag Harald Claes and Carl Henrik Knutsen.
p. cm. -- (Routledge/Warwick studies in globalisation)
1. International economic relations. 2. Economic policy. 3. International agencies. I. Claes, Dag Harald. II. Knutsen, Carl Henrik.
HF1359.G688 2011
337--dc22
2010050823

ISBN: 978-0-415-66535-3 (hbk)
ISBN: 978-0-415-66536-0 (pbk)
ISBN: 978-0-203-81374-4 (ebk)

Typeset in Baskerville by Prepress Projects Ltd, Perth, UK

Printed and bound in Great Britain by
TJ International Ltd, Padstow, Cornwall

This book is dedicated to our good colleague, supportive mentor, and dear friend Helge Hveem on the event of his seventieth birthday.

CONTENTS

PART III
Corporate strategies in the globalized economy   245

FIGURES

TABLES

CONTRIBUTORS

Daniel C. Bach is Professorial Fellow at CNRS and Professor at Sciences Po, Bordeaux, France. He has published extensively on, for example, the political economy of Nigerian federalism; regionalism, regional institutions, and region-alization process.es in Africa; and the relations between France, the European Union, China, and Africa.

Christian Bellak is Associate Professor of Economics at the University of Economics and Business, Vienna, Austria. Research interests include international factor flows and economic policy. He is the author of several articles published in international scientific journals and of several book chapters.

Dag Harald Claes is Professor at the Department of Political Science, University of Oslo, Norway. His publications include studies of oil-producer cooperation, energy security, and European integration. At present he heads a work package on energy under the research program "Geopolitics in the High North."

Eric Helleiner is CIGI Chair in International Political Economy and Professor at the Department of Political Science, University of Waterloo, Canada. His most recent books are the co-edited volumes *Global Finance in Crisis* (2010) and *The Future of the Dollar* (2009).

Peter J. Katzenstein is the Walter S. Carpenter, Jr. Professor of International Studies at Cornell University, U.S.A. His research and teaching lie at the intersection of the fields of international relations and comparative politics, and address issues of political economy, security, and culture in world politics.

Robert O. Keohane is Professor of Public and International Affairs, Princeton University, U.S.A. He is the author of *After Hegemony: Cooperation and Discord in the World Political Economy* (1984) and co-author of *Designing Social Inquiry* (1994). He won the Johan Skytte Prize in Political Science in 2005.

Carl Henrik Knutsen is PhD Fellow at the Department of Political Science, University of Oslo, Norway. He has published articles in the *Journal of Development Studies*, *Electoral Studies*, *International Political Science Review*, *European Political Science Review*, and *Business and Politics*.

Karl Ove Moene is Professor in Economics at the University of Oslo, Norway, and leader of the research center ESOP, funded by the Research Council of Norway as a center of excellence. He has written on the political economy of welfare states, wage bargaining, governance, and society models in rich and poor countries.

Chung-in Moon is Professor of Political Science at Yonsei University, South Korea. His recent works include *Exploring China's Tomorrow* (2010 in Korean) and the *U.S. and Northeast Asia* (2008, co-edited with John Ikenberry).

Rajneesh Narula is Professor of International Business Regulation at the Henley Business School, University of Reading, UK. He has published extensively on internationalization of innovation, R&D alliances, and the role of multinational firms in industrial development.

Andreas Nölke is Professor of Political Science at Goethe University, Frankfurt. He is co-editor of *The Transnational Politics of Corporate Governance Regulation* (2007), and *Transnational Private Governance and Its Limits* (2008). He has published in journals such as *World Politics*, *Review of International Political Economy*, and *Journal of Common Market Studies*.

Morten Ougaard is Professor of International Political Economy at the Department of Business and Politics, Copenhagen Business School, Denmark, and Director of the BSc and MSc programs in International Business and Politics. He has published on, among other things, political globalization, corporate social responsibility, business and global governance, and the OECD.

T. J. Pempel is Professor of Political Science at the University of California, Berkeley, U.S.A. He has written extensively about Japan's political economy, Asian regionalism, and security in Northeast Asia. His latest book is *Crisis as Catalyst: Asia's Dynamic Political Economy*.

Rudra Sil is Associate Professor of Political Science at the University of Pennsylvania, U.S.A. His research interests encompass qualitative methodology, philosophy of social science, comparative labor politics, Russian/post-communist studies, and general theories of comparative politics and international relations.

Georg Sørensen is Professor of Political Science at the University of Aarhus, Denmark. His books include *Changes in Statehood: The Transformation of International Relations* (2001); *The Transformation of the State: Beyond the Myth of Retreat* (2004); and *Liberal Dilemma: The Making and Unmaking of Liberal World Order* (forthcoming).

Arild Underdal is Professor at the Department of Political Science, University of Oslo, Norway. He has published extensively on international cooperation and international institutions with empirical focus primarily on environmental governance. He has made significant theoretical and methodological contributions to the study of international regimes.

Geoffrey R. D. Underhill is Professor of International Governance at the Amsterdam Institute for Social Science Research, University of Amsterdam, the Netherlands. He has published widely on the governance of international trade, international financial governance, and theories of political economy. His latest book, edited together with Jasper Blom and Daniel Mügge, is titled *Global Financial Integration Thirty Years On: From Reform to Crisis*.

Rob Van Tulder is Professor of International Business-Society Management at the Rotterdam School of Management/Erasmus University Rotterdam, the Netherlands. He has published on, for example, European business, high-tech industries, CSR, and network strategies. His latest books include *Corporate Responsibilities in Turbulent Times* (2010), *Skill Sheets* (2007) and *International Business-Society Management* (2006).

Dae-yeob Yoon is a Doctoral Candidate at the Department of Political Science, Yonsei University, South Korea, and a visiting fellow at the Center for Korean Studies, Keio University, Tokyo, Japan. He is currently writing a doctoral thesis on the political economy of the economic crisis in Northeast Asia.

PREFACE

This book is dedicated to Professor Helge Hveem on his seventieth birthday. We can think of no one more deserving of a celebration like this than Helge. Academics tend to gain friends and enemies during their careers. Some gain neither and some end up with nothing but enemies. Helge has made the rare achievement of gaining only friends along the way – and a great collection of friends indeed. When we invited Helge's friends, an impressive list of scholars responded to our invitation and agreed to take part in this festschrift. These scholars, coming from various disciplines such as political science, economics, and business studies, have made great contributions to the study of political economy. We hereby extend our warmest thanks to all the contributors. Not only have they produced magnificent chapters for this volume, but they have also assisted us with generous support and advice throughout. It has been a true pleasure for us to work with all of them.

Helge Hveem graduated from the University of Oslo in 1968. He was then a Research Fellow at the International Peace Research Institute in Oslo (PRIO) from 1968 to 1979. In 1980 he was senior research adviser in the UNCTAD Secretariat, Geneva, and from 1981 he was employed at the Department of Political Science, University of Oslo. From 2002 to 2006, Helge was Director of the Centre on Technology, Innovation and Culture at the University of Oslo, before returning to the Department of Political Science. Helge has also held several prominent board and committee positions in Norwegian and international academia, and has had visiting research assignments at Makerere College, Kampala, Université des Sciences Sociales, Grenoble, London School of Economics and Political Science, Harvard University, European University Institute, and Sciences Po Bordeaux.

During Helge's period as a researcher at PRIO, his main field of study was the relations between rich and poor countries, in particular aspects related to international institutions such as UNCTAD and the negotiations regarding a new economic order. His study on Third World producer associations (Hveem 1977) is an impressive study that even today provides empirical insight regarding conditions for the establishment of cooperation among Third World countries. The study also precedes core theoretical perspectives in the field of international political economy (IPE) regarding state–market relations and the role of international economic institutions. Working on primary commodity industries, Helge recognized early the need to include an understanding of the behavior of multinational enterprises (MNEs). Three main components of Helge's academic universe were thus already established by the late 1970s: the role and working of international institutions, the interests and policies of Third World countries, and the behavior of MNEs. Later Helge extended the set of countries he studied. He has conducted a number of studies on the foreign economic relations of Norway, and lately taken an interest in Asian economies that today can hardly be described as Third World countries. As part of his perspective on the role of international institutions Helge has emphasized the importance of the regional level and regionalization processes (Hveem 2006). A fascinating aspect of Helge's writing is how he is able to find interesting parallels and discover dynamics between different sectors and topics. As mentioned above, he has studied primary commodities, but he has also written on the technology sector (Hveem 1982), the oil sector (Heradstveit and Hveem 2004), and lately the knowledge sector (Hveem and Iapadre 2011). In addition he has conducted general studies, covering the relationships between public policy and globalization (Hveem and Nordhaug 2002) and between globalization, governance, and economic development (Hveem 2002). He has also written a popular introduction to IPE (Hveem 1996), and later a similar book together with two of his former students (Claes et al. 2006).

As indicated above, Helge's perspective preceded how the nexus between international institutions, domestic politics, and MNEs became a cornerstone of the academic field of IPE. This book is organized accordingly: Following the introductory chapter, Chapter 2 contains a discussion of theoretical perspectives. The rest of the chapters in this book include a discussion of systemic characteristics of the liberal world order (Chapter 4), discussions on the role of international institutions (Chapters 3 and 5), and studies of the behavior of individual states (Chapters 12 and 13). A special emphasis is put on financial aspects, as they have been particularly important in the recent economic crisis (Chapters 6, 7, and 14). The book also discusses economic politics and policies more generally (Chapters 8–11), and finally it emphasizes the role of MNEs and their interaction with governments and international institutions (Chapters 15 and 16). Obviously, a single volume such as this cannot cover all important aspects of the complicated world of global political economy. On some topics we can provide only a superficial account, although such topics deserve a book in themselves. Regarding state behavior we can provide only sample case studies, although the internal and external economic behavior of ten or twenty countries (such as all the G20 members) could very well have been discussed in individual chapters. Nevertheless, we hope this book can be a valuable companion for all readers interested in one of the greatest challenges of our time: the governance of the global economy.

A special thanks to the series editors and staff at Routledge, in particular Hannah Shakespeare and Harriet Frammingham, and Deborah Bennett and Andrew R. Davidson at Prepress Projects for their very kind cooperation in producing this volume. We would also like to thank Richard Higgott for his generous help and advice in the early phase, and series editors Leonard Seabrooke and Shaun Breslin. We are very grateful to Nils Olve Gillund and Andreas Hvidsteen for excellent research assistance. Thanks also to Ingrid Hjertaker for valuable advice in the finishing stages of this process. We are also very thankful to UNCTAD for granting us permission to publish Chapter 11, which is a revised version of an article that has previously appeared in *Transnational Corporation*. Thanks also to the Norwegian Research Council for their generous support to a launching seminar for this book in May 2011. We have the pleasure of sharing with Helge the Department of Political Science at the University of Oslo as our workplace. The head of the Department, Øyvind Østerud, has provided important moral support and facilitated funding for this project.

Last, but definitely not least, we would like to thank Helge Hveem. Without his academic influence, his generous help and advice for us as students and later colleagues, and his vast network of friends, this book would never have been produced. This book can be considered a well-earned present for him on his seventieth birthday on May 17, 2011.

1

THE GLOBAL POLITICAL ECONOMY

International institutions, states, and multinational enterprises

Dag Harald Claes and Carl Henrik Knutsen

Introduction

Following the G20 meeting in Seoul in November 2010, the website www. CNNMoney.com posted a commentary with the following headline: "It's the global economy, stupid." Showing the parallel movement of the U.S. S&P 500 and the Chinese Hang Seng stock indexes, the conclusion was: "You need me. I need you." In the same internet posting a portfolio manager is quoted as saying:

> It all boils down to jobs whether you are in the U.S., Europe or China. One of our biggest concerns is politics . . . If the subpar recovery in the U.S. were to translate into protectionist policies, that would be bad news. Bad things happen in the long-term if you put up barriers to global trade.[1]

In 2008–9 the world experienced the worst financial and economic crisis since the great crash of 1929 and the depression of the 1930s. The recent crisis has demonstrated how more and more people are part of an integrated global economy and that the level of integration is deeper than ever before. It also illustrates the intrinsic link between economics and politics, nationally and internationally. Job creation, a key political aim for most governments, is dependent on the economic policies of other states and the behavior of non-state actors in global industries and in the financial sector. The worries of the portfolio manager show the other side of the coin: how private actors are influenced by political decisions.

In 2011 we can celebrate, or mourn, the fortieth anniversary of the breakdown of the Bretton Woods system. For the founding members of the Bretton Woods institutions these forty years have been less stable than the twenty-seven-year-long Bretton Woods period, but far more stable than the forty years preceding it. On the other hand, developed countries and several developing countries are far richer today than they were at the end of the Bretton Woods period, partly because of increased global trade and foreign investment since 1971. Nevertheless, over the last five years the global economy has experienced more turmoil than for decades. This has made politicians, columnists, and analysts reflect over the fundamental robustness of the current liberal economic system. In this book we provide an academic approach to present challenges of governing the global economy. Without prejudice, with no quick-fix solutions, without expressing political convictions, and without trying to benefit particular interest groups, we do what academics do: We provide our best judgments based on our accumulated empirical knowledge and guided by our various theoretical perspectives. Central to this book is our ambition to study "*governance* of the creation and distribution of wealth through linking (in different ways) the international systemic, the national state, and the sector societal levels" (Hveem 2009: 369).[2]

The title of this book, *Governing the Global Economy*, indicates our interest in the dynamic interaction between politics and economics, between states and markets. Economics can be defined as "how societies use scarce resources to produce valuable commodities and distribute them among different groups" (Samuelson 1988: 5). At least the latter part of this definition is strongly related to an old but still popular definition of politics as "who gets what, when, how" (Lasswell 1935). The topics discussed in this book are important to economists and political scientists alike. The differences between the two disciplines are of little relevance for the purposes of the studies conducted in this book. In general it is easy to side with Robert Gilpin (2001: 33) when he argues that "the differing analytical approaches and conclusions of the economists and the political scientists are actually complementary rather than contradictory."

In real life the connections between economics and politics are many. A couple of examples indicate how symbiotic the relationship actually is. For instance, markets presuppose political institutions. Imagine trade of land, bonds, or stocks if there were no state able to define and guarantee property rights. After the collapse of the Soviet Union the situation in Russia resembled this example, with detrimental consequences for the economy, the political system, and the welfare of the citizens. On the other hand, imagine a state without any income from its citizens. The taxation of citizens and firms is a defining characteristic of the modern state (e.g. Schumpeter 1954). From the Boston Tea Party we know the political implications of this in the phrase "no taxation without representation." There are exceptions to this particular type of economic connection between state and society. Some states are self-financed by ownership of and revenues from the extraction of natural resources. We call these states rentier states, a group of states in which democratization is particularly hard to achieve (see, for example, Boix 2003). Also at the international level politics and economics go hand in hand up through recent world history. In the following section we will briefly point out some recent major historical changes that constitute a background for the chapters in this book.

Historical changes in the international political economy

Economic interaction across national borders has existed for centuries. Particularly, international, and even intercontinental, trade has a long history (e.g. Greif 1993; Maddison 2007); but also foreign direct investment (FDI) has a history before the twentieth century (e.g. Lipson 1985; Wilkins 2001). Through the ebbs and flows of the history of economic interaction, politics has caused economic prosperity and disaster, as is illustrated, for example, in Chapters 8, 9, and 10 in this book. At the same time, economic changes have constrained and enabled political ambitions of state leaders, as is highlighted, for example, in Chapters 3 and 13. Norms, rules, and other regulatory mechanisms are vital preconditions for economic interactions. For example, the historical development of contract rights and property rights systems were important for trade, and related division of labor, as well as various types of investment (see, for example, North 1990). Ensuring a proper regulatory framework becomes harder when dealing with transnational economic interactions, as they extend beyond the jurisdictional borders of any one polity. Therefore, groups residing in different polities have sometimes interacted under an implicit framework consisting of norms and the disciplining of actors through repeated interaction and reputation building (see, for example, Greif 1993). At other times, powerful states have sought to unilaterally enforce the property and contract rights of their national firms abroad (see, for example, Lipson 1985).

The chapters of this book mostly focus on post-World War II (WWII) history; this goes for analyses at the systemic level (e.g. Chapter 4), of particular sectors (Chapter 16), and of the strategies of individual countries (Chapters 12 and 13).[3] Although powerful states had regulated international economic affairs for centuries, the institutional system set up after WWII became an important milestone in the history of the international economy. As noted by Underhill (2006: 103): "Although World War II is slowly sinking deeper into our past, it remains one of the most important punctuation marks in human history in terms of both economic and security matters."

Three related aspects of the post-WWII embedded liberal economic order are important for the overall perspective of this book: first, the creation of a set of international institutions, in particular the free trade regime known as GATT (General Agreement on Tariffs and Trade) and the monetary regime governed through the international monetary fund (IMF); second, how these institutions on the one hand constrained states' foreign economic policy and on the other hand affected state interventions in domestic economic affairs; and, third, how these institutions created an environment for the global operations of multinational enterprises (MNEs).

The post-WWII political order of the international economy was manifested through the establishment of international institutions, although not necessarily international organizations.[4] An important motivation for establishing these institutions was the lessons from the experiences of the Great Depression and World

War II. An important factor behind the Great Depression was the inability of Britain and the unwillingness of the United States to stabilize the world economy: "for the world economy to be stabilized, there has to be a stabilizer – one stabilizer" (Kindleberger 1986: 304; but see Keohane 1984). After WWII, the United States took on the role of leader.

Another lesson from the interwar period was that trade barriers and competing currency devaluations had been the main contributors to the economic disaster of the 1930s. This made it important to constrain the ability of states to use protectionist instruments. On the other hand, what had arguably been a successful experience were the active fiscal policies associated with the "New Deal." The government as a potential positive force in the economy was obviously essential to both of the key architects at Bretton Woods: Harry Dexter White and John Maynard Keynes. Keynes (1997), for example, forcefully argued that governments should be able to intervene in the domestic economy by public spending in order to avoid severe economic downturns. In addition a political demand for the development of welfare states emerged, in particular in Europe (Esping-Andersen 1990; see also, for example, Moene and Wallerstein 2003 and Chapter 9 on the politics of redistribution). However, there were tensions between the goal of achieving full (or almost full) employment at home and pursuing policies compatible with free, international trade. For example, high government spending could jeopardize the stability of the exchange rate, and changes to the exchange rate could impact on production and employment levels domestically and abroad among major trade partners. In this respect, the combined effect of the international free trade regime and the system of fixed, but adjustable, exchange rates under the supervision of IMF, and with the U.S. dollar as the de facto "reserve currency," was vital.[5] With increasing free trade under GATT and a stable exchange rate system under IMF, capital movement across borders had to be restricted in order to avoid the danger that capital movement would counteract the effect of government intervention.[6] The free trade regime of GATT and the fixed exchange rate system of Bretton Woods were thus combined with political leeway for domestic economic interventions. Inspired by Polanyi (1957), John Ruggie (1982: 393) later denoted this combination of international free trade and government's domestic monetary control as "embedded liberalism."

The Bretton Woods regime collapsed in 1971. The Marshall Plan, U.S. defense spending, and Americans buying large amounts of foreign goods increased the number of U.S. dollars in circulation. By the end of the 1960s the amount of dollars held outside the United States was eight times the amount of gold held by the Federal Reserve to back up the fixed exchange rate between dollar and gold. The need for dollars in order to create liquidity weakened the trust and confidence in the value of the dollar (Triffin 1960). The international monetary regulatory regime was never to return. From now on, the U.S. government treated U.S. monetary policy as a national affair. Furthermore, the amount of capital in global circulation had increased, and was now far beyond the control of individual governments.

A wave of deregulation of domestic and international capital markets followed in the late 1970s. A key feature of the Bretton Woods system was that capital movements were constrained. During the late 1970s and early 1980s a financial revolution took place. Innovations in electronic communication made it possible to transfer financial capital across the globe in a matter of seconds. At the same time, Keynes' perspective on regulation of international economic activities (see, for example, Best 2004) was surpassed by economic policy perspectives arguing for the benefits of free flow of capital, domestically as well as internationally (see, for example, Stiglitz 2006). This has been a double-edged sword:

> Removal of capital controls . . . resulted in increased integration of national capital markets and creation of a global financial system . . . [which] has greatly facilitated efficient use of the world's scarce capital resources . . . on the other hand, international capital flows have increased the instability of the international economy.
>
> (Gilpin 2001: 261)

Sørensen characterizes such instability as a "transnational bad" (Chapter 4), and in the post-Bretton Woods era several crises have rocked the global economy, for example the Asian Economic Crisis of 1997 (see, for example, Pempel 1999a). The recent financial crisis of 2008 again demonstrates the consequences of the instability of the present financial system. The challenges of global governance in the financial sector are discussed in Chapters 6 and 7.

Following from free trade and increased international communication, a potentially powerful set of actors gained importance on the international scene: the multinational enterprises, "with structures that take only casual account of the way in which sovereign states have drawn their national boundaries" (Vernon 1968: 114).

> MNEs have come to be regarded as the primary shaper of the contemporary global economy [due to their] ability to coordinate and control various processes and transactions within production networks, ability to take advantage of geographical differences in the distribution of factors of production, ability to switch and to re-switch resources and operations between locations.
>
> (Dicken 2003: 198)

Perhaps, especially from the 1980s, the MNEs gained importance in the global economy not only through their *direct* investment abroad, but also through their public relations strategies and strategies to affect international regulation.[7] MNEs' role in affecting the make-up of the TRIPS Agreement is one prominent example of the latter type of influence (see, for example, Hveem 2007a). Both financial and direct investments abroad have increased dramatically since 1980, and they have become more geographically dispersed, in terms of both origin and destination, in recent years. This book contains analysis of the strategies that MNEs employ to face the challenges of globalization, for example related to economic crisis (Chapter 14), the strategies of emerging MNEs outside the United States, Europe, and Japan in affecting international regulation (Chapter 15), and the investment and other foreign operations of MNEs in the oil sector (Chapter 16). However, other chapters in this book also point to important aspects related to MNE activities and national politics, for example the institutional characteristics of states that tend to attract foreign direct investment (FDI) (Chapter 10) and the strategies of governments that enhance FDI's economic benefits (Chapter 11).

The volume of global exports, measured in constant 2000 U.S. dollars, increased sixfold from 1975 to 2005 according to data from the World Development Indicators (WDI), and global exports as a percentage share of global gross domestic product (GDP) also increased from 13.6 in 1970 to 28.7 in 2007. However, the increase in FDI volume has been even more staggering than the increase in trade, at least since the early 1980s.[8] This is illustrated by Figure 1.1, which shows global outward FDI (flow) as a percentage share of global exports. This share was just above 2 percent in 1982, falling from around 5 percent in the 1970s, and peaked at just below 20 percent before the dot-com bubble burst in the early 2000s. FDI flows are more volatile than trade flows, and both greenfield investments and mergers and acquisitions (M&As) tend to react sharply to global business cycles. Thus, as seen from Figure 1.1, outward FDI flows as share of exports sank to the

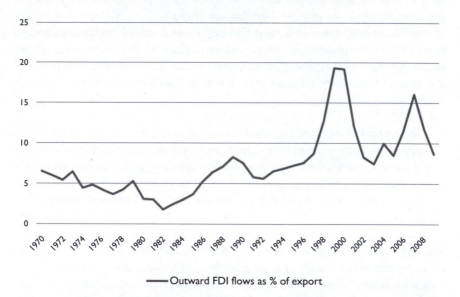

—Outward FDI flows as % of export

FIGURE 1.1 Global outward FDI flows as a percentage share of global exports. Source: Data are gathered from UNCTAD, Foreign Direct Investment Database, last accessed October 1, 2010. The data are now available at UNCTAD's UNCTADSTAT online database, http://unctadstat.unctad.org/ReportFolders/reportFolders.aspx (accessed January 25, 2011).

levels of the early and mid-1990s as a response to the recent financial crisis. Both the general growth over time and the volatility of FDI flows is also evident when considering global FDI flows as a percentage share of global GDP. This metric increased from around 0.5 in the mid-1980s to 3.8 in 2007, but fell to 1.9 in 2009, largely as a result of the financial crisis. In this year, the global FDI stock was 31 percent of global GDP.

Today private firms can operate globally on an unprecedented scale. Thus, economic integration may take place without the direct involvement of governments, although some types of government policies and institutional structures, from both the host country and the home country side, may more indirectly facilitate FDI (see, for example, Blonigen 2005; Knutsen et al. forthcoming). For the study of the international political economy this implies that the understanding of inter-*national* relations has to be supplemented by an understanding of inter-*firm* relations and the relationship between firms and governments (Stopford and Strange 1991). As an illustration of the latter aspect, at the G20 meeting in November 2010 the state leaders interacted with a business summit consisting of chief executives of 100 MNEs.[9]

Perspectives on the politics of economic relations

A possible starting point for developing the theoretical background of this book is the evolution of the academic field today known as international political economy (IPE). The field is defined not by method or theory but by its empirical theme: "it concerns the social, political and economic arrangements affecting the global system of production, exchange and distribution, and the mix of values reflected therein" (Strange 1988: 18). In this section we do not intend to give a full account of this field of study.[10] Rather, we will briefly show how the core topics of this book, the formation and role of international economic institutions, their relations to domestic politics and to MNEs, also have been focal points in the academic debates in IPE over the last forty years.

After WWII the dominating perspective in the field of international relations was realism (e.g. Morgenthau 1948). Realism emphasized security issues, had governments as the key actor, and made separate analysis of international and domestic politics. Presumably, realists were marked by the Cold War, with its highlight during the Cuban Missile Crisis in 1962, and thus found international relations as prone to conflict, not cooperation. At the end of the 1960s, some political scientists observing the changes described above started to question the validity of realism. They were inspired by Richard Cooper's study *The Economics of Interdependence* (1968) and Raymond Vernon's (1968, 1971) work on MNEs (Katzenstein et al. 1998: 655). This group of political scientists took an interest in economic relations and started to investigate the political consequences following from how non-state actors, such as the MNEs, related to each other across national borders, denoted by the phrase "transnational relations" (Keohane and Nye 1972). Keohane and Nye (1977) developed the concept of interdependence, signifying that also governments were exposed to "reciprocal costly effects" (Keohane 2002: 14). This was soon followed by a fresh view on international institutions in the study of so-called international regimes, defined by Keohane and Nye (1977: 19) as "governing arrangements that affect relationships of interdependence."[11]

A prominent challenge to this new perspective was the work of Robert Gilpin (1975, 1981): "Gilpin showed how realism's emphasis on power could provide both a political explanation of the emergence of liberal principles and practices in U.S. foreign economic policy and a parsimonious critique of liberal scholarship" (Katzenstein et al. 1998: 656). Following the observation of Kindleberger described above, the theory of hegemonic stability was developed in line with realism. The core hypothesis was that international economic cooperation presupposes the presence of a hegemonic power with the ability and willingness to maintain peace and economic stability, and that any international economic regime will mirror the interest of the most powerful state. Keohane (1984) suggested that the stabilizing role of the hegemonic power can be filled by international institutions, which may ease coordination and subsequent cooperation between the various stakeholders. Keohane (1984: 85) developed what he called "a functional theory of international regimes" by applying concepts from institutional economics such as transaction costs, uncertainty, and political market failure. With the work of Kenneth Waltz the classical realism of Morgenthau was developed into a more structural realism putting more emphasis on the consequences of the anarchic structure of the international state system (Waltz 1979; Mearsheimer 2001). The debate between neorealism and neoliberalism dominated the field of international relations for several years (see, for example, Baldwin 1993; Mearsheimer 1994).

This debate took attention from the dynamics of the relationship between international and domestic politics. This was soon corrected: "students of comparative politics focused their attention on the connections between domestic structures and international relations, which were bracketed by neoliberalism and realism" (Katzenstein et al. 1998: 667).[12] Katzenstein (1978) explored how varieties of the state–society relations of industrial states had implications for their foreign economic policies and thus for the international economic system as such. Gourevitch (1978) turned the table and studied how international factors affected domestic structures and interest groups. This opened a new field of study exploring the dynamics between the international system and various aspects of domestic economic policies (e.g. Katzenstein 1985; Rogowski 1989; Keohane and Milner 1996). Several studies following the innovative work of Peter Katzenstein contributed to mitigate the differences between international and comparative political economy:[13] Putnam (1988) showed that domestic institutional structures may have a strong impact on bargaining outcomes related to international agreements; Rogowski (1987) showed that there are important interlinkages between domestic institutional structures, such as the nature of the electoral system, and trade policies; Rodrik (1999) convincingly argued that democratic countries are better able to manage different types of economic shocks that emanate from an open world economy; whereas the Asian developmental regime literature (see, for example, Johnson 1982; Wade 1990; Evans 1995; Pempel 1999b), however, indicates that some types of authoritarian regimes may be better at conducting certain types of industrial policies that enhance exports and maybe even economic growth (see also, for example, Sørensen 1998; Mo and Moon 1998; Leftwich 2000). A discussion related to the latter point is found in Moon and Yoon's chapter on the South Korean experience in this volume.[14]

Above, we have provided some highlights from *former* theoretical debates. In Chapter 2, Katzenstein and Sil explore one important aspect of the *present* theoretical (and methodical) debates. In their chapter titled "Toward analytic eclecticism: the political economy of an integrated Europe," Katzenstein and Sil note that the IPE literature is characterized by different researchers applying the assumptions, methods, concepts, and analytic frameworks of distinct research traditions. To some extent, they argue, competition among research traditions generates progress within each tradition. However, Katzenstein and Sil argue that the sharp boundaries between research traditions also serve to prevent more inclusive dialogues and collaboration. Moreover, the sharp boundaries lead to a multitude of different concepts and arguments that seem incommensurable, despite the interconnectedness of empirical observations and substantive arguments found in different research traditions. Katzenstein and Sil argue that "analytic eclecticism" offers a practical means to explore such interconnectedness; analytic eclecticism is a "problem-driven approach," which includes extraction, adaptation, and integration of concepts, empirical observations, and theoretical interpretations from distinct research traditions. Katzenstein and Sil exemplify this approach by considering three pieces of research on the European political economy. More specifically they consider studies on the political strategies of European policy makers to strengthen EU institutions, the EU enlargement process, and European firms' responses to liberalization.

This very brief exposition of some highlights from the development of the academic study of IPE shows that international institutions, domestic politics, and MNEs, and the relationships between them, have been important for many scholars before us. In order to more fully understand the functioning of the global political economy, one should analyze both how various actors respond to supranational regulatory frameworks (and global economic developments), *and* how these same actors try to influence the regulatory frameworks. The global economy has become a highly complex system with linkages between trade and finance, between international and national politics and policies, between firms and states, and so on.

One book can hardly cover the politics of all aspects of this complex system. However, for organizational purposes we propose a model consisting of three components: (1) international institutions and the related economic environment, (2) the politics and policies of states and their related economic performance, and (3) the behavior of MNEs (including their FDI decisions). These three components

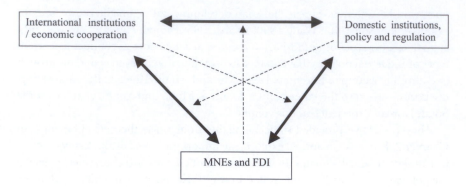

FIGURE 1.2 A simplified sketch of the types of relationships investigated in this book.

are highly interrelated, as the solid arrows in Figure 1.2 indicate; international institutions and economic cooperation, domestic institutions and policy, as well as the behavior of MNEs, may all mutually affect each other in various ways.

Several examples of such linkages are discussed in this volume. For instance, Keohane and Underdal (Chapter 3) argue that economic development in, for example, China and India will increase their power in the international system, thus enabling them to more easily affect international institutional structures according to their preferences. Sørensen (Chapter 4) argues that domestic groups in developed countries may influence their elected politicians to pursue protectionist policies, thereby undermining a liberal international economic order. Knutsen (Chapter 10) argues that the economic benefits of having democratic institutions have increased in the last thirty years compared with previously because of several international political and economic developments. Moon and Yoon (Chapter 13) argue that the industrial policies followed by South Korea have changed as a result of South Korea's place in the international political and economic system.

Moreover, the dotted arrows in Figure 1.2 indicate that there may be important interaction effects. For example, the international political-economic environment may mediate the effect of domestic institutional structures, such as democratic institutions, on FDI allocation (Busse 2004). One example of such interaction effects discussed in this volume is Nölke's (Chapter 15) argument that the nature of domestic institutions in non-triad home countries will affect their MNEs' behavior toward the setting up of international institutions. Another is Narula and Bellak's (Chapter 11) argument on how the changing global political economic environment affects the way domestic policies should be designed in order to attract and properly utilize FDI for development purposes.

Thus, the discussions and analyses in the chapters of this book contain various mixtures of the three components and relations between them. However, these three components are chosen as an organizing principle for Parts I–III. As indicated above, the three components also contain important topics of scholarly debate concerning the international political economy. Our intention for the rest of this introductory chapter is to briefly explore the three components and their interrelations by integrating empirical observations and scholarly perspectives.

International institutions and global economic governance

The first part of this book, titled "International Institutions and Global Economic Governance," deals with some important questions that are extensively discussed in the IPE literature. For example, how do international institutions affect the probability of achieving efficient solutions to global problems, and how do they affect the distribution of different goods? Which institutional and other factors are important for maintaining a stable, liberal world economic order? How do emerging powers affect the shape and functioning of international institutions and networks? These general questions underlie the analyses in Chapters 3, 4, and 5. Moreover, the section contains two chapters (Chapters 6 and 7) that analyze the global finance system. Both these chapters focus on the relatively recent and dramatic events of the global financial crisis.

There currently exists a plethora of bilateral, regional, and global regulatory frameworks that impact on international economic transactions (see, for example, Hveem and Iapadre 2011). Some of these frameworks enhance international transactions, some deter them, while others may not impact much on aggregate volumes but rather alter the composition of actors in such transactions. This book deals with such economic effects of global and regional regulatory frameworks, assessing how various actors, from firms to national governments, adapt to them, and also how such actors adapt to developments in the global economy.[15] However, this book also considers the endogeneity of such regulatory frameworks, for example by investigating how governments of powerful states seek to affect the governance of the global economy.

The high economic growth rates of some populous and relatively poor countries has led to a higher share of global production being located in the developing world today than was the case twenty or forty years ago. Regarding trade, the main bulk of global trade was conducted by Organisation for Economic Co-operation and Development (OECD) countries in 1970, and this was still the case in 2007. However, according to WDI data, the share of exports coming from high-income OECD countries dropped from about 0.7 to 0.6 during that time period. Particularly China has increased its share of global GDP. Moreover, China, partly because its production level has increased and partly because its economy has become more integrated in the global production system, has dramatically increased its share of global imports and particularly exports. Currently, China has surpassed Japan in terms of total exports, and may soon surpass the United States.

The changing geographical distribution of global production is illustrated in Figure 1.3, which in descending order presents the twenty largest economies in terms of total GDP (exchange rate adjusted) in 2008. The figure also shows these

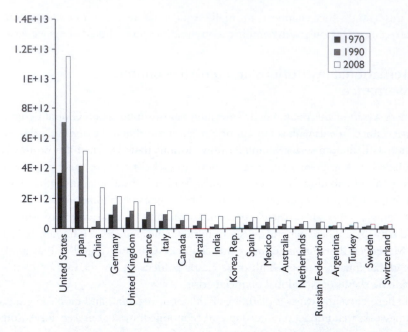

FIGURE 1.3 GDP in the world's twenty largest economies in 2008 (GDP measured in 2000 U.S. dollars). Source: World Development Indicators. Available at http://data.worldbank.org/data-catalog/world-development-indicators (accessed October 1, 2010).

countries' GDP in 1970 and 1990. The list would have included even more large developing countries if we had used purchasing power parity (PPP)-adjusted GDP, as price levels are lower in relatively poor countries. However, even the exchange rate-adjusted data show that China has become an economic giant, being the third largest economy in 2008. In 1970, China's total GDP was well below that of Switzerland, which was the twentieth largest economy in 2008. Should China continue its rapid growth, it may soon surpass Japan, which has experienced rather poor economic performance since the early 1990s. As Pempel reminds us in Chapter 12, Japan was one of the greatest global economic success stories from the end of WWII to 1990, but a

> classic asset bubble popped in Japan during the early 1990s and since then the country's once staggering growth has stagnated. Nothing more indicates that stagnation than the fact that its share of world GDP has now returned to roughly the same level as the country enjoyed thirty years ago.

Other populous countries have also increased their shares of global GDP: Brazil was the ninth largest economy in 2008 and India the tenth. Should these countries continue their recent high growth rates they will relatively soon surpass less populous OECD countries such as Canada and Italy in terms of total GDP. As Keohane and Underdal and Nölke note in their chapters, this may also impact on the development of global political institutions as their increased economic production yields more power resources that can be used to influence global regulation according to the preferences of these countries' governments.

In Chapter 3, Keohane and Underdal describe the post-WWII development of the global political economy, and some of the most vital institutional structures regulating it. In particular they describe how the United States and other Western countries created a set of multilateral institutions that governed the post-WWII global economy. They also generate some predictions, based on theoretical and historical insight, on how the global economy and institutional frameworks will develop over the coming decades, focusing on the likely important role of large developing countries such as China. Keohane and Underdal's main argument is that, although global institutions and networks regulate the common global economy, the shape of these structures is highly responsive to the preferences of actors with high relative power in the system. Relative power is to a large extent a function of asymmetrical interdependence:

> Asymmetrical interdependence – having others more dependent on oneself than vice versa – constitutes a crucial source of power, defined as the ability to pursue autonomous policies, on the one hand, and the ability to get others to do what one wants them to do, at feasible cost, on the other.

Keohane and Underdal evaluate various sources of asymmetric interdependence and argue that the previous hegemonic position of the United States is being eroded on many, but not all, accounts. This leads them to predict that the U.S. position of power, which also means the power to shape international institutions according to its preferences, is being challenged by some emerging actors. China is the most important, but also India will likely become an important player in affecting the rules that govern the global political economy. Keohane and Underdal also consider the role of non-governmental organizations (NGOs) in affecting global institutional structures, and how NGOs interact with states in this regard, and they discuss normative issues of leadership and legitimacy when it comes to shaping global institutions.

As discussed above, international trade and FDI volumes have been on the rise in recent decades. This is partly facilitated by the liberal world economic order, with the World Trade Organization (WTO) being one vital ingredient. However, history has taught us that international integration, and trade more specifically, may not develop in a monotonic fashion. Global trade, as a share of global GDP, was also very high in the period leading up to WWI (see, for example, Findlay and O'Rourke 2007), but trade volumes were reduced as a result of the war. Furthermore, the interwar period brought about increases in tariffs and other protectionist measures that reduced trade volumes. Thus, as economic historians like to point out, the history of transnational economic interactions, and related regulations and policies, is not one of ever-increasing integration. This point is appreciated in Chapter 4, in which Sørensen points to the many difficulties of maintaining a liberal economic order. Several international and domestic political factors may in the near future endanger the institutional framework that has allowed the recent expansion in world trade.

Sørensen focuses on various obstacles to maintaining a liberal global economy. Among such obstacles he discusses the interests of main state actors in the system when it comes to preserving or undermining a global economy with free markets and general property rights protection. As Sørensen acknowledges, the global economy, and thus the regulatory system that affects its functioning, affects the welfare of voters in liberal states. This means that economic issues are also often hotly contested political issues; voters and other groups that expect to lose out from a liberal global economy therefore have strong incentives to "modify the rules of the economic game in their favor." This fact puts states and governments that vocally support a liberal global economic order in a dilemma, as following these principles may lead to reduced political support from important groups. Sørensen further argues that the powerful, rich countries have in later decades professed and imposed liberal economic policies in developing countries, despite the likelihood that such policies may have negative economic consequences. He thus argues that the recent "Liberalism of Imposition" has resulted in "state–market matrixes" that have hurt rather than helped economic development in many countries. Sørensen also discusses some transnational bads of a liberal global economy, such as financial crises. All these factors lead him to predict that a liberal world economy will be difficult to maintain in the future.

The dynamics between "old" international institutions and emerging economies are further discussed by Ougaard in Chapter 5, using the OECD's relationship to five emerging economies as a case. In 2007 the OECD extended an invitation to Brazil, China, India, Indonesia, and South Africa to participate in a so-called Enhanced Engagement program. This initiative has been followed up and enlarged, proposing a structured and coherent partnership between the OECD and these five emerging economies. The Enhanced Engagement Strategy acknowledges the importance of the domestic economic policies in emerging economies for global economic interaction, interdependence, and integration. The overarching aim of the Enhanced Engagement Strategy is to integrate the emerging economies into the institutional structures of international economic relations that dominate among market economies, although as a long-term project. Through the Enhanced Engagement program, the non-members are invited to participate in OECD committees, are subject to regular economic surveys, are obliged to adhere to OECD instruments, and are supposed to integrate into the OECD statistical reporting and information systems. Ougaard conducts a detailed study of how this cooperation actually works and to what extent the non-members actively participate in OECD committees.

Arguably, international economic institutions are more vibrant today than they were in the 1930s. One very recent example of this is related to the international financial system. In order to reform the IMF to accommodate the emerging economies, the G20 meeting in Seoul in November 2010 gave emerging econo-mies stronger representation in the IMF, by changes in voting rights and board members. The recent financial crisis has spurred popular, political, and academic interest in questions related to the structure of the financial system, and the causes and consequences of financial crises. One important challenge is that the after-math of the financial crisis of 2008–9 may see countries resorting to financial instruments that are intended to accelerate domestic economic growth, although such policies may include measures that reduce exchange rates and thus appear as unfair competitive instruments against other countries. To some extent we are back to a parallel situation as described by Kindleberger's thesis regarding the situation in the interwar period: the United States is unable to stabilize the world economy, at least on its own; and China is unwilling to take on global leadership, at least so far. This book contains two analyses of various aspects of the global financial system, with a focus on the determinants and effects of the recent crisis.

Underhill's chapter, "Paved with good intentions: global financial integra-tion, the eurozone, and the hellish road to the fabled gold standard," first briefly describes the development of the global political economic system after WWII, and then focuses on the causes of, and especially the responses by various actors to, the recent crisis. Underhill draws four general lessons from the political-economic literature on the financial system and financial regulation. His main argument is that the crisis to a large extent is due to the specific nature of regulation, and lack of such, prior to the crisis, but that knowledge needed to avoid such a crisis was available. He further argues that it was rather the influence of specific private actors, in finance, with well-specified private interests, that led to the pre-crisis financial system's particular make-up, and thus the crisis itself. Underhill thereafter analyses and evaluates the responses to the various phases of the crisis, indicating that political actors constructed a quite proper political response in the first phase, rescuing various financial institutions on the brink of collapse, and thus avoiding the exacerbation of the crisis. However, Underhill argues that European govern-ments', Germany's in particular, and the EU's responses to the latter phase of the crisis, the sovereign debt phase involving among others the economic problems of Greece, were quite weak, and contributed to a worsening of the situation.

Helleiner's chapter, "Reining in the market: global governance and the regula-tion of OTC derivatives," focuses more specifically on the regulation of particular financial instruments, derivatives. Helleiner provides an introduction to the regu-latory instruments in this area, a narrative of the recent crisis, and the political responses and proposed and actual changes to the regulation after the crisis hit. Helleiner analyses both political responses in the United States and the EU, and the attempts to provide international regulation in the area. Helleiner asserts that:

> [b]efore the crisis, the OTC derivatives sector provided theorists of globali-zation with the one of the most extreme cases of powerful global markets largely outside of official regulation. For this reason, it has been tempting

to portray their rapid growth as evidence of a broader revolution in world politics involving the rise of unaccountable transnational private power. This interpretation no longer looks so convincing. Since the start of this crisis, states have started to cooperate to rein them in through public regulation in an internationally coordinated manner. Their actions suggest that power in global governance remains firmly in the hands of public authorities working through the state system.

Thus, Helleiner takes a stance against more structuralist views that consider private, financial interests to be dominant. Once regulation of derivatives gained the public's and politicians' eyes, political actors were indeed able to impose regulation in this important issue area.

Domestic institutions and policies in the globalized economy

The book's second part, titled "Domestic institutions and policies in the globalized economy," analyses how states and governments adapt to and act within the current global political economic framework. What strategies do governments employ, and how does the nature of these strategies interact with the global political economic environment to produce specific outcomes? Moreover, how do particular political institutional structures affect economic policies and outcomes in an integrated world economy? Such questions are central to the fields often referred to as comparative political economy and political economics (see, for example, Persson and Tabellini 2000), which have included contributions from several academic fields, notably political science and economics (see, for example, Dewan and Shepsle 2008a,b).

Domestic political events in large countries may more or less directly affect the international political-economic environment. For example, the collapse of the Soviet Union, largely a function of domestic political structures and economic policies and outcomes, had tremendous repercussions for the international political economic environment. Domestic political structures are also a function of broader international factors and trends. For example, the nature of colonial expansion and the institutions designed by colonial powers have a strong influence on the present domestic political institutions and economic outcomes in many countries around the world (see, for example, Acemoglu et al. 2001). Also, the EU, and more specifically the prospect of EU membership, has had an important effect on domestic political institutions and economic development in Central and Eastern Europe over the last two decades (see, for example, Chapters 2 and 11).

Political economic processes are often complex and hard to grasp. Ideal types, or prototypes, serve an important role for organization and specification of our knowledge of such processes, and may ease cross-country and intertemporal comparisons. Concepts such as "the developmental state" (see, for example, Evans

1995; Chapter 13 in this volume) have informed thinking and theorizing about the relations between political and economic processes and structures. In Chapter 8, Bach conducts a discussion of the Weberian-based concept of neopatrimonialism and how it has been used to analyze the linkages between African politics and economic factors. As Bach writes:

> Neopatrimonialism in Africa is still classically viewed as the outcome of a confusion between office and officeholder within a state endowed, at least formally, with modern institutions and bureaucratic procedures . . . Unlike patrimonialism, conceived by Weber as a traditional type of authority, neopatrimonialism combines the display of legal-bureaucratic norms and structures with relations of authority based on interpersonal rather than impersonal interactions.

One of the key variables of interest in this regard, Bach argues, is the degree to which a state has the capacity to produce public policies. Bach further argues for a nuanced approach to analyzing states, and state–society relations, under the heading of neopatrimonialism. Indeed, this is an ideal type, and different empirical cases exhibit weaker or stronger degrees of neopatrimonial characteristics of governance. Bach stresses that one should distinguish between political systems in which patrimonial practices tend to be regulated and cases in which the patrimonialization of the state has become all-encompassing, with a resulting loss of public space and public policy. The concept of neopatrimonial rule has been frequently invoked to understand African politics, and politics–development relations. However, the concept has recently also been used to study the politics of other regions, and Bach evaluates the strengths and limits of such analysis.

In Chapter 9 Moene asks whether "good policies are good politics." As Moene asserts, crucial issues for political actors are strategies related to how to become the incumbent and how to remain in position (how to be re-elected in democratic polities). Successful politics is thus about obtaining and maintaining power. Policies, on the other hand, are recipes for economic and social performance. Strongly related to the question of whether good policies are good politics is another: Is it rational for politicians, who want to obtain or maintain power, to pursue efficient economic policies or proper distributional policies? As Moene argues, the answer to this question is highly context dependent, and a range of factors affect whether politicians have incentives to pursue "good policies." Moene applies this framework to two different contexts. First, he analyses the political plausibility of targeted income transfers in well-established democracies. Although such transfers may be superior in reducing poverty levels, Moene argues that it is politically easier to implement more universal income redistribution schemes. Although universal redistribution schemes are not optimal for poverty reduction, they work quite well, and have other advantages. Thus, in this case political incentives may induce politicians to employ fairly good policies. This is not true for Moene's second example, that of politics in (neo)patrimonial systems, which is also extensively discussed in Bach's chapter. In such contexts, leaders have incentives to enact policies that are quite detrimental to economic performance.

The political incentives to conduct development-enhancing policies are thus dependent on contextual factors, importantly including the structure of political institutions in a country. Democratic institutions and rights, such as elections and political participation rights, are among these contextual factors that determine whether good policies are good politics (see, for example, North 1990; Bueno de Mesquita et al. 2003; Rodrik 2007a). However, the effect of democratic institutions on politicians' incentives to conduct good policies may itself be dependent on other factors, for example factors related to the structure of the international political economy.

In Chapter 10, Knutsen analyses whether the effect of democracy on economic growth has changed over the last decades. Knutsen presents various reasons why a potential positive effect of democracy on growth may have increased after the changes in international political and economic contexts that took place in the 1980s and 1990s. For example, Knutsen argues that the increase in global FDI after 1980 may have contributed to an extra advantage for democracies in terms of economic growth, as democracies attract more foreign capital than dictatorships. Moreover, the sectors that are predominant in a modern knowledge economy require a substantial amount of human capital and relatively free flows of ideas, which are two areas in which democracies generally outperform dictatorships. Knutsen's empirical analysis finds evidence for the hypothesis that the effect of democracy on growth increased after 1980, compared with the time period from 1820 to 1979. However, some of the empirical models also show that democracy had a positive effect on growth rates even before 1980.

Thus, "globalization" may have increased the economic benefits of having a democratic regime. Still, a key question is whether increased economic integration has coincided with, and maybe even contributed to, increasing global production and income. Indeed, PPP-adjusted real global GDP increased by a factor of 2.4 from 1980 to 2009, according to data from the WDI. The simultaneous growth of global trade, FDI, and GDP is likely to be due in part to other factors such as new production and organization technologies, and perhaps also an improved domestic institutional environment in many countries. Trade and FDI are likely also endogenous to GDP (see, for example, Rodrik 1999). Nevertheless, it is plausible that increased trade, and resulting international specialization and increased economies of scale, as well as allocation of capital to countries where it can be more effectively put to use, have contributed to increased global production and income.

A heated discussion has taken place on whether globalization benefits the already rich (individuals and countries) or the poor relatively more (see, for example, Bhagwati 2003 and Wade 2008 for two very different positions). When it comes to the economic growth of rich and poor countries, one important prediction from neoclassical economic growth theory is that of (conditional) convergence (see

Barro and Sala-i-Martin 2004). Starkly simplified, poor economies are expected to grow relatively fast compared with rich economies. This prediction has not found much empirical support when tested on global data samples. After WWII there has been convergence among OECD countries (Barro and Sala-i-Martin 2004), and some poor countries, such as Botswana, Mauritius, South Korea, and Taiwan, have over long periods of time grown much faster than already-rich European and North American countries. However, most poor countries, especially in the 1970s and 1980s, had quite low GDP growth rates. This is shown in Figure 1.4, which indicates divergence rather than convergence in income; countries with low initial GDP per capita grew slower on average from 1970 to 1990 than those with high initial GDP per capita. The x-axis measures the logarithm of GDP per capita at the beginning of the period, and initially rich countries are therefore placed to the right in the diagram. The y-axis measures the average GDP per capita growth rate during the period, and fast-growing countries are therefore placed to the top of the diagram. The upwards sloping line therefore indicates that there was a positive correlation between income in 1970 and average growth rate between 1970 and 1990.

Several different factors have been proposed to explain the lack of economic development in poor countries (see Adelman 2001 for an overview). International structural factors, geographic factors, cultural factors, and market failures in poor

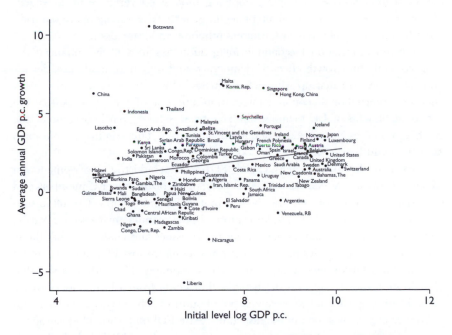

FIGURE 1.4 Economic divergence between 1970 and 1990. Log real GDP per capita in 1970 and average annual real GDP per capita growth rate from 1970 to 1990. Source: Knutsen (forthcoming), based on data from the World Development Indicators.

countries are among the proposed explanatory variables. One of the predominant explanations in political science and economics today is that the nature of domestic political and economic institutions starkly affects the prospects for economic development in poor countries. This type of explanation is exemplified by Bach's, Moene's, and Knutsen's chapters in this volume. As Moon and Yoon's chapter argues, particular economic policies may also have an important impact on development prospects.

Nevertheless, the last few years have witnessed extreme growth rates in some poor countries such as India and China, and in some medium-income countries such as Brazil. Might increased global economic integration affect the prospects for economic convergence? Indeed, the neoclassical economic growth framework predicts more rapid convergence in a world in which capital flows more freely (Barro and Sala-i-Martin 2004). Moreover, and perhaps more importantly, increased trade and FDI increases the prospects of rapid diffusion of ideas and technologies (e.g. Hveem and Iapadre 2011), which are vital to poor countries' economic growth prospects (e.g. Easterly 2001). Thus, one may expect that the general economic divergence identified in Figure 1.4 has been altered in more recent years, as the global economy has become more integrated. Indeed, this seems to be the case, as indicated in Figure 1.5; there was no general divergence in incomes taking place between 1995 and 2005.[16] If anything, the "best-fit" line is now slightly downward sloping, implying modest convergence on average.[17] However, there is still a large discrepancy in growth rates among poor countries: some become rich relatively fast, whereas others seem to stay poor.

Increased international economic integration has thus likely enhanced the positive economic growth effect of democracy and may have made it easier for poor countries to catch up with rich countries. However, there are other likely effects of international economic integration, and one of these may be that the economic benefits of EU membership have been reduced, partly because of the catching up by, especially, Asian developing countries. This argument is put forth by Narula and Bellak.

Narula and Bellak's chapter is called "FDI-assisted industrial development and EU enlargement." As Narula and Bellak note, many of the new EU members and candidate and accession countries believe that EU membership will result in substantially increased inward FDI, for example in the manufacturing sector. Narula and Bellak's chapter analyses the various policy issues and challenges that these, and some other, countries face regarding attracting inward FDI, and regarding utilizing this FDI for generating economic development. The authors argue that globalization has impacts on the benefits that come from EU membership for these, in a European context, relatively poor countries. The reason is that in a globalized economy, these countries must compete for FDI both with other European countries *and* with non-EU emerging economies. Narula and Bellak derive several policy recommendations from their analysis. For example, they argue that new EU members and accession countries should not base their industrial development

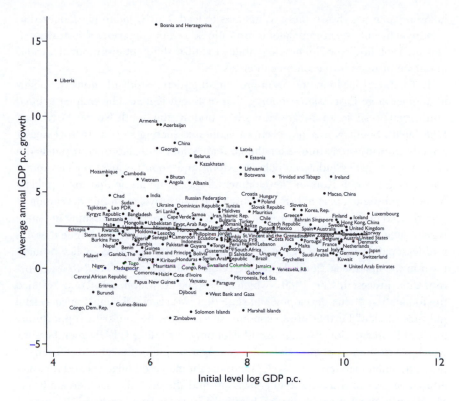

FIGURE 1.5 Slight convergence between 1995 and 2005. Log real GDP per capita in 1995 and average annual real GDP per capita growth rate from 1995 to 2005. Source: Knutsen (forthcoming), based on data from the World Development Indicators.

strategy on passive reliance on FDI flows without considering how to intentionally link the type of FDI they attract to their wider domestic industrial development.

Pempel's chapter, "Japan: dealing with global forces: multilateralism, regionalism, bilateralism," also considers the interesting and complex interactions between government strategies and international institutions, including those at the regional level. Pempel presents a thorough case study of one of the most important economies in the world. Coming out of WWII with a defeat by the United States and its former expansionistic policy scandalized, a de facto demilitarized Japan put all its effort into creating economic growth. The country achieved an exceptional growth rate, especially from 1970 to 1990. During the whole period from WWII, Japan has been active in bilateral, regional, and multilateral fora. The bilateral relationship with the United States has been infused by security connotations. Although Japan was eager to participate in multilateral cooperation after WWII, it did not take on a role as leader. However, in regional cooperation in Asia, Japan has shown more willingness to lead. Lately, Japan has emerged as a more active player in multilateral institutions. Pempel describes the strategy as "forum flexibility," a willingness and ability to utilize different institutional formats in pursuit of one's own economic interests.

In Chapter 13, Moon and Yoon present an in-depth study of industrial policy in another large East Asian economy, that of South Korea. The chapter is titled "Industrial policy in an integrated world economy: the South Korean paradox." Like Japan, South Korea has been an economic success story with spectacular growth rates in the decades after the Korean War. South Korea also pursued a vast range of active industrial policies. Moon and Yoon tie these policies to the nature of the South Korean "developmental state" and argue that these policies played a substantial part in bringing about the impressive economic development experienced in the country. However, South Korea is no longer pursuing the same type of activist industrial policies it once followed. Moon and Yoon argue that this is at least partly explained by the economic success that industrial policy brought forth in the first place. South Korea's economic success contributed to a democratization process in the 1980s, which according to Moon and Yoon "eroded the foundation of the developmental state that was crucial for making successful industrial policy." Furthermore, economic success gave the country an opportunity for further integration into the world economy, including OECD membership, which restricted the policy options of South Korean policy makers. Moreover, the newly attained high level of development meant increased bilateral and multilateral trade pressures for trade liberalization and the end of "neomercantilism." However, South Korean policy makers have in latter years pursued a range of other available policies that may be considered a kind of "new industrial policy." More specifically, science and technology policy has emerged as an alternative to the more traditional industrial policy followed in the past. To sum up, Moon and Yoon's chapter analyses crucial interactions between political factors, domestic and international, and economic factors, domestic and international, in the issue area of industrial policy.

Corporate strategies in the globalized economy

Important questions addressed in Part III of this book, "Corporate strategies in the globalized economy," are how and why do MNEs develop different strategies, for example related to corporate social responsibility (CSR) and public relations? What are the opportunities and constraints facing MNEs, and how do they adapt to and act within these opportunities and constraints? How do MNEs seek to influence these very same constraints in the longer run? Another important question related to MNEs is how they allocate FDI in the global economy.

The study of FDI in particular has exploded over the last few years. Theoretical and empirical contributions have come from various fields, such as business studies, economics, and political science. We will not review the literature on FDI here (see, for example, Blonigen 2005), but provide only a short discussion. However,

FDI is not the only type of international activity conducted by MNEs. For example, several firms *license* production to entities abroad (see, for example, Feenstra 2004), and several MNEs engage in *strategic alliances* and other forms of cooperation with foreign firms to reap various benefits, for example in the area of R&D (e.g. Dunning and Narula 2004; Hveem and Knutsen 2011). Moreover, intra-firm trade across borders makes up a very large share of total international trade for many countries (see, for example, Dunning and Lundan 2008; Chapter 14).

When it comes to investing abroad, MNEs' motives for conducting FDI may vary and include for example a desire to seek resources or market outlets. Dunning's (1980) famous OLI framework focuses on three factors that separately or in combination promote FDI: ownership advantages (O), location-specific advantages (L), and internalization advantages (I). Dunning's framework was set out to account for firms' FDI strategies, but Dunning expanded this perspective to the national level with the international development path theory (Dunning 1981a,b), later expanded by Narula (1993). This framework relates countries' net outward investment to their level of development (see Dunning and Narula 1996a).

Returning to the OLI framework, O includes assets specific to firms, such as superior technologies that make them more productive, and such O-factors are the reasons why foreign firms are able to successfully compete against local firms with better knowledge of the situation on the ground. Recent empirical studies indeed find that only the most productive firms invest abroad (see, for example, Helpman 2006). L-factors are various factors that make some locations more attractive as destinations for FDI than others. The literature, both theoretical and empirical, for a long time focused mainly on "economic" L-factors, such as a large home market, abundance of human capital or specific natural resources (see, for example, Blonigen 2005). However, a host of recent studies have focused on the L-factors stemming from particular host country institutional structures, for example related to rule of law, control of corruption, degree of democracy and human rights protection (see, for example, Knutsen et al. forthcoming). I-factors refer to factors that make direct investment a more profitable alternative for firms than other options for serving foreign markets, such as trade and licensing. I-factors are often factors that point to the benefits of exercising direct control over production abroad, and are often related to relatively high transaction and monitoring costs associated with trade and licensing (e.g. Coase 1937; Williamson 1985; Feenstra 2004; Helpman 2006).

As noted above, the decisions on whether to invest abroad or not, and on where to allocate FDI, are not the only important dimensions of firm behavior. For example, there is a growing interest in corporate social responsibility issues (e.g. Vogel 2006), and the CSR literature often focuses on the behavior of firms investing abroad. Even if corporate managers should be motivated by profit, an increased societal focus on CSR norms, for example fronted by NGOs, could induce behavior in accordance with such norms. One reason is that consumers may buy less goods and services from firms that are known to violate CSR norms.

Van Tulder with van der Zwart (2006) analyze the importance and functioning of this so-called "reputation mechanism." However, having previously pursued active CSR strategies may also have effects on other aspects of firm behavior, as van Tulder shows in his chapter.

Van Tulder's chapter, "Crisis . . . what crisis? (revisited): exploring multinational enterprises' responsiveness to the financial crisis," assesses how MNEs are dealing with two challenges of globalization. The first is globalization's (perceived or real) unfairness of economic outcomes. The second is the large economic crises presumably associated with globalization. Van Tulder draws on a sample of the world's 100 largest MNEs to illustrate how they publicly deal with these two challenges, and he classifies MNEs' strategies as either passive or active. The chapter first discusses how MNEs deal with CSR. Thereafter, van Tulder documents how MNEs have responded to the recent global financial crisis, and explores whether this response has been influenced by earlier positioning on internationalization and CSR issues. Van Tulder finds a "prevalence of relatively inactive and reactive approaches toward globalization and the financial crisis. The determinants of these approaches can be found in national regulation, sector origins, degrees of internationalization, and/or previously implemented CSR strategies." However, van Tulder also identifies several factors that enhance the likelihood of transnational companies taking a more active approach to the problems related to globalization, such as having had active CSR strategies previously, having a higher degree of internationalization, and originating from Europe.

As was discussed above, several large developing countries have rapidly increased their shares of global GDP. When it comes to FDI, the United States and European countries have dominated historically, both as sources and destinations of FDI. This is still the case, particularly for outward FDI. However, developing countries as a group have been catching up in the last ten years, at least in relative terms, as suppliers of FDI. Developing countries have, especially over the last decade, increased their share of *inward* FDI flows even more. This is exemplified by the volume of FDI inflows to China in 2009 almost equaling the volume going to the United States; the latter volume was however sharply reduced from previous years because of the financial crisis. Figure 1.6 shows the distribution of inward FDI to developed economies and to developing and transition economies. These two groups of countries received almost equal shares of global FDI flows in 2009, highlighting the point made in Chapter 11 that EU member countries nowadays compete to a larger extent with countries such as China and India for foreign capital.

We noted above that the United States and European countries still dominate as sources of FDI. However, several companies from developing economies have increased their FDI dramatically in recent years. This is described in Nölke's chapter, "Non-triad multinational enterprises and global economic institutions." Here, Nölke analyses the recent surge in MNEs coming from outside the United States, the EU, and Japan, so called non-triad countries. Nölke shows that the number of large, non-triad MNEs (NTMNEs), and the sizes of their investments, have

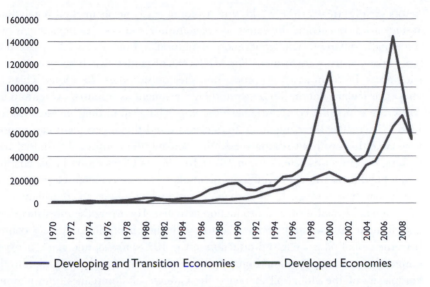

Developing and Transition Economies **Developed Economies**

FIGURE 1.6 Inward FDI flows in millions of U.S. dollars at current prices and current exchange rates. Source: Data are gathered from UNCTAD, Foreign Direct Investment Database, last accessed October 1, 2010. The data are now available at UNCTAD's UNCTADSTAT online database, http:// unctadstat.unctad.org/ReportFolders/reportFolders.aspx (accessed January 25, 2011).

increased dramatically since the early 1990s. Many of these NTMNEs come from India and particularly China. As Nölke shows, these corporations have to a large extent preferred brownfield investments through M&As, many of which have taken place in OECD countries. Nölke further analyses how NTMNEs may be expected to affect global business regulation, for example in the areas of financial regulation, corporate governance, labor standards, intellectual property rights, and competition policy. As Nölke acknowledges, there is yet limited empirical evidence on this issue, and there is seemingly "minimal participation of NTMNEs as transnational actors in global economic institutions." However, Nölke argues that we may obtain solid predictions by investigating the domestic political and economic institutions from which NTMNEs originate. Nölke's core argument, drawing on a "varieties of capitalism" framework (see Hall and Soskice 2001; Nölke and Taylor 2010: 162–70), is thus that domestic institutional structure will shape the interests and strategies that NTMNEs pursue regarding global business regulation. Moreover, Nölke shows how NTMNEs "operate in closer collaboration with national governments than triad MNEs. Correspondingly, they are more inclined to further their interests through governmental channels, rather than by transnational participation in global economic institutions."

One of the sources of MNEs' power, mentioned above, is their geographical flexibility, making them able to switch between investments and operations across various areas of the world, thus avoiding costly governmental regulations. In industries concerning the extraction of natural resources, this flexibility is fundamentally different. The exploration of natural resources can take place only where the resources are located. The MNEs can of course switch between various such areas, but cannot set up production sites outside these locations. This creates a particular relationship between the government as resource owner and the MNEs, in which the companies have the upper hand until their investments are made. Thereafter the companies are locked in and the government can impose new conditions without risking the MNEs' leaving the country. The initial bargaining becomes obsolete (Vernon 1971: 46–59). As Claes shows in his chapter, "States and firms in the international oil market," this puts increased pressure on the cooperation among MNEs in the international oil market to coordinate their international exploration and production activities. Following the most successful cartelization of a natural resource sector, with the oil producers taking control over the global oil price and production in the 1970s, a dynamic game between companies and both host and home countries emerged. A recent addition to the complexity of the global oil market is the Chinese oil companies' international strategy. Developments in the global oil market are thus linked to the observations made by Nölke regarding the role of home country domestic political institutions in MNEs', including NTMNEs', international commercial activities.

Summing up

As illustrated in this chapter, the global political economy is a complex system incorporating a variety of different actors and processes. Different metrics suggest that the global economy has become more integrated over the last decades, and this may have a range of important effects, for example on various national economic policies and prospects for economic development. As illustrated by recent efforts to reform the financial system, there is also an ever-continuing effort, for example by states and MNEs, to shape and reshape regulation of the global economy. The actors that are likely to be shaping such regulation according to their preferences will probably change with the changing distribution of global production and other economic resources.

The following chapters focus on different types of relations between international institutional structures, domestic political processes and government policies, and the behavior of MNEs. However, we will first turn to a discussion of how insights from diverse theoretical and methodical perspectives may be combined to enhance the validity of studies investigating the types of relationships we are concerned with in this book.

Notes

1 Rob McIver, manager of the Jensen Portfolio in Portland. CNNMoney.com. Article by Paul R. La Monica, first published November 12, 2010. http://money.cnn.com/ 2010/11/12/Markets/thebuzz/index.htm.
2 The quote is Hveem's definition of the analytical core of IPE.
3 For an extensive account of the historical development of the politics of the international economy see Schwartz (2000).
4 Although the IMF obviously counts as an international organization, GATT lacked several features of formal international organizations. See Keohane (1989) for a discussion of the terms "institution" and "organization" at the international level. Keohane defines institutions as "persistent and connected sets of rules (formal and informal) that prescribe behavioral roles, constrain activity, and shape expectations" (Keohane 1989: 3). Keohane further considers formal intergovernmental organizations and cross-national non-governmental organizations as a subcategory of international institutions. For another interesting discussion on the conceptual distinctions between "institutions" and "organizations," see, for example, North (1990). Very simply put, North considers the former as "the rules of the game" and the latter as the "players of the game."
5 For a detailed account of the development of the financial regime, see Helleiner (1994).
6 According to the "monetary policy trilemma," there is a stark trade-off among exchange rate stability, monetary independence, and capital market openness. Only two of these desired policy goals can be achieved simultaneously (e.g. Obstfeld 1998).
7 See Ougaard (2008) for a review of different aspects of business influence in global governance.
8 There is a large literature on the relationship between trade and FDI, and whether they are complementary or supplementary activities (see, for example, Norman and Venables 1995; Brainard 1997; Feenstra 2004). Although horizontal FDI, still the most voluminous type of FDI, arguably functions as a substitute for international trade, both FDI and trade have grown since 1980. A part of the explanation of this "dual growth" is the sharply increased international division of the production chain, with the localization of production at different stages of the production process in different countries (e.g. Hummels et al. 2001). Such international vertical specialization is related to both increased foreign trade (in inputs) and FDI.
9 The business meeting even has its own website: http://www.seoulg20businesssummit. org/en/.
10 There are a number of textbooks providing good introductions to the field; for a small collection see Ravenhill (2010), Oatley (2009), Frieden et al. (2009). For accounts of the theoretical evolution of the field the following articles are suggested: Katzenstein et al. (1998), Underhill (2000), Zürn (2002). Furthermore, some of the leading academics have provided their own account of the development of the field and evaluation of the state of the art: Keohane (1989, 2002), Cohen (2008a).
11 A more elaborate definition was provided by Krasner (1982). The study of international regimes has developed into a field of research in its own right (Hasenclever et al. 1997; Underdal and Young 2004). The approach of Keohane and Nye also differed from traditional formal studies of international organizations, in which the focus had been on the structure and processes within organizations such as the UN (Cox and Jacobson 1973).
12 Although the realist–liberalist dispute can be said to have immediate implications also for the domestic level:

The sharp disagreement between Realism and Liberal theory is overstated. In fact, the two approaches can be complementary. Sophisticated versions of Liberal theory address the manner in which interactions among states and the development of international norms interact with domestic politics of the states in an international

> system so as to transform the way in which states define their interests. Transnational and interstate interactions and norms lead to new definitions of interests, as well as to new coalition possibilities for different interests within states.
>
> (Nye 1988: 238)

13 The volume edited by Frieden et al. (2009) contains several such analyses. See also, for example, some of the studies discussed in Lake (2009a).

14 Several other strands of literature have also focused on the complex linkages between political and economic factors and processes, for example the "varieties of capitalism" literature (e.g. Hall and Soskice 2001) and the "domestic institutions and development" literature (e.g. North 1990; Acemoglu et al. 2001). The latter literature has focused on how domestic political institutions, which to some extent are a result of international political developments (e.g. Acemoglu et al. 2001; Huntington 1991), provide incentives for rulers, other policy makers, and individuals to engage in productive or unproductive activities.

15 Although most contributions in this book mainly consider regulatory frameworks that are global in scope, the development of various regional regulatory frameworks has been a very prominent feature in later decades (see, for example, Hveem 2006). The most well-known and probably most effective regional regulatory frameworks have been established in Europe. However, regional regulatory frameworks, particularly in the area of trade, have also been formed in, for example, East Asia (see, for example, Pempel 2004) and sub-Saharan Africa (see, for example, Bach 1999).

16 2005 is the latest year of data in the data set developed by Knutsen (forthcoming), which Figure 1.5 is based on.

17 We urge caution when interpreting these results. A possible change in the convergence/divergence properties among economies globally is still very much an uncertain, but interesting, hypothesis. The change is not very large, and other factors may have impacted on the result discussed cursorily in this section.

2

TOWARD ANALYTIC ECLECTICISM

The political economy of an integrated Europe

Peter J. Katzenstein and Rudra Sil

The naturalist and sociobiologist Edward Wilson (1998: 8) insists that the "fragmentation of knowledge and resulting chaos in philosophy are not reflections of the real world but artifacts of scholarship." The study of international political economy (IPE) appears to confirm this observation when we consider the earlier competition between realist-mercantilist, liberal-institutionalist, and Marxist approaches as well as the current debates among various strands of rationalist and constructivist scholarship. We do not assume, as Wilson does, that the remedy for this state of affairs must be a unified effort at "consilience" across all branches of learning. We do, however, view the boundaries separating contending schools of thought – variously referred to as paradigms or research traditions – as artificial constructs that illuminate certain aspects of social reality while obscuring the complexities and messiness of everyday political economy as experienced by policy makers and other actors.

What we have called analytic eclecticism (Sil and Katzenstein 2010) is intended as a complement to established scholarly traditions, designed specifically to gain traction on this complexity and messiness. We define as analytically eclectic any approach that seeks to extricate, translate, and selectively integrate analytic elements – concepts, causal logics, mechanisms, and interpretations – of theories or narratives that have been developed within separate paradigms but which address related aspects of substantive problems that have both scholarly and practical significance. In the context of contemporary IPE, an eclectic approach refuses to advance programmatic versions of either rationalism or constructivism. Instead it extricates and combines elements of theories developed within both research traditions, and it generates middle-range causal accounts about the complex interconnections between material and ideational factors and between local, national, and transnational processes. Although its epistemological agnosticism and intrinsic heterogeneity makes analytic eclecticism unsuitable as a unifying paradigm for political economy, it opens the door to the creative exploration of the variety of complex processes that cut across or connect multiple levels of analysis and multiple dimensions of social reality.[1]

This chapter is divided into two parts. In the first part, we develop the general rationale for analytic eclecticism insofar as it applies to the study of IPE. We consider the shifting fault lines between different schools of political economy, and then elaborate on the rationale for analytic eclecticism, stressing its potential value-added and downplaying overblown concerns about incommensurability. In the second part of the chapter, we turn to three recent examples of eclectic scholarship on different aspects of European political economy: Nicolas Jabko on the relationship between neoliberal reforms and European unification; Frank Schimmelfennig on the manner in which member states ended up supporting the risky venture of eastward enlargement of key European institutions; and Cornelia Woll on how European firms adjusted their preferences in surprising ways to cope with liberalization. The conclusion considers what the three otherwise disparate studies have in common, distilling three generalizable attributes that make each a reasonable approximation of eclectic scholarship on European and international political economy.

Dueling traditions and analytic eclecticism in international political economy

During the Cold War, Robert Gilpin's (1975, 1981, 1987) seminal writings both reflected and shaped a generation of scholarship organized around three paradigmatic approaches – realist-mercantilist, liberal, and Marxist – each with domestic and international variants. Realist-mercantilist theories put the state at the center of economic life, viewing state calculations and interests as derivative of the international balance of power. Liberal theories focused on the significance of individual and corporate interests in the domestic arena, and on the evolution of these interests in response to the growth of trade and interdependence in the international economy. And Marxist theories operated more freely across the domestic–international divide, linking the dynamics of class conflict in capitalist societies to the perpetuation of inequalities in the international capitalist system.

This map of the field of IPE has now become outdated. Although Marxist scholarship is still visible in many places and elements of neo-Marxist analysis can be found in critical perspectives on the global economy, Marxism no longer constitutes one of the prevailing schools in the analysis of IPE. Moreover, since the late 1980s, many (but not all) neorealists and neoliberal institutionalists have gravitated toward a "neo-neo synthesis" (Waever 1996), marked by a common set of rationalist-materialist assumptions (Keohane 1989; see also Katzenstein et al. 1999). At the same time, drawing upon sociology, new constructivist approaches to political economy have gained currency, forcing the field to consider the significance of ideational factors alongside the traditional focus on state power in realist thought and on economic incentives in liberal thought. These shifting intellectual traditions have also been intersecting with evolving methodological debates on the relative merits of different types of quantitative and qualitative approaches.

Fault lines of contemporary IPE: American versus European, rationalist versus constructivist

In trying to make sense of these recent currents, Benjamin Cohen (2007, 2008a,b) has suggested that the most significant divide in the study of IPE is now between an economic–rationalist–quantitative American research tradition and a socio-logical–non-rationalist–qualitative British one. Seeing merits and limitations in both approaches, Cohen's analysis has managed to attract critics on both sides of the Atlantic. Although he flatly contradicts the notion of a single unified approach touted by some proponents of the American research tradition (Frieden and Martin 2002), British scholars have taken him to task both for accepting the American research tradition as a baseline against which to judge other approaches (Higgott and Watson 2008) and for overlooking American-inflected work within the British tradition (Ravenhill 2008). Cohen's characterization of the evolution of the field of IPE has continued to be a lightening rod for ongoing debates over the possible existence and consequences of a trans-Atlantic divide, as evident, for example, in a special issue of *Review of International Political Economy* from 2009. Although not always explicitly acknowledged, the debates reveal fundamental differences over ontology (the basic units that make up the global political economy), epistemology (the foundations on which we make knowledge claims), and methodology (such as the choice between "counters of beans" and "tellers of stories").

To the extent that there is an "American school" of IPE, its epicenter is a model grounded in rational expectation theory – open economy politics (OEP), as outlined by David Lake (2009a). OEP resonates with sweet common sense, at least on the American side of the Atlantic. On economic issues, actors who are price takers with clearly ordered preferences will rank policies and outcomes based on how they affect their expected future incomes. OEP analysis seeks to make special adjustments for situations in which one or several of these assumptions are not met. OEP scholars start with sets of individuals "that can be reasonably assumed to share (nearly) identical interests . . . Deducing interests from economic theory was the essential innovation of OEP" (Lake 2009a: 50). In this formulation, individual (not social) interests are stipulated to exist (not inquired into). Although this is also a cause of worry to many students of politics, the great innovation of OEP is that it enables scholars to derive parsimonious theories of politics entirely based on economic theory.

The theories on which OEP relies are presumed to be falsifiable and empiri-cally robust for explaining economic outcomes. Whether they offer any new insights into significant *political* outcomes, however, is a matter of considerable dispute. OEP generally brackets interests and preferences by taking them as given. Interests may be "aggregated" institutionally and "translated" via institutions into policy outputs and outcomes, but the interests themselves are not problematized. Moreover, OEP subscribes to a truncated view of what institutions are and do, focusing exclusively on their regulative power. In doing so, it neglects altogether the possibility that institutions, in conjunction with identities, may shape actors' preferences and interests as well as their capacities for acting on them. As Robert Keohane (2009: 38) notes, although it has contributed to the integration of comparative and international political economy, OEP has turned out to be "too materialistic and much of it is too inclined to identify rationalism with egoism – an analytical mistake." OEP's dependence on the rational expectation assumptions in economic models means that it reproduces the limitations of those models when it comes to making sense of complex or unexpected phenomena, including the most recent economic crisis.

The rationalist underpinnings of OEP are being directly challenged by an emergent sociological perspective on IPE. Stability and instability in the economy, in this view, are inherently social phenomena, open to individual and collective irrationalities that are not shaped by or subordinate to market dynamics but deeply intertwined with them (Beckert 2002). Of course, this is not a completely novel proposition. In fact, as Rawi Abdelal, Mark Blyth, and Craig Parsons (2010) point out, it is one of the deep insights of John Maynard Keynes. Keynes was not a mechanic who simply instructed the government to spend money during economic downturns to cover the shortfall of private purchasing power. He was a student of the complex social interactions that offer crucial insights into the functioning of markets. Materialist and individualist theories are not tailored to capturing social and ideational changes. The material infrastructure of the global economy, understood in terms of the distribution of resources and the existence of standard individual motivation, does not tend to vary much either across space or over short expanses of time. In contrast, the *social* infrastructure of conventions, norms, ideas, and identities tends to vary considerably across both time and space. This was reflected, for example, in very different definitions of what constituted the latest financial crisis in the first place: liquidity (United States), capitalization (United Kingdom), or Anglo-Saxon capitalism (Germany). Furthermore, in times of enormous uncertainty, expectations are not stable. Growing uncertainty can lead to a redefinition of identities and interests among a whole array of economic actors, from investors to more or less risk-averse individuals.

This fundamental difference between the OEP research tradition and the sociological perspective is a development of the last two decades. The mainstream extends the liberal research tradition but also incorporates insights from economics, viewed as the model social science that is admired and often copied by political scientists. In response, a distinct alternative has begun to crystallize, combining constructivist epistemology with insights from economic and historical sociology (Abdelal et al. 2010). We have no interest in mediating this debate; we do, however, seek to leverage and combine the theoretical intuitions and empirical findings generated by both camps.

Cautioning against a monoculture in the study of political economy, Keohane

(2009: 40) calls for a "synthetic interpretation of change" in which ideas, structural power, and diffusion processes all play crucial roles. He acknowledges that scholars now confront a larger volume of work and a greater degree of complexity, but he insists that "those of us who are not in the field of IPE – scholars, policy-makers, or citizens – need to know what the best research says about the big questions." This does not imply the need for an alternative unifying paradigm that can subsume rationalist and constructivist elements. Indeed, both camps have produced work of exceptionally high caliber, and it would be an intellectual loss to trade in diversity in perspective for the sake of a new unified framework that informs any and all studies of political economy. We suggest instead a third alternative: analytic eclecticism.

The rationale for analytic eclecticism

Scholarship embedded in different research traditions has produced valuable insights. And the competition among traditions has served to motivate progress and knowledge cumulation within each tradition. However, this competition also takes on a life of its own, supported by normalized institutional practices in regard to hiring and promotion, the review of academic publications, and competitions for grants. These practices serve to reify the artificial boundaries between scholarly traditions, which, in turn, prevent more inclusive dialogues, more expansive networks of collaboration, and more useful forms of cumulative knowledge that are intelligible to policy makers and those engaged in public debates. These contending traditions also leave adherents of particular scholarly traditions using seemingly incommensurable theoretical vocabularies and speaking past one another even when they are addressing related aspects of the same phenomena (Adler and Pouliot 2008). Rigid commitments to paradigms or research traditions not only constitute a "hindrance to understanding," as Albert Hirschman (1970) noted long ago; they also account for what Ian Shapiro describes as a "flight from reality" (Shapiro 2005) among academics and an ever-widening gap between academic scholarship and the worlds of policy and practice (Calhoun 2009; Nye 2009).

In advancing the case for greater analytic eclecticism in the study of IPE, we begin with the obvious. Although they are based on competing epistemic commitments, paradigms and research traditions are not usually so rigid as to produce uniform research products that predictably converge on substantive interpretations, explanations, or prescriptions. In engaging particular problems, it is entirely possible for constructivists and rationalists to disagree amongst themselves while some types of constructivists and rationalists may end up converging upon substantive characterizations of, and prescriptions for, a particular problem in international life. Such convergence points to the possibility and utility of eclecticism in the study of world politics.

Eclectic modes of inquiry increase the chances that students of world politics, and the ordinary actors they claim to study, generate more useful theoretical and empirical insights. These insights can elude adherents of paradigms who view their problems through distinct lenses that are specifically designed to filter out "inconvenient" facts to enable a more focused analysis. The very features that enable proponents of a paradigm to delimit the objects of their research entail that the research will not speak to a range of potentially relevant phenomena, processes, and mechanisms. Analytic eclecticism forgoes the simplifications required by paradigmatic boundaries and permits a more comprehensive assessment of the practical relevance and significance of findings generated within multiple paradigms.

Significantly, eclectic scholarship does not require that research traditions be disbanded or their scholarly output discarded. It does, however, require that scholars leave behind the rigid meta-theoretical principles upon which paradigms rely in the process of bounding and framing empirical problems. Analytic eclecticism seeks to expand the opportunities for engaging relevant theories produced by competing paradigms and for creatively utilizing elements from these theories to generate useful insights about complex social phenomena. At the same time, a commitment to an eclectic style of inquiry does not suggest that a scholar has carte blanche to pursue each and every imaginable lead. Rather, analytic eclecticism is obligated to appreciate and engage scholarship embedded in established paradigms. Its value-added stems from its ability to expose previously hidden connections between the findings and theories generated by those same paradigms.

Our defense of eclectic analysis has multiple roots. One is Hirschman's (1970: 341) observation that experienced politicians, whose intuitions are more likely to take into account "a variety of forces at work," frequently offer more useful conjectures and forecasts in a given situation than do adherents of paradigms, who necessarily ignore some of these forces and run the risk of many errors in their efforts to explain phenomena and forecast large-scale transformations. Paradigms can be useful in identifying certain aspects of significant transformations; even so, Hirschman (1970: 343) insists that proponents of specific paradigms have no reliable blueprints to offer to actors seeking to engineer social change.

More recently, Philip Tetlock (2005: 214) has argued that a single analytic framework "confers the benefits of closure and parsimony but desensitizes us to nuance, complexity, contingency, and the possibility that our theory is wrong." Tetlock's study of decision making demonstrates that grossly inaccurate forecasts are more likely when experts employ a single parsimonious approach or excessively generalized abstractions. Conversely, better forecasts are more likely when experts rely on various kinds of knowledge and information to improvise ad hoc solutions in a rapidly changing world. Adapting the famous reference from Isaiah Berlin's work, Tetlock (2005: 91) suggests that, all other things being equal, "eclectic foxes" tend to do better than "intellectually aggressive hedgehogs" because the former refuse "to be anchored down by theory-laden abstractions," and are instead ready "to blend opposing hedgehog arguments." Analytic eclecticism represents such an effort at blending, a means for scholars to guard against the risks of excessive reliance on a single analytic perspective. This is particularly true when it comes to understanding intersections and interactions among multiple social processes in different domains of reality.

Analytic eclecticism is also in part an effort to reverse the trade-offs that accompany simplifications characteristic of research embedded in paradigms. Although such simplifications are fruitful at certain stages of research, it is also true that the ontologies guiding the study of politics and political economy are increasingly characterized by "more extensive endogeneity and the ubiquity of complex interaction effects" (Hall 2003: 387). Along similar lines, Bernstein et al. (2000) argue that the study of international relations should be modeled not after physics but after evolutionary biology, which features a more open-ended system in which specific mutation and interaction processes cannot be foreseen in light of uncertainty regarding contingencies. Under these conditions, a practically useful approach is oriented not toward point predictions based on rigid theoretical principles but rather toward scenarios that require "the identification and connection of chains of contingencies that could shape the future" (Bernstein et al. 2000: 53). This suggests that international relations theories are likely to do better when they take into account the wide-ranging causal factors from diverse paradigms and then demonstrate how these factors affect one another or combine to generate specific outcomes under certain conditions.

Three distinguishing features of eclectic scholarship

We employ three criteria for distinguishing eclectic scholarship from scholarship embedded in paradigms or research traditions. The first has to do with the manner in which research problems are formulated. Research questions within paradigm-bound projects tend to be formulated to test theories derived from that paradigm, to fill in gaps thought to exist among theories constructed within the paradigm, or to explore anomalies or new phenomena that these theories have yet to account for. This has certain benefits, but, as Shapiro (2005: 184) argues: "If the problems posited are idiosyncratic artifacts of the researcher's theoretical priors, then they will seem tendentious, if not downright misleading, to everyone except those who are wedded to her priors." Analytic eclecticism features the articulation of problems that reflect, rather than simplify, the complexity and multidimensionality of social phenomena of interest to both scholars and practitioners. Eclectic research thus does not seek to develop better answers to questions already identified by specific research traditions. Its value-added lies instead in expanding the scope and complexity of questions so as to facilitate a more open-ended analysis that can incorporate the insights of different paradigm-bound theories and relate them to the concerns of policy makers and ordinary actors. Thus, eclectic analysis is not only problem driven; it also makes a conscious effort to stretch the domain of analysis so that it is not limited by the need to adopt a specific ontology or a specific set of epistemic norms.

Second, analytic eclecticism is self-conscious in its effort to incorporate causal mechanisms, broadly defined, drawn from separate research traditions within novel recombinant mid-range theories responding to concrete problems. For the kinds of complex problems likely to be tackled by eclectic scholarship, it is important that assumptions about the ontological primacy of agency/structure or of material/ideational factors not be conflated with the causal primacy of either side of these dyads. Eclectic research considers the different ways in which individual and collective actors in world politics form and pursue their material and ideal preferences within given environments. It also draws attention to the manner in which external environments influence actors' understandings of their interests, capabilities, opportunities, and constraints. And it considers the extent to which the material and ideational components of these environments are reproduced or transformed as a result of those actors' varying preferences and varying abilities to act upon those preferences. That is, eclectic styles of analysis seek to develop mid-range theories that train their sights on those processes that cut across different levels of analysis, that connect domestic and international factors, and that link material and ideational elements. Put differently, analytic eclecticism assumes the existence of complex interactions among the distribution of material capabilities (typically emphasized in realism), the gains pursued by self-interested individual and collective actors (typically emphasized by liberals), and the role of ideas, norms, and identities in framing actors' understanding of the world and of their roles within it (privileged by constructivists).

Finally, analytic eclecticism is motivated by a desire to close the growing gap between theoretical debates within the academe and demands for policy relevance and practicality outside it (Calhoun 2009; Nye 2009). We are not suggesting here that all academic scholarship be reorganized so as to cater to the existing agendas of policy makers. Indeed, academic research designed solely to serve those in power can reinforce acceptance of particular worldviews and uniform modes of inquiry at the expense of critical thinking in relation to existing policy agendas and practices. At the same time there exists a very real danger of scholarship becoming overly preoccupied with purely academic disputes that are hermetically blocked off from public discourse and policy debates about important issues of interest to both scholars and practitioners. Analytic eclecticism is part of a wider effort to restore "the balance between detachment and engagement, between withdrawal behind the monastic walls of the university and the joys and dangers of mixing with the profane world outside" (Wallace 1996: 304). This implies that eclectic research, even when it is not offering explicit policy prescriptions, should have some clear implications for some set of policy debates or salient normative concerns that enmesh leaders, public intellectuals, and other actors in a given political setting.

Anticipating eclectic scholarship in international political economy

Although our particular formulation of analytic eclecticism is original, it is not difficult to find examples of scholars, including prominent ones frequently identified with an established school of analysis, who have acknowledged the limitations of paradigm-bound research and hinted at the value of eclectic styles of inquiry. In the context of political economy, Robert Gilpin's (1975, 1987) attempts to grapple systematically with competing perspectives led him to draw upon liberal, realist, and Marxist analytic principles in order to shed light on different facets of the international political economy. In his more recent work, characterized as a "state-realist" approach to political economy, Gilpin goes on to challenge the stark separation of constructivism and realism. He notes:

> Ideas are obviously important, but the world is composed of many economic, technological, and other powerful constraints that limit the wisdom and practicality of certain ideas and social constructions. Any theory that seeks to understand the world must . . . seek to integrate both ideas and material forces.
>
> (Gilpin 2001: 20)

Frequently associated with the neoliberal camp, Robert Keohane also acknowledges the importance of approaching problems from multiple vantage points, as is evident in his analysis of cooperation without a hegemon. Keohane (1984: 39) accepts the realist theory of hegemonic stability as "a useful, if somewhat simplistic starting point." But he then goes on to construct a framework of analysis that not only combines elements of realist and liberal theory but also borrows extensively from Antonio Gramsci's theory of hegemony as well as the work of Karl Kautsky (Keohane 1984: 43–5). Keohane (1986) and John Ruggie (1986), although thought of as critics of neorealism, do not discard Kenneth Waltz's structural realism. Instead, they view it as an essential and valuable foundation for the building of more complex frameworks, in which Waltz's notion of structure coexists with other non-systemic factors that can better capture the effects of growing interdependence and the dynamics of system change.

A strong proponent of liberalism, Andrew Moravcsik (2008), has also called for de-emphasizing theoretical parsimony and ontological consistency in order to facilitate synthetic analyses featuring causal factors drawn from different theories. Moravcsik (2003: 132) notes:

> The complexity of most large events in world politics precludes plausible unicausal explanations. The outbreak of World Wars I and II, the emergence of international human rights norms, and the evolution of the European Union, for example, are surely important enough events to merit comprehensive explanation even at the expense of theoretical parsimony.

The basic notion underlying all of these quotes is that no one approach can offer all the tools needed to make sense of political economy. And yet, there has not been a concerted effort to define and articulate the rationale for a coherent, pragmatic alternative to paradigm-centered research. Analytic eclecticism is one such alternative. Intended to complement and draw upon existing research traditions, eclectic scholarship is not only problem driven, but also emphasizes the extraction, adaptation, and integration (but *not* synthesis) of discrete concepts, mechanisms, observations, and interpretations normally embedded in the various traditions. Focusing on the relationships among empirical referents used to operationalize concepts in various theories and narratives, analytic eclecticism seeks to reveal hidden theoretical and empirical connections across research traditions while also having relevance for the management of substantive real-world problems that ordinary actors are trying to solve in particular contexts. The following section offers a small sample of scholarly analyses pointing to the potential value-added of analytic eclecticism in relation to the study of European political economy.

Analytic eclecticism and European political economy

Anticipating today's canonical distinction between realism, liberalism, and constructivism, European integration theory during the 1950s and 1960s had three main strands. In their analysis of European affairs, realists were skeptics who insisted that states would not relinquish their sovereign prerogatives on questions that mattered most (Hoffmann 1966). In contrast, neofunctionalists such as Ernst Haas (1958, 1964) argued that the logic of integration was dynamic and would convince states to surrender more of their sovereignty claims as the efficiency costs of not doing so became clearer. Finally, communication theorists such as Karl Deutsch (1957) remained skeptical that any progress in European integration was actually occurring, as underlying rates of national communication, trade, and integration outpaced observable international ones, suggesting that collective identity formation at the European level was going to be a very slow affair at best. Although the interparadigm debates of the 1960s were spirited and strong, they were somewhat mitigated by the fact that all the major protagonists shared a strong substantive interest in Europe, to which each had strong personal ties. Hoffmann, Haas, and Deutsch were all brilliant first-generation immigrant scholars who had made it to the United States between the 1930s and 1950s. Their debates reflected distinct analytic prisms that would shape later debates on the possibilities for governance, in Europe and elsewhere.

Half a century later, EU member states are coordinating their foreign policies more effectively than ever before, and the European Commission is engendering a far higher level of harmonization than Deutsch, Haas, or Hoffmann could have anticipated. Scholars, however, continue to study the political economy of European integration through sharply different theoretical lenses, each offering important insights into different parts of the story. Realists are correct in pointing to the lack of any substantive evidence indicating that any state is willing to relinquish sovereign control over the many issues it considers to be vital to its national security. The emergence of a multilevel European governance system in the EU, liberals correctly insist, is pooling sovereignty across numerous policy domains that once had been under sole national control. Thanks to a shared rationalist ontology, it has been possible for some neorealists and neoliberal institutionalists to set aside their differences and gravitate toward open economy politics. However, whatever rationalist consensus exists is confronted by constructivists who highlight the emergence and significance of shared European identities in response to the growing density of social interactions and subtle cultural transformations among the people of Europe.

Thus, although the particular manner in which we draw fault lines between schools of IPE have evolved, the boundaries between contending paradigms or research traditions remain quite entrenched, as the most recent TRIP surveys indicate (Jordan et al. 2009; Maliniak et al. 2007). At the same time, not satisfied with the rigid separation between constructivism and rationalism, a growing number of scholars have been seeking to bypass rigid commitments to particular approaches in favor of problem-driven approaches that we view as analytically eclectic. In the remainder of this chapter, we consider book-length studies by three such scholars who work on different aspects of European political economy but evince a similar style of inquiry in search of eclectic middle-range theoretical formulations.

Nicolas Jabko (2006) on the European Union

Europe's quiet revolution during the 1980s and 1990s, Jabko argues, was not inevitable. Rather, it was the result of a political strategy devised by initially weak and opportunistic political actors. This was true, specifically, of the European Commission, which smartly deployed ideas about market liberalization to build a broad-based coalition in favor of deeply institutionalized integration. The plasticity of the market concept proved to be a crucial component of a political strategy calculated to produce a broadened coalition that could support the strengthening of European institutions.

In developing his argument, Jabko challenges, but also borrows from, three conventional arguments of European integration in the 1980s and 1990s. According to the most prevalent view, European integration is fundamentally intertwined with, and driven by, the inexorable process of market globalization. Globalization has shifted interests and power relations, enabling European multinational corporations and financial actors to gain influence and to promote market-friendly policies through the European Union. A second view is institutionalist. It emphasizes the path-dependent processes of change through which the European Union has expanded and become more deeply institutionalized, sometimes quickly and at other times more slowly. A third view is constructivist. It emphasizes the centrality of key ideas that became decisive in moments of uncertainty. In this view, the apparent failure of Keynesian policies in the 1970s paved the way for a more market-driven program for relaunching Europe in the 1980s. Each of these views captures aspects of the broad structural and ideational context of late twentieth-century Europe, but, as Jabko notes, none manages to fully account for the complex processes that account for "the path breaking nature of change in European economic governance in the 1980s and 1990s" (p. 3).

Jabko's own argument proceeds eclectically, drawing upon constructivist and rationalist perspectives to formulate a perspective he refers to as "strategic constructivism." Contra simplified utilitarian or institutionalist perspectives, Jabko sees ideas as playing a pivotal role in marking key shifts in both the evolution of the material interests of key actors and the development of institutional characteristics. At the same time, he veers away from typical constructivist treatments of ideas by emphasizing that "ideas are important not so much as pure beliefs but because, in any given policy area, the parties involved must resort to ideas to articulate and advance their interests" (p. 8). Moreover, Jabko is wedded to middle-range theorizing, limiting his investigation to the European context in order to "disaggregate the various elements of that process and evaluate theoretically derived hypotheses at a more concrete level" (p. 20). At the same time, he notes that the EU's quiet revolution is not idiosyncratic. It represents an instance of contemporary institutional change and, as such, offers analytical observations that are potentially transferrable to other situations – particularly the insight of the strategic opportunities opened up by institutional tensions and incongruities (p. 9).

Jabko argues that the simultaneous pursuit of market liberalization and deep regional integration during the 1980s and early 1990s was aided by a broad coalition of political actors with disparate political objectives and divergent attitudes toward market reforms. Although there had always been a core elite committed to the idea of a unified Europe, the new converts to the idea included supporters and opponents of free markets, adherents of the political Left and Right, bureaucrats and business leaders, and highly placed government officials in all countries. The formation of so heterogeneous a political coalition was not a chance event but the result of a political strategy led by the European Commission, which fully understood the need to rally a broad constituency in support of its ambitious plans. Specifically, it engaged in a creative crafting of new institutional rules that were broadly acceptable to a heterogeneous coalition of actors under the rubric of a market-based Europe.

In effect, the market became a "talisman of political discourse" (p. 7), a political metaphor that served to bridge the chasm between those who ardently supported markets and those who were less committed but were willing to accept it as a pragmatic necessity in the pursuit of higher, normative goals. For some, the market was a constraint that undermined existing institutions, but it was accepted on pragmatic grounds in the form of a single European entity. For others, it was understood as the most legitimate norm for organizing economic life, even in sectors such as energy that had been shielded from market competition for decades. For many, the market facilitated an energetic pursuit of economic prosperity for all, but only as part of a broader EU strategy that would limit market-based inequalities. For all of these groups, the market provided a "conveniently broad repertoire of justifications" for a diverse set of actors who "were given a stake in the European Union's quiet revolution and thus encouraged to reframe their interests around the achievement of Europe's market and monetary integration agenda" (p. 6).

Two features of the integration process are better explained by Jabko's argument than by prevailing explanations. First, Europe's shift toward market-based governance does not correspond neatly with the strength of market pressures in various sectors, as a neo-utilitarian argument might suggest. In the fast-changing sectors of finance and telecommunications, for example, the move toward a single market only accelerated domestic regulatory reforms already in progress. In other sectors that provided collective goods or services, such as energy, the effects of a single market were far more significant and dramatic. Second, the shift of policy making from national capitals toward Brussels went hand in hand with a reassertion, not dilution, of public power. For example, the Economic and Monetary Union (EMU) created a powerful European Central Bank (ECB) rather than transferring authority to markets. Indeed, inasmuch as the EMU protected the European economy against currency fluctuations, it dampened rather than reinforced the operation of free markets. Europe's shift to market-based governance thus represents a conundrum (pp. 24–5). The resulting story goes beyond Europe's responses to market globalization and the ascent of neoliberal ideology; it reflects the operation of "strategic constructivism" in different contexts and environments.

Jabko's eclectic approach also points to some real-world scenarios with policy implications. Most significantly, the historical specificity of the political processes that gave momentum to European integration implies that there is no guarantee that this momentum will continue in a radically different environment. It is even possible that "the remarkable success of the integrationist strategy of the 1980s and 1990s could become a liability for future political integration" (p. 186). Jabko also notes that, although the EU may have strengthened its capacity for supranational governance, this has not been at the expense of the member states' capacities, even in the area of monetary policy. Thus, the EU, although more powerful than was anticipated in the 1970s, remains vulnerable when it comes to the legitimacy of its decision-making processes in the eyes of Europeans. This explains why the EU's key actors tend to approach conflict resolution through deferment, approaching their separate agendas in roundabout ways to avoid the risks of popular backlash against the decision-making process. These observations suggest that, under different conditions, the "progressive decomposition" (p. 186) of the EU may not be as unthinkable as assumed by some of its backers.

Frank Schimmelfennig (2003) on European enlargement

For Schimmelfennig, "the most consequential political project" (p. 2) undertaken by European organizations in the last decade has been the post-Cold War eastward enlargement process of the EU and NATO. Why Central and East European Countries (CEECs) would want to join these organizations in the wake of the Cold

War is not particularly puzzling for Schimmelfennig. Rationalist arguments suffice to explain this development. What is more interesting is why Western member states in these organizations bothered to embark on the complicated and risky course of steady enlargement when there is no clear indication of the gains from doing so. Why did the EU and NATO decide to acquiesce to the CEECs' desires for membership? How did the members arrive at their decisions to support eastward expansion? And how did they decide on the criteria for accession? Driven by these questions, Schimmelfennig's analysis gravitates toward two novel theoretical arguments. The first stresses the significance of "the constitutive liberal rules of the Western international community" in explaining expansion; the second the significance of "rhetorical action" in explaining how these liberal rules have affected the enlargement process (p. 3). Although the first argument does not stray too far from its constructivist origins, the second is more self-consciously eclectic in seeking to connect rationalist and sociological-institutionalist perspectives. It is this argument we focus on here.

Schimmelfennig notes that, for most EU and NATO members, eastward enlargement imposed significant transaction, autonomy, and crowding costs. Furthermore, both had at their disposal more efficient and less risky institutional mechanisms to address the issues of new member states – associate membership in the case of the EU, and the Partnership for Peace in the case of NATO. And although it is true that some EU and NATO member states such as Germany would derive great benefits from enlargement, neither they nor the CEECs had the bargaining power to impose enlargement on a reluctant majority of EU and NATO members. Put differently, the standard arguments advanced by neoliberal institutional analysis do not hold. Yet there is little evidence to suggest that the logic of appropriateness stressed in constructivist analysis trumped material interests or egoistic action among Western states. In fact, distinctive of the enlargement process is the fact that neither member nor applicant states acted in accordance with either rule-based enlargement routines or internalized membership norms.

In analyzing the process by which the decision to enlarge came about, Schimmelfennig examines the relative significance of four modes of social action. Each rests on different cognitive mechanisms that can be measured against the null hypothesis of rational action in which outcomes reflect actors' fixed preferences and bargaining power. *Habitual* action leaves the least room for individual agency. Goals and behavior that result from unreflective habit will necessarily conform most closely to collective rules because these already influence social action at the cognitive level. *Normative* action gives more play to agency. Although an actor's goals are rule-based, the rules reflect the actor's normative reasoning and thus are a matter of reflected choice that may deviate from collective rules. *Communicative* action assumes that actors have conflicting preferences, and that their conflicts cannot be resolved by habit or norms but by entering into deliberation following standards of true reasoning and rational argumentation. These standards reflect social rules that directly influence actors' behavior, including behavior that contradicts initial preferences. *Rhetorical* action is "the strategic use and exchange of arguments to persuade other actors to act according to one's preferences" (p. 5). It is distinguished from communicative action in that it accepts individual and instrumental choice as the starting point of analysis. Actors employ rhetoric that invokes social rules, which, in turn, affects their interaction and ultimately influences collective outcomes.

In the processes of EU and NATO enlargement, rhetorical action proved to be the most original and significant mode of action in Schimmelfennig's analysis. Building on the sociology of Erving Goffman's (1959) classic study on the "presentation of self in everyday life," Schimmelfennig's conception of rhetorical action relies on a scale rather than a dichotomy to examine the variable mix of social and rational mechanisms at play in the behavior and interaction of actors. For Schimmelfennig, "the strategic conception of rules combines the social and ideational ontology of constructivism – in a non-structuralist, processualist variation – with rationalist instrumentalism" (p. 198). Without an analysis of rhetorical action, the gap between rule-ignoring individual preferences and rule-conforming collective outcomes could not have been bridged. The processes of EU and NATO enlargement reveal the complex interplay of material interests and power differentials (stressed by rationalists), community rules and norms (stressed by sociological institutionalists), and the strategic deployment of rhetorical action making reference to those rules and norms.

Yet, as Schimmelfennig emphasizes, whether or not rhetorical action is sustainable and effective depends on the availability of formal and informal mechanisms to induce cooperation among opponents. In the context of EU and NATO enlargement, formal mechanisms such as institutional sanctions and decisions were not as significant as informal mechanisms involving social pressure and social influence. These informal mechanisms encompass cognitive and emotional reactions triggered by social rewards (such as popularity and respect for compliance), and punishments (such as shaming and shunning for non-compliance). What boosted the prospects for eastward enlargement was the ability of CEEC governments and their Western supporters to invoke rhetorical action in order to overcome an unfavorable constellation of preferences and power inside the EU and NATO. They based their case for enlargement on the constitutive liberal values and norms of the community of states that both organizations represented, and to which all member states professed to adhere. They emphasized the inconsistency between members' reluctance to enlarge and the organizations' liberal rules of membership as well as past rhetorical commitments and treatment of outsiders. This proved to be an effective shaming strategy in getting reluctant states to cross over and support enlargement. States opposing enlargement could not afford to veto it, as such an act would have been immensely costly for their credibility and standing in the West. In the end, "opponents of Eastern enlargement found themselves rhetorically entrapped" (p. 5).

Schimmelfennig's eclectic approach also provides a basis for engaging in practical political action in the international arena without waiting for the conditions that rationalists and constructivists posit as necessary for building a viable international order. Rationalism views such an order as epiphenomenal to elusive power- or interest-based dynamics that tend to make international cooperation elusive. Constructivism relies on the equally elusive internalization of norms that are thought to define and encourage "appropriate" behavior in the international arena. These are high thresholds for the creation of effective forms of governance. For Schimmelfennig, a "strategic conception of rules and the story of Eastern enlargement draw a more optimistic picture" (p. 287). This is because of the possibilities opened up by rhetorical action even when the constellation of power and interests, or the diffusion of shared norms and conceptions of appropriateness, is not sufficient to enable cooperation. Even among selfish actors and in the absence of coercive institutional power or egoistic incentives to comply, rule-based collective outcomes are possible as the consequence of such forms of rhetorical action. As long as an international community has rules that are considered constitutive, legitimate, and salient, the absence of self-interest or deep socialization does not constitute an insurmountable barrier to the construction of international normative order. Rhetorical action and strategies of entrapment provide political substitutes for unlikely coalitions that can sustain such an order.

Cornelia Woll (2008) on European firms

When setting out to study the responses to liberalization in various sectors, Woll was surprised to find that European firms, far from fearing loss of markets and resisting liberalization, expressed happiness with new agreements liberalizing services in telecommunications and international aviation. Woll initially suspected that her interview subjects were trying to cover up a past policy defeat, after failing to protect their large home markets. However, as she delved into the problem it became increasingly clear that a genuine shift in perspective had taken place: her interview subjects admitted that they had been wary of liberalization at first, but that they and the world had changed (p. xiii). Thus, the central question of Woll's book is: "Why had preferences evolved so decisively over such a short period of time? What did it take to move a business actor from protectionism to support for liberalization?" (pp. xiii–xiv).

Confronted by the very different kinds of advice offered by economists and sociologists, Woll set out to write a self-consciously eclectic book that would seek to build bridges between dueling analytical traditions. In doing so, she found inspiration in Max Weber's understanding of economic action as a type of social action, setting her sights on understanding how economic action under conditions of uncertainty can defy expectations based on the standard rational actor model (p. 7). Woll readily acknowledges that firms act rationally in seeking to maximize their goals, once these goals are clear. However, she emphasizes that, "since identities, beliefs, and political opportunities depend on the political and regulatory contexts, business lobbying varies between cases, even when material conditions would indicate that behavior should be similar" (p. 5). At the same time, merely "recognizing that interests are intrinsically bound up with ideas is of little analytical value if scholars cannot specify when and how these mechanisms operate and what this implies for an understanding of policy change" (p. 17). Thus, it is essential to track how political stances emerge in interaction with competitors and government representatives, with crucial shifts often hinging on ideational and strategic conditions.

For Woll, it is significant to conceive of corporate interests under conditions of uncertainty within a specific political and regulatory context that includes their historically embedded relations with governments and competitors (p. 8). Although neoclassical economists often pay close attention to uncertainty, Woll finds that they tend to adopt a very narrow conception of the term, focusing on costs or benefits given the likelihood that an anticipated event will occur. Economists working in fields such as transaction costs or signaling attempt to model firms' confusion about their interests by predicting a time lag for informational updating. Building on these models, uncertainty is often reduced to a world of computable probabilities and risk assessments in the literature of IPE. Assuming that actors share the same information and the same subjective probabilities, this statistical form of computational rationality permits the calculation of risk in an uncertain environment.

Following the work of Jens Beckert (2002) and Mark Blyth (2006), Woll differentiates between situations involving risk, which allow for the assignment of probabilities over a set of outcomes, and situations involving extreme uncertainty, in which there is no information on which to base calculations of probabilities. In complex environments, actors do not calculate in isolation but make sense of their self-interests through their interactions with others. These interactions define, preserve, and transfer ideas about the proper relations between means and ends; shape which means to pursue; and predict the most likely courses of behavior. Such a socially and historically embedded conception of agency implies that the very notion of self-interest lacks purposeful content and thus is radically indeterminate in what it can tell us about the choices of individuals, firms, and other actors in the world.

Woll's empirical study focuses on the liberalization of trade in services in the United States and Europe, specifically negotiations related to the Basic Telecommunications Agreement of the World Trade Organization (WTO) and the liberalization of international aviation. Her analysis and evidence confirm her intuition that traditional economic and sociological approaches cannot by themselves predict which actors ended up supporting liberalization. In contexts in which new trade issues have arisen, the logic of international exchange is not yet clear, and firms may be operating in regulatory contexts in which they are not necessarily in direct competition but do face extreme uncertainty. Under such conditions, traditional trade models, although helpful for predicting tariff negotiations in the trade of goods, come up short. Instead, it is necessary to develop "a nuanced conceptualization of business interest in international trade that takes into account ideational and strategic changes induced by firms' political and regulatory interactions" (p. 25). This process is shaped by contests, not over *whether*, but over *how* to liberalize in a given sector.

Woll's analysis points to two more specific conclusions. First, the political and institutional arrangements in Europe and the United States differ significantly. Europe's multilevel polity gives trade negotiators more liberty to ignore interest group pressure and to work selectively with those supporting their own objectives. For business lobbyists, this means that some demands are difficult to voice or simply unfeasible. This creates strategic constraints that shape outcomes in important ways, causing European firms to embrace policy positions that one would not expect in the American context. Varieties of political systems and regulatory regimes thus have a significant but often unacknowledged impact on preferences. Second, since political context is so important to preference formation, atomistic models are misleading. Governments are not merely arbitrators of competing demands, and government strategies do not merely conform to pressures from firms and other social actors. Rather, in the case of service trade liberalization, large service companies frequently shifted their positions, often in response to strategies and ideas coming from the government. The case studies and comparisons suggest that business demands do not merely determine, but are formed in response to, government policy. In the process, ideas and strategies interact to produce a more complex evolution of preferences on both sides: "ideas explain how firms reorient their policy demands, while strategic changes trigger often profound transformations of firm preferences" (p. 19).

The final chapter of Woll's book takes up the implications of the study for normative and policy questions. Specifically, Woll points to the importance of democratic decision making and accountability in international trade negotiations. Among other observations, she notes that the fluid nature of business interests in negotiations over new issue areas potentially enables greater participation in a more pluralist approach to global public policy. Although multinational firms still retain advantages over smaller businesses, NGOs, and social movements, trade negotiations increasingly take place in a more public sphere, enabling a more diverse set of actors to participate in the debates (p. 158). Moreover, in the case of the European Union, although European negotiators seek to expand their capacity to bargain with U.S. counterparts, they also risk attenuating the already limited level of democratic accountability evident in EU trade policy decisions. Thus, Woll's analysis points to the need for formal rules that facilitate greater transparency and wider participation among all relevant actors in trade and other policy areas (p. 160).

Conclusion

Analytic eclecticism not only takes into account a wide range of causal factors from diverse paradigms, but also seeks to demonstrate how these factors affect one another or combine to generate certain specific outcomes under certain conditions. In so doing, analytic eclecticism enables us to add new layers of complexity to phenomena that paradigm-bound research must necessarily over-simplify. It provides opportunities to recognize or uncover hidden possibilities and connections that frequently elude researchers who have come to take for granted the artificial boundaries of the research traditions within which they work. In addition, it offers hope that perhaps academic scholarship can constitute "usable knowledge" (Lindblom and Cohen 1979) from the vantage point of those engaged in policy making or public debates.

We view the quite different studies discussed above as approximations of such eclectic work. Jabko studies the evolution of a distinctive political strategy that enabled key actors to promote market liberalization while engineering support for supranational governance structures; Woll inquires into the changes in politics and perceptions accompanying the liberalization of telecommunications and air transport; and Schimmelfennig analyses how the injection of "rhetorical action" helps to clarify some of the choices and processes accompanying the eastward enlargement of European governance institutions such as the EU and NATO. All three works fall outside the "American IPE monoculture" (Weaver 2009: 1), at least insofar as this it is currently identified with the open economy politics embraced by Lake (2009a) and others. And all three, whether explicitly intended as a contribution to eclectic scholarship or not, help us to make a strong case for the promise of analytic eclecticism in analyzing not only European political economy, but IPE writ large.

It is impossible to derive from these different studies a uniform guide on how to conduct eclectic research on global political economy. Although it is conceivable that further evolution of international relations scholarship away from paradigm-centered to eclectic work might generate greater demands for such a guide, we remain skeptical about the possibility and desirability of developing one. Analytic eclecticism as we define it is incompatible with the idea of rigid injunctions or formulas for how to define and analyze political economy. At the same time, the three studies do evince three common characteristics that we believe may be used to generally distinguish eclectic scholarship from conventional scholarship embedded in paradigms or research traditions.

First, each has identified and articulated problems that extend beyond the theoretical scope of competing research traditions in IPE. Each is creative in its effort to identify a question of broad scope that is substantively interesting and not bounded restrictively to facilitate the testing of existing theories or to fill in gaps in intraparadigm scholarship. Second, in their theoretical aspirations, all of the authors operate at or near the level of middle-range theory, taking spatial and temporal contexts seriously but seeking out mechanisms and processes that are, at least in principle, portable to comparable cases. The authors do not always use the language of causal mechanisms in formulating their arguments. They do, how-ever, forgo the search for parsimony and instead offer complex causal stories that draw together a wide range of factors and logics drawn from diverse research traditions. Third, the studies generate findings that are explicitly or implicitly related to the practical challenges that policy makers and ordinary actors encounter. The authors do not necessarily start off with the intention of offering policy prescriptions; but they are self-conscious about how the problems they investigate and the analytic frameworks they offer bear on important issues of policy and practice.

As the studies suggest, the point of analytic eclecticism is not merely to articulate a new argument for the sake of novelty; nor is it simply to carve out a line of analysis that defies classification under the existing set of contending paradigms. It is also to generate "pragmatic engagement" with the social conditions within which prevailing ideas about world politics have emerged (Haas and Haas 2009: 101). In keeping with the Aristotelian notion of *phronesis* (Flyvbjerg 2001; Schram 2005), analytic eclecticism embraces a flexible pragmatist ethos to grapple with concrete problems of wide scope, not narrowly sliced intellectual puzzles formulated on the basis of the theoretical priors of a single research tradition. Alongside, and in dialogue with, scholarship embedded in discrete research traditions or paradigms, analytically eclectic scholarship can qualitatively improve the state of theoretical and practical knowledge about political economy and the social sciences writ large. In the process, it can also help to bridge the gulf between academic scholarship and the "everyday politics of the world economy" (Hobson and Seabrooke 2007).

Note

1 Because it traffics in theories premised on different ontologies and epistemological perspectives, eclectic scholarship does run into the challenges raised by the incommensurability thesis as articulated by Paul Feyerabend (1962) among others. However, as we have argued elsewhere (Sil and Katzenstein 2010: 13–16), these challenges are not insurmountable provided care is used to recognize the metaphysical orientations undergirding the use of concepts and analytic principles in contending theories. Moreover, as Donald Davidson (1974) and Hilary Putnam (1981) have argued and even Feyerabend has acknowledged (cf. Oberheim 2006), there is the possibility of translation of terms and concepts across different types of theories. To this, we would add that, since all theories must ultimately operationalize their key terms through empirical referents, these referents provide a shared basis for clarifying and standardizing terms drawn from contending scholarly traditions. This does not guarantee conceptual equivalence in all cases, but it does point to possibilities for mitigating the problem of incommensurability.

PART I

International institutions and global economic governance

3

THE WEST AND THE REST IN GLOBAL ECONOMIC INSTITUTIONS

Robert O. Keohane and Arild Underdal

Introduction: power shifts and institutional change

The global economy is now so tightly linked that state policies, to be effective, have to be coordinated with one another. Coordination takes place most efficiently through established institutions: persistent sets of rules, procedures, and practices designed to govern particular sets of issues. Some of these institutions take the form of organizations, such as the International Monetary Fund (IMF), World Bank, and Bank for International Settlements, and have legal status. Many of the most important institutions, however, are not built around formal organizations but constitute networks with regular patterns of interaction: networks of central bankers have long existed, and now the G8 and G20 government networks play a major role, to the extent that economic coordination among major powers takes place. Although these institutions are designed to govern economic relations, they are intensely political: They are shaped by configurations of power and their politics reflects the domestic politics of their members. Their members act on the basis of their interests, as they perceive them, and make agreements on the basis of reciprocity. Asymmetrical interdependence – having others more dependent on oneself than vice versa – constitutes a crucial source of power, defined as the ability to pursue autonomous policies, on the one hand, and the ability to get others to do what one wants them to do, at feasible cost, on the other (Coleman 1973; Keohane and Nye 1977).

As patterns of interdependence change, so do power relationships. Immediately after World War II, the United States was hegemonic in the world economy: it had strong control over raw materials, including Middle Eastern oil resources; it was the major source of capital and by far the most important market in the world; and it was highly competitive in goods production, as indicated by its large current account surplus. Over the next forty years, all of these advantages eroded, although it continued to be by far the most important player in the world economy, and benefited as well from its leading political role in the Cold War. After the collapse of the Soviet Union, the United States became politically and militarily even more dominant than before: the world became, at least for a while, "unipolar" in strategic terms. In the 1990s, its economy was more dynamic than those of Europe and Japan, and so it regained its economic lead over its nearest competitors as well.

Since the end of the Cold War, however, economic growth has been extraordinarily rapid in much of Asia and in a number of developing countries elsewhere. Asia especially has generated huge current account surpluses, making China and Japan the largest holders of dollar reserves. The United States has run very large and persistent current account deficits. Meanwhile, state oil companies have taken over the major Middle Eastern oilfields, and in some of the oil-producing countries the United States wields little influence. In raw materials, goods production, and capital the United States has lost its hegemonic position, although it remains the most important market in the world and the country to which many others look for leadership.

Institutions are shaped not just by state interests and power but also by the activities of non-governmental organizations (NGOs). Most of these organizations are weak in material resources but are often able to influence public attitudes in democratic countries through the use of mass media and the internet: Insofar as they are seen as advocates for the poor, or protectors of the natural environment, they may wield symbolic influence. Two decades of spreading prosperity, and the impact of the fax machine and the internet on the cost of communication, have created auspicious conditions for the growth in the number and impact of NGOs. Yet patterns of participation and influence *within* NGO networks correlate strongly with the patterns found for intergovernmental organizations (IGOs): Rich democratic societies tend to be the most active.

Because institutions are shaped by power and power is shaped by patterns of asymmetrical interdependence, the "rise of the rest" has major implications for global economic institutions. China and India are now able and willing to block Western initiatives in the World Trade Organization (WTO). The IMF and World Bank have belatedly adjusted voting shares in these organizations to accommodate their strengthened Asian members. Even more importantly, the United States has become dependent on Chinese purchases of Treasury bonds to finance its deficits; hence, Chinese influence in global economic institutions will continue to rise. Yet there is a tension here with the symbolic politics of NGOs: China's foreign and energy policies are strongly at odds with the recommendations of Western NGOs, and, in general, developing countries have resisted the incursion of NGOs into multilateral institutions. Multilateral institutions are like "coral reefs" for NGOs, which gather around them; but some of the states occupying these coral reefs are hostile to the new organisms.

This essay explores, with a broad brush, the past and future of global economic cooperation by focusing on shifts in power, and in the activities of NGOs, in shaping the practices and policies of multilateral economic institutions. In so doing, we discuss tensions as well as cooperation between NGOs and states, especially developing countries; the power shift from Western countries and Japan, on the one hand, to developing countries, especially in Asia, on the other; and the issues of leadership that arise in such a time of transition. Our essay is divided into two major sections. The first describes how the West, led by the United States, created a set of multilateral institutions. The second discusses two trends that are both important but point in different directions: the increase in economic capacity and influence of rapidly growing developing countries; and the vast expansion in the number and activity levels of non-governmental organizations. Our conclusion speculates on future authority relationships, which are likely to depend both on the legitimacy of institutions and on the capacity of leadership to adapt them to rapid shifts in wealth and power.

How the West shaped multilateralism

American hegemony and the American vision

In 1953, when recovery in Europe had only begun after World War II, the United States controlled over 40 percent of world manufacturing production, and even in the 1980s that proportion remained over 30 percent (Nye 1990: 76, 109). Throughout the period of the Cold War, therefore, the United States was hegemonic within the non-communist world: that is, it had "control over raw materials, control over sources of capital, control over markets, and competitive advantages in the production of highly valued goods" (Keohane 1984: 32). Between 1945 and 1970, the United States played the central role in building and maintaining a stable international monetary system, a regime of liberal trade, and dominance in world oil markets leading to stable prices and open access to supplies. American partners and allies benefited from these arrangements, and in return for their provision deferred to the United States on crucial issues. American hegemony reduced uncertainty because the United States had incentives both to enforce rules and, on the whole, to fulfill its commitments (Keohane 1984: ch. 8). Furthermore, the United States was democratic and prosperous, and therefore an object of emulation. United States "soft power" – the ability to shape the preferences of others – reinforced its material power (Nye 2004: 5). The United States had a vision of an alliance system of prosperous, democratic states – along with some convenient non-democratic and not necessarily prosperous allies and dependents – and the means to implement it. It did so not merely through alliances but through international regimes – sets of rules, norms, and practices, open to a wide variety of states – that regulated relationships among states.

U.S. hegemony was consistent with – indeed fostered – multilateralism. The United States found that multilateral institutions could perform valuable functions for it, reducing the costs of making and enforcing agreements, providing information and therefore credibility, and legitimizing practices consistent with U.S. values and conducive to American interests. There were some costs – the United States did not control all outcomes and had to make compromises at the margin – but the overall gains well outweighed these costs.

Throughout the period of American dominance, it faced an external challenge from the Soviet Union, which preoccupied the American government and public. However, the attempt by the Soviet Union and other Communist countries to establish an alternative international system had little impact beyond the Communist bloc itself. In the 1970s, however, in the wake of the Vietnam War and inflationary pressures that it helped to create, the United States faced new economic pressures.

Two major sets of events occurred in the first half of the 1970s that reflected these new pressures: the dollar crises of 1971 and 1973, and the oil crisis of 1973. Until 1971 the United States had exchanged gold for dollars at a fixed price of $35 per ounce, making the dollar "as good as gold." A successor regime, created at the end of 1971, fell apart in 1973, leaving the dollar to float against other currencies. Although the floating regime reflected U.S. interests in a changing world, the inability of the United States to maintain a fixed value of the dollar was a sign of the relative weakening of its position. It was still hegemonic, but less in control than it had been earlier. Likewise, the Arab oil embargo of 1973 reflected a new inability of the United States to control events. In some ways the United States benefited, because it was even clearer than before to Europe and Japan that they depended on the United States for their oil lifeline; but the structural control exercised by the United States was nonetheless diminished.

The rise and fall of the NIEO

In the wake of the monetary and oil crises came another challenge, from Third World countries arguing that the existing order and the policies pursued by major countries in the North had negative effects on economic development and human well-being in the South. This campaign also failed, and that failure offers some important lessons.

A concerted and ambitious effort by Third World countries to change the ground rules for trade and investment laid down by the West is known as the program for a New International Economic Order or NIEO (Bhagwati 1977). Launched in the mid-1970s, this program included four main categories of demands. One aimed at securing for developing countries effective control over natural resources and economic activities within their own territories. Arguing that foreign companies had been granted privileges unfair to the host country, Third World governments demanded the right to nationalize foreign companies that were not prepared to accept "fair" terms and a new code of conduct. A second set of demands called for measures to improve terms of trade. For raw materials, such measures included the right to form producer associations and an indexing device linking the price of raw materials exported to the price of manufactured goods imported. For manufactured goods, Third World governments demanded open access to and preferential treatment in northern markets. A third set of demands focused on debt relief, technology transfer, and development assistance more generally. Finally, developing countries demanded institutional reforms giving them a "fair say" in decision-making processes of important economic organizations such as the World Bank and the IMF.

Much of the political energy behind the NIEO campaign seems to have been generated by a rare combination of dissatisfaction and self-confidence. As Stephen Krasner wrote, "the unity of developing countries is a product of their objective situation and subjective self-understanding" (Krasner 1985: 308). In many African and Asian countries, independence had created great hopes of rapid economic development and improvement in the quality of life. These hopes proved hard to fulfill. Part of the blame was put on the Western powers and the international institutions that they had created. At the same time, self-confidence was boosted by events such as the dismantling of colonial rule, the establishment of a politically significant coalition of Third World states (known as G77), and the success of Arab oil-exporting countries in organizing and implementing an embargo that raised prices significantly and proved Western economies vulnerable to concerted action by a small group of commodity producers. Moreover, the UN Conference on Trade and Development (UNCTAD) served as a useful arena for and facilitator of Third World coordination.

Despite some favorable conditions and sustained efforts over several years, results were meager, at least compared with ambitions. By the mid-1980s it was clear that no major reform of the international economic order would be accomplished. The fall of NIEO suggests four important lessons about institutional reform.

First, at least in the absence of hegemonic leadership, a solid base of consensual knowledge seems to come close to being a necessary condition for effective cooperation (see Breitmeier et al. forthcoming). The proponents of the NIEO never succeeded in building such a platform; in fact, the diagnosis of the problem as well as the essence of the cure remained contested. Second, dynamics of coalition building may serve to polarize positions (Rothstein 1984: 316–18). Within the G77 demands were to a large extent aggregated by simple addition. This approach left the industrialized countries with a rather bulky package. The inclination of some radical G77 governments to frame NIEO demands in terms of ideological principles that did not resonate well with political developments in the West strained negotiations further. Around 1980 voters in major Western countries turned to leaders with market-oriented reforms high on their agendas (notably President Reagan and Prime Minister Thatcher). Third, "votes count, but resources decide" (Rokkan 1966: 106–7). Although successful in mobilizing the majorities required to win contested decisions in the UN General Assembly and other similar bodies, G77 was much weaker when it came to power in the basic games of international trade and finance. The success of the oil-exporting countries in using control over important resources to extract concessions proved hard to replicate elsewhere.[1] Finally, although arguably "unfair" to the South in some important respects, the institutional system established by the West goes further than imperial orders of the past in "creating conditions for rising states to advance their expanding economic and political goals within it" (Ikenberry 2008: 29). For countries capable of taking advantage of such opportunities – such as China and India – this makes it more attractive to join. For the rest it becomes harder to overturn (Ikenberry 2008: 24). As a consequence, the internal cohesion of G77 itself proved hard to maintain as negotiations dragged.

The apogee of Western power and the creation of the WTO

The collapse of efforts for a NIEO was followed by the Latin American debt crisis of the early 1980s, which further weakened these economies and made them more dependent on the United States for debt relief. At the same time, as noted above, the economically advanced countries turned toward more neoliberal, market-oriented policies both at home and abroad. One reaction of developing countries was to move more strongly toward trade openness in an attempt to promote exports. Mexico, for example, joined the GATT (General Agreement on Tariffs and Trade) in the mid-1980s and began to push for what became the North American Free Trade Area (NAFTA). India fundamentally changed its policies with market-oriented reforms in 1990.

The trade negotiations that concluded the Uruguay Round illustrate how the impact of the end of the Cold War enhanced the bargaining power of the United States at the expense of developing countries. In the run-up to the Round, developing countries had been able to block the beginning of negotiations conditional on concessions by the rich countries about the agenda. However, as the Round neared conclusion, the United States and the European Community agreed on the Single Undertaking, which some U.S. officials referred to as "the power play." The Uruguay Round Final Act bound all members to all of its parts, including the controversial TRIPS Agreement on intellectual property. Furthermore, "after joining the WTO (including the GATT 1994) the EC and the United States withdrew from the GATT 1947 and thereby terminated their GATT 1947 obligations (including its MFN guarantee) to countries that did not accept the Final Act and join the WTO" (Steinberg 2002: 360).

The period of negotiation of the WTO, which was finalized in 1994, represents the high-water mark of U.S. power in the world. The Soviet Union had collapsed. The United States therefore no longer had to compete with the Soviets for the favor of developing countries, and had only the European Community as an effective economic competitor. Japan had already entered its recession of the 1990s and China was not yet a major economic power. As the WTO negotiation shows, the United States did not miss its chance: on the contrary, it took advantage of the situation to institutionalize its favored rules in the WTO.

Major changes: transnational and transgovernmental relations; the rise of the East and South

Broadly speaking, multilateralism between 1945 and 1990 was state led and formally structured. The United States was hegemonic, but other states played a role. International cooperation took place largely through formal multilateral institutions such as the United Nations, the IMF and World Bank, and the GATT. Since 1990, however, two major shifts in the conditions underlying world politics have altered this picture; neither is closely related to the end of the Cold War.

The first major set of changes has derived from the rapid growth since the 1980s of China, and since 1990 of India, along with relatively rapid growth rates for some other major developing countries. As China, India, Brazil, and other developing countries have become more important in the world economy, decisions that do not include them have decreasing effect. As a direct result, the multilateral system of the late twentieth century has been restructured to provide more access and influence for newly large economies that have a major impact on outcomes worldwide. These countries are typically strongly committed to traditional conceptions of sovereignty. They are willing to cooperate on the basis of specific agreements and very limited delegations of authority to multilateral institutions, as states traditionally have. The economic, and therefore political, rise of these countries has strengthened rather than shaken the state-led structure of world politics.

The second of these major changes, whose early signs were evident twenty years earlier, is very different, as it challenges the traditional conception of world politics as essentially involving relationships among sovereign states. Non-governmental organizations operating on a transnational basis have vastly expanded in numbers and scope during the last twenty years. They form networks of relationships among NGOs and between them and other entities, including firms and states, that are much more varied and complex than traditional interstate relationships. These relationships include what have been called "transgovernmental relations" (Keohane and Nye 1974) or "government networks." Transgovernmental relations and government networks involve semi-autonomous or autonomous government agencies, and judicial bodies, that coordinate activity across national lines. Anne-Marie Slaughter has described the activities of government networks composed of regulator, legislators, and judges (Slaughter 2004).

"The rise of the rest": economic growth in Asia, Africa, and Latin America

The world economy is undergoing significant change, arguably amounting to a "tectonic shift" (Haas 2008: 44). Over the ten-year period 1995–2005 the developing countries as a group increased their share of the total value of goods and services produced in the world from 39 percent to 46 percent (World Bank 2007:

185). Developing economies in East Asia and the Pacific account for most of this increase, raising their aggregate share from 13 percent to 19 percent. China recorded an impressive economic growth of nearly 10 percent annually over the six years 2003–8. Also other major Asian countries can point to growth rates far above those of North America and Western Europe: India nearly 8 percent, Pakistan and Iran about 6 percent. Major African countries report similar achievements, with Ethiopia at 7 percent, Nigeria at 6 percent, and Egypt at 5 percent. Major Latin American economies have been growing at a pace between 5 percent (Argentina) and 3 percent (Brazil, Mexico) annually. Although pale by Chinese standards, these figures compare well with those of major Western European countries, where economic growth fell below 2 percent in France, Germany, and Italy. A quick look at growth rate rankings drives home the message. Whereas China's *worst* performance in the 2003–8 period leaves it in place 17, the *top* rank for the United States is 100 and for Germany 167. Should the Chinese economy continue to grow at a pace of 9 percent per year and the U.S. economy at a rate of 3 percent, the GDP of China (adjusted to purchasing power parity or PPP) would surpass that of the United States in about eleven years.[2]

Linear extrapolation of recent growth trends is, however, not a reliable method for predicting future developments (Olson 1982). Economic models – referring to mechanisms such as diminishing returns to capital and diffusion of technologies – predict per capita growth rates to be higher for poor than for rich countries. Empirical studies offer conditional support; when important other factors such as initial levels of human capital and government policies are controlled for, growth rates tend to vary inversely with initial levels of income (Barro and Sala-i-Martin 2004: 14; see also Jones and Romer 2010). Country-specific studies identify other factors that may slow down future growth. In the case of China, these factors include environmental damage, depletion of natural resources, and demographic change raising the proportion of elderly people from 10 percent in 2000 to about 24 percent in 2035 (Riley 2004: 27); perhaps also social strain and political conflict spurred by increasing income inequalities. China may be "destined" to become the world's largest economy, but recent performance, however impressive, provides no guarantee that the ride will be smooth and fast in the future.

Moreover, to understand the implications of the pattern described above we have to couple growth rates to absolute numbers. Many of the rapid growth countries are still poor by Western standards. The larger the gap between rich and poor, the more the latter will have to outpace the former in order to catch up. In fact, even with a growth rate only one-third of that of China, the annual increment added by the U.S. economy to the nation's wealth, measured in terms of GDP per capita, is still larger. Countries with high population growth, such as Ethiopia and Nigeria, will have to add about 3 percent per year to the aggregate value of goods and services produced just to keep GDP per capita constant. For these and many other countries it will take a consistently superior performance over several decades to close the income gap to North America and Western Europe. Such an achievement would be truly remarkable.

Two interrelated consequences of the development described above are particularly important here. One concerns the distribution of power; the other pertains to the configuration of interests.

Uneven economic growth is likely to affect the *distribution of power* in the world economy. First, rapid economic growth makes a country more important as producer, market, and investor. The political significance of this change cannot be understood merely by looking at aggregate figures; as important may be particular bilateral relationships of (inter)dependence. One example is the large Chinese investment in U.S. securities since 2002, leaving China in control of U.S. Treasury bonds worth about $800 billion (Morrison and Labonte 2009). Even though China's control over U.S. securities may not be an effective tool of financial coercion, it has generated considerable concern (Drezner 2009a). Second, a higher income enables a country to acquire new capabilities such as more advanced technologies, better education, and better health services. Third, success tends to enhance prestige and in some instances also other forms of "soft power" (Nye 2004).

Also *configurations of interests* will likely be affected. With large investments in U.S. securities comes a positive interest in a healthy U.S. economy. As the Western champions of the liberal economic order see their competitive position weaken in important sectors, their concern with terms of trade and investment is likely to increase. Conversely, at least some of the countries that enjoy rapid economic growth find themselves reaping benefits of the open and rule-based order established by the West. As their competitive positions improve, these countries are likely to benefit more from the liberalization of trade and investment.

Institutional dispersion and adjustment to change

The impact of changes in the structure of the world political economy is clearly indicated by changes in the configuration and practices of multilateral institutions. Two patterns are particularly evident. On the one hand, various institutions are undergoing changes in their composition and the distribution of authority within them. This is particularly true of the G7 and the IMF. On the other hand, in certain issue areas we are seeing a dispersion of institutions, either diminishing the dominance of a single institution such as the WTO or reflecting the failure to agree on a single institution for the issue area.

Let us first consider the G7. As we have seen, the 1973 oil crisis and the global recession in the mid-1970s spurred the leaders of the major Western powers – the United States, the United Kingdom, Japan, France, West Germany, and Italy – to meet in order to coordinate policy responses. The parties agreed to meet annually under a rotating presidency. Canada was soon added (1976) to form the G7, and later Russia, and – on special terms – the EU, have been invited to join, creating what is today known as the G8. The G8 summits constitute a forum in which the leaders can exchange views on important challenges and search for common response strategies, usually outlined in the form of rather general principles or guidelines.

The G7 was founded as an exclusive "club" of the most important democratic industrialized countries. Its expansion to the G8 with the inclusion of Russia in 1997 was a response to the democratization of Russia. However, it has become somewhat anomalous for two reasons. The presence of Russia, at best semi-democratic and certainly not a political ally of the other seven members, constrains discussion of sensitive issues. And the fact that China has outstripped Russia in gross domestic product means that the G8 no longer includes all of the largest economies in the world.[3]

Recognition that the G8 omits major countries – including also Brazil and India – has led to the inclusion of other countries in "G8+" meetings over the last few years. In November 2008, during the global financial crisis, heads of state for the first time met as the G20, which includes nineteen countries plus the European Union; and in September 2009 its leaders designated it as the "premier forum for international economic coordination."[4] The current G20 is an outgrowth of the G20 created in 1999 as a semi-formal network providing a forum for finance ministers and central bank directors, which, unlike the G8, included the most important emerging economies of the South (Argentina, Brazil, China, India, Indonesia, Mexico, Saudi Arabia, South Africa). All of its members are among the top thirty-two economies of the world, measured by GDP in current dollars, and among the top twenty-four countries measured by purchasing power parity. The G20 members were selected through a political process. Some European countries that rank higher than some G20 members are represented only through the EU. Of the non-European countries, Iran and Taiwan are the only ones among the top twenty states in PPP-based GDP who are not included in the G20.[5]

The transition from the G8 to the G20 as the principal forum for international economic coordination is a clear mark of the rise of certain developing countries to positions of economic prominence.

The more highly institutionalized multilateral institutions have been slower to adjust, but adjustment is occurring. Both the World Bank and the IMF have made adjustments recently in their voting rules in favor of the South. As of this writing, the IMF is in the midst of a rather wrenching debate about these changes, which will cost the European countries some of their seats on its Executive Board. These changes may not be sufficient to convert developing countries into staunch supporters of these institutions, but at least they show that the rules of the liberal order can to some extent be used to their advantage (Ikenberry 2008). Yet they involve trade-offs. As Ngaire Woods has written, the Bank and the Fund "are trying to incorporate 'ownership' into the way they do business at a time when nonborrowers are also demanding that the institution be yet more accountable and responsible to them" (Woods 2006: 208). With respect to the policies of states, at any rate (as opposed to advocacy groups), demands for fundamental change of the international economic order have seemed to give way to proposals for more moderate reforms. From the standpoint of the newly powerful, inclusion in the "clubs" of powerful state is clearly preferable to fighting a difficult and uncertain battle to restructure multilateral arrangements. Institutions, as we have learned, are "path dependent." The shadow of former Western dominance persists in the orientation of these institutions (toward liberal openness), in their membership (with heavy European representation throughout), and in their voting rules. "Informal governance" in the IMF, as Randall Stone has shown, heavily favors the United States (Stone 2002, 2011).

Nevertheless, the gradual opening of major multilateral institutions to developing countries is likely to enhance the support of developing countries for established international economic regimes. Indeed, export-dependent industrializing countries are in many ways the greatest beneficiaries of a system that combines liberal trade with lack of constraint on their ability to manipulate their own exchange rate to enhance exports and build up foreign exchange reserves. It would be hard to think of a plausible global economic regime complex that would be better in economic terms for China and a liberalizing India than one that encourages exports and, as a result of competition among Western firms, enables access to technology and sophisticated organizational techniques provided by multinational corporations. The current system meets these requirements.[6]

In a variety of issue areas, however, global institutions with universal rules have lost ground to more decentralized or even fragmented sets of institutions. Notably, the WTO has been stalled since its formation in 1994 by conflict between the West and developing countries. Now, unlike the early 1990s, developing countries are able to block Western initiatives, although they are both too divided and too weak to push through measures that they favor. As a result, we have seen the proliferation of bilateral investment agreements (BITs) with "TRIPS-plus" agreements that favor powerful developing countries. With the option of pushing through their preferred rules in global institutions rendered unavailable (as indicated by the concessions made by the rich countries at Doha in 2001), powerful states have increasingly resorted to a "divide and rule" strategy.

In other issue areas the increasing power of the developing countries, in the context of continuing conflicts of interest, has contributed to the proliferation of institutions that are connected in systematic and mutually supportive ways. Instead of coherent regimes on such issues as plant genetic resources and biodiversity, climate change, and energy we see the emergence of "regime complexes": collectives of non-hierarchical and partially overlapping regimes (Raustiala and Victor 2004; Keohane and Victor 2011; Colgan et al. 2010). The emergence of such regime complexes in place of coherent regimes is likely to reduce constraints on governments, enabling them to "forum shop," searching for the institution that enables them to best pursue their self-interests (Alter and Meunier 2009; Drezner 2009b).

So we see a changing world order. The developing countries have greater ability than before to shape the agendas and structures of major international institutions; yet the deadlocks that result from their greater power have generated a proliferation of institutions that may weaken their authority overall. Furthermore, the power of developing countries to shape this new world order is limited by their internal disagreements. Indeed, as the Copenhagen Conference on climate change in December 2009 indicated, beyond opposition to many of the plans of the West, there is little unity of interest or strategy among the developing countries. But, to borrow a phrase from Asia, they are now "the developing countries that can say no," which they were not in 1994.

The combination of stability with increasing institutional complexity or even fragmentation and a lack of the conditions for leadership – with the weakening of the dominant position of the United States and the absence of a coherent strong coalition – seems quite unique in modern history. Broadly speaking, the era between the Crystal Palace Exhibition of 1851 and World War I beginning in 1914 was a period of British leadership – perhaps not hegemony, as the United States passed Britain in industrial power midway through this period, but clear leadership nonetheless. The pound sterling was the world's most important currency, London was the center of international financial activity, and the British Empire still spanned the globe. So, broadly speaking, 1851–1914 was a period characterized by both stability and leadership. In contrast, the interwar period was the opposite: lack of leadership was coupled with instability. In Charles Kindleberger's analysis, Great Britain was unable and the United States unwilling to lead by performing the key functions of maintaining open markets for goods, engaging in stable long-term lending, policing a relatively stable system of exchange rates, ensuring the coordination of macro-economic policies, and acting as a lender of last resort (Kindleberger 1973: 289). Between 1947 and 1973, the United States, aided by multilateral institutions that it had taken the lead in creating, played these roles. The patterns were modified after 1973 – in particular, the United States no longer led in long-term lending and exchange rates floated, but the combination of effective leadership and stability lasted at least through the end of the Uruguay Round and the formation of the WTO in 1994.

Now, however, the world economy is entering into uncharted waters. If global stability requires "a stabilizer – one stabilizer" (Kindleberger 1973: 304), we are in for trouble. However, if the complex of organizations and networks that have emerged – that is, the "regime complexes" – can perform these tasks, we may see stability without hegemonic leadership. From the standpoint of policy makers these will be frustrating times, as initiatives can easily be blocked, even by majorities. Still, despite divergent views on a number of specific issues, the level of mutual interest in keeping the system from collapsing is very high. No major state wants to bring it down, or is ideologically committed to its collapse. In an era of rapid change, therefore, we could paradoxically see considerable stability.

The NGO system: modifying or amplifying the Western order?

Intergovernmental regimes, organizations, and networks provide the basic institutional infrastructure for governing transboundary economic activities. Much of the cooperation that takes place at the global level is, however, initiated and organized by non-governmental actors; and much intergovernmental coordination takes place informally among subunits of governments. For each intergovernmental organization there are about ten international non-governmental organizations, and over the past four to five decades the growth rate has been significantly higher in the latter sphere.[7] Most NGOs have small budgets and secretariats and little or no political significance. But some stand out; the Catholic Church counts more than 1 billion "members," the largest humanitarian organizations have billion-dollar budgets and thousands of employees, and some advocacy organizations are significant voices in the domains of, inter alia, human rights and environmental protection. Moreover, transnational corporations play important roles in the global economy.

To what extent and how is this system of non-governmental organizations and informal networks modifying the interstate order developed by Western great powers?

If we compare the populations of IGOs and NGOs, similarities are as striking as differences. The growth rates are strongly correlated (Boli and Thomas 1999: 28). For both, patterns of participation reflect the stratification of world society: "old" and well-established countries are more actively involved than "young" countries, rich participate more than poor, and democracies more than countries under authoritarian or totalitarian rule (Boli et al. 1999; Shanks et al. 1996). In fact, the difference between rich and poor seems to be larger in the non-governmental sphere than for IGOs. It is also greater within the domains of industry and trade than in other issue areas such as education, culture, and sports. Moreover, the discrepancy between center and periphery becomes even more conspicuous if we look at the location of headquarters. At the turn of the century about two-thirds of NGO headquarters were found in Europe. The corresponding figure for IGOs was below 50 percent (van der Wusten 2004). In some respects, the center–periphery discrepancy is diminishing. Most importantly, participation rates have been significantly higher in other parts of the world at least since the 1980s, and meetings are now far more dispersed than secretariats. Nevertheless, the NGO system at large still reflects the stratification of world society more sharply than the system of IGOs.

In social science research non-governmental organizations and networks are sometimes seen as a positive transformative force, "engaged in a longer-term project to modify what can be regarded as the underlying constitutive basis of modern civilization and to develop new modes of local as well as transnational governance" (Lipschutz with Mayer 1996: 2). At least three more specific propositions may be distinguished. One says that civil society organizations overall provide a more genuine and direct representation of the "will of the people." Another claims that the overall thrust of these efforts is to promote *universal* values (such as basic human rights) and *common* interests (such as protection of nature's life support systems). Finally, some see the growth of transnational cooperation as fostering a new *world culture*, characterized by more inclusive conceptions of identity ("world citizen") and acceptance of a combination of reason and voluntarism as a basis for authority (Boli and Thomas 1999).

It is easy to identify transnational organizations and networks that fit at least one of these images very well. As general statements, however, they should still be considered as bold hypotheses. Skeptics can point out that, as the membership of most NGOs is made up of non-representative subsets of the world's population, even perfect internal democracy would not guarantee that their aggregate voice is that of "the people." They will also find that the largest subcategories of NGOs are established to promote specific group interests rather than universal values. And with regard to the world culture hypothesis, they may note that much of the growth in the NGO system in recent decades has come through further differentiation and specialization – a trend that is not particularly conducive to fostering more inclusive identities.

Indeed, a close look at NGOs suggests that many of them play roles that are much more mundane than some of the more enthusiastic commentary suggests. Jessica Green has analyzed what she calls "the emergence of private authority" along two dimensions: delegated and entrepreneurial. States often delegate authority to non-governmental organizations (Green 2010). For instance, the Clean Development Mechanism of the Kyoto Protocol regime delegates the key task of monitoring and certifying emissions reductions to non-governmental organizations, typically accounting firms such as KMPG Peat Marwick. When authority is delegated by intergovernmental organizations to NGOs they should be viewed as partners in an agency relationship rather than as competitors or carriers of different cultural values. Entrepreneurial authority, by contrast, derives from initiatives taken by the NGO. For instance, the Forest Service Council certifies forests as managed in sustainable ways and the International Standards Organization (ISO) has established a variety of standards with respect to environmental as well as other values.

The shift in the structure of the global political economy toward rapidly growing large developing countries provides a striking contrast with the rise in NGOs, mostly based in the West. The "rise of the rest" reinforces statism and traditional conceptions of sovereignty. The policies of these states can principally be understood as self-interested, adopted in the shadow of their conception of how much influence they can wield, and in the service of increasing that influence over time. When they support multilateralism, we can understand it as a reflection of the functional value of multilateralism. In other words, traditional methods of analysis of world politics apply; one only has to change the focus of one's attention.

In contrast, the rise of NGOs leads us to ask whether there really is something "new under the sun." Their prominence is clearly evident in certain fields, human rights arguably being the most celebrated case. Until the 1990s the Human Rights Committee of the United Nations – a committee of experts established in 1977 to oversee national policies with respect to the International Covenant on Civil and Political Rights – never took formal notice of information provided by NGOs. Now the Committee "openly solicits information from non-governmental organizations" and "devotes the first morning of every session to a meeting with representatives of NGOs" (Kretzmer 2010: 48). To take another example, the newest human rights convention is the Convention on the Rights of Persons with

Disabilities (CERD), which came into force in 2008. At the conference where the Convention was negotiated, representatives of accredited NGOs received official documents, participated both in public and informal/closed meetings, had extensive formal representation in the working group, and were permitted to make substantive statements on the floor as well as to actively lobby state delegations (DeBurca 2010: 184). And it appears that, in many respects, the final Convention mirrors many of the demands of the NGO community focused on disability rights. Finally, it was well publicized that the Copenhagen climate conference of December 2009 had 40,000 authorized participants. NGO representatives roamed the floor and apparently played a major role in formulating the policies of a number of small states.

These three examples illustrate the close connection between NGO activity and transgovernmental networks. In none of these situations could NGOs make policy on their own. However, they could exercise influence by aligning themselves with government agencies or with officials who had similar objectives. The "mixed transnational–transgovernmental coalitions" that Keohane and Nye (1974) observed over thirty-five years ago are now commonplace at conferences hosted by international organizations.

So far, the rise of the non-West and the very Western rise of NGOs have seemed to proceed on parallel tracks. NGOs have obtained most prominent roles in areas such as human rights and environmental protection. Both of these issue areas are secondary concerns to the governments of most emerging economies, and the strengthening of human rights norms and rules may even be seen as threatening by some of these governments. There have been some civil society protests against the IMF, World Bank, and WTO, but what is most striking about these protests is that there has been no alignment between First World activists, concerned about issues of (global) justice, and developing country governments, seeking specific economic benefits from the international economic order and greater access to its major institutions. In any competition on these issues between China, India, and Brazil on the one hand and Western NGO activists on the other, we think that the advantages are almost all on the side of the developing countries, particularly in view of the fact that elites in rich countries have more interests in common with them than with their protesting fellow citizens.

Conclusion: legitimacy and leadership in the twenty-first century

We end this paper with some reflections on prospects for global economic institutions in a world in which the dominance of the West is eroding and "the rest" are becoming more important.

Global economic institutions operate, as before, within a system of sovereign states, but there are clear tensions around the classic conception of sovereignty, under which sovereignty is indivisible and excludes other authorities from the sovereign's territory (Bull 1977: 8; Lake 2009b: 46–7). As Stephen Krasner has brilliantly argued, "the characteristics that are associated with sovereignty – territory, autonomy, recognition, and control – do not provide an accurate description of the actual practices that have characterized many entities that have been conventionally viewed as sovereign states" (Krasner 1999: 237). In the current era, sovereignty along some dimensions is being rapidly altered by globalization. The state seems to have been able to cope with competing authority structures such as multinational enterprises – as indicated by their replacement in petroleum politics by state-owned companies. However, norms against the prosecution of state officials for crimes such as torture and murder – formerly entirely blocked by conceptions of sovereignty – have eroded dramatically during the last thirty years (Sikkink forthcoming). Sovereignty is malleable and dynamic; so its current form should not be taken for granted.

Within the persistent system of states that are sovereign (but subject to changing notions of the concept), international order, and the authority patterns that establish it, will in turn depend on two essential pillars: legitimacy and leadership. Hedley Bull (1977: 8) defined international order as "a pattern of activity that sustains the elementary or primary goals of the society of states." Thus defined, order in world politics depends to a considerable extent on whether the institutions that make and enforce rules are regarded as legitimate by those to whom they are subject. That is, do the subjects of rule regard these institutions as having the right to carry out these functions? In other words, authority in world politics – as opposed to sheer coercive power – depends on legitimacy. The hierarchy of international relations rests on such authority (Lake 2009b).

The legitimacy of an institution, in turn, reflects both its procedures and its outputs (Scharpf 1998). The main question asked about procedures is whether they are "fair." Any student of politics understands that "fairness" is an elusive goal in a system lacking a people with common values or a comprehensive system of global governance. Yet certain basic norms of equal treatment seem to be frequently invoked and rarely disputed. Although widely considered imperfect by these standards, the institutional framework created by the West after World War II is an open and rule-based system, providing opportunities for countries enjoying rapid economic growth to enhance their influence. In the words of Ikenberry (2010: 514), this system is "distinctive in its integrative and expansive character." The inclusion of major developing countries in the G20 network reinforces this impression. Moreover, one of the factors making for compliance with international law is what Hedley Bull called "acceptance by the parties of the ends of values underlying the agreement." International law, for Bull, should be seen as a "means by which states can advertise their intentions . . . provide one another with reassurance, . . . and specify precisely what the nature of the agreement is" (Bull 1977: 141–2). Again it seems that the institutional framework established by the West goes some way to meeting these requirements. The heavy and profound criticism launched against this system by developing countries during the NIEO campaign is now more muted, particularly as far as the governments of major countries such as China, India, and Brazil are concerned.

In a strategic environment such as world politics it may be very difficult to ascertain whether there is a shared belief that a particular institution has the right to make and enforce rules (Buchanan and Keohane 2006). The reason for the difficulty is itself strategic: Actors have an incentive to disparage the legitimacy of institutions that they wish to influence, by claiming that this supposed "illegitimacy" requires reform in the direction preferred by the actor. Caution is therefore required in using the frequency of illegitimacy claims to measure the actual legitimacy of an institution. In contemporary world politics, willingness to join and willingness to pay are probably more reliable indicators. Despite Kofi Annan's statements about the "unique legitimacy of the United Nations," the fact that the resources at its disposal are very small – compared not only with those of states but also with those of the IMF and World Bank – suggests that rich states have reservations. Yet membership is virtually universal and states – with the exception of Indonesia briefly under Sukarno – have shown no inclination to leave or have not threatened to leave either the UN or the IMF and World Bank. In the 1980s and 1990s there was a wave of applications to join GATT and the WTO, and states still clamor to join the EU.

Compare this situation with the wave of departures from the League of Nations in the 1930s, when the legitimacy of multilateral institutions genuinely was challenged – by the United States (which never joined), the Soviet Union (which was long excluded), and later by the fascist countries. The League's difficulties were a reflection of underlying fissures that weakened any general agreement on legitimacy. One of the striking features of contemporary multilateralism is the *absence* of such fundamental dissension, despite rapid change, disagreement over a number of specific issues, and deadlock. Despite rapid change, the current system is not a "revolutionary system" in the sense used fifty years ago by Stanley Hoffmann (1961). Among major states, purposes are often at odds but are not fundamentally incompatible; and the means used in relations among them do not include extreme measures such as massive violence. When such means are used – as by al-Qaeda – they are virtually universally condemned.

Legitimacy is one thing; leadership is something else entirely. The increasing dispersion not only of power but also of authority in world politics means that leadership is difficult to exercise. Sovereignty, of course, limits the extent of international leadership. But even more so does independence: more precisely, the relative lack of dependence of most major states on *one* particular other and more powerful state for protection or for economic support. For example, in the winter of 2009–10 the United States had difficulty getting universal support for sanctions against Iran, even given considerable evidence that Iran was defying UN inspectors and trying to develop the capacity to build nuclear weapons. The President of Brazil said no directly to the American Secretary of State when she asked for support on sanctions. In multilateral institutions governed by consensus, as we have noted about the WTO and the Framework Convention on Climate Change (FCCC), it is very difficult indeed to obtain any meaningful agreements, particularly any which would be legally binding.

The resulting institutional system, then, combines structural stability, massive changes in relative capabilities, and political deadlock on major issues. Order is maintained by convergent interests and to some extent by shared values that bolster legitimacy and authority; but power resources are too dispersed to facilitate strong leadership.

The performance of this "stable but stuck system" will vary, depending on features of the problems to be solved. First, as Barrett (2007) reminds us, some collective action problems (such as the eradication of a highly contagious disease) require universal participation whereas others can be solved by a "coalition of the willing" and some even by one single actor (but not *any* actor). Second, we may safely assume that such a system will be more effective in managing business as usual than in responding to new challenges requiring bold or innovative action. Third, with regard to new challenges, we expect more success in dealing with acute common threats than in responding to threats that are seen as differentiated and challenges that require proactive, long-term policies. For instance, the Great Recession of 2008–10 (an acute common threat) was met, admittedly with only partial success, by a mix of unilateral and loosely coordinated measures; but the unity of 2008–9 has dissipated as states have reverted to unilateral measures to depreciate their currencies, or at least to slow their appreciation. At the same time, there has been little progress in developing a common strategy for mitigating the impact of human activities on the global climate system – a particularly demanding challenge, calling for proactive and long-term policies (Underdal 2010; Keohane and Victor 2011).

Responses are one thing; reactions and unintended effects are something else. In this regard, how institutionalized an issue area is may be important. For example, the Great Recession seems not to have profoundly disrupted patterns of liberal trade, which are bolstered by WTO as well as by widely shared elite attitudes; but there are clear signs of possible currency wars, as various countries manipulate the value of their currencies to gain export advantages. Currency manipulation is easier to conduct than trade manipulation because of the weak institutionalization of international monetary relations: the lack of clear rules and authoritative dispute-settlement procedures.

Ultimately, whether one considers the contemporary system to be satisfactory by normative standards depends on three factors: (1) how satisfied one is with the status quo in a given issue area; (2) how stable one regards the system as being, so that it inhibits retrogression toward unilateralism and associated conflict; and (3) how optimistic one is about the prospects for change. Those who are satisfied with the status quo, regard it as stable, and are pessimistic about prospects for change – the position of classic conservatives – are quite satisfied. Radicals are dissatisfied with the status quo and optimistic about prospects for change; and for them the stability of current practices is negatively valued. There may be a few people who are both satisfied with the status quo and optimistic about the prospects for change; whether they regard current institutions as stable or not, they are probably happy, but it is doubtful that they understand world politics very well.

The situation is more difficult for those of us who combine dissatisfaction with the status quo with pessimism about prospects for fundamental transformation. With part of our being, we want to "reform world politics altogether," to change the stark inequalities of power and wealth and foster new policy measures to combat global dangers such as climate change. However, our pessimistic side warns that rapid reform is difficult and risky. Unintended consequences are likely to appear, and self-interested or even malign actors may hijack reform for their own purposes. We therefore hope for institutional stability, and try to maintain established institutions as constraints on abuses of power, even as we advocate their gradual reform. Our hope is that our own generation's search for cooperation even in the face of continuing discord (Keohane 1984) will yield incremental improvements for the benefit of future generations.

Notes

1 For a comprehensive analysis of the prospects of Third World producer cooperation, see Hveem (1977).
2 Chan (2008: 14) reports a similar estimate, but concludes that about forty years would be a more plausible prediction.
3 According to the IMF and the World Bank (Wikipedia, accessed March 9, 2010), in 2008 China was the fourth largest economy in the world, if one includes the EU, and was poised, at its 10 percent annual growth rate, to pass Japan. Russia was eighth or ninth, depending on the list, with less than half the GDP of China.
4 G20 website (http://www.G-20.org, accessed March 9, 2010).
5 Wikipedia (accessed March 9, 2010).
6 China's sudden restrictions in the fall of 2010 on exports of rare earth elements to Japan and more generally suggests that a note of caution with respect to this optimistic prognosis would be appropriate. If the Chinese elites decided that disrupting the international economic order would be worthwhile to advance their political interests, or in response to nationalist pressure at home, the prognosis would be much less rosy.
7 The standard source of reference is *Yearbook of International Organizations*, published by the Union of International Associations (http://www.uia.be/yearbook, accessed January 14, 2011).

4

FREE MARKETS FOR ALL

The difficulties of maintaining a stable liberal world economy

Georg Sørensen

I want to propose a basic tension in liberal thought that also has consequences for a global economic order based on liberal principles. It flows from two major modalities of a liberal posture. One can be called Liberalism of Restraint: it emphasizes tolerance of diversity, moderation, holding back, empathy, non-intervention, and peaceful cooperation. Pluralism rather than universalism will be at the heart of this posture and negative liberty a preference over positive liberty even though that might not always be the case and there can be different priorities in domestic and international politics. The other posture can be called Liberalism of Imposition: it accentuates that liberal principles are morally superior to other principles and universally valid. It supports activism, intervention, and, in the international realm, the change of non-liberal regimes to liberal regimes, not excluding the possible use of force. Universalism is stressed over pluralism, but there is not necessarily agreement among impositionists on the relative importance of negative versus positive liberty (Sørensen 2006). I apply these postures to the current world economic (dis)order; that leads to a pessimistic conclusion concerning the future prospects for a stable liberal world economy. My theoretical basis is that of a skeptical liberal: the progress in the global political economy that liberals talk about is in principle possible, but by no means assured or guaranteed. In relation to this, liberal theory and liberal politics contain tensions and problems that have not been sufficiently recognized. The ambition is to analyze and evaluate these tensions and problems in order to consider the implications for liberal economic order. So the liberal stance needs, true to the pluralism advocated by Helge Hveem (2009), to be supplemented with insights originating in other theoretical traditions.

A stable global economy based on liberal principles of free markets and private property is a cornerstone of liberal world order. Some will see the economy as the easy part of the liberal project; there is, after all, almost universal support today for a liberal-capitalist free market arrangement. Even classical, die-hard opponents of a liberal economy, such as North Korea and Cuba, are slowly coming around to move in that direction. However, the economy directly affects the well-being of citizens around the world, including people (and voters) in liberal states. Therefore, economic issues are easily transformed into topics of political contestation: Less satisfied individuals and groups will seek to change or modify the rules of the economic game in their favor. On the one hand, then, liberal states support the universal principles of "an open, equitable, rule-based, predictable, non-discriminatory and multilateral trading and financial system" (United Nations 2000: 4). On the other hand, liberal states frequently seek to preserve, and even expand, special economic arrangements that support domestic groups and often protect them from the vagaries of international competition.

The following section specifies major dimensions of the relationship between politics and economics, that is, between states and markets. The meaning of Liberal Imposition and Liberal Restraint in the economic sphere is examined. Restraint dominated in the first decades following World War II: the Bretton Woods system of "embedded liberalism" was, in the terminology of this book, a Liberalism of Restraint system as it combined open markets with domestic autonomy in economic policy making. It was a successful system for the Western countries. I will, however, argue that it cannot be restored under the current conditions in the globalized economy.

A Liberalism of Imposition system has taken the driver's seat since the 1980s, under the heading of "Washington Consensus" principles. However, these principles cannot sustain a stable global economy because they do not sufficiently address major problems in weak and modernizing countries. For latecomers, there is less room for developmental choice today, and full participation in neoliberal economic globalization is the recommended, if not mandatory, option. At the same time, leading liberal states themselves uphold significant non-liberal elements of protectionism. These states have long practiced double standards: advocating neoliberal principles to others that they do not abide by themselves, not now and not in their earlier phases of development.

Finally, instead of delivering transnational goods, the liberal world economy is increasingly producing transnational bads, with financial crisis, environmental problems, and illegitimate transactions involving people, drugs, and money. So three major problems obstruct the establishment of a stable liberal world economy: (1) construction of an appropriate state–market matrix: liberal states have imposed neoliberal principles on the rest of the world, but it has not worked well and the establishment of a Restraint order with higher flexibility in the adaptation of liberal principles is not likely; (2) the lack of leadership: there is no strong coalition of liberal states today ready to take the lead in consistent economic policy making with universal appeal; even in a time of serious crisis, hegemonic management is absent; (3) there are no coherent strategies for confronting transnational bads. The three sets of problems hang together, of course; hegemonic leadership requires hegemonic power, but the economic leadership of liberal states is increasingly challenged in a world where rising economic powers do not necessarily support liberal values. Economic disaster is probably not on the cards; rather a simmering crisis exacerbated by the current downturn of the world economy.

States and markets: restraint and imposition

Since the end of the Cold War, the expansion of market-based economic relations across borders has entered a new and more intense phase, often labeled economic globalization. For the first time ever, there is an international market for goods, money, and finance with a truly global reach (Held et al. 1999; Dicken 2003); a large number of countries that had planned economies have transformed into market economies and are integrating them in the global market. This recent process of economic globalization is not a pure market phenomenon: A significant enabling condition of current globalization consists of changes in political regula-tion in the direction of a more "market-friendly" state–market matrix that helps market-based economic activity to expand.

It follows that the "globalization pressures" faced by single countries are not purely economic, but also political and expressed through the policies of the dominant coalitions in such organizations as the International Monetary Fund (IMF), the World Bank, and the World Trade Organization (WTO). In sum, eco-nomic globalization adds a new dimension to the state–market interplay because different national modes of that relationship are opened up to each other (Hveem 1994). That raises anew the issue of the proper mode of regulation for that larger context, including the basic question about the extent to which markets should be more or less closely integrated. In the global context, political power is decentral-ized or fragmented in so far as it is unevenly distributed among sovereign states. However, at its core, the global topic is a replication of the national one: a struggle between different political and social coalitions that want to move in different directions. Some claim that they want an unfettered market whereas others claim that they want a market regulated according to certain socio-political objectives. In spite of this, the former frequently aim to preserve certain elements of protec-tionism while the latter also seek to achieve the benefits that free market dynamics can create.

With this in mind, it is clear that any agreement among liberal states about "free markets" must always be accompanied by potential disagreement about who gets what, that is, about relative and absolute advantages for countries and groups flowing from any specific state–market matrix. Therefore, strong leadership in the making of a stable liberal economic order with potential benefits for all partici-pants emerges only under special circumstances. Such was the case after World War II: The United States (and the democratic West) faced a serious security challenge from the Soviet Union, and Germany and Japan had to be rebuilt into solid members of the community of democracies. The democracies in Western Europe faced significant economic difficulties as well and the United States was by far the strongest economy in the world. Security interests, national economic interests, and a concern for the Western democratic community came together in motivating the United States to create a Western economic order. It also provided great incentives for Western democracies to successfully manage their collaboration and avoid serious splits and divisions among them.

Today these conditions are no longer present. There is not a common security challenge that gives the United States a clear role as security provider for the Western alliance. The liberal economic order is now a global system with a great many different stakeholders who do not easily agree on the precise set-up of the economic order. The economic superiority of the United States – and also of the entire community of Western democracies – is much less pronounced than earlier. Principal support for a liberal "free market" system still exists, but, within it, each participating state is much more conscious about its national economic interests.

Restraint and imposition since World War II

The principal postures of Liberalism of Restraint and Liberalism of Imposition can now be defined in relationship to the international economy. Both positions agree on the fundamental advantages of an economy based on free markets and private property, but they combine it with markedly different positions regarding the freedom of single states to decide on the make-up of the state–market relationship. The Liberalism of Restraint, on the one hand, is pluralist: It seeks to leave very substantial political-economic decision power in the hands of individual states; they should comprehensively participate in international economic exchange at all levels, but they should also be given maximum freedom to construct their own preferred version of the state–market relationship, be it "social democratic," "catholic conservative," or "neoliberal." The Liberalism of Imposition, on the other hand, is universalistic: It aims at imposing a certain set of market economic principles in all countries. These principles are drawn primarily from the neoliberal understanding of the state–market relationship, and that means they include liberalization of investment inflows and interest rates, competitive exchange rates, fiscal discipline, deregulation, and tax reform (Williamson 1990).

When the international framework for economic exchange had to be reconstituted after World War II, great emphasis was put on the preservation of domestic policy autonomy. Under the joint leadership of the United States and Britain the Bretton Woods conference in 1944 set out that new framework. The dollar was tied to gold at a fixed rate of $35 per ounce, and other states pegged their currencies to the dollar. However, it was not a return to the discipline of the gold standard. On the one hand, countries could adjust the value of their currencies when they encountered a "fundamental disequilibrium." On the other hand, countries were also given the right of enforcing capital controls. Finally, currency convertibility was not introduced until 1958. Under these conditions, countries were given a free hand domestically to pursue appropriate macro-economic planning and decide the optimum interest rate; in other words, liberal openness was combined with domestic autonomy in a system of "embedded liberalism" (Ruggie 1982). In the terminology of this article, it was a Liberalism of Restraint system.

A similar development took place in the area of trade. The United States government initially sponsored the establishment of an International Trade Organization (ITO) that should seek to provide the widest possible freedom of movement for goods and services, but Europeans were not ready to let go of preferential trade agreements and subsidy systems. The support for some protectionism was also strong in the U.S. Congress. The less ambitious GATT (General Agreement on Tariffs and Trade) system came to be the vehicle for tariff reductions and free trade, but special national support arrangements in agriculture and elsewhere were allowed to continue (Spero and Hart 1997).

On one level, the Liberalism of Restraint system worked very well for the United States, Europe, and Japan. Trade barriers were reduced, economic interdependence for mutual benefit increased dramatically, short- and long-term liquidity was made available, and the European and Japanese economies quickly recovered from the war. On another level, however, it is clear that the system depended on the benevolent management of the United States, including a willingness to forgo short-term national interest for the sake of the larger arrangement. First, the United States provided liquidity for the system by promoting a huge outflow of dollars; the Marshall Plan and U.S. military expenditures in NATO countries were important elements in this. Second, the United States accepted Japanese and European trade restrictions while encouraging exports from these countries to the United States. Finally, the United States supported a range of measures to increase the competitiveness of Europe and Japan (Mastanduno 2008).

In the longer term, these initially successful policies contained their own inbuilt problems. In order to provide sufficient international liquidity, the United States needed to run a balance of payments deficit; but doing so on a more or less permanent basis would inevitably undermine the confidence in the dollar's convertibility into gold. That would lead to runs on the dollar in which speculators converted their dollars into gold; a first occasion of this occurred already in the fall of 1960.[1] During the 1960s, large military expenses in relation to the Vietnam War contributed to inflationary pressures and an overvalued dollar. By 1971, the United States showed a trade deficit for the first time in the twentieth century.

At that point in time, President Nixon announced a new policy that reflected immediate U.S. priorities: the dollar would no longer be convertible into gold and a 10 percent surcharge would be imposed on dutiable imports. Two major pillars of the Bretton Woods system were thus removed: the dollar was no longer convertible into gold, and instead of fixed exchange rates the major world currencies now floated with management left to market forces and occasional interventions by central banks. It made the system markedly more unstable, but it also increased flexibility. The continued economic strength of the United States kept confidence in the dollar at a high level, while floating exchange rates at the same time removed the need for adjustment through trade restrictions and capital controls, thereby enabling rapid growth of financial and commodity flows. However, it was also a volatile system of "casino capitalism" (Strange 1986) with ordinary producers and consumers exposed to dramatic currency changes brought about by speculators seeking short-term gain. Capital controls were abolished by the United States already in 1974 and by Britain in 1979; the other advanced capitalist countries followed suit in the 1980s. In a short period of time, private actors massively entered the field of international finance, and they quickly began to develop financial derivatives (futures, forwards, options, swaps) that boosted the level of activity. Foreign exchange trading had a daily size of $15 billion in 1973; by the late 1990s that figure was $1,500 billion and world financial flows exceeded trade flows by a factor of at least thirty to one.

The 1970s was a period of economic slowdown exacerbated by two rounds of sharply rising prices of oil. The advanced liberal countries increasingly became subject to a combination of stagnation and inflation. When Ronald Reagan became president in 1981 he initiated a program of neoliberal "supply-side" economics that involved tax cuts for the wealthy and deregulation of the economy. With decreasing inflation the dollar appreciated; high interest rates attracted very large inflows of capital, in spite of the twin deficits of, on the one hand, the U.S. trade and balance of payments and, on the other hand, the federal budget. During the Reagan presidency, the United States would move from being the world's largest creditor to being the world's largest debtor nation. Regardless of some initial attempts, the leading liberal states were unwilling to control the large financial fluctuations through a more tightly managed system. Taking that road would have sharply decreased their macro-economic policy autonomy and they were not inclined to accept that. As a consequence:

> the period since 1976 has been one of muddling through, characterized as much by national and regional management as by multilateral management . . . Despite the growth of interdependence, national governments have been either unwilling or unable to adjust national economic policies to international economic needs.
>
> (Spero and Hart 1997: 30)

The large amounts of capital coming into the United States, attracted by low inflation and high interest rates, contributed to problems elsewhere in the system. Many developing countries had borrowed heavily during the 1970s, when inflation was high and real rates of interest were low, even negative. Now these countries faced sharply rising real interest rates, frequently combined with expensive oil imports. Mexico declared its inability to service its debt in 1982, and a large number of countries soon faced similar problems.

The 1980s, then, was a decade of debt rescheduling in which the Bretton Woods financial institutions – the World Bank and the IMF – played a central role. Pushed primarily by the United States under Reagan and Britain under Thatcher, but also by other advanced industrialized countries, these institutions took the lead in advocating a policy of structural adjustment in the Third World. The new policy followed the principles of what would be termed the "Washington Consensus" (Williamson 1990). It was strongly felt that "government failures" were a more serious problem than "market failures"; consequently, the policy of structural adjustment aimed at liberalizing economic exchange. Regulations should help set economic flows free by removing the heavy, and distorting, hand of direct state intervention. In concrete terms that meant (1) lifting trade restrictions and currency regulations; (2) public sector cutbacks, fiscal discipline, and tax reform; and (3) removal of industrial and agricultural protectionism, privatization of state enterprises, and support for establishment of private enterprises (Taylor 1997: 148–9).

The Washington Consensus represented a turn to a Liberalism of Imposition system. At its core is a common set of neoliberal principles believed to be appropriate for promoting economic growth and social welfare in any economy. However, the endorsement of these principles by leading liberal states took place in a highly selective manner. The neoliberal principles were imposed on less developed and developing countries with major external imbalances; they were highly indebted and/or ran large balance of payments deficits. Neoliberal imposition was therefore a disciplining instrument aimed at correcting the external imbalances of these countries so that they would be able to meet their international obligations. Julius Nyerere of Tanzania stated the issue in no uncertain terms:

> The IMF has an ideology of social and economic development which it is trying to impose on poor countries irrespective of their own clearly stated policies. And when we reject IMF conditions, we hear the threatening whisper: "Without accepting our conditions, you will not get our money and you will get no other money." . . . When did the IMF become an International Ministry of Finance? When did nations agree to surrender to it their power of decision-making?[2]

There was initially no external imposition of neoliberal economic principles on the liberal states themselves; they continued to freely organize their state–market matrices as they saw fit. Since the 1970s, then, global liberal economic order is to a much larger extent than earlier a field of contestation, in which countries and groups of countries attempt to influence the regulatory framework in a way that best suits their interests.

The promotion of neoliberal principles by leading liberal states took place at a point in time in which various groups of countries in the world were moving in different directions. The developing countries, who had stood together in the 1970s in demanding a "New Economic World Order" from the rich countries, were now increasingly differentiated into separate groups: very weak and poor states, many of which were in sub-Saharan Africa; newly industrializing countries (or "emerging markets") in Southeast Asia, parts of Latin America, and most recently also in Eastern Europe; oil producers in the Middle East; highly indebted countries; less indebted countries; and so on.

It would soon be clear that the neoliberal principles contained in the economic Liberalism of Imposition were not an adequate answer to the challenges faced by these different groups of states. At the same time, a return to the previous Liberalism of Restraint system is not feasible because the old preconditions are now absent: on the one hand, the economic system is now so integrated across borders that some substantial coordination of policies is required; on the other hand, the United States is less willing and able to supply the benevolent management of earlier days. The following section demonstrates the flaws of the Liberalism of Imposition system in relation to various groups of countries. Because a clear-cut Liberalism of Restraint is not feasible either, the global economy will remain a serious challenge in the quest for a stable liberal world order.

One size does not fit all: economic liberal imposition in the developing world

In the economic realm, Liberal Imposition is about imposing the principles contained in the Washington Consensus. John Williamson coined the term "Washington Consensus" in 1990; it was meant as specific advice to a number of Latin American countries in order to promote macro-economic discipline, a market economy, and openness to the world in respect of trade and investment. In that sense, he said in 2002 that the term is "motherhood and apple pie and not worth debating" (Williamson 2002: 4). But the consensus did take on a life of its own. It became a set of neoliberal principles with universal application, and, on that basis, a series of measures focused on fiscal discipline, privatization, and economic openness were promoted around the world by the international financial institutions (the IMF and World Bank), backed by the leading liberal states. In many cases, the measures did have some positive effects in terms of growth and macro-economic stability, but it was soon clear that there were also considerable negative effects (Taylor 1997). In the weak and poor states, attempts to increase exports had to rely on one or a few primary products that accounted for more than 90 percent of total export production in sub-Saharan Africa in the 1990s. These were goods for which long-term global demand was shrinking in an increasingly technology-intensive world economy.

Nor was it easy for weak states to attract great amounts of foreign direct investment (FDI). These countries have never been able to create coherent national economies. They are disjointed amalgamations of traditional agriculture, an informal petty urban sector, and some fragments of modern industry. Political institutions are inefficient and corrupt, frequently run by self-serving elites offering what state services there are to the highest bidder. FDI is not very interested in coming into these countries in the first place because of the lack of stability and attractive conditions of operation; by the turn of the century less than 2 percent of total FDI (World Bank 2000: 38) went to sub-Saharan Africa.

In the domestic realm of weak states, a dramatic slimming down of the public sector had negative consequences for employment and welfare. Public sector workers either were laid off or had their pay frozen. The cutting back of government spending in education, health, and other areas of basic infrastructure together with increasing prices for food and other basic necessities meant falling social standards for those already in need. These short- and medium-term consequences were indicative of a larger problem that Liberal Imposition did not address: Weak states were in need of more rather than less state capacity in order to be able to promote long-term development. Trevor Manuel, South African Minister of Finance, pointed to the predicament in 2003:

> The problem in Africa is that most states are weak and limited, not that states try to do everything . . . Most states need to expand, not contract, their public sector – and dramatically improve its efficiency in delivering quality public services. This demands institutional capacity, especially in the areas of regulation, service delivery, and social spending . . . Technical capacity needs to be combined with transparency and representation in public institutions.
>
> (Manuel 2003: 19)

In other words, capable states are needed to set up the rules that enable the market to function properly. However, to the extent that weak states have actually set up and enforced rules governing the market, these regulations have often been counterproductive in terms of long-term growth and welfare. Instead, they have benefited leaders and their select groups of clients. For many rulers, the game became one of extracting as much as they could in terms of new aid and loans while offering as little as possible in terms of actually implemented policy reform; "a perfectly understandable attitude for African rulers, who were anxious to get their hands on the money, but whose long-established practices and possibly political survival were threatened by the conditions which accompanied it" (Clapham 1996: 177).

In sum, the economic Liberalism of Imposition did not sufficiently aim at addressing the major problems impeding long-term economic development in weak states: the promotion of stronger institutional capacities combined with more transparency and accountability. Nor did the neoliberal principles sufficiently address underlying problems connected with human capital creation and technical and social infrastructure, especially related to the large informal sectors in weak states. Macro-economic discipline, a market economy, and openness to the world might be economic "motherhood and apple pie," but dressed up in a narrow framework of neoliberal economics it was not well suited to address the economic development problems of weak states (Toye 2003).

In relation to the transition from planned economies to market economies in Eastern Europe, including Russia, Liberal Imposition economics was no great success either. The Washington Consensus proscribed a "shock therapy" (World Bank 1996) aimed at quickly installing the institutional and regulatory framework of a market economy (Stiglitz 2001: 153). The reformers "underplayed the importance of social, organizational and informational capital; they underestimated the impediments to the creation of new enterprises; and perhaps most importantly, they paid too little attention to the issues of corporate governance"

(Stiglitz 2001: 158; Woodruff 1999). However, the challenges of the transition to a market economy cannot be reduced to technicalities concerning regulations and institutions: A well-functioning market depends on a well-functioning state, and a well-functioning state depends on a well-functioning civil society. So a market economy entails both a new economic order (market building), a new political order (state building), and a new basis for social order (civil society building). The harmonious development of these three interrelated transformations is highly complex: on the one hand, they depend on each other; on the other hand, market actors, state actors, and groups in civil society have interests of their own that are not necessarily conducive to a smooth process of transition. In short, Liberal Imposition economics does not have a comprehensive answer to the challenges of transition from plan to market.

We now turn to the emerging markets in Latin America and Southeast Asia. One should expect the neoliberal economic principles to work better here as these countries have much stronger domestic economies and substantially higher capacities for designing and implementing policies. Adopting the principles of openness in trade and finance combined with sound money, meaning a stable exchange rate, should mean that "capital flowed into a country that was following the right path" (Krugman 1995: 38). True enough, money poured into these countries during the first half of the 1990s. From a very low level in the 1980s, private capital flows to developing countries reached a staggering $130 billion in 1993 and $236 billion in 1996 (the abundance of available capital is explored in Wade 1998a). The bulk of the money "went to countries that had done poorly in previous years, but whose new commitment to Washington consensus policies was believed to ensure a dramatic turn-around" (Krugman 1995: 40). They included many Latin American countries plus Thailand, Malaysia, the Philippines, and a few others. But already by 1994 investors were fleeing from Mexico and a few years later the crisis hit in Asia. What went wrong?

First, expectations were probably too high. Abandoning protectionism and embracing free trade might support faster growth, but the precise magnitude of that move is hotly contested. A World Bank (1987) study concluded that open economies performed better in terms of economic growth, but the results of this type of analysis are far from clear because of the conceptual and empirical problems involved (Edwards 1993). Furthermore, stable exchange rates curbed inflation and increased international confidence, but they also led to overvalued currencies, decreasing ability for export sectors to compete, and a boom in cheap imports.

Second, the capital coming into these emerging markets was more short term than earlier. In what was known as carry-trade, financial institutions borrowed in yen and dollars and invested in short-term notes in Southeast Asia that were paying much higher interest rates. "There was less and less compulsion on the part of lenders, borrowers or governments to improve financial supervision or control bank asset quality" (Wade 1998b: 1539). The system could function only to the extent that countries receiving large capital inflows could maintain a stable exchange rate. Capital abundance fueled domestic prices at a time when inflation in the United States and Japan was at a much lower level. With currencies pegged to the dollar in order to create stability, real exchange rates (the ratio of prices in dollars in emerging markets to those in the United States and Japan) increased dramatically. The Mexican peso revalued by 28 percent in 1994; in Southeast Asia, inflationary pressures were put in relief by a Chinese devaluation of the yuan in 1994 that further enhanced China's relative capacity to compete. In Thailand, inflation and the availability of capital led to speculation in real estate. Property prices went up more than 40 percent per year in Bangkok in the early 1990s.

This could not go on; a crisis of confidence seemed unavoidable. In Mexico it came when the government attempted to boost economic growth; the loss of credibility meant that investors

> became unwilling to hold peso assets unless offered very high interest rates; and the necessity of paying these high rates, together with the depressing effect of high rates on the economy, increased the pressure on the government to abandon the fixed exchange rate – which made investors even less willing to hold pesos.
>
> (Krugman 1995: 42)

In Thailand, the property market bubble burst and slowed down economic growth; again, the prospect of devaluation made investors unwilling to hold the local currency, baht. By July 1997 the Thai central bank had to give up defending the currency, letting it float, and sink. Higher real interest rates and cutbacks in domestic demand led to a massive contraction in economic activity.

In sum, Liberal Imposition economics was not an effective way forward for emerging markets. Economic openness and the aspiration of "sound money" eventually led to enormous capital outflows rather than inflows and a large number of local companies could be bought up by outsiders at fire-sale prices. This opens the question about the appropriate framework of regulation for international finance, an issue that reappeared in 2008 when a real estate bubble in the United States sparked off a financial crisis in the global economy. The economics editor of the *Financial Times*, Martin Wolf, made the following comment in the context of the crisis a decade ago:

> It is impossible to pretend that the traditional case for capital markets liberalization remains unscathed. Either far greater stability than at present is injected into the international monetary system as a whole or the unavoidably fragile emerging countries must protect themselves from the virus of short-term lending . . . After the crisis, the question can no longer be whether these flows should be regulated in some way. It can only be how.
>
> (quoted from Wade 1998b: 1550)

A similar argument about the need for regulation is frequently voiced in the context of the 2008 financial crisis. Overall, then, one size does not fit all. Liberal

Imposition economics have revealed serious flaws in dealing with the challenges of different types of developing and transition economies. The problems point in the direction of returning to a strategy based on a Liberalism of Restraint, allowing much more space for adapting general liberal principles to the particular situations in different states. However, such adaptation may also involve deviations from strictly liberal economic principles and the leading liberal states have not been able to agree on how to go about doing that. The liberal strategy as regards the developing world is spearheaded by the World Bank, and, on the one hand, most of the critique mentioned here has been recognized by the bank (World Bank 2005); the current emphasis is on "the need for humility, for policy diversity, for selective and modest reforms, and for experimentation" (Rodrik 2006: 3). On the other hand, "there is little evidence that operational work at the Bank has internalized these lessons to any significant extent" (Rodrik 2006: 7); therefore, neoliberal imposition policies, with their recognized flaws, continue to dominate in the process of actual policy implementation.

Do as I say, not as I do: rhetoric and reality in the promotion of neoliberal standards

Neoliberal standards are not being imposed on developing and transition econo-mies because they represent the development experience of the advanced liberal states themselves. The now developed countries did not rely on trade and invest-ment liberalization, privatization, and deregulation during core phases of their of development trajectories (Chang 2002). They instead used interventionist policies related to support of domestic industries, regulation of trade and foreign invest-ment, and promotion of national capacities in technology and research. Britain became the first industrially advanced country; it did so by vigorously pursuing infant industry protection and export subsidies, and building "high and long-lasting tariff barriers" (Bairoch 1993: 46). The repeal of the Corn Laws in 1846 did represent a significant turn toward free trade, but this happened at a point at which British economic supremacy was now so well established that free trade would be to British advantage. In that sense, economic openness and deregulation are fair-weather principles: They work well in the context of economies that are already well established and ready to face the international competition that such principles must imply.

Nor was the United States for a considerable period any champion of eco-nomic openness. On the contrary, it should be viewed as "the mother country and bastion of modern protectionism" (Bairoch 1993: 30). Alexander Hamilton, one of the founding fathers of the United States, was a strong proponent of mercantilism in the form of protectionist policies aimed at promoting domestic industry in the United States. It was only after World War II, when the United States was established as the industrial powerhouse of the world, that it liberal-ized trade, acting according to fair-weather principles. There has always been substantial political support in the United States for the mercantilist view that economic activity is and should be subordinated to the primary goal of promoting a strong state.

A German economist, Friedrich List, developed a theory of "productive power" in the 1840s. It stressed that the ability to produce is more important than the result of producing. In other words, the prosperity of a state depends not primarily on its store of wealth, but on the extent to which it has developed its powers of production:

> A nation capable of developing a manufacturing power, if it makes use of the system of protection, thus acts quite in the same spirit as the landed pro-prietor did who by the sacrifice of some material wealth allowed some of his children to learn a production trade.
>
> (List 1966 [1885]: 145)

These mercantilist principles were much more dominant as guidelines for the now developed countries than were Ricardian and Smithian recommendations of comparative advantage and economic openness. List remarked that the secret of the "cosmopolitical doctrine of Adam Smith" lies in the fact that the country that has advanced by mercantilist means now *"kicks away the ladder"* (List 1966 [1885]: 296; italics in original) for latecomers, denying them similar advance by imposing on them principles of free trade.

The argument is not that protectionism and import substitution is always so much better for developing nations than free trade; on several occasions, protec-tionism has gone too far and led to inefficiency and lack of innovation. But import replacement remains a relevant part of a larger industrial strategy "to nurture the capabilities of domestic firms and raise the rate of domestic investment in the context of a private enterprise, market-based economy" (Wade 2003: 634). Import replacement and export development can go together, as the Southeast Asian "tiger economies" have demonstrated.

By imposing neoliberal principles, strategic options in economic development are substantially narrowed down, and that also violates another lesson from the experience of the now developed countries (NDCs): their history demonstrates "a considerable degree of diversity . . . in terms of their policy-mix, suggesting that there is no 'one-size-fits-all' *model* for industrial development" (Chang 2003: 27; italics in original). Sequencing – the notion that some policies are relevant for certain phases of a country's development but not for others – is part of this diversity. Both the NDCs and the successful late developers in Asia made extensive use of sequencing.

The narrowing down of development options in the current international system proceeds in other ways from the ones described above. Current interna-tional regulations of intellectual property rights (TRIPS), of investment measures (TRIMS), and of trade in services (GATS), can be seen as a contemporary way of "kicking away the ladder" by constraining national development strategies for latecomers. Trade-Related Aspects of International Property Rights (TRIPS) introduce standards for intellectual property protection. Developed countries are net producers of patentable knowledge; developing countries are net consumers. TRIPS make it more expensive and more difficult for latecomers to get access to advanced technology. The United States in its time, and later Japan, Taiwan, and South Korea, made ample use of duplication in their early phases of development. TRIPS, by contrast, "raises significant development obstacles for many countries that the earlier developers did not face" (Wade 2003: 626).

Trade-Related Investment Measures (TRIMS) prevent host countries from demanding performance requirements from foreign investors. Such requirements may include locally produced inputs, export targets, or joint venturing with local firms; they are important elements in securing that foreign investment will contribute to domestic industrial upgrading. Successful late industrialized countries, including Taiwan, South Korea, China, India, and Brazil, have all made extensive use of these performance requirements (Amsden and Chu 2003). The General Agreement on Trade in Services (GATS) stipulates market liberalization in services (e.g. health care, sanitation, education, banking, insurance). Governments are not allowed to protect their service industries from foreign competition. Again, this puts developing countries in a worse position than previously successful developers.

In sum, the three agreements are much more favorable to the advanced countries than they are to latecomers. They put serious limitations on the rights of developing countries to "carry through policies that favor the growth and technological upgrading of domestic industries and firms" (Wade 2003: 630). The advanced liberal states, by contrast, continued to make use of protective measures, even in recent times. The Multi Fiber Arrangement (MFA), operating between 1974 and 2005, protected labor-intensive textile industries in the North from more competitive imports from developing countries. Tariffs and quotas continue to protect textile and apparel markets in the North. Agriculture is another area in which the developed world offers a high level of subsidies to its own producers.

The United States has supported the establishment of a stronger WTO whose role it is to promote free trade principles. As a consequence of this, the United States itself has had to comply with WTO measures toward openness (Chorev 2005). At the same time, the United States and other advanced liberal states have found new ways of domestic promotion of advanced, knowledge-intensive undertakings. The WTO playing field, it turns out, is not level: according to Linda Weiss:

> the measures now *prohibited* under the WTO are those of *diminishing importance* to a relatively *advanced* level of development, which depends increasingly on knowledge-intensive technologies. Second, the measures *permitted* – or at least not explicitly prohibited – are *advanced country friendly*: they enable the industrialized state to align its national growth goals with significant support for industry, technology, and export.
>
> (Weiss 2005: 724; italics in original)

In other words, high-tech capabilities and innovative technologies are the core areas of interest for the advanced countries. Even under the new global rules of economic openness, there is ample room for advanced countries' public efforts to promote these areas through public–private partnerships, the development of information infrastructures, environmental upgrading, technology diffusion, and other means. Such "strategic activism" (Weiss 2005: 731) in combination with a substantially more restricted development space for the latecomers shows that the new rules appear to have served "more generally as an *upgrading device* for the *developed* economies" (Weiss 2005: 725; italics in original).

One important element of "strategic activism," which is of increasing importance, is government procurement, that is, public purchase of goods and services from the private sector. A recent study of the United States demonstrates that the effort to promote openness and non-discrimination abroad is combined with an emphasis on "Buy American" at home. The United States, according to one recent study:

> has no equal in the extent to which it preserves the home market against foreign incursions. Here the Buy American principle – both as legal and social norm – offers a robust form of protection. . . . In the hand of the world's superpower, government procurement has moved on from being an important mechanism for nurturing national champions to become a major instrument of trade policy.
>
> (Weiss and Thurbon 2006: 713, 719)

In sum, there is a gap between the advanced liberal countries' rhetorical support for neoliberal principles of economic openness and free trade and the development experience of the developed countries themselves; the advanced countries in practice relied very much on mercantilist principles of state activism and intervention in support of domestic industry promotion. Today, such principles carry little weight in the liberal economic world order; here, the emphasis is on "market access" and full participation in economic globalization. There are not many serious debates on development strategies and state–market frameworks specifically tailored to meet development needs in countries at dissimilar levels facing a variety of different challenges.

At the same time, the neoliberal rhetoric on the part of the advanced liberal states is combined with substantial policies that tilt the playing field in favor of further economic upgrading of the highly developed countries and against the development aspirations of the latecomers. The unequal development prospects that result from this situation may perhaps be seen as a manageable problem in a period in which the world economy has been expanding to the benefit of most states, a group of weak states being the exception to the rule. However, in a prospective period of severe recession the question is whether this unbalanced framework is sufficient to sustain a stable liberal economic order. We now know that the more troubled times for the liberal world economy have already begun.

Fall 2008: financial crisis and impending recession

A financial crisis is "a disturbance to financial markets that disrupts the market's capacity to allocate capital – financial intermediation and hence investment come to a halt" (Portes 1998: 1). Most financial crises emerge and disappear without being much noticed; they are part of the rhythm of capitalist development. However, big financial crises are relatively rare; they simultaneously involve "foreign exchange market disturbances, debt defaults (sovereign or private), and banking system failures" (Portes 1998: 1). It was a general international crisis of this kind that engulfed the advanced liberal states and much of the rest of the world in the fall of 2008 (for detailed description of the crisis, see Chapters 6 and 7).

Even if the financial system is so globalized today that it acts as a real-time, twenty-four-hour integrated organism in which exchange rates and interest rates are determined in the context of the global market, there was no cooperating political center, no common global or even Western institution of financial governance that could adequately respond to the crisis. The financial system is deeply integrated on a global scale, but regulation and control remains almost purely national. It was thus left to national governments, beginning with the United States where the crisis broke, to work out responses to the crisis and to coordinate those responses with other national governments to the extent that they deemed necessary and expedient; "at moments of confidence-withering crises, who would ultimately be responsible for bailing out financial institutions confronting the prospect of collapse? . . . Lender-of-last-resort facilities remain under the exclusive purview of individual states themselves" (Pauly 2005: 188).

Therefore, the national reactions came country by country: Germany set up a €500 billon stabilization fund, France pledged €360 billion, the Netherlands €200 billion; and the United States would invest $250 billion in its banks and has extended guarantees for new bank debt as part of a larger rescue package. Almost all of the advanced liberal countries have proposed similar measures. Will they solve the problem? The system currently appears to unfreeze, but the question remains whether the measures taken are sufficient to stop the credit crunch. On the one hand, neither consumers nor companies are likely to begin large-scale lending and banks will themselves be holding back in order to meet new demands for capital ratios. On the other hand, the rescue package itself comes at a cost and "investor's nerves are shot. . . . Concern about banks' creditworthiness may yet morph into worry about sovereign risk as the full cost of the various bail-outs becomes clearer" (*The Economist* 2008).

And so it happened; the enormous financial commitments by countries seeking to mitigate the economic crisis had to put their financial stability under immense strain, thus risking a sovereign debt crisis. It began with Greece in late 2009 when investors suddenly and without warning dumped their Greek bonds and drove its market value into a free fall. Weaker versions of the crisis emerged in Portugal, Spain, Ireland, and other countries in Europe that were under similar financial stress. A comprehensive disorder now threatened the entire eurozone and the

European Central Bank had to mount a rescue operation in the spring of 2010 (*The Economist* 2010). Together with severe public austerity measures in the most affected countries it has managed to restore a relative calm to financial markets but the risk of a meltdown in Europe's financial system has not gone away.

Because of the dollar's status as a reserve currency, the United States does not face a similar sovereign debt crisis. However, the Chinese Central Bank Governor, Zhou Xiaochuan, has recently suggested that a dollar-based international monetary system is inherently unstable. "Issuing countries of reserve currencies are constantly confronted with the dilemma between achieving their domestic monetary policy goals and meeting other countries' demand for reserve currencies," he wrote. "They may either fail to adequately meet the demand of a growing global economy for liquidity as they try to ease inflation pressures at home, or create excess liquidity in the global markets by overly stimulating domestic demand."[3] In other words, we have a return of the Triffin dilemma mentioned earlier. China wants the debtor to bear the burden of adjustment; the United States is not enthusiastic about a tighter monetary and fiscal policy under current conditions; taking that road would also aggravate the threat of a global economic slump.

One alternative for China, which it already pursues with Brazil and Russia, is trading without dollars. However, the only way to do this is to balance trade bilaterally.

> This would mean systematic trade discrimination, and the beginning of the end of the multilateral trading system built up painstakingly since the 1950s. . . . In those days, it was a dollar shortage that destroyed multilateral trading. Tomorrow it may be a dollar glut that does it. There is no escaping the Triffin dilemma.
>
> (Steil 2010: fn. 3)

In sum, the financial and economic crisis may re-erupt at any point. The crisis has, over a very short period of time, led to a level of state involvement in the advanced liberal economies – including the United States – that nobody could have expected or foreseen, even a short while ago. The advanced liberal states themselves have become living proof that the state–market relationship must develop and change over time in order to meet new challenges and new conditions. They are now in uncharted territory in which densely integrated economies are combined with political frameworks that are overwhelmingly national and accustomed to put national economic priorities over international ones. Neither liberal economic theory nor liberal economic politics provides good guidelines and answers to the problems raised by this situation.

Conclusion

An international economic order based on liberal principles cannot create itself. It must be supported by a political framework of appropriate regulation that allows the free market economy to function. This opens the issue of the appropriate nature of a state–market matrix for the liberal economy: how much room for market forces versus how much scope for state intervention and control, and what is the nature of the proper framework in more detailed terms? The principle of domestic policy autonomy underpinned the reconstitution of the liberal economic system after World War II; it was a Liberalism of Restraint system that lasted until the early 1970s. The coming to power of Ronald Reagan in the Unites States and Margaret Thatcher in Britain helped usher in a Liberalism of Imposition system in the 1980s. The aim was to set market forces free in the developing world through the lifting of trade restrictions and currency regulations, public sector cutbacks, and removal of industrial and agricultural protectionism.

In the context of these developments, global general support for a liberal state–market arrangement based on private property and "free market" exchange has increased. Processes of economic globalization have amplified the level of interdependence among many nations. However, the neoliberal principles in the economic Liberalism of Imposition did not represent a coherent answer to the problems faced by different groups of countries. In the weak states, economic liberalization did not have the desired effects and the neoliberal measures did not address core issues of lacking state capacity and infrastructure improvement. Nor did they give a sufficient answer to the complex challenges of transition from planned to market economies. In the "emerging markets" of Latin America and Southeast Asia, the rapid influx of short-term capital ended in capital flight and economic crisis.

The advanced liberal states had not themselves relied on neoliberal principles in their own processes of development. They instead turned to mercantilist policies of support for domestic industry and regulation of trade and foreign investment. Only when their domestic industries were robustly competitive did they begin to strongly support economic openness and free trade. The current imposition of neoliberal standards on latecomers "kicks away the ladder" under them as they are denied certain ways forward. This is exacerbated by rules and measures that tilt the economic system in favor of the developed countries; TRIPS, TRIMS, and GATS constrain the development options of latecomers, forcing them in a neoliberal direction. At the same time, the current system leaves space for new inventions in "strategic activism" for the advanced countries.

The current financial crisis has opened up an even larger gap between advanced liberal countries' rhetorical support of neoliberal imposition economics and their actual deeds. Deregulation of the financial system led to solvency and liquidity imbalances that could not be absorbed by market adjustments, nor was there any multilateral institutional framework among liberal states ready to face the problems; they had to be handled through national reactions in terms of country-specific rescue packages.

In the liberal tradition, an open international market economy based on free trade was always a force for cooperation, progress, and peace. The removal of economic barriers and the establishment of an equality of trade was a central element in Woodrow Wilson's peace program. The Liberal International Manifesto from 1997 also emphasizes its support for free trade, an open economy, and resistance to protectionism. The notion of progress promoted by free men pursuing peaceful economic intercourse not interrupted by governments is a core belief in the liberal tradition.

The actual trajectory of liberal economic development has not corresponded with the liberal vision. There is more broad support for a liberal state–market arrangement than ever before, but progress is very unevenly distributed; some groups benefit more than others. It is a key element in this that the advanced liberal states attempt to bend the rules in the sense that they support a system in which the playing field is not level: It is tilted toward the advantage of the advanced states and the disadvantage of the latecomers. It imposes constraints on latecomers not faced by the advanced states, and in this basic sense the system is not liberal. Strong reactions from the disadvantaged may yet intensify the contestation over liberal economic order.

Even with such inequalities, the system can potentially provide benefits for all participants; the question is whether this will be sufficient to uphold and develop a stable global economy based on liberal principles. There are three major reasons to believe that it is not. First is the issue of the appropriate state–market matrix. It has become increasingly difficult to formulate a set of substantial liberal economic principles that can be fully supported by the vast majority of countries. Countries at different levels require dissimilar answers to their economic development problems, depending on the specific challenges they face. There is not a one-size-fits-all imposition model that all can embrace; on the extreme end of this insight is the fact that successful development strategies, such as the one currently pursued by China, do not pass through the liberal West. They sooner combine elements of capitalism and a market economy with authoritarian government, political control, and a quite substantial role for the state in the regulation of economic development. They are not a version of development that owes much to the liberal idea of free men pursuing peaceful economic intercourse not interrupted by government. As far as the weak countries at the bottom are concerned, liberal economic principles alone will not solve their problems; they need much more effective and responsive statehood, and there is no straightforward path to that.

Second is the lack of leadership. The largest difference between now and the previous post-war period of successful Liberalism of Restraint is the lack of a leading country or group of countries able and willing to take responsibility and go in front. Liberal states on both sides of the Atlantic are looking inward, focusing on their own problems.[4] The International Civil Society, a global organization of NGOs, recently complained that, instead of repairing the global economy, G20 leaders had

injected 1.1 trillion dollars into many of the same institutions whose economic, finance, and trade policies exacerbated the speed, scale and impact of the crisis. Reforms have been superficial, and any shifts to the current economic paradigm still seem temporary, rather than long term.[5]

Focusing on trade, Ian Cambell made the following statement already in 2004:

> the world no longer has a leader in economic policymaking. Nowhere is that lack of leadership more evident than in trade. The failure of the ministerial summit meeting of the WTO in Cancun, Mexico in September was prepared by the prior positions adopted by the main players: the United States, the European Union and developing countries. The positions of all were characterized by hypocrisy. Perhaps the greatest hypocrisy, however, was that of the United States, which preaches the merits of free trade more strongly than almost any other country and yet spends tens of billions of dollars to prevent its own markets from being free and has taken fresh measures in recent years to discriminate against other countries' producers. . . . Developing countries that depend utterly on agriculture are forced to compete with a U.S. agricultural sector that is hugely subsidized. Yet the United States constantly urges countries to open their own markets and allow freer access to U.S. goods and services. . . . What the United States and the European Union bring to trade meetings at present is not a willingness to do what is right but a determination not to give anything away.
>
> (Campbell 2004: 111–12)

Last is the issue of transnational bads, where I have focused on the economic crisis; the indicators of economic downturn and crisis are presently stronger than they have been at any point since the 1930s. A complete breakdown of the liberal economic order will probably not take place, if the early reactions are valid indicators of what is going to come. However, in a period of severe crisis, countries will be less willing to forgo what they see as core national economic interests. This is no less true for finance than it is for trade, or any other major economic domain. At the same time, a period of severe crisis can spark more profound institutional change, as happened after World War II. The current economic crisis, however, does not appear to have led to initiatives for major reform; emphasis is on minor adjustments aimed at "restoring confidence" in existing markets.

Liberal states appear comprehensively unready, unable, and unwilling to construct a stable economic order based on liberal principles. The financial and economic crisis has been met with piecemeal reform aimed at national challenges in single countries; it can break out again at any time. Instead of conducting leadership in economic policy making, liberal states focus on their own short- and medium-term troubles. And it is not at all clear what the principles of a reformed order should be – neo-liberal Imposition will not do, and a return to classical Restraint is not feasible. Today's globalized world economy is no easy part of the liberal project; on the contrary, the world economy will continue to pose serious difficulties for any aspiration to a stable liberal world order.

Notes

1 Diagnosed by the American economist Robert Triffin, this became known as the Triffin Dilemma: the international economy needs dollars for liquidity and reserves, but this undermines domestic economic stability and leads to large current account deficits. Triffin argued that this would eventually put pressure on the dollar and undermine its position as a reserve currency (Campanella 2010).
2 Nyerere in 1980, quoted from http://taifaletu.blogspot.com/2009/03/nyerere-and-imf-will-our-leaders.html (accessed March 11, 2010).
3 Quoted from Benn Steil (2010).
4 President Obama spent seven minutes out of seventy-one on issues outside American borders in his 2010 State of the Union address. The EU has just come out of a long process of adopting the Lisbon Treaty and is presently preoccupied with the economic stability of South European members.
5 http://www.halifaxinitiative.org/content/towards-a-global-leaders-forum   (accessed May 20, 2010).

5

A NEW ROLE FOR THE OECD?

The "Enhanced Engagement" strategy toward emerging economies

Morten Ougaard

In 2007 the Organisation for Economic Co-operation and Development (OECD) extended an invitation to Brazil, China, India, Indonesia, and South Africa to participate in "Enhanced Engagement programs with a view to possible member-ship" (OECD 2007a). A few years later the OECD's Secretary-General Angel Gurria labeled this "a fundamental proposal by the OECD member countries to forge a more structured and coherent partnership, based on mutual interest, with these five major economies" (OECD Secretary-General 2010: 5), thereby signal-ing that this is neither an unambitious nor a peripheral initiative.

This is not the organization's first and only engagement with non-member countries. Indeed, already at its inception in 1961 it was mandated to promote growth in the world economy and a rising living standards among member and non-member states (OECD 1960), and structured and formalized involvement of non-members can be traced back to the 1980s (Ougaard 2010; Woodward 2010). Still, the 2007 initiative to pursue enhanced engagement, concurrent with the opening of accession talks with another group of emerging economies – Chile, Estonia, Israel, Russia, and Slovenia – marks a clear departure. After all, the OECD is widely perceived as a club of rich capitalist and democratic coun-tries, and closer cooperation "with a view to possible membership" with the five enhanced engagement countries has the appearance of a break with the past as they, their enhanced status as emerging economies notwithstanding, are normally considered parts of the developing world, and in China's case it lacks democratic credentials and is not a fully fledged market economy.

In what follows I will take a closer look at the Enhanced Engagement Initiative (EEI), suggesting a theoretical interpretation of the phenomenon and offering some initial observations on how the invitation has been received by the countries chosen. I will do this in the context of an understanding of the OECD's role in global politics, which in turn requires a brief presentation of the theoretical perspective on global governance informing the discussion. I will, in other words, first offer some theoretical comments on global governance, then move on to situate the OECD in this context, summarizing some of the salient features of the organization and its work along the way. After this the chapter takes a closer look at the EEI and offers a theoretical interpretation of it based on a range of policy statements. Then I will offer some tentative comments on the reception of the initiative and conclude with a discussion of the perspectives entailed for the organization.

A perspective on global governance

One of the better definitions of the discipline of international political economy (IPE) is that its core concern is "the study of global governance of the creation and distribution of wealth" (Hveem 2009: 368). "Wealth" is not to be taken narrowly in this context. IPE is concerned with "power and welfare in world society" as articulated by the title of Hveem's comprehensive 1996 discussion (Hveem 1996) and the discipline investigates how governance arrangements affect the distribution of societal values in the broad sense of "values" that was implied by Easton's classical definition of politics (Easton 1953). IPE investigates how such governance arrangements are created, developed, and changed.

Hveem's above definition can be read as calling attention to *all* institutions and practices that impact "the creation and distribution of wealth," or in Eastonian terms the allocation of values in society. Thus it would encompass governance exerted through market mechanisms and private actors, such as large business enterprises – a phenomenon that has drawn much scholarly attention in recent years under such headings as private authority (e.g. Cutler et al. 1999; Hansen and Salskov-Iversen 2008), private institutions (Pattberg 2007), or business practices as governance (Leander 2010). These are unquestionably important phenomena and there are good reasons to define the field of IPE broadly and include purely private arrangements and practices under the heading of global governance.

On the other hand, however, there is also merit in restricting the definition to governance arrangements that directly or indirectly involve political institutions in the normal sense of the term; in other words to governance that is related to public authority. Thus, for instance, in a recent contribution Avant, Finnemore, and Sell, although accepting that corporations and other private actors can be "global governors," defined such governors as "authorities who exercise power across borders for purposes of affecting policy" (Avant et al. 2010: 2). Referring again to David Easton, what is involved is the "*authoritative* allocation of values for society" (Easton 1953: 129–31; emphasis added), in which "authorities" refer to authority that is backed up one way or the other by the power of the state. Non-state actors are not excluded, but they are only included to the extent that they have a bearing on policy.

Building on this line of arguing, the phenomena that often are descriptively referred to as global governance could also be designated in an Eastonian sense as "the global political system," encompassing those aspects of cross-border societal institutions and practices that are involved in the authoritative allocation of values for world society or large parts thereof (Easton 1953; see also Strange 1996: 34). This implies that a direct or indirect presence of public authority or state power is part of the definition. Of course the normal empirical reference for the notion of a "political system" is the territorial nation-state and in this sense there is no global political system. Global governance lacks the essential centralization of power, it is less unified, less formalized, less constitutionalized, and so on. It is, in the words of Jan Aart Scholte, poly-centered and multilayered and has a highly varied geographical reach across political issue areas (Scholte 2005). Yet it is an ensemble of institutions and practices that involve public authority – or rather public authorit*ies* – and do have major implications for the allocation of values among and within countries. In this sense and with these qualifications there is a global political system and the present question is, first, how to theorize it further and, second, how to situate the OECD within it.

For the purpose of theorizing global governance further, I find certain themes in a particular strand of state theory in the tradition of historical materialism useful, namely some elements inspired by the work of Poulantzas (1973). Broadly speaking, in the conceptual language of this tradition, global governance or the global political system can at the most aggregate level of theory be conceived as an evolving global political superstructure, and it should be noted that among contemporary writers it is debated whether such a phenomenon really is evolving, indeed whether it is possible at all in the context of capitalist societies, and it is debated how to analyze it if its existence is acknowledged. For some it is simply not possible – capitalism can function only within a system of autonomous nation states (Wood 2002); for others it is theoretically a possibility but not yet a reality (Lacher 2006); and for yet others it is an important reality (e.g. Cox 1987; Robinson 2002; Ougaard 2004). Within the last of these groups, however, there are important differences in the way the phenomenon is theorized. Robinson, for instance, emphasizes the role that the "transnational state" plays in providing institutional, regulatory, and other conditions that are required for capitalism to continue to function. The transnational state is essentially at the service of transnational capital. In contrast to this, I find that, although accepting that business can be and often is a powerful force in global governance, through direct action and indirect structural effects, a more nuanced and complex understanding is more adequate, and I argue that a critical engagement with some of Poulantzas' contributions can provide this. His complex understanding of the state, rather than being a problem, is an advantage because it opens up several different but complementary analytical perspectives on the state that usefully can be applied also to politics at the global level (for more see Ougaard 2004).

A central reason for the complexity in Poulantzas is that his concept of the state encompasses several analytical aspects: the state functions, state power, and what he called state apparatuses, a notion that again covers both the executive and other "apparatuses" and the state as an institutionalized arena for political contestation. Another contribution to the complexity is his understanding of state functions, and this requires a few critical comments.

Poulantzas defines the overall function of the state as being the factor of cohesion in a society. He has a tendency to equate this with the function of power, that is, with maintaining a social order that is in the interest of dominant classes, but at the same time, by focusing on cohesion, he also points to the continued reproduction of society as part of the state function. Arguably there is a tension here, and, drawing on Engels, this leads me to adopt a dual perspective on the overall function of the state: It is both to secure the continued existence of society, and to reproduce relations of power. The duality is succinctly expressed by Engels in a comment on "the Asiatic mode of production": "the exercise of a social function was everywhere the basis of political supremacy; and further that political supremacy has existed only for any length of time only when it discharged its social functions" (quoted from Poulantzas 1973: 51). I refer to this as the power–persistence duality. Both aspects are always present in any state's mode of operation except when the social order breaks down, and the extent to which one aspect constrains or supports the other is contingent and requires historically concrete analysis, in which both aspects have to be examined.

From Poulantzas, then, we get several analytical perspectives on the state: as a set of material institutions, as a structured political arena, as a dual state function with several modalities, and as a materialization of relations of power. Applying this to the "continuing increase in the number and complexity of international institutions, and in the scope of their regulation" (Keohane 1993: 285), global governance is theorized as the partial and uneven globalization of the several aspects of statehood (Ougaard 2004). It is an ensemble of institutions and institutionalized practices involving national state apparatuses and international organizations as central components; it is a set of unevenly developed state functions in relation to world society, developed and implemented through these institutions; it is an ensemble of political arenas in which policies are subject to political contestation by state and non-state actors; and it embodies global relations of power between states and social forces (for more see Ougaard 2004). A central analytical point here is that, from the perspective of state functions, the global governance system should be examined *both* from the aspect of persistence, that is, the function of securing the persistence and sustainability of global society, of humankind *in toto*, and from the aspect of power, that is, reproducing global relations of power.

The OECD in global governance

How then to situate the OECD in this system? It is not an organization that is easily summarized and some indicators of the nature of its work are required (see Martens and Jakobi 2010; Woodward 2010; Ougaard 2010). First, in addition to being a formal international organization with a governing council and a permanent staff of close to 2,500, of whom about 700 are professional economists, lawyers, and scientists (Woodward 2010: 50), it is also the hub of a series of transnational networks, bringing together a much larger number of officials and experts from member and increasingly also non-member countries. In the words of Anne-Marie Slaughter, it is "the quintessential host of trans-governmental regulatory networks, as well as a catalyst for their creation" (Slaughter 2004: 46). There also is a significant participation of non-state actors from business communities and civil society in general in many of these networks (Ougaard 2011).

Second, the OECD is also densely networked with other international organizations, providing various kinds of input and services to their operations and receiving contributions from them as well. Secretary-General Angel Gurria's 2010 Report to Ministers emphasized several recent examples of this: the OECD was represented at the 2009 G20 summit and had a "Sherpa" contributing to preparations; it was invited to the G20 finance ministers' meetings; it works with the Financial Stability Board; and it provides analytical input to ongoing global negotiations on climate change (OECD Secretary-General 2010: 7–8). The OECD has formal partnership agreements with several international organizations and close and regular cooperation with even more, and more than seventy international organizations participate as observers or members in work at the OECD (Ougaard 2010: 43–4). The organization is, in other words, an integral part of the larger system of global governance.

Third, it is a distinctive feature that the organization covers so many policy areas, enabling it to work across the functional divisions that define specialized organizations such as the World Bank, the International Monetary Fund (IMF), and the various bodies of the UN system. As pointed out by Salzman and Terracino, one reason for its significance is simply the scale of its activities (Salzman and Terracino 2006: 394), standing out among intergovernmental organizations in terms of the number and scope of issues it works with, the cumulated experience from decades of working with them, and the number of persons involved in its work. In these issue areas, work at the OECD can combine analytical work that is generally highly respected for its quality, discussions of best practices and policy options, mutual policy surveillance and peer review, and in some areas the setting of authoritative standards of various kinds.

Fourth, it is worth noting that work at the OECD is characterized by a multi-stakeholder consensus-seeking mode of operation that utilizes mutual surveillance and peer review as important techniques, enabled by the high degree of "like-mindedness" among members – a like-mindedness that the organization itself has helped to cultivate over its more than fifty years of operation. In this regard the respect surrounding the quality of the secretariat's analytical work is also important as a shared foundation for policy discussions. At the same time, however, it is also important that there are real political discussions going on in the OECD and consensus can be difficult to achieve. In such situations the organization as such does not always speak with a single voice; rather, as shown by Jacobsson and Noaksson, conflicts between different constituents can be reflected within the

OECD as disagreements between different sections of the secretariat (Jacobsson and Noaksson 2010). Therefore, and more generally, the OECD is also a set of arenas for political contestation among state and non-state actors.

What are the implications of these features for the OECD's role in global governance? Compared with other intergovernmental institutions, the OECD is not much involved in formal decision making, operational activities, and policy implementation. However, through its network activities and analytical work it is strongly involved in other sequences of international policy cycles, in particular agenda setting, strategy formulation, provision of analytical input, and performance evaluation. It provides mechanisms for nation-states jointly to negotiate convergence and develop coordinated responses to new challenges. It does so not only in relation to specific policy areas but also as a strategic direction setter, providing overall direction for societal development, or more precisely for the way in which states and political institutions seek to influence societal development (Ougaard 2010). It is occasionally a site for negotiation of hard international law, but more importantly it is a mechanism for soft convergence and integration, for fostering "a common mindset" among participating government officials (Martens and Jakobi 2010: 261) and, one should add, representatives of other international organizations.

In summary, the OECD is in multiple ways a part of the global governance system. It represents an institutionalized internationalization of the government machineries of member states, participating in and contributing to transnational policy processes across a range of issue areas. It embodies the internationalization of several aspects of statehood – the internationalization of administrative state apparatuses that play roles in agenda setting, development of policy proposals, and policy evaluations; the structuring of political arenas for contestation and bargaining among state and non-state actors; and the shaping of internationalized state functions in their dual aspects, namely the function of societal persistence and the reproduction of relations of power.

At the outset these functions were mainly related to the states and societies of member states, the industrialized countries in North America, Western Europe, and East Asia, which today constitute a core of developed capitalist and democratic societies in the global order – a community of market democracies, whose internal coherence and integration the organization has helped to strengthen, as indicated by the high degree of like-mindedness that is both a result of and a contributing factor to its work. Over the years, however, membership has expanded and the organization has increasingly developed the global dimension in its work, including its engagement with non-members, to which I now turn.

The OECD's engagement with non-members

The OECD had, as already noted, a concern with the entire world economy built into its mandate right from the beginning, but beginning in the 1980s it embarked on a more systematic involvement of non-members. One key reason for this first wave of outreach activity was the rise of new dynamic economies outside of the OECD area (the newly industrializing countries, in particular in Southeast Asia) associated with an early concern with what later became labeled as "globalization" (Ougaard 2010: 36–7). Another reason was the emergence, a few years later, of a group of transitional economies on Europe's eastern border, eager to join the institutions of the West, as a result of the breakdown of the Soviet bloc. Several of these countries have now joined the organization, and after the latest round of accessions – Chile, Estonia, and Israel in 2010 – the membership has reached thirty-three at the time of writing. The latest accessions resulted from the 2007 decision to open membership discussions with Chile, Estonia, Israel, the Russian Federation, and Slovenia. At the same time the decision was made "to strengthen OECD co-operation with Brazil, China, India, Indonesia and South Africa through enhanced engagement programs with a view to possible member-ship" (OECD 2007a). These decisions mark the beginning of a second wave of outreach activities, which is the focus of the remainder of this chapter.

In the preparatory work the political reasoning behind the decisions was clearly laid out. It was noted that the rise of new "significant players" in the world economy weakened the organization's agenda-setting role in other international organizations because it "does not today have the required membership to influ-ence the international economic order as effectively as in the past" (OECD 2004: 13). The combined membership of the organization was no longer as dominant in the world economy as it had been previously; the international relations of economic power had changed, creating a new situation to which the OECD had to react. Furthermore, there was now perceived to be a direct link between the interests of present members and the *domestic* policies of the emerging economies. As stated explicitly: "the economic growth and environmental policies of present Members depend to a certain extent on their capacity to influence the domestic policies of other significant players" (OECD 2004: 13).

The two explicitly stated reasons for the new wave of outreach – the rising power of emerging economies and the significance of their domestic policies – are easily accepted as causal explanations in the theoretical framework applied here. However, it is worth adding another element, namely that hitherto central institutions in North–South economic diplomacy such as the World Bank, the IMF, and some of the specialized UN agencies derived much of their leverage over developing and emerging economies from these countries' dependence on short- and long-term credits and development assistance. In a situation in which several of these countries have reduced this dependence considerably and perhaps to the level of political insignificance, the more indirect and subtle mechanism of engaging them in OECD's processes of mutual policy review and "peer pressure" can be a more promising venue for influencing their domestic policy choices.

Relating the above OECD statements to the analytical notion of the power–persistence duality – maintaining power relations versus securing societal sustainability – they are clearly leaning toward the power side: They are about strengthening the present membership's capacity to influence the governance of the global economy according to its own interests and strategies. They indicate a strategy for co-opting the emerging economies into the institutional machinery of the community of industrialized marked economies under terms and conditions set by this community. Thus the rise of emerging economies and the OECD's response to this implies the potential adding of a significant new dimension to the organization's work.

However, it is worth noting that the process leading up to the 2007 decisions began formally in 2003 after some years of preparatory work (Ougaard 2010: 38), in other words before it became widely recognized that global economic power relations had shifted somewhat in favor of emerging economies. But soon after the 2007 decisions the global financial crisis began to unfold and ensuing events – the global recession and the potential contributions of emerging economies to counteracting it, as well as the disappointing COP (Conference of the Parties) 15 on climate change in 2009 – accentuated the enhanced standing of the "new significant players" in global governance and strengthened the incentive for the OECD to develop constructive engagements with these countries. Therefore a look at recent developments in the enhanced engagement program and the discourses surrounding it is useful before developing the theoretical interpretation further.

In the wake of the crisis: increased emphasis and adjustment

Secretary-General Gurria's section on enhanced engagement in his 2010 Report to Ministers is worth quoting at some length:

> In fact, if the OECD is to remain the home of best practices, we need to reinforce our links with key emerging economies which bring very valuable lessons to the table, without compromising our values or diluting our standards. Working with these countries is essential to finding common responses to global challenges. This is all the more important as we face the consolidation of a new global governance architecture, in which both developed and emerging economies have an important role to play. But, clearly, our success in this endeavor depends crucially on the commitment and support of our own member countries to this concept. It also depends on the interest of and response by the Enhanced Engagement partners to our offers for further co-operation.
>
> Much has been accomplished since the Enhanced Engagement Initiative was launched in 2007. Now, after three years, we need a "Quantum Leap" to improve the quality, depth, breadth and level of trust with our Enhanced Engagement partners. We must create what Prime Minister Gordon Brown described as a "comfort zone" with Enhanced Engagement countries, both bilaterally (MCM, ECSS, Committees) and in multilateral fora such as the G8, the G20 and the many specialised high-level and ministerial meetings in which we participate.

This "Quantum Leap" does not necessarily mean a fast track for membership, although it suggests that we need to significantly upgrade our work and integrate those countries into our analysis. It also calls for the OECD to be more proactive in support of these countries' efforts to consolidate their own development paths. We must therefore seek to develop agendas that are of joint interest and upgrade our dissemination efforts, contacts and presence in Enhanced Engagement countries, including by having OECD officials located in some capitals.

(OECD Secretary-General 2010: 15)

Several observations can be made. First it is recognized that the emerging economies "bring very valuable lessons to the table." In other words, the process of mutual learning among peers that often is flagged as a core OECD working method implies that current members also must be willing to learn. It is not just a matter of non-members converging toward already established principles and policies of the current membership; it must be a two-way process if the principles of mutual learning, peer review, and consensus are to be taken seriously. But, second, Gurria also emphasizes that this should happen "without compromising our values or diluting our standards." He signals in other words that there is a limit to the lessons that the organization and its present members are willing to take from the new partners in the enhanced engagement process. "Our values and standards" still represent a clear line of demarcation.

Third, there is no doubt that the process of enhanced engagement has now become even more important, among other things because of the heightened role of the new players in the global governance architecture. In line with this Gurria signals several concrete steps to be taken to affect a "quantum leap" in the enhanced engagement process.

The fourth and final observation to be made here is that Gurria acknowledges, indirectly at least, that this process may not turn out to be smooth sailing. It depends on the continued support from members and, significantly in the present context, on "the interest of and response by the Enhanced Engagement partners to our offers for further co-operation." This, combined with the choice of language – the need to improve the "quality, depth, breath and level of trust" and to create a "comfort zone" – signals that there may be an element of distrust and discomfort in present relations, and that the interests of the emerging economies may not always be compatible with the interests and strategy of current members.

Relating this to the power–persistence duality, there is in this discourse a clear concern with the sustainability of world society – economically, socially, and environmentally. There is also recognition that there has been a change in power relations, that now it is important to work with countries that see their interests as different from OECD preferences, and there is an openness to accommodate such interests but in a highly circumscribed fashion. The basic interests and strategy of the community of market democracies are not to be compromised, and in that sense the discourse also reflects the function of reproducing existing relations of power.

"For a stronger, cleaner, and fairer world economy"

What, then, are the overall guiding principles or strategy that the OECD has set for its work, including its engagement with non-members? The declared goals of the organization, as stated in Article 1 of the convention, are to

> promote policies designed (a) to achieve the highest sustainable economic growth and employment and a rising standard of living in Member countries, while maintaining financial stability, and thus to contribute to the develop-ment of the world economy; (b) to contribute to sound economic expansion in Member as well as non-member countries in the process of economic development; and (c) to contribute to the expansion of world trade on a multi-lateral, non-discriminatory basis in accordance with international obligations.
>
> (OECD 1960)

These goals have served as an overall guiding framework for the organization's activities throughout its history. However, over the years they have been developed and operationalized across a growing range of policy areas, and they have been adapted to shifting economic and political circumstances, for instance with a con-tinuously growing emphasis on environmental matters, and, as this paper focuses on, with a heightened interest in non-member countries (see Ougaard 2004, 2010; Woodward 2010 on previous stages in OECD strategy).

At the time of writing, the catchphrase "For a stronger, cleaner, and fairer world economy" summarizes the organization's strategic direction. It headlined the Secretary-General's 2010 annual report (OECD Secretary-General 2010: 6) and it was emphasized in the statement from the June 2009 Ministerial Council Meeting:

> we, Ministers, assembled in the midst of the worst global financial, economic and social crisis since the Great Depression [. . .] agreed to do all that is necessary to overcome the crisis and go beyond to build a stronger, cleaner, and fairer world economy.
>
> (OECD Secretary-General 2010: 24)

The statement speaks seriously about all three aspects (strong, clean, fair), pointing out inter alia concerning fairness that "Recovery plans should serve people by addressing the social and human dimensions of the crisis, through support for the most vulnerable, including active labour market policies, skills development, income support, effective social safety nets, pensions, education and enhanced training projects" (p. 25). There is also a special concern with the plight of devel-oping countries: "It is vital that we support measures to mitigate the impacts of the current recession on the world's poor and vulnerable and that we step-up efforts to ensure developing countries are well-placed to participate in the eventual recovery of the global economy" (p. 26). On the environment it is stated that "We commit to ensuring that the economic recovery and future economic growth are consistent with sustainable development" and a reference is made to the Declaration on Green Growth, which also was adopted at the June 2009 meeting (p. 26).

Economic growth is also central and here the statement holds on to principles that have been part and parcel of OECD strategy for decades. Free trade and investment are central in this regard. The ministers agreed that "We shall resist protectionism. The free flow of trade and investment is essential to ensure a return to sustainable economic growth and improved standards of living for all, particularly for developing countries" (pp. 26–7). Equally important is structural reform and macro-economic stability: "swiftly implementing structural reforms that enhance the flexibility and productivity of our economies, such as in product and labour markets, will be essential to address the deterioration of our public budgets and the loss in living standards caused by the crisis" (p. 26).

These elements – economic, social, and environmental – are not competing goals in OECD's understanding; rather they are mutually supporting provided that clever policies are crafted: "We are convinced that the current crisis can act as a catalyst for much needed policy reform, generating both environmental, employment and economic gains" (OECD Secretary-General 2010: 26).

The link between environmental sustainability and economic growth is further stressed in the Declaration on Green Growth:

> Economic recovery and environmentally and socially sustainable economic growth are key challenges that all countries are facing today. A number of well targeted policy instruments can be used to encourage green investment in order to simultaneously contribute to economic recovery in the short-term, and help to build the environmentally friendly infrastructure required for a green economy in the long term, noting that public investment should be consistent with a long-term framework for generating sustainable growth.
>
> (OECD Council 2009: 1)

Although declarations are not formal agreements, it is worth noticing that they do have a special significance. They are "solemn texts [. . .] which set out relatively precise policy commitments [. . .] they are not intended to be legally binding, but they are noted by the Council of the OECD and their application is generally monitored by the Committees" (OECD Legal Directorate 1996: Preface). Thus, the intention to embark on a green growth strategy is a relatively strong policy commitment by member countries, and it should also be noted that non-members are invited to "cooperate with the OECD in line with the Declaration" (OECD Council 2009: 2).

One further document can help illuminate OECD's strategy toward "a stronger, cleaner, and fairer world economy," namely the Declaration on Propriety, Integrity and Transparency in the Conduct of International Business and Finance from May 28, 2010 (OECD 2010a). This declaration states that "Propriety, integrity and transparency are the keystone of an economy which commands the support and confidence of the people and serves their needs and aspirations" (p. 1), and it goes on to list key principles that companies should adhere to in order to live up to this. Among the principles are respect for the rule of law; not engaging in anti-competitive behavior; good corporate governance; and "disclosure of timely and accurate information regarding their activities, financial situation, non-financial performance, adherence to responsible investment principles, foreseeable risks (including social, ethical and environmental risks)" (p. 1). The declaration further states that "Standards of responsible business conduct should be reflected in corporate decision-making. Corporate responsibility entails timely and accurate fulfillment of tax obligations wherever a company operates. Companies should comply with both the letter and the spirit of the tax law" (p. 1).

The declaration also addresses public governance. Governments should, for instance, punish anti-competitive business behavior and remove unnecessary restrictions on competition, take effective measures to prevent bribery in international business transactions, and provide "business and market regulatory frameworks" that serve "clearly identified policy goals and produce benefits that justify costs" and "are submitted to a systematic assessment of their impact" (p. 1).

In two annexes the declaration lists all of the legal OECD instruments (recommendations, guidelines, decisions standards, and so on) and initiatives that address these issues, covering competition, corporate governance, tax cooperation, anti-corruption, interaction between government and business (e.g. integrity in public procurement, integrity in lobbying), and quality of regulation (OECD 2010a). This amounts to the cumulative result of the organization's work over decades with setting and specifying ground rules and principles for the proper behavior of business and governments in market economies. It amounts to a program for a world economy in which responsible and law-abiding private businesses operate in competitive markets underpinned by appropriate and effective government regulations and services adhering to principles of good public governance as developed by the OECD and its members.

How to characterize this? In critical IPE studies it is often asserted (or assumed) that international institutions dominated by the capitalist North pursue an agenda of neoliberalism. Clearly, many of the elements associated with the neoliberal agenda and the Washington Consensus are present in the OECD's strategy: macro-economic stability, emphasis on long-term growth, structural reform, free international trade and investment flows, and a bias against government regulation. Still, the OECD agenda is not a market fundamentalist one. It accepts public services and social safety nets, it accepts government regulation (if it serves clearly defined policy goals cost-effectively), indeed it calls for strong regulation in several regards, it accepts government policies to stimulate the economy when required, and it accepts government interventions to redirect the pattern of economic growth toward a cleaner economy. Therefore I find it more adequate to label it a *green social-liberal agenda*, one that is firmly committed to the basic principles of a capitalist market economy, but one that also includes public policies to address problems that are not solved adequately by market forces alone.

This social-liberal agenda is rooted in the domestic social orders of the OECD member states. It reflects the social compromise between capital and labor and other social forces that have shaped the modern welfare states in these countries, where the basic premises for the compromise are those set by the principles of capitalism and democracy. Furthermore, with the steadfast adherence to the principles of an open world economy with free trade and investment flows, the OECD agenda also reflects the economic and political weight of transnational capital in the OECD member countries.

This compromise, however, is not a static balance; on the contrary it is continuously subject to adjustments and renegotiations that reflect both new economic and societal developments and changes in the relative strength of the social forces involved. Such underlying changes are also reflected within the OECD, where both the overall strategic orientation and the approach to more specific policy issues are adapted and adjusted on an ongoing basis through political multi-actor processes that can be more or less contentious. Examples of this can be found in Jacobsson and Noaksson's (2010) analysis of shifting emphasis in the jobs strategy or more generally in the approach to economic governance (Woodward 2010) – and of course also demonstrated by the adaptation to the rise of emerging economies and the adjustment of this particular strategy to the post-crisis situation.

What is implied here is exactly the duality inherent in the overall state function – societal persistence and reproduction of relations of power – and the fact that this dual function is continually reproduced and modified through political agency in processes in which state institutions are important both as embodiments of the dual function with an agency of their own and as structured political arenas.

Against this background, when examined in the light of the notion of the inherent duality of the overall state function, the offer of enhanced engagement to selected emerging economies – the proposal "to forge a more structured and coherent partnership, based on mutual interest" (OECD Secretary-General 2010: 5) – is a strategy for the gradual and stepwise integration of them into the institutional machinery of the community of developed market democracies and the functions performed by and through this machinery. This implies several things. It is an attempted, long-term outward projection of the social-liberal social order, securing the persistence and ongoing reproduction of this order and its inherent relations of power at a global scale. Furthermore, in this social order the state's function of persistence has acquired a global dimension, a concern with the persistence – or, in OECD terminology, economic, social, and environmental sustainability – of world society. The EEI is therefore also an effort to further integrate the states in emerging economies in the performance of this global function of persistence. But again, this is on terms defined by prevailing relations of power and in particular the international dominance of the "community of market democracies" and the balance of social forces within them. And there is still more to the story. The EEI also implies that the "new significant players" are invited to join political arenas in the OECD as "peers" and thereby – at least in principle – to participate in the ongoing shaping and adjustment of this order. Secretary-General Gurria's words, quoted above, about present members' willingness to learn from the enhanced engagement countries, if taken at surface value, signal a willingness to listen and perhaps accommodate and adjust in ways that reflect interests and preferences of the new players. Thus, within the parameters set by the basic principles of the OECD, reflecting fundamental features of the social order in the present OECD membership, a possibility for adjusting to changed global relations of power is acknowledged.

The prospects for this project, as also stated by Gurria, hinge very much on how the EEI is received by the invited countries. On this I will offer some preliminary observations in the next section.

Responses

The EEI is still an unfolding process and it would be premature to offer more than some preliminary observations. It seems fair to say, though, that the initiative has been met with varying degrees of enthusiasm by the invitees, but that they all in practice are willing to engage with the OECD, although their level and pattern of participation is markedly different.

South Africa seems to be the most enthusiastic, as evidenced by the large number of OECD bodies in which it participates (Table 5.1). It is also the country that has most vocally embraced the EEI and its underlying rationale. In July 2008 the South African Minister of Finance and the OECD's Secretary-General issued a joint statement that, inter alia, said that:

> The ongoing partnership between South Africa and the OECD has proven to be deep, strong, enduring and mutually beneficial . . . The South African Government welcomes the enhanced engagement process and we believe that this is an opportunity to build our partnership with the OECD through a strengthened relationship and a more structured interaction, based on mutual interests . . . In the long term, a programme of greater convergence is envisaged between South Africa's social, economic and political structures and the generally accepted standards established by the OECD.
>
> (OECD South Africa 2008)

Similar ringing endorsements of the project were not found for the other four invited countries. For example, the two official visits that Secretary-General Gurria paid to India in October 2007 and December 2009 (OECD 2007b, 2009a) have not led to similar joint declarations – indeed no official statements seem to have emerged from these occasions.

Still, if we look at the actual engagement with the OECD – as indicated by the data on participation in OECD bodies in Table 5.1 – India is not passive. It is not surprising that Russia, which is engaged in accession talks, tops the list, but next come three of the five EEI countries, with China not far below. Only Indonesia has a rather low level of participation. The numbers in the table should be seen

TABLE 5.1 Most active non-members' participation in OECD bodies, October 2010

Country	Number of OECD bodies in which non-members participate		
	Member	Observer	Total
Russian Federation	15	93	108
South Africa	17	58	75
Brazil	13	40	53
India	9	28	37
Argentina	8	28	36
Egypt	9	23	32
Romania	14	14	28
People's Republic of China	3	25	28
Morocco	9	6	15
Bulgaria	8	6	14
Ukraine	4	10	14
Lithuania	8	5	13
Singapore	5	8	13
Serbia	10	2	12
Latvia	4	8	12
Croatia	8	2	10
Lithuania	5	6	11
Indonesia	2	5	7

Source: "OECD On-line Guide to Intergovernmental Activity." Available at http://webnet3.oecd. org/OECDGROUPS/Bodies/ListByRoleView.aspx?book=true (accessed October 15, 2010).

in the light of the fact that member states on average participate in the work of 200+ OECD bodies (Ougaard 2010: 41); the participation of non-members is still therefore limited. It is also evident that the EEI invitees are not the only non-members who participate and that the involvement of a broad circle of countries goes back to the 1980s. Thus the level of participation revealed in Table 5.1 is not only the result of the EEI. Still, three of the five EEI countries top the list if Russia is excluded, and China's position can actually be considered surprisingly high in view of the fact that it probably is the country whose domestic structures are most different from established OECD standards. Furthermore, there are also indications that at least South Africa and India have stepped up their engagement in recent years; a similar table based on July 2008 data showed a total of twenty-eight bodies for India and fifty-six for South Africa, compared with the present thirty-seven and seventy-five respectively (Ougaard 2010: 42).

Another indicator of the invitees' willingness to engage with the OECD is their participation in mutual surveys and peer reviews, which are among the most important mechanisms for influencing the domestic policies of participating countries. Among the five, Brazil has gone most extensively into peer review processes. Economic surveys have been made in 2001, 2005, 2006, and 2009, and there have been another eight peer reviews, covering inter alia budgeting systems, regulatory reform, implementation of the anti-bribery convention, and competition law and policy. China has had economic surveys in 2005 and 2010, a survey of regulatory reform in 2009, of eco-innovation policy in 2009, budget reform in 2009, the shipbuilding industry in 2009, and the innovation system in 2009, and investment policy reviews in 2006 and 2008, and environmental performance reviews in 2006 and 2007 (OECD 2010b). The first economic survey of India was completed in 2007 and the second is foreseen for the end of 2010 (OECD CCNM 2009: 8), and so far only one sectoral policy review has been made, the investment policy review concluded in 2009 (OECD 2009b). South Africa has had two economic surveys in 2008 and 2010, and has further submitted to peer review of its "public expenditure management system," its outlook in science and technology, and its implementation of the Anti-Bribery Convention (information from OECD 2010b), whereas Indonesia has published a public procurement self-assessment in 2005, an anti-corruption self-assessment in 2005, an energy policy review in 2008, and an economic assessment in 2008 (OECD 2010b).

This evidence shows that all five have accepted the peer review process in some policy areas, but also that there is variation in both the number and the nature of policy areas they have engaged in. Thus a second observation is that the participation profiles – the policy areas in which they are interested – of the EEI invitees are quite different. This is further evidenced by Table 5.2, which shows how participation in OECD bodies is distributed across OECD committees. (Table 5.2 is based on a different data set from the OECD from Table 5.1 and therefore the numbers are not quite consistent.) It is evident, for instance, that Brazil is alone in taking a strong interest in the Public Governance Committee, that South Africa has a strong interest in the Environment and Chemicals Committees, that Brazil and to some extent South Africa, in contrast to India, are interested in OECD work on investment and competition, and that China's interest is concentrated on taxation (fiscal affairs), science and technology, and education.

This high degree of variation is important in itself because it shows that the EEI is a very flexible mechanism. OECD and individual non-member countries can engage with each other in a pattern that is tailored specifically to each particular relationship – focusing on some policy areas while avoiding others – and the pattern revealed by the information presented above shows precisely that each invitee has engaged in such a selective fashion.

The conclusion to these preliminary observations is that the five countries – Brazil, China, India, Indonesia, and South Africa – have responded positively to the Enhanced Engagement Initiative (although it should be remembered that they already were involved with the OECD before the 2007 initiative), but they have

TABLE 5.2 Participation in committees and subsidiary bodies, as of February 1, 2010

OECD Committee	Brazil	China and Hong Kong	India	Indonesia	South Africa
Trade Committee	O	O	–	–	–
Participation in subsidiary bodies	3	3	–	–	–
Investment Committee	O	–	–	–	–
Participation in subsidiary bodies	4	–	1	–	2
Competition Committee	O	–	–	O	O
Participation in subsidiary bodies	2		–	2	2
Committee for Agriculture	–	–	–	–	–
Participation in subsidiary bodies	8	1	6	–	10
Committee on Financial Markets	–	O	–	–	–
Participation in subsidiary bodies		2	–		
Environment Policy Committee	–	O	–	–	–
Participation in subsidiary bodies	3	1	2	–	8
Chemicals Committee	–	–	–	–	F
Participation in subsidiary bodies	–		–	–	5
Steel Committee	F	–	F	–	F
Participation in subsidiary bodies	–		–	–	–
Committee for Information, Computer and Communications Policy	–	–	O	–	O
Participation in subsidiary bodies	–		4	–	4
Committee on Industry, Innovation and Entrepreneurship	–	–	–	–	–
Participation in subsidiary bodies	1		–	–	–
Insurance and Private Pensions Committee	–	–	–	–	–
Participation in subsidiary bodies	1	–	1	–	1
Public Governance Committee	O	–	–	–	–
Participation in subsidiary bodies	9	–	–	–	–
Committee on Fiscal Affairs	–	O	O	–	O
Participation in subsidiary bodies	–	10	10	–	10
Committee for Scientific and Technological Policy	O	O	–	–	O
Participation in subsidiary bodies	8	8	–	–	8
Education Policy Committee	–	–	–	–	–
Participation in subsidiary bodies	2	5	–	1	–

(continued)

TABLE 5.2 Continued

OECD Committee	Brazil	China and Hong Kong	India	Indonesia	South Africa
Committee on Consumer Policy	–	–	*0*	–	–
Participation in subsidiary bodies	–	–	–	–	–
Territorial Development Policy Committee	–	–	–	–	*0*
Participation in subsidiary bodies	–	–	–	–	3
Employment, Labour and Social Affairs Committee	–	–	–	–	*0*
Participation in subsidiary bodies	–	–	–	–	–
Committee on Statistics	*0*	–	*0*	–	*0*
Participation in subsidiary bodies	3	3	3	–	3
Governing Board of the Development Centre	F	–	F	F	F
Participation in subsidiary bodies	–	–	–	–	–
Number of high-level participations	8	0	6	0	10

Source: OECD (2010c: Box 4, p. 15–21).

Notes
Number in italics: number of subsidiary bodies in which the country participates. (It is possible to participate in a subsidiary body without being a formal member of that committee and without participating at committee level.)
O, observer in committee; F, full participant in committee.

done so selectively, with varying degrees of open enthusiasm, and with rather different levels of intensity, ranging from a very active and enthusiastic South Africa to a much more timid response from Indonesia.

Let me on this basis offer some concluding thoughts on the prospects for this new and apparently growing role for the OECD. First, in relation to the theoretical interpretation of the EEI initiative developed above, that is, a long-term strategy for the integration of the emerging economies in the institutional machinery of the community of market democracies and the state functions associated with it, this must be seen precisely as a long-term project – very long-term indeed. It could be argued that the project of fostering societal convergence between such vastly different societies is far too ambitious a goal to be taken seriously and it certainly is a daunting project.

On the other hand, based on the same analysis, it is a project that corresponds to basic strategic interests of the current membership and therefore it is a project that is likely to remain on the agenda in the long term. But then the OECD is not the only international organization that can and does address the multiple policy issues that are involved in the project and so the question is also whether the OECD will remain an important site for policy processes in all of these issue areas.

Indeed it is likely that issues will migrate to other fora such as the WTO, the IMF, the Bank of International Settlements, or parts of the UN system – but based on experiences so far it is also likely that in many cases this will happen on the basis of groundwork laid in the OECD, and that this organization in many cases will continue to play a key role in some stages of international policy cycles.

In the context of institutional competition between international organizations, it should be remembered that the OECD has some distinct advantages. One is the flexibility pointed out above. Another is the fact that the organization apparently has the strength of being quite attractive. In spite of the occasional voicing of doubts about the OECD's diminished relevance, the fact remains that no member country has left the organization and that many countries have been eager to join it, bringing the membership up to the current level of thirty-three. In this context it is also worth noting that the OECD offers to both new members and enhanced engagement partners the status of peers, signaling participation on an equal footing. A final advantage is that the OECD has the capacity to deal with such a broad range of policy areas, which sets it apart from most other, more specialized international organizations. Indeed, the only organization with a similar broad remit is the United Nations, which in principle, through the Economic and Social Council and the large array of special organizations and programs, has a comparable wide remit – and even broader if the Security Council is included. However, considering the well-known weaknesses of the UN system and the level of discord among its members, the OECD is a more likely contender to play a key role in the gradual and stepwise integration of emerging economies in the institutional machinery of transnational governance – at least if that integration is to take place under conditions set by the de facto community of developed market democracies. Therefore I consider it plausible, and indeed likely, that the engagement with emerging economies and other non-members will remain and perhaps even grow as a major new role for the OECD.

6

PAVED WITH GOOD INTENTIONS

Global financial integration, the eurozone, and the hellish road to the fabled gold standard

Geoffrey R. D. Underhill

Helge Hveem, to whom this volume is dedicated, argued that regional integration projects were governance arrangements the recent proliferation of which was closely related to the pressures of global integration (Hveem 2006). Thorough-going global market integration might prove economically efficient, yet the outcome confronts democratic demands for a reasonable distribution of wealth that implies redistributive or other interventions in the market necessary to the legitimacy of authority: "when the self-regulating market produces systemic instability . . . democratic governance is threatened. The authority of the system loses legitimacy; it is challenged and may eventually break down" (Hveem 2006: 300). Meanwhile, national authorities as the locus of political legitimacy in democratic systems have diminished capacity to deal with this problem on their own while preserving the efficiency benefits of market integration. Hveem saw region building as a potential compromise that might deal successfully with this dilemma: "*the comparative advantage of the regional project is that it may be more effective in governing globalization than the nation-state, while at the same time potentially offering more legitimacy and collective identity than globalization itself*" (Hveem 2006: 301; italics in original).

The EU with its single currency is surely the archetype of this sort of compromise. The recent financial crisis has certainly produced systemic instability and drawn attention to the highly unequal distribution of benefits brought about by interacting national, regional, and global patterns of liberalization, and this has been exacerbated by the subsequent and related sovereign debt crisis in the eurozone. The debt crisis therefore provides a test of Hveem's proposition wherein two conditions might confirm that he was on the right track. First, successful cooperative resolution of the debt crisis would require that the EU as a regional project had achieved sufficient levels of cross-national legitimacy and shared identity (in the EU referred to as "solidarity") to produce a solution in the first place. In turn, the solution would need to demonstrate to member citizens and national governments alike that a common solution was more effective than a national one, thereby strengthening the collective identity and legitimacy of the EU as a regional project. The outcome so far tells us that Hveem may, sadly, have been overly optimistic. As he himself foreshadowed, "authority relationships in regional action are both more complex and more unpredictable at the end of the third-generation [regional] projects than was previously the case" (Hveem 2006: 310). If so, the financial crisis has landed the EU in greater trouble than we may yet realize.

The first section of this paper will briefly establish the context in terms of financial liberalization and its collapse. The second section will examine the pre-crisis literature that warned of the potential dangers of the emerging liberal order, demonstrating that the crisis was less a result of bad bankers than of bad public policy driven by policy rent seeking and based on blithe assumptions with no historical evidence to support them. A third section will address the crisis of the eurozone and the reaction to it in the light of this literature, demonstrating that lessons available pre-crisis remain poorly learned. The paper will conclude with further reflections on the requirements of successful and legitimate financial and monetary governance.

Global financial integration

Global financial integration became a defining feature of the late twentieth and early twenty-first centuries, along with a somewhat less consistent push for a more open trading order. This market-oriented trend in economic policy was largely justified in terms of the broad, aggregate economic benefits that it might bring to both the developed and the developing world, differentially distributed though they might be. The general turn toward more liberal market-based strategies followed the apparent exhaustion in the crises of the mid-1970s and early 1980s of the thirty years of post-war economic miracle fostered by often interventionist reconstruction and development policies and the rise of the welfare state as a political imperative in many lands.

Taken up to varying degrees depending on the country, this policy turn made considerable sense for national economies in search of the future through widening the market while forcing necessary adjustments by increasing the competition in some way or other. Post-war reconstruction was long over and the sectors that had fueled the boom had reached maturity. New sectors and technologies sought widened access to world markets, and the revolution in services industries was part of the trend.

Most importantly, there were the unintended consequences of wealth in the developed world. Many of the policies that had been set in place in the aftermath of war were policies aimed at the economic transformation of poor societies. Europe west of the Berlin Wall was suddenly far from poor, likewise Japan. The successful and rapid growth of productivity had meant that wages rose and organized labor enjoyed the political benefits of full employment combined with rising consumerism. People lived longer, were healthy, and sought pleasures in consumption and returns for their surplus wealth. Population growth in the developed world came to an end, school rosters shrank, and a wealthy new generation less chastened by the Depression and the war took power and began to move about the planet with increasing frequency.

These changes greatly altered the needs of these societies in terms of demand for products, finance, and public services, and of government budgetary priorities. Trade agreements had brought down many of the trade barriers to manufactured products, and the rise of off-shore capital markets in London and elsewhere provided the functional equivalent of increased capital mobility. The end of the boom saw high labor costs juxtaposed on industrial crisis in the developed economies. A yearning for industrialization elsewhere presaged a shift in the more labor-intensive segments of the production chain that also served the cause of price competition. In response, multinational enterprise began to implement more global production and corporate strategies as increased economic openness provided new incentives, often to the cost of those without the resources and know-how to adapt. The European Union was indulging in yet more radical experiments with regional liberalization across state boundaries.

Perhaps most importantly, states emerged from the 1970s and 1980s downturn with vast mountains of debt. This had to be financed, and once Paul Volcker ruled out inflation as a solution an adventure with financial internationalization seemed a good bet. OPEC oil surpluses provided markets with a massive increase in capital just as recession had dampened private appetites for investment. The public sector could conveniently fill this gap (Cohen 1982: 471) as state treasuries and increasingly independent central banks discovered the delights of access to international capital markets. The major international banks were hardly averse to such a strategy. Governments and their economies gained enhanced access to international capital while large financial institutions facing market saturation at home gained access to new public and private markets. Cross-border coalitions formed to press their own and foreign governments to engage in cross-border financial liberalization (Underhill 1993) and this proved an enduring alliance for the promotion of cross-sectoral and cross-border financial market integration.

Given the very real costs, financial and other forms of globalization would not have happened had this not served material interests by providing an adequate range of (unequally distributed) benefits (Rodrik 1998a). This period of rapid financial integration came to be punctuated by frequent and severe episodes of financial crisis (Bordo et al. 2001). For a while these crises appeared limited to the "emerging markets," which led to the implementation of reforms in these "weakest links." This market-based "New International Financial Architecture" emerged as the underpinning to asset bubbles and economic imbalances in the global economy (Guttman 2009).[1] In the end the weakest link proved to be the financial system and payments imbalances of the United States (Schwarz 2009). The booming market for securitized mortgage-based assets became unstable and by the summer of 2007 an avalanche of misunderstood risks metamorphosed into demon uncertainty, paralysing the interbank market. The entire edifice collapsed and deflation and depression threatened to possess the spirit of the age.

Public authorities re-established a modicum of financial stability by mid-2009 and an internationally coordinated fiscal stimulus appeared to have launched a fragile recovery. Worries began to shift away from the health of the financial sector to the rising public debt burdens exacerbated by the financial sector rescue and cost of the recession. By late 2009 this was focused on the weaker economies of the eurozone, particularly post-election Greece (the outgoing government of which had been highly economical with the truth about its debt burden). Governments squabbled, and publicly assigned blame while remaining inactive, worsening an otherwise containable situation, which required another dramatic rescue under crisis conditions. The jewel in the crown of European integration, economic and monetary union and the single currency, seemed to be, and may still be, under threat.

Distilling the lessons of a crisis well-enough deserved (by some)

We know and have long known that liberal financial markets are potentially unstable. There is historical evidence a-plenty (Kindleberger 1989; Galbraith 1993, 1995), and adequate theoretical explanations of the phenomenon.[2] The case for adequate governance in the form of supervision and regulation is well understood and entrenched in the fabric of post-Depression, post-war economic systems. There are those who argue it was the most warned-of crisis in history,[3] and others who claim that no one saw it coming. The latter have little evidence on their side. A brief examination of some twenty years of research findings and scholarly analysis should allow one to review the record of our prior understanding of the matter.[4]

Among the most consistently prescient of political economists was Susan Strange. The rise of off-shore and deregulated financial markets outside national systems of governance had largely been responsible for the breakdown of the international monetary system during the 1970s (Strange 1976: ch. 6). In *Casino Capitalism* Strange (1986) argued persuasively that the increasing liberalization of capital markets and their cross-border integration was transforming and risked disrupting the system of states and the global economy. Despite the increasing prevalence of arguments concerning the importance of financial market discipline for government finances and macro-economic policy, the increasing availability of private finance arguably postponed or allowed states to avoid altogether the required adjustment to international imbalances (see also Cohen 1982: 471–5). The distortionary growth of the financial sector was skewing incentives in Western societies, destabilizing the international monetary system, and was an inherently unstable enterprise. This *Retreat of the State* (Strange 1996) in favor of markets not only increased the risk of major financial crisis, but also, by enhancing private power, correspondingly disarmed crucial instruments of public policy, which risked delegitimizing government over time. Her last book was appropriately entitled *Mad Money* (Strange 1998) and was published at her death and just in time to welcome the dot-com bubble and crash, in retrospect a forerunner of the crisis of 2007–10.

A range of scholars followed Strange's lead (e.g. Cerny 1993; Moran 1991) to focus on this "phoenix risen" (Cohen 1996) of global finance and the domestic dimensions of policy change (Moran 1984; Pauly 1988; Rosenbluth 1989; Coleman 1996). Many of the works emerging at this time focused on the causes of this major shift in global order, while others debated the balance of economic costs and benefits of financial openness (King and Levine 1993; Demetriades and Hussain 1996) and/or possible systems of regulation and supervision (Steil 1994; Barth et al. 2006). Often enough, cautionary messages in the literature emerged that should have served as ample warning that global financial market integration was potentially problematic. At least four such messages can be distilled from the literature (Underhill et al. 2010).

Lesson 1: financial instability prevalent

A first message has already been alluded to: that a liberal or market-based order of cross-border and cross-sectoral financial integration underpinned by a high degree of capital mobility constitutes an inherently unstable system. As mentioned, this was a point emphasized by Strange and based on historical research (Strange 1976; also Kindleberger and Laffargue 1982), but there were prominent economists who also argued this point well before the crisis of the twenty-first century (see, for example, Minsky 1982; Rodrik 1998a; Bhagwati 1998; Stiglitz 2000, 2002). In particular, the consequences of financial liberalization for developing countries were always in serious dispute. Despite the predictions of "standard" economic theory, empirical research revealed that net capital flows to developing countries over time mostly flowed "uphill" from poor to developed economies, with (fortunately) foreign direct investment as a major exception (Prasad et al. 2007). If one adds to this "Lucas paradox" (Lucas 1990) picture the frequency of crises in emerging market economies,[5] then it was highly likely that capital market integration would develop as an erratic system, potentially destabilizing for exchange rates and other macro-economic variables, and often costly for economic development. Although there were identifiable longer-run benefits to financial openness, these might require considerable and successful institutional development and governance in developing countries if the benefits were to be realized properly (Kose et al. 2006).

There is in any event no real-time historical case of successful economic development under conditions of financial openness. On the contrary, successful development strategies in nineteenth- and twentieth-century Europe, and from the United States to Japan to the Asian tigers to contemporary China, rather demonstrate that economic development is accompanied by a range of strategic state intervention measures: capital account and/or exchange controls, selective protectionism, and measures to attract and shape foreign direct investment flows to national advantage.[6] The clear conclusion was that financial openness would most likely turn out badly if insufficient attention were to be paid to governance and if there were to emerge an over-reliance on the market as the core mechanism of the system.

Lesson 2: constraints on policy space

This brings us to the second cautionary tale of the literature: This institutional fabric of financial governance must be consciously developed, and cross-border market integration will require substantial levels of international cooperation if national policy goals are to be achieved. A crucial element of this institutional underpinning concerns the macro-economic policy framework, particularly in the domain of monetary and exchange rate policy, and public debt. The macro-economic environment and the autonomous use of national policy instruments will be rendered more difficult through the introduction of a high degree of capital mobility, especially in the domain of monetary and exchange rate policy. The dilemma is what Cohen has called the problem of the "Unholy Trinity" (Cohen 1993, 1996: 280–5) based on the long-standing work of Mundell and Flemming. Capital mobility can also increase constraints on the fiscal options available to governments: the redistributional and social welfare policy choices crucial to domestic political legitimacy, placing governments between often-incompatible global market pressures and national political imperatives (Underhill and Zhang 2003; Rodrik 2007b). Managing these trade-offs is far more difficult for poor and emerging market economies than for the developed world and often challenges their historical economic development models (Underhill 1999), but the pressure is felt by all. Achieving the benefits of better access to international capital frequently involves trade-offs against other policy options, yet far too often regulatory change was implemented without due consideration for the macro-economic consequences, and capital market regulation and macro-economic considerations involved quite different policy communities and processes wherein the gains of the financial sector were not measured against potential losses for others (Underhill 1996).

The reform of the international financial architecture, undertaken in the shadow of the serial emerging market crises from 1994 to 2002, was designed to deal with these growing tensions. What is interesting is the way in which this problem was addressed and why. The approach at Bretton Woods in 1944 had been to render the international monetary and financial order compatible with creating for national governments the policy space required to make, in their own way, according to their internal politics, the difficult choices involved in adjustment to international imbalances. In other words, the aim was to make the world compatible with the political vagaries and legitimacy requirements of national democracy. The financial architects of the 1990s saw the problem the other way around: The focus was on adapting and strengthening the "weakest links" in the global chain, the developing and emerging market economies, to the pressures of a market-based and integrated global financial system. There was no provision for macro-economic stability or monetary order; on the contrary, the monetary system and system of international adjustment was de facto simply a derivative of the market-based financial order. Volatile capital flows were seen as constituting useful pressure to develop sensible norms and standards to underpin macro-economic policy compatible with the global system. Because national financial regulation and monetary governance was increasingly ineffective, a market-based system strengthened by sound domestic regulation, better crisis prevention mechanisms, and better national macro-economic policies and related international monitoring and coordination was billed as the solution.

Therefore a major plank in the reform process was the promulgation of a range of "global" standards in the domains of macro-economic policy, financial stability, accounting, and corporate governance to which emerging markets and poor countries with weak institutional capacities were to conform and adapt by means of new international standards and codes (Tirole 2002: 18–22). In this way the "new" international financial architecture focused on facilitating the free flow of capital across borders, preserving the same market-based characteristics that emerged in the 1980s and 1990s while aiming to render national economic policy and space more compatible with the demands and pressures of financial integration. If the rules were right and properly applied, the market would function in a stable manner.

A range of initiatives was taken in the field of crisis prevention, with a focus on improving transparency in financial markets and macro-economic governance (International Monetary Fund Reports on the Observance of Standards and Codes or ROSCs). New consultative forums emerged as a response to the exclusion of emerging markets (G20) and the need for better overview and supervisory coordination of globally integrated markets (Financial Stability Forum or FSF – recently renamed and strengthened as the Financial Stability Board or FSB). Yet none of these bodies had or have real power to set rules for global financial governance; the key still lies with the major G7/G10 economies despite the new role for the G20 and the major emerging market countries therein. The one serious institutional innovation in the field of crisis resolution, the Sovereign Debt Restructuring Mechanism (SDRM), failed to materialise and was replaced by the incremental and voluntary Collective Action Clauses (CACs) and the non-binding private sector "principles" promulgated by the Institute for International Finance (IIF 2006). These and other private sector initiatives were as much an attempt to pre-empt public intervention as they were attempts to fill gaps in governance. The subsequent "period of calm," 2002–7, bred a sense of complacency that the new global financial architecture was working and was successfully preventing the outbreak of new major crises. Nonetheless, less positive signs were visible to those who wished to see them: Capital flows to emerging markets and poorer developing countries remained volatile and unpredictable over time (World Bank 2006), and a deadly toxin was accumulating in Western banking systems.

Lesson 3: skewed policy input

Perhaps more important is how demands for these new forms of international financial governance initially emerged and were adopted as policy. Financial firms and their associations have historically close and relatively exclusive relationships with elite state policy makers and with the key international organizations, together responsible for the design of the reforms. There was already a private sector–state agency coalition in favor of liberalization, the policy preferences of which were observable in the norms and rules of the new architecture. G7 governments generally backed the preferences of their corporate financial sectors (Baker 2005) in an increasingly transnational policy community. Cooperative institutions of global financial governance, such as the Basel Committee and the International Organization of Securities Commissions (IOSCO), were characterized not only by exclusive policy communities, but also by virtual separation from accountable political processes (Underhill 1995, 1997), a problem further exacerbated by frequent recourse to self-regulation. As a result, the transnational financial system is increasingly regulated by agencies constituting regimes that are more responsive to private interests than to providers of collective goods (Cerny 1996: 96–9; Porter 1999).[7]

Evidence indicates that crucial multilateral international financial institutions, such as the International Monetary Fund, were part of this constellation of interests (Wade 1998a; Stiglitz 2002). Private institutional investors have attempted to shape the investment environment in emerging market economies by pressing these countries to adopt policy frameworks favorable to their interests (Maxfield 1998; Porter 1999), even though such policies might exacerbate problems of economic development and socio-political stability. The emerging system of financial governance across national and global levels was thus flawed in important ways in terms of input-side, policy-process legitimacy. The guardians governing the monetary and financial order had become relatively autonomous from the traditional mechanisms of (democratic) accountability and control as well as from the influence of broader social constituencies. The point here is not that there should be no private sector involvement in financial governance, but that such involvement is problematic if it aligns notions of the public interest with those who not only profit most from financial markets, but also represent the greatest risks to the financial system as a whole.

Lesson 4: policy rent seeking and capture

This brings us to the fourth cautionary tale that was reflected both in the literature and on the ground. The problem of narrow, exclusionary policy communities that generated the international financial architecture is anchored at the domestic level of the countries that host the principal financial centers. Skewed policy input results in a skewed balance of public versus private authority and interests in the fashioning of both supervisory/regulatory policy and the financial order itself. As a result, the output side of policy making becomes flawed in terms of legitimacy *and* effectiveness: Liberalization and market-based financial architecture did not improve the stability of the system, and ultimately raised the costs for ordinary citizens. Financial liberalization and the subsequent establishment of a market-based approach to financial governance constituted a process of policy rent seeking that yielded important competitive advantages for the major international investment banks and financial conglomerates who pursued the policy in the first place. State agencies involved in financial governance also had a crucial interest in financial liberalization and frequently made common cause with the financial sector.

This private dominance at the domestic level of decision making is based on the close relationship between private financial institutions and supervisory and regulatory agencies, with frequent delegation of oversight to self-regulatory processes (Baker 2005). Most often statutorily independent from politicians and other state institutions, regulatory agencies are highly responsive to the preferences of private financiers, their main domestic political constituency. In fulfilling their regulatory and supervisory functions, they draw much of their legitimacy, and work in close concert with, private financial firms. Regulators also collaborate with national firms to adopt policies that promote their competitiveness in the transnational market place. Close public–private ties are further reinforced by common professional norms, the specialized and technical nature of expertise in the financial sector, and the shared need to maintain public confidence in the financial system itself.

The Basel II Supervisory Accord (B-II) was perhaps the best example of the problem. Oatley and Nabors (1998) document how the original Basel I Accord was created to respond to the rent-seeking demands of private financial firms in leading industrial nations. The process through which B-II was formulated was a second example of policy rent seeking by financial interests seeking liberalization and lower regulatory charges.[8] Basel II capital requirements were formulated in a relatively exclusionary and closed policy community consisting of regulators and supervisors from the G10 leading industrial nations and their private sector interlocutors. In these networks, private market interests found respondents in finance ministries and central banks and have thus been able to shape policy at the global level. The final rules and standards sanctified by B-II tend to award competitive advantages to powerful market players with little regard for either their smaller (systemically less significant) competitors or developing and emerging market economies, and the impact of B-II is far wider than the banking institutions and markets of G10 committee members. The bottom line is that private actors, in particular large internationally active financial institutions, had more influence on pre-crisis financial architecture reform than developing country members of the Bretton Woods institutions.

To conclude this section, it had become clear at the very least through the regularity and persistence of crises that a liberal financial order posed important risks to developing and developed countries alike in terms of market instability and risk management. No one denied the need for better national-level governance and greater levels of cooperation at the international level. The result, however, was a crisis-prone system of "governance light" that delivered material advantages to those who had proposed it and unduly constrained the policy space available to the very governments in whose name it was promulgated. Private preferences dominated the making of public policy in the new financial architecture and at the domestic level.

This section has demonstrated that the literature had warned policy makers representing the public interest of these problems. Policy makers and private interests chose to listen to arguments in favor of financial integration and market-based governance, putting other people's money and futures at serious risk. There was no serious evidence that untrammeled capital mobility was either universally or unmitigatedly beneficial; and, even if beneficial, it was clear that these benefits were not straightforwardly to be achieved. Regulatory and supervisory policy change was required, but policy capture ensured that this went awry. Even major industry players warned policy makers of the problem, for example hedge fund luminary George Soros (2005) and the president of State Street Bank, Avinash Persaud (2000).[9] We knew all we needed to know in order to prevent the outcome we achieved.

Ultimately the costs of the system were born by poor country and developed country citizens alike through the public rescue of the banks and the recession that followed. The lesson is that well-placed private interests win out against common sense and scholarly understanding and also win out against the dispersed and unorganized interests of the general public unless specific measures to prevent such an eventuality are positively developed. This outcome again should not surprise us and we were so warned by Adam Smith some 240 years ago: "People of the same trade seldom meet together, even for merriment and diversion, but the conversation ends in a conspiracy against the publick" (Smith 1937 [1776]: 128). The inherent interest in financial stability of those who ultimately bear the risks and pay for policy failure should be reflected in the content of policy. As Louis W. Pauly (1997) asked some time ago, "who elected the bankers?"

Euroland in search of the lost gold standard

The lessons that were well known but unlearned prior to the credit crunch should have increased in importance as the recession closed in upon developed economies. This section looks at the onset and initial EU member country and European Central Bank (ECB) reaction to the broader financial crisis, and then focuses on the reaction to the sovereign debt crisis in the eurozone of spring 2010. It will be argued that EU financial integration and the eurozone were very much part of the adventure of global financial integration, with similar assumptions that "governance light" was a workable option and that monetary and financial stability could be automatically achieved, given the correct rules and proper application by governments and financial institutions alike. I called this "the political economy of the stability culture" (Underhill 2002).

This combination of intense integration into the liberal financial order plus weak institutional fabric rendered the EU and the single currency in particular vulnerable to either monetary or financial crises. The subprime crisis, credit crunch and banking collapse, and sovereign debt problem focused on Greece were the first major test, and they were a major one indeed. The available lessons were of course no better learned by the EU than anyone else, and so the crisis caught the authorities by surprise. The section will nonetheless demonstrate that the financial crisis and banking collapse phase was extraordinarily well managed under the circumstances, with the ECB at the helm, whereas the highly predictable sovereign debt phase was a lamentable policy failure that still risks unraveling the accomplishments of the single currency. The EU as a collectivity proved ready and willing to bail out banks with trillions of euros, but bailing out the citizens of vulnerable developing member state economies, citizens who had helped bail out the banks and were already paying the price as such, was not worthy of prompt or proper action.

Even after the onset of the sovereign debt phase of the crisis, the lessons concerning the need for better and *different* financial architecture (in this case better EU machinery for crisis management and prevention) were poorly absorbed. Nor were lessons learned concerning the need to expand member state policy space, especially in relation to particular needs of the weaker (developing) members of the Union. There has been little attention to the need to think about, and to respond decisively in relation to, the domestic political imperatives of political systems experiencing the turmoil of crisis wherein a fragile political legitimacy may be breached. The EU emerged from the crisis divided between rich and poor, institutionally in disarray, and demonstrating a poor understanding of successful crisis management. The solution developed will likely lead to further division and difficulties in the future. In short, the direction of policy at the moment still yearns for an automatic solution akin to the myth of the nineteenth-century gold standard: If only the correct rules and standards of behavior are adopted and followed, all will be well in the not-so-stable "stability culture." This situation belies a profound misunderstanding of monetary governance deep within the EU and its member governments.

EMU: global finance, the "stability culture," and institutional lacunae

It is useful at this point to review four observations made at the inception of the Economic and Monetary Union (EMU) (Underhill 2002). First, there was and remains a central paradox concerning the place of the eurozone as an economic unit in the structures of the global monetary and financial system: The EU is relatively self-sufficient in terms of international trade, but is deeply integrated into the structures of global financial markets and investment flows. Capital flows, not trade pressures, will mediate between EMU and the rest of the world. This means that, although EMU member states are subject to all of the market adjustment pressures of capital mobility, the exchange rate matters a lot less and there is also insulation from at least short-term current account constraints among members (Jones 2003).[10] Second, although there is a clear legal institutional mandate in terms of managing the eurozone's monetary policies, it is unclear how other policy domains such as international monetary relations or the nature of global financial architecture are to be managed. There is also a dearth of collective EU machinery for managing internal or externally induced crises. Both of these characteristics, it is argued, tend toward the neglect of the exchange rate as a tool of macro-economic policy and a reliance on rules and macro-economic standards that are easily and perhaps necessarily breached under pressure. The theory was that of the German Bundesbank: If policy remained resolute and free of political interference, a "stability culture" could be achieved quasi-automatically. This was an unfortunate misinterpretation of post-war German economic success,[11] but the case appeared well grounded in experience and was anyway politically unassailable if the German government were to agree to the Union in the first place.

Third, financial integration and EMU on the one hand confronts members with considerable pressure for convergence in terms of macro-economic management and corporate governance practices, but on the other there are the intense bottom-line pressures of political legitimacy in terms of social policies, national (and other) identities, and the role of national democracy in an increasingly integrated economic unit. This is often perceived as the "sovereignty issue," although the debate is probably better characterized as one concerning identity and policy autonomy, which are not the same as sovereignty. Fourth, following from the third point, the eurozone can be seen as a radical extension of the single market. EMU enhances the cross-border market forces already at work and was explicitly intended to do so. Yet this integration process is juxtaposed on what remain distinct political systems with their own internal dynamics. The economic development and adjustment process associated with the single currency would furthermore prove highly asymmetrical with the greatest adjustment pressure on the weaker economies (Padoan 1994; Feldstein 1997, 2000).[12] The eurozone was consequently likely to encounter its share of disagreements among its members as the asymmetrical distributional consequences of integration became clear. As we now know, it did, and crisis made this worse.

As already implied, EMU was very much unfinished business that suffered from institutional lacunae which would make the collective management of these problems a serious challenge. Dealing with its interrelated policy dilemmas would require EU-level institutional development and further compromise in terms of national policy autonomy, and failure would render the future of the single currency a difficult one. The unknown factor in the eventual success of the stability culture would likely be external to the eurozone itself: the periodic eruption of monetary and financial crisis at the global level. Would the eurozone be the island of monetary and financial stability its architects had hoped? Given the transmission mechanism for contagion and spillover provided by the process of global financial integration, of which EMU was an intentional part, there was insufficient attention to this problem, as we now know. The institutions and coordinating mechanisms for prudential supervision and oversight of the financial system and eventual crisis management were woefully underdeveloped at the level of the eurozone and even after post-crisis reform still remain essentially the stuff of national jurisdiction.

The Maastricht Treaty itself reinforced what the logic of global financial integration already implied: a reliance on market forces to provide discipline and stability. The only collective mechanism for dealing with crises was the Stability and Growth Pact that accompanied the treaty. This was essentially an agreement on sovereign debt burdens, less inflexible than many thought, but the overall framework implied that governments, not financial markets, were the problem: If the rules were properly applied, stability would prevail. The treaty thus favored price stability and the fight against inflation over growth, employment, and social policies. Monetary policy and day-to-day exchange rate management would be in the hands of a highly independent central bank, not at the discretion of elected governments or an integrated Council-based mechanism.

Of course there were also substantial benefits. Members of the euro would gain weight in global financial and monetary affairs. Those who had been subject to German monetary policy would now have a voice at the ECB table. Internal exchange rate crises would be a thing of the past, and the most competitive economies (Germany, the Netherlands) would no longer suffer the devaluations of others. Member states would have better access to cheaper capital, a serious benefit for the poorer and weaker economies. Given that by far most EU member trade was with other EU partners, eurozone participants would be sheltered also from global exchange rate volatility. Members would be relatively free of current account constraints as well (Jones 2003), although (no devaluations!) *less* free of the need to adjust to competitive pressures in the long run. Last but not least, and in retrospect perhaps the most important, national central bank reserves and resources that might be required for adjustment or in a financial rescue would be pooled: Large and stable economies could, and *would* (it was assumed), support the weaker links. The stability culture was a safe harbor from the winds of financial, exchange rate, and monetary instability, and this was central to the compromise. What political and institutional machinery was to manage the process when push came to shove was unclear, but over time there was as much talk of solidarity as of the need for discipline.

At the very least, if one institutes an essentially federalized monetary union, then under the threat of crisis the union must act in a functionally federal manner even in the absence of sufficient institutions to do so. This means central (ECB) guarantees to the "provinces," and adequate internal resource transfers to compensate for the fully predictable adjustment asymmetries in the absence of intra-eurozone devaluations. How did the eurozone and EU perform in the crisis, particularly relative to the lessons of the literature rehearsed in the first section of this chapter?

Crisis: the financial phase

The ECB largely compensated for the lack of collective federal-like machinery by exceeding its mandate so as to resolve what might have been severe collective action problems across the EU banking and financial system. Although member states of course played a role at the national level, the European System of Central Banks proved a miracle under fire, pooling resources and cooperating with the U.S. Federal Reserve among others. The ECB rapidly developed a repo market for distressed assets, eased the terms of refinancing for banks in difficulty, and eased monetary policy without running out of ammunition from the start by approaching zero interest rates too soon, and early in the process introducing quantitative easing techniques. Trillions were put up to restore confidence in the stricken banks and national governments chimed in with nationalizations under fire where necessary.[13] The ECB took the lead in ensuring that national systems of deposits were protected and there was an initially shaky but eventually systematic move toward 100 percent coverage for the duration of the crisis. Panic avoided, despite some initial bank runs, the interbank market was slowly resuscitated, and the ECB coordinated the effort internationally with the Federal Reserve system of the United States, the Bank of Japan, and other major players. Much largesse was shown to the new members and neighboring economies, although one might have wished for yet more. Budgetary rules were loosened for the crisis, and fiscal stimulus was encouraged and coordinated, although of course implemented at the national level. Finally, the EU Commission and the Bank also took their place in the new G20 context and there was an open admission that the institutional lacunae in terms of EU financial regulation and supervision required filling in without delay: National autonomy would give way to collective comfort and insurance.[14]

There was of course plenty of drama, but the markets and the banks stayed open and recovered substantially from March 2009. Overall, and given the institutional weaknesses, the financial crisis management phase could have been expected to be much worse. In contrast to the 1930s, public authorities largely did the right thing and kept lines of credit open to each other. Beggar-thy-neighbor policies were notable for their absence despite the extreme pressure on national governments. ECB and national outlays may yet be recuperated as the Bank's balance sheet is slowly restored to its normal state.

What then of the sovereign debt phase of the crisis, which emerged well into the recession and a year or so after the peak of the financial crisis? The result was a lamentable policy failure largely directed and motivated by the German government, supported by the proportionately largest net contributor to EU finances, the Netherlands.

Crisis: the sovereign debt phase

A first point to be established is that the sovereign debt crisis was no surprise, or at least should not have been. There are two phenomena that made it obvious that national debt burdens would become a concern to the financial markets that were financing these deficits: (1) there had been a stupendous transfer of private debt and toxic assets to national central banks and to government balance sheets; (2) fiscal stimulus measures and automatic stabilizers built into welfare systems added to the government debt burden. These facts were no mystery,[15] and the G20 summits and IMF meetings resounded with talk of "exit strategies" and the risks of inflation associated with deficits and monetary easing. A second point is that it was hardly unexpected that the weaker economies in the eurozone would be the worst hit: The effects of EMU and of financial integration were known to be asymmetrical. The experience in the euro and non-euro new members of Central and Eastern Europe was there for all to see, with considerable national variation depending on context and on the quality of domestic policy. National choices mattered, and Greece did "cheat," and proportionately by a considerable amount, but this behavior was well established (see Jones 2010: 26–7) and was also largely forecast by IMF country reports in the public domain (International Monetary Fund 2009: 20–1). Anyone who should have known could have known.

The next problem was an apparent failure to separate out the debt crisis and crisis management phase from the rules of the game under normal circumstances. The German government consistently drew attention to the Growth and Stability Pact and the imperative that it implied. Yet already the G20, EU, and other bodies had accepted that for some time exceptions to normal fiscal prudence would have to be allowed (again, see Bank for International Settlements 2009a: ch. VI). International cooperation would be required to ease the burden for the hardest hit, usually the poorest. Aid should not be cut, welfare provision would continue. There would be solidarity.

But suddenly within the eurozone this was all to be denied by one country showing the most abject lack of understanding as to why the financial rescue had been mounted at all: to safeguard citizens whose future was threatened by monetary Armageddon, and whose individually meagre but pooled resources of course also provided the ultimate guarantee for the banks in the first place. Trillions had been thrown at the banks in the face of moral hazard problems and the greedy snatching of salary bonuses, but citizens of the poorest of the "old" EU members were not worth as much care even when the price was a paltry amount in relative terms. Bond spreads relative to German Bunds in November–December 2009, as the crisis began to break, were still a modest 200–250 points (Bank for International Settlements 2010b: 3; *Financial Times* Lex column, December 15, 2009), and the most pessimistic talk was of a potential rescue in the €20 billion range. Far from acknowledging de facto federal obligations, Germany was saying publicly that weaker economies in predictable difficulty should look to themselves for help. The problem soon began to spill over to Portugal and other eurozone countries, and by April–May 2010 Greek bond yields were at one point over 1,000 basis points above German levels with Greek (and other) debt loads commensurately higher. In the end the German government did begin to worry, but that was once it was hastily and quietly informed by its own banks (not to mention alarm from the U.S. president) that Greek bonds about which the default debate was taking place were largely held by, yes, German, French, and other banks (Bank for International Settlements 2010a: 27).[16] The prospect of simultaneously dealing with a sovereign default and collapsing banks as well was somber, and this time German and eurozone public finances in Germany were also denuded because of the crisis. Whatever the political climate in Germany, which at the time included tense provincial elections that stimulated Merkel's party to appear tough on Greek "cheaters," a prompt and decent policy reaction could have avoided the problem altogether and a crisis-avoidance solution would surely have bolstered her political fortunes too.

This was all the more ironic in view of the past record of Germany on the observance of the maximum 3 percent of GDP budget deficit provisions of the Stability Pact. Germany and France taught everyone in the EU that the pact was to be ignored and that cheating was acceptable in times of fiscal difficulty: After the bursting of the dot-com bubble and subsequent recession the German deficit 2002–5 was respectively –3.7 percent, –4 percent, –3.8 percent, and –3.3 percent of GDP; France was above the limit in 2002–4, and Italy from 2003 to 2006. These large countries even caused the terms of the Stability and Growth Pact to be softened in 2005 to help themselves out.[17] The rules are for the small and weak, and discretion remains in the hands of the powerful member states. The pact was after all a largely German idea, which only increases the irony.

Next, Greece did cheat and the deficits grew alarmingly fast (largely on account of widening bond spreads), but in absolute terms the Greek economy is small and poor, and has little weight in the eurozone or global scheme of things (see discussion in *Financial Times*, Lex column, December 15, 2009). The initial market reaction to the crisis was relatively calm as a result. As Jones (2010: 27–9) points out, Greek debt auctions continued to be oversubscribed until the end of April 2010. However, time was increasingly of the essence, as was a clear policy line from the EU and eurozone members. To the bewilderment of all, the German Chancellor declared that there would be no rescue until the capacity of Greece to finance its debt was exhausted. By that time, as we soon saw, it would be too late and the problem would be spiraling out of control. There was high-handed talk of temporary expulsion of eurozone members (taking away their Council vote remains another favorite of the German Chancellor) who failed to deliver on policy promises. Even in March 2010, when panic was clearly spreading and the question was no longer whether a bailout but what sort and how large, Merkel astounded all by insisting that the crisis should not be discussed at the EU summit because there was no crisis and Greece had not requested help.[18] Greece learned to its horror that internal political constraints from riots to strikes were unimportant to Germany and others, although German political constraints had been imposed on all when Germany violated the pact a few years earlier.

The German approach clearly made the problem rapidly and terrifyingly worse. If the problem was largely dismissed by commentators in December 2009, or bailouts were discussed at around the €20 billion mark, by April 11, 2010, a €45 billion joint EU–IMF package was on the table. Too late: The April 27 ratings downgrade of Greek and Portugese bonds to BB+ sent Greek spreads to 1,200 points and debt also skywards. A Greek bond auction failed. The next (May 2, 2010) package that temporarily stopped the rot was €110 billion, some €32.5 billion extra per week or €4.6 billion a day! (Bank for International Settlements 2010b: 3–4), plus a combined EU–IMF standby bailout fund of €750 billion (Bank for International Settlements 2010a: 26). The failure to adopt an appropriate and *timely* solution also meant playing huge risks with contagion for other EU member states: Ireland, the U.K., Portugal, Spain, the new members. As of writing an €85 billion Irish bailout was announced (see, for example, *Financial Times*, November 29 and 30, 2010), an agreement not without default and further contagion potential. Policy space for the Greek and Irish governments and (through spillover effects) much of the eurozone will be constrained for years to come. The markets trump the people, especially if it is not initially understood that under conditions of EU financial and monetary integration it is only a matter of time before they are also *your* people.

Three final points may be made to round off this section. First, one cannot but most unwisely on the one hand condemn the markets for "causing" the financial crisis, as the German government has been wont to do (ignoring official policy failure), while at the same time exposing eurozone partners to cold market forces in dealing with the very debt born of rescuing the financial markets in the first place. In the end, is there public authority and policy in the EU financial and monetary system, or only the rules of private competition and declaratory national self-interest? Why would small and vulnerable economies want to lose their monetary and exchange rate policy autonomy and join the euro, as new members are obliged to do, if the protection of pooled reserves is demonstrably to be denied in the most crucial of moments?

Second, and even in the face of serious institutional lacunae, if one has a single currency then in a crisis one must behave as though the eurozone were a single economic entity. During the *financial* phase of the crisis the EU led by the Bank behaved in just such a "federal" fashion, violating its own rules to take on all sorts of dubious collateral from banks. A repeat performance on sovereign debt was not to be and instead loans with stringent conditionality attached were hastily arranged. Ironically, the eurozone demonstrated very publicly to all that the IMF, not the EU, was the source of a real rescue. European "solidarity" proved non-existent at first, and its delayed and weak return has since most likely worsened the problem for all. Returning to the points raised in the introduction to this chapter, EMU did not prove particularly effective for its member states in dealing with the sovereign debt phase of the crisis. Neither national nor EU institutions have seen their legitimacy enhanced as a result, and it is unclear whether the eurozone will yet survive. The most worrying development is that the German (and other, for example Dutch) creditor government reactions have now infected national electoral politics with the centrifugal forces of populist beggar-thy-neighbor sentiment, making future rescues even more problematic.

Finally, Germany and other eurozone current account surplus economies refuse to look at their position as at least in part a problem for the creditors. The terms of the rescue show that debtor citizens are to bear the burden of loan repayment and adjustment essentially alone, even in a monetary union. Yet who buys creditor exports, if not the deficit countries? In a crisis one should stimulate them to maintain a reasonable level of consumption so that trade recovers for all, and that means internal transfers, one version of which might be a (timely) rescue. And who benefits most from monetary union in a crisis if not the surplus economies (because the others cannot free ride through devaluation)? In the end, there was a clear belief that pouring sterilizing and cleaning fluids on the guilty country will resolve the problem. If all eurozone members behave like Germany then the stability culture will be achieved. However, even in the most virtuous of all possible worlds it is impossible for all economies to have a current account surplus simultaneously, or has Chancellor Merkel not yet learned of this fundamental axiom of international economics? The issue will be back to haunt us when the loans come due, perhaps sooner.

Meanwhile, what should have been done? The first point was to remain calm at the outset (October–November 2009), to deal with the matter quietly behind closed doors, and to actively demonstrate to the markets that there was no danger of default. This would have prevented the whole unhappy train of events and Greece and others would have had smaller (if still large) debts to deal with. The starting point could have been a simple press conference in early December 2009 with ECB President Trichet, the Commission President, the Commissioner for Monetary Affairs, and the Greek premier:

> "Welcome ladies and gentlemen of the press, thank you for coming. There will be no sovereign defaults in the eurozone. European institutions and partners will ensure that deficit finance and financial sector liquidity remain available under all circumstances, until crisis circumstances have eased. That is all we have to say and there will be no questions. Thank you."

Next, official loans are a poor solution in a monetary union in which the central bank can indulge in quantitative easing as it is called, or printing money, as in a domestic economy. Loans with interest only add to the debt burden and allow markets to focus on the risk of default once again when loans are due. The logic of the loan approach is that it will remind profligate governments that they spent too much, a punishment logic that fails to understand the problem as rooted in the bailout of the banking system. Further lending also does little to restore the confidence in the bond market, the scene of the carnage. The ECB should have adopted immediately the same strategy it adopted in relation to rescuing the banks: unlimited repo operations in the asset markets concerned (this is now indeed taking place). That places a floor under the price of bonds and brings the yields down, easing the increase in debt load. This is also a highly profitable operation if one understands the one and only rule of successful investment: buy low, sell high. The ECB can finance itself for nothing indefinitely (as it did for the bank rescue, danger of eventual inflation duly noted). Distressed sovereign bonds can be purchased at all-time low prices, while income from yawning yield spreads is generous. As the market stabilizes and the situation eventually approaches resolution, spreads will come down and bond prices will rise, just in time to unravel ECB positions. For the monetary sadists out there, the price for Greece (and now Ireland) would have remained very high, but no German or Dutch taxpayer would have been asked to lend directly, thus depoliticizing what became an ugly, populist row across several EU countries with serious centrifugal results for the eurozone. Of course this strategy carries with it risks, and an exit plan would be required, but the risks were rather less than they were in the case of the insolvent banks (Greece is after all sovereign, not very large, and EU resources can be pooled). Indeed such a strategy would have been against the ECB's own rules, but no more so than was the acceptance of essentially toxic collateral from private banks in the context of the ECB's Covered Bond Purchase Programme. Purchasing sovereign bonds before they are distressed is of course not about saving risk-taking financiers, but about stabilizing the future of those whose resources already have been called upon and who have done their duty. Somehow one should really prefer people to banks, at least if democracy and citizenship are to have any meaning.

Conclusion

This chapter has shown that there was more than sufficient knowledge of the problems inherent in a liberal and integrated financial order to alert private and public authorities to the predictable dangers of financial instability. There was no historical evidence to support the approach adopted to liberalization and cross-border financial integration, nor for the theories that underpinned market-based "governance light." This knowledge was not brought to bear and taxpayers and future generations are to suffer as a result. Nonetheless, important policy lessons from the 1930s appeared to have been well learned during the financial market phase of the crisis. The financial system was successfully rescued albeit at a considerable cost, and a serious depression and deflationary episode have hopefully been avoided as well.

Unfortunately, during the EU sovereign debt phase of the crisis, more primitive instincts prevailed. Domestic political dynamics stimulating centrifugal tendencies among eurozone members were stoked up not just by a frequently jingoist press but by the very member governments who claim to be committed to an "ever closer union." What might have been a noble exercise in ad hoc EU governance innovation, demonstrating the validity of Hveem's claims concerning the efficacy of regional arrangements, instead ran seriously aground. A poor strategy was eventually adopted that saddles Greece among others with yet more debt and at the time of writing had far from removed market doubts concerning the possibility of default for a range of weaker eurozone economies. The proposed reforms to the Stability Pact aim to constrain national policy space yet more and to punish errant debtors, with likely consequences for the political legitimacy of both the single currency and debtor governments.

Of course, Greece should long ago have reformed its system of tax collection, its accounting procedures, the audit and relative size of its civil service, but France and Germany cheated just as blatantly from 2002 to 2005, albeit in better economic times. Perhaps there is something wrong with the assumption that the origins of the crisis lay in the failure of government fiscal policy, rather than in the way in which an integrated and liberal financial and monetary order works. In 2009, only six of the twenty-seven EU members held to the Stability Pact budgetary norm, and Greece did not end 2009 as the worst offender. At the very least, current account weakness, budgetary problems, and a fragile financial system are all well-known characteristics of small, open emerging market economies such as Greece or the next potential domino in the eurozone, and the financial crisis simply accentuated these problems by rather a lot. Under duress, stricter rules are no more likely to work in the future than in the past two years. The burden of adjustment to global market pressures must be rendered more compatible with the requirements of national political legitimacy, and a sensible and predictable debt crisis management mechanism making sensible use of eurozone resources and the ECB needs to be put in place.

The EU appears for a long time to have been looking for some functional equivalent of the lost, mythical gold standard: If only the rules are the right ones, and everyone behaves properly, stability will be achieved automatically. The literature analyzed and historical experience tells us that this is unlikely to be achievable. There is as yet no sign of an adequate debate or proposals concerning the further development of EU institutions to prevent and/or manage crises in the future. The risk of sovereign default had already returned at the time of writing, and purely national solutions may yet prove the only option and the European dream would then die. The eurozone hangs in the balance as a result of serious policy mistakes led by the largest economy in the Union, Germany. The worst is that banks turned out to be more important than fellow citizens of the Union, especially citizens in poorer economies. The poor and the "other" too frequently appear expendable in our world. There are somber days ahead of us yet where regional governance in the EU is concerned.

Notes

1 See also 2005 articles by Cooper, Roubini and Setser, Mann, and Gray in a debate on the matter in "Focus: Sustainability of the US External Deficit," CESifo Forum, volume 6, 1. Available at http://www.cesifo-group.de/pls/guestci/download/CESifo%20 Forum%202005/CESifo%20Forum%201/2005/Forum1-05.pdf (accessed December 15, 2010).

2 See among others Minsky on Keynes (Minsky 1975) and also on the financial instability hypothesis (Minsky 1982); and Kindleberger and Laffargue (1982) and Galbraith (1993) on the psychology of speculation.

3 The 2006 warnings of "Dr. Doom" Nouriel Roubini were famously dismissed; see Mihm (2008).

4 See an analysis of the origins of the crisis in Schwarz (2009: 27–38).

5 The concept of "original sin" developed by Eichengreen and Hausmann (2005).

6 See Schwartz (2010) on late industrialization.

7 Oatley and Nabors (1998) document how the original Basel Accord was created to respond to the rent-seeking demands of private financial firms in leading industrial countries, especially the United States.

8 For a more substantial account of this point, see Claessens et al. (2008), especially pp. 318–27.

9 Persaud's essay criticizing the market-based approach to financial supervision even won in the year 2000 the high-profile Jacques de Larosière essay prize issued by the Institute for International Finance and was promoted widely on that basis.

10 *Within* the eurozone of course there is no longer any exchange rate fluctuation at all.

11 This stability culture version of German monetary history in the post-war period left out many factors such as successful industrial renewal and development in which government policy played a central role, externally supported political stability and democratic development, post-war Deutsche Mark undervaluation, EU integration as a growing market for German export success, and the refusal to recognize the German current account surplus as a problem for anyone but Germany's trading partners.

12 Although these have also of course experienced the fastest growth. Developing economies that do well often experience severe short- and medium-term external imbalances, difficulties with public debt, and perhaps inflation. This phenomenon is well known in the literature and should surprise no one.

13 See Bank for International Settlements (2009a: ch. 6) for a comprehensive survey of policy responses to the crisis including government and central bank outlays.

14 Although the promises of reform at time of writing were far from fulfilled.

15 See Bank for International Settlements (2009a, 2010a); see also the annual and per country IMF *Staff Report for the [e.g. 2009] Article IV Consultation* on Greece.

16 70 percent of Greek debt was held by non-residents in 2010 (Bank for International Settlements 2010a: 68), and so someone out there thought the bonds were a decent investment.

17 Deutsche Bundesbank, 'Monthly Report, April 2005'. Available at http://www.bundesbank.de/download/volkswirtschaft/mba/2005/200504mba_en_changes.pdf (accessed November 15, 2010).

18 Richard Wray, *The Guardian* online, March 21, 2010. Available at http://www.guardian.co.uk/business/2010/mar/21/eu-greece-angela-merkel (accessed November 15, 2010).

7

REINING IN THE MARKET

Global governance and the regulation of OTC derivatives

Eric Helleiner[1]

A century ago, the Canadian political economist and humorist Stephen Leacock (1910) wrote a famous essay describing how banks rattled him. If he were alive today, he would no doubt be even more rattled by over-the-counter (OTC) derivatives. So too, it seems, are scholars of global governance. A search of considerable literature on the politics of international financial regulation turns up only a few sources examining these complex financial products. A more charitable interpretation might be that scholars have neglected the subject because they thought there was so little to study; OTC derivatives, after all, have been one of the most unregulated realms of global finance. However, those brave few scholars who have explored the subject have shown how the absence of regulation is just as interesting to try to explain as its presence (e.g. Coleman 2003; Tsingou 2006). As Susan Strange (1986) reminded us years ago, non-decisions are in fact often more much worthy of study than decisions.

The 2007–8 global financial crisis has acted as a catalyst for policy makers to finally bring OTC derivatives under the public international regulatory umbrella for the first time. This policy shift makes the OTC derivatives sector particularly interesting for scholars of global governance. Because of their enormous size and unregulated nature, global OTC derivatives markets have often been a kind of poster child for arguments that a structural transformation in world order is under way involving the rise of private transnational power and the eclipse of the sovereign state system (e.g. LiPuma and Lee 2004). The arguments have been reinforced by the fact that it has been private industry groups, rather than public authorities, that have often been key rule makers for these markets. If states are suddenly asserting their regulatory authority in this realm in an internationally coordinated manner, these broader arguments are called into question and states have more enduring power than many thought.

How do we explain this policy shift in international regulatory politics? In this chapter I address this question focusing on the results of the first three G20 leaders' summits between November 2008 and September 2009, which were the key meetings at which this international policy shift was endorsed.[2] I argue that the international regulatory initiatives can be explained with reference to several developments that took place during the 2007–8 crisis: the politicization of OTC derivatives within leading states, the shifting ideas of policy makers, changing private industry interests, and interstate rivalries. This explanation suggests the need for a more contingent conception of the public/private divide in global governance than the kinds of structuralist accounts that highlight the growing power of financial capital, transnational neoliberal technocratic networks, and international competitive pressures. At the same time, I note that structuralists are partially right about one thing. Although states are asserting their regulatory authority over global OTC derivatives markets, they have done so in a manner that continues to delegate some tasks to industry-led international initiatives.

The chapter is organized as follows. The first section describes the lax regulation of OTC derivatives before the crisis as well as some of the structuralist explanations that were offered by scholars to explain this phenomenon. The second section provides a brief overview of the international official endorsement of regulation between November 2008 and September 2009. In the third section I begin to explain that outcome by highlighting the importance of the politicization of OTC derivatives within the United States in this period as well as the changing ideas of top U.S. officials. The fourth and fifth sections offer further explanations, pointing, respectively, to the significance of the changing position of the financial industry as well as the role of European politics. The chapter concludes with a brief discussion of the broader theoretical significance of the argument for global governance debates.

Global OTC derivatives markets leading up to the current crisis

Derivatives include a wide range of products – futures, forwards, options, and swaps – whose value is derived from the performance of another asset or even an index of asset values. Some classes of derivatives have long been traded primarily on exchanges, with the largest exchanges being in London (Liffe) and Chicago (the CME Group). The vast majority of derivatives, however, have been traded over the counter; that is, they have been negotiated privately on a bilateral basis between the buyer and the seller. Most of this OTC trading takes place in the world's major financial centers of London and New York (with the former being the more important site at the moment).

The size of outstanding OTC derivatives contracts has grown enormously since the 1970s, and particularly over the past decade (until the second half of 2008 when it declined somewhat). At the end of 2008, the total notional size was $592 trillion, which was about sixteen times the global equity market capitalization or ten times the global GDP. If the cost of replacing all existing contracts is measured, this "gross market value" was much smaller at \$34 trillion, but this is still a very large number.[3] The largest portion of the notional total consists of interest rate derivatives (\$419 trillion), followed by currency derivatives (\$50 trillion), credit derivatives (\$42 trillion), equity derivatives (\$6 trillion), and commodities derivatives (\$4 trillion) (Bank for International Settlements 2009b).

Because of their role in the current crisis, credit default swaps (CDS) have attracted most of the regulators' attention recently. They first emerged in the mid-1990s and grew very rapidly to a peak of \$62 trillion at the end of 2007 (although net exposures were probably closer to \$4 trillion; Financial Services Authority 2009). The purchaser of a CDS pays the seller a fixed fee every quarter in return for the promise that the full value of a bond on which the contract is written will be paid if that bond is defaulted upon. The product enables the purchaser of the underlying bond to insure themselves against default. However, many buyers of CDS do not in fact hold the underlying bond; purchasers of these "unattached" contracts are simply speculating on the likelihood of default. Indeed, in recent years, CDS contracts have even been created on indexes of bonds; their notional value has grown close to \$10 trillion. The CDS market has also become highly concentrated with a small number of large U.S. and European banks controlling the vast majority of the dealing in CDS contracts. These same banks are also active as major buyers, alongside hedge funds and other institutional investors. As of December 2008, only \$0.5 trillion of the \$42 trillion in notional CDS contracts outstanding was with non-financial customers.[4]

Despite their size, OTC derivatives markets have remained largely outside the various official international rules and standards that have been developed to govern financial markets since the 1980s. There have, however, been a number of efforts to change this situation before the current crisis. U.S. policy makers – prompted particularly by members of Congress – discussed derivatives regulation extensively in the wake of financial crises in 1994–5, the East Asian and LTCM crises of 1997–8, and the Enron crisis of 2001 (Coleman 2003; Tsingou 2006). At the international level, an initiative within the International Organization of Securities Commissions (IOSCO) in the late 1980s to develop international capital standards for securities firms was driven in part by the goal of prompting authorities – particularly U.S. authorities – to pay more official attention to derivatives activity (Singer 2008: 81–4). One of the early drafts of the Basel II agreement also included a provision for a credit charge on banks for derivatives exposure (Wood 2005: 138, 141). In the end, however, these efforts to bring OTC derivatives markets directly under the international regulatory umbrella failed. Instead, international regulatory bodies such as IOSCO, the Basel Committee, and the Joint Forum largely encouraged private actors to regulate themselves in various ways and they restricted official focus to the task of strengthening supervisory cooperation.

What explains this outcome? Several themes emerge from existing work on this topic (as well as my own reading of the history). The first was the strong opposition of the derivatives industry itself. Like other parts of the financial industry, the derivatives sector has benefited from close access to policy makers. However, the complex nature of derivatives has given the industry particular strength to fend off regulation in this sector. Their almost exclusive expertise gave them a unique ability to shape the discourse and debate. As Tsingou (2006) notes, their close involvement with and support for an influential G30 report in 1993 was particularly important; its analysis and advocacy of industry self-regulation set the tone for policy discussions over the next decade and a half.

The industry's demonstration that it could respond to the G30's suggestions and those of governments also helped pre-empt official regulation (Coleman 2003; Tsingou 2006). Created in 1985 and now with 830 member institutions from fifty-seven countries, the International Swaps and Derivatives Association (ISDA) played a lead role in coordinating self-regulation at the international level. It standardized documentation across the industry through its master agreement and it played a leading role in coordinating other forms of collective action and lobbying efforts. Other groups were also important in generating voluntary standards, such as the Derivatives Policy Group (involving six major dealers), which set out in 1995 detailed voluntary standards to implement the G30 recommendations.

Tsingou suggests that the absence of official regulation was linked not just to private sector influence but also to that of a broader "transnational policy community" which included top technocratic financial officials and policy makers alongside market participants. She argues that this community was bound together by shared expertise, the regular interaction generated by international networks, and a common culture (forged through Anglo-American education and experience in both the public and private sectors), as well as similar neoliberal ideology that prioritized the values of economic efficiency and stability. The community had considerable autonomy from domestic legislative politics; as she puts it, "public regulators and supervisors are much closer to the private sector and their counterparts in other countries than they are to other national public actors such as legislators" (Tsingou 2006: 182).

Tsingou highlights how the preferences of this community for self-regulation reflected not simply the material interests of industry but also a broader ideational consensus about the virtues of self-regulation. Leaving OTC derivatives largely free from official regulation stemmed partly from a broader confidence in the Anglo-American model of light-touch regulation and neoliberal ideas. It also reflected confidence in, and even enthusiasm for, securitization, which saw financial risks unbundled and repackaged in increasingly complex ways. According to proponents, securitization was boosting the stability and resilience of the financial system as a whole as well as promoting efficiency.

It is important not to overstate the consensus among technocrats among this international policy community in this period. At a number of moments over the past two decades, various officials expressed concerns about the unregulated nature of OTC derivatives markets. However, ideational support for self-regulation was particularly strong among key U.S. policy makers, particularly Federal Reserve

Chair Alan Greenspan. Their views precluded any serious international regulatory initiatives. Indeed, when the chair of the U.S. Commodities Futures Trading Commission, Brooksley Born, raised concerns about OTC derivatives markets in 1998, Greenspan – along with Larry Summers in the Treasury and the head of the Securities Exchange Commission, Arthur Levitt – mobilized strongly against regulation. In late 2000, Congress even passed a bill that locked in the deregulatory domestic environment by precluding the regulation of OTC derivatives markets (Johnson and Kwak 2010).

U.S. opposition to official regulation at that moment and others reflected one final factor: international competitive pressures. Concerns about business fleeing to London helped to strengthen U.S. policy makers' opposition to domestic and international regulatory proposals as far back as the late 1980s (Coleman 2003) and played a particularly important role in the thinking of U.S. policy makers around the time of the 2000 bill (e.g. U.S. Government 1999). The reverse was true as well. London financial interests successfully invoked the competitive threat from the United States in mobilizing against regulation in their country.

The international endorsement of regulation

The first signal of a change to the hands-off approach to the international regulation of OTC derivatives came at the first G20 leaders' meeting in mid-November 2008 in Washington. The meeting had been hastily called to address the global financial crisis and the meeting concluded with a long communiqué in which leaders outlined a detailed road map for the reform of international financial regulatory standards. Derivatives were specifically mentioned in the following passage:

> Supervisors and regulators, building on the imminent launch of central counterparty services for credit default swaps (CDS) in some countries, should: speed efforts to reduce the systemic risks of CDS and over-the-counter (OTC) derivatives transactions; insist that market participants support exchange traded or electronic trading platforms for CDS contracts; expand OTC derivatives market transparency; and ensure that the infrastructure for OTC derivatives can support growing volumes.
>
> (G20 2008)

Backing for international regulatory action on derivatives was apparent again at the second and third G20 leaders' summits in April 2009 (London) and September 2009 (Pittsburgh) respectively. At the former, the leaders declared:

> we will promote the standardisation and resilience of credit derivatives markets, in particular through the establishment of central clearing counterparties subject to effective regulation and supervision. We call on the industry to develop an action plan on standardisation by autumn 2009.
>
> (G20 2009a)

By September in Pittsburgh the leaders announced their agreement on the following points:

> All standardized OTC derivative contracts should be traded on exchanges or electronic trading platforms, where appropriate, and cleared through central counterparties by end-2012 at the latest. OTC derivative contracts should be reported to trade repositories. Non-centrally cleared contracts should be subject to higher capital requirements.
>
> (G20 2009b: 9)

Taken together, these announcements signaled an important shift in international policy under which public authorities accepted a responsibility to regulate derivatives markets. To be sure, some of the past reliance on the private sector remained, particularly in the encouragement of industry to develop a plan for standardization of credit derivatives. But the G20 leaders were also now instructing their regulators to act directly in a number of areas.

Most attention was given to the need for more use of central counterparties (CCPs), which serve as intermediaries between the seller and the buyer of a contract. When a CCP is involved in a trade, the seller sells a contract that has been negotiated to the CCP, which in turn sells it on to the buyer. The CCP forces all participants to put up collateral against their trades and then draws on this pool of capital to cover the losses if a counterparty collapses. The benefit of a CCP is that it minimizes systemic risks that can be generated by the failure of a major counterparty, not just by covering these losses but also by eliminating broader uncertainty about counterparty risks in OTC markets that can easily generate cascading contagion. The CCP can also help regulators and supervisors monitor the build-up of risks as well as implement rules concerning such things as margins, capital, position limits, and even who is able to participate in the markets. CCPs have been used to clear derivatives products such as U.S. futures for many decades, and the G20 leaders were now insisting that they be used more generally. At the Washington and London summits, their focus was on the CDS market. By Pittsburgh, the leaders called for the use of CCPs for "all standardized OTC derivative contracts" and declared that all other derivative contracts "should be subject to higher capital requirements" (G20 2009b: 9).

The G20 leaders' insistence in London that CCPs be subject to "effective regulation and supervision" was also important. At the time of the London summit, the G20's Working Group 1 gave more details about the kinds of regulations that CCPs would be subject to: They would have to "meet high standards in terms of risk management, operational arrangements, default procedures, fair access and transparency" (G20 Working Group 1 2009: xvi). A subsequent report from IOSCO in May also recommended that CCPs for CDS should be required to cooperate with regulators and "make available transaction and market information that would inform the market and regulators" (IOSCO 2009: 31). The insistence on regulating CCPs was logical as counterparty risk becomes concentrated in

CCPs when markets rely on them. As G20 Working Group 1's suggestions highlighted, however, officials recognized that this regulation could have other benefits as well. Officials could encourage CCPs to address other issues relating to default procedures and operational processes in the OTC market that had troubled them for some time. CCPs could also be prompted to share the centralized information about OTC transactions with authorities – as IOSCO recommended – in ways that enabled supervisors to monitor risks in the previously opaque markets.

In addition to the focus on CCPs, the G20 leaders also sought to increase the transparency of derivatives markets in other ways. Their insistence at the Pittsburgh summit that all OTC derivatives should be reported to trade depositories had this objective. So too did the promotion of the trading of derivatives on exchanges or electronic trading platforms (which would enhance transparency not just to regulators but also to the market participants themselves). In the latter case, the G20 leaders' ambitions were initially restricted in November 2008 to the trading of CDS contracts, but they had widened to include "all standardized OTC derivative contracts" by September 2009 (although subject to the important proviso "where appropriate") (G20 2009b: 9).

These various developments did not go as far as many wanted. Critics argued that the G20 leaders should have been more forceful in insisting on the wider use of exchanges. Large potential loopholes were opened by the language that required only "standardized" contracts "where appropriate" as well as the acceptance of "electronic trading platforms." The G20 leaders also did not attempt to enforce margins on OTC derivatives in this period,[5] or position limits on the participants in the markets.[6] Some were also critical of the failure of the G20 leaders to regulate specific derivative products – such as unattached CDS – which, as noted below, were seen to have contributed to the severity of the crisis. Despite these limitations, however, the G20 leaders' actions had established new international commitments of public authorities to regulate OTC derivatives markets directly. Why had this international policy shift taken place?

Changing U.S. domestic politics

To begin with, the severity of the financial crisis in the United States prompted an important domestic political shift in favor of direct regulation. The public bailout of Bear Stearns in March 2008 first put the issue of derivatives regulation on the U.S. policy agenda in a serious way. Bear Stearns' difficulties highlighted how risk had become highly concentrated in large counterparties that dominated the OTC CDS market. Because of its extensive interconnections with other institutions via CDS contracts, the collapse of Bear Stearns risked triggering a chain reaction. As two economists noted in June 2008, "danger of a cascading failure makes intermediaries linked by these [OTC derivative] instruments appear like a convoy that swims or sinks together" (Alexander and Schoenholtz 2008).

The spotlight on the OTC CDS market only intensified with the collapse of Lehman Brothers in September 2008. At the time of its collapse, Lehman

Brothers was believed to be a counterparty to around $5 trillion in CDS contracts. Its CDS exposures were approximately eight times its balance sheet and involved hundreds of counterparties. At the time, no one knew the size of the CDS on its own debts or who held those contracts. Thus, even if one did not hold a CDS contract on Lehman and did not have direct counterparty risk to the institution, there was still reason to panic because of the possibility that its collapse would trigger problems elsewhere (Haldane 2009: 30). The situation appeared to vindicate Warren Buffett's warning from 2003 that derivatives were "financial weapons of mass destruction" (quoted in Oldani 2008: 38).

The massive bailout of AIG soon after provided one further blow to the reputation of derivatives. AIG once again highlighted how the CDS market had concentrated risk rather than dispersed it. At the time of its rescue, AIG had over $2.7 trillion in notional derivatives exposure from 12,000 contracts (of which $1 trillion was with only twelve financial firms) (Sorkin 2009: 236–7). It had also sold $446 billion in CDS contracts without enough capital or liquidity reserves to back them. Indeed, U.S. Federal Reserve Chair Ben Bernanke later described AIG's Financial Products division in London as acting "like a hedge fund sitting on top of an insurance company" (quoted in Paulson 2009: 236). Its failure to meet payments posed a serious systemic risk, given the exposure of the many large financial institutions that had bought credit protection from it.

These events provoked a widespread political backlash within the United States against the lack of regulation of derivatives markets, particularly the OTC CDS market. Few suggested that these markets had *caused* the crisis alone, but OTC derivatives were widely blamed for having intensified it. In the years leading up to the crisis, their opacity had enabled actors to hide risks and accumulate excessive leverage (e.g. Morris 2008: 135; Soros 2008). When the bubble burst, OTC derivative markets had then acted as a key mechanism of contagion because of the uncertainties about counterparty exposures and the dense interconnections between top market actors. In the words of the New York insurance superintendent Eric Dinallo, "credit default swaps are the rocket fuel that turned the subprime mortgage fire into a conflagration" (Dinallo 2009).

Derivatives markets were also accused of distorting markets in other ways. Large-scale speculative activity in commodity futures markets was widely blamed for the sharp increase in energy and food prices in the summer of 2008 (Clapp and Helleiner 2010). CDS contracts were also blamed for creating perverse incentives among investors who might be tempted to push for defaults in order to cash in on the contract.[7] Unattached CDS contracts, in particular, came under fire because they were, in the words of Dinallo, the equivalent of "taking out insurance on your neighbor's house and maybe hoping it blows up" (quoted in Gapper 2009). Since insurance law bans the purchase of insurance when there is no underlying interest, many joined Dinallo in asking why restrictions were not imposed on unattached CDS contracts. George Soros reinforced these calls with a high-profile argument that CDS contracts offered speculators convenient ways to short bonds with limited risk. This feature, he argued, encouraged self-reinforcing bear raids, a phenomenon that he believed helped to explain the collapse of Lehman and AIG. Taking these two arguments together, many concluded along with Soros (2009) that CDS contracts were intrinsically "toxic" and required regulation.

Finally, there were new concerns expressed about how the opacity and complexity of many OTC derivatives markets were often used simply to circumvent taxation and regulation. Regarding the latter, many argued that the rapid expansion of CDS products had reflected the efforts of banks to get around Basel capital requirements by purchasing products that allegedly eliminated the risk of default (e.g. Dinallo 2009). One self-described "conservative libertarian" ex-banker told the American Enterprise Institute in February 2009 that "in my view, CDS and the entire OTC derivatives market represents a form of regulatory arbitrage – a retrograde and deliberate evasion of established prudential norms masquerading under the innocent guise of innovation" (Whalen 2009: 1). More generally, many complained that customers for OTC derivatives were left reliant for price and trading information on the large dealers who were able to derive excessive profits from their asymmetric access to information (e.g. Das 2006, 2009). These critics called for greater standardization of contracts and exchange trading as the tools to boost transparency.

As public anger about the financial crisis grew, many members of Congress took up the cause of regulating derivatives and proposals of various kinds began to be discussed in the fall of 2008. Some bills went so far as proposing to force all OTC derivatives onto exchanges and enabling officials to ban unattached derivatives. This was not the first time that Congress had considered derivatives regulation, but the issue was now politicized to an unprecedented degree. Never before had a crisis involving derivatives provoked the need for such massive taxpayer support. Fueling the fire in early 2009 was the revelation that AIG had not only continued to pay bonuses to employees in the Financial Products division that was at the source of the troubles, but also paid in full the big dealer banks – including some foreign banks – that had been AIG counterparties.

When members of Congress had pushed for regulation in the past, the executive branch had been more reluctant. Now, however, the Bush administration signaled their support for some regulatory action. The Bear Stearns crisis had already prompted officials to push the industry to reform itself by addressing various weaknesses in the OTC market. In the immediate wake of the Lehman collapse, the head of the Securities and Exchange Commission (SEC), Christopher Cox (2008), urged Congress to give regulators the power to oversee CDS, arguing that the market was "completely lacking in transparency" and was "ripe not only for rumor and misinformation, but potentially fraud." New York officials also announced plans for insurance regulators to define some kinds of CDS as insurance in order to bring them under regulatory controls (plans that were then delayed in November in order to allow for regulatory coordination with the Fed and SEC) (van Duyn and Davies 2008, van Duyn and Chung 2008). By November, on the day before the G20 summit, the Bush administration's President's Working Group on Financial Markets announced detailed policy objectives for the OTC derivatives markets, which included explicit regulatory goals such as (1) required public reporting of prices, trading volumes, and aggregate open interest for CDS, (2) access for regulators to trade and position information regarding CDS at CCPs and central trade repositories (with one objective being that of "preventing market manipulation"), (3) standards (particularly regarding risk management) for regulated entities that transact in OTC derivatives, and (4) review by regulatory agencies to determine if they have adequate enforcement authority to police against "fraud and market manipulation" (U.S. Government, President's Working Group 2008).

The new Obama administration accelerated the move toward regulation. Treasury Secretary Tim Geithner outlined a detailed regulatory agenda for derivatives in May 2009, an agenda that went well beyond the G20 summit statements. The proposed reforms included (1) introducing mandatory use of CCPs (which must have margins requirements) for all standardized OTC derivatives and registration for all other trades, (2) requiring CCPs and trade repositories to make public aggregate data on open positions and trading volume, and to provide regulators with data on individual trades and positions, (3) authorizing regulators to impose requirements for capital, reporting, initial margins, and business conduct for all OTC dealers "and all other firms who create large exposures to counterparties," (4) empowering authorities to force all standardized trade onto exchanges and electronic trade execution systems, and to encourage all regulated institutions to make more use of exchange-traded derivatives, (5) policing against fraud and market manipulation, and (6) giving regulators the power to set position limits on OTC derivatives that influence price discovery with respect to regulated markets (U.S. Government, Department of the Treasury 2009). Some of these provisions were watered down somewhat when Geithner released detailed legislation in August 2009. However, the broad push for regulation remained; the legislation was designed to overturn large portions of the U.S. legislation from 2000 that had exempted OTC markets from regulation.

In 2005, when he was head of the Federal Reserve Bank of New York, Geithner had showed an early interest in derivatives reform when he had encouraged the industry to address operational risks by embracing electronic platforms/processing for CDS. He had also taken a lead role in pushing the industry to reform itself after the Bear Stearns crisis. In developing these much more ambitious and official rules in 2009, Geithner noted the limitations of his past approach: "I wish I had worked to change the framework, rather than to work within that framework" (quoted in Gerth and O'Harrow 2009). He was not the only person to acknowledge past mistakes. Some other prominent officials in the Obama administration had been involved in the U.S. Treasury's push against regulation in the late 1990s, such as Gary Gensler (named head of the Commodity Futures Trading Commission by Obama) and Larry Summers (named chair of the National Economic Council by Obama). During his confirmation process in February, Gensler now urged that OTC derivatives be regulated and signaled support for position limits on some futures trading as well as the move of OTC derivatives to exchanges and clearing houses (Chung 2009). Larry Summers, too, acknowledged that he had not had "perfect foresight" on this issue (quoted in Hirsh and Thomas 2009). Even those out of office admitted their past mistakes. Arthur Levitt was particularly forthcoming about his role opposing regulation in the late 1990s: "All tragedies in life are preceded by warnings. We had a warning. It was from Brooksley Born. We didn't listen" (quoted in Hirsh and Thomas 2009). Alan Greenspan also acknowledged in October 2008 that he had been "partially" wrong to oppose regulation of CDS (quoted in Das 2009).[8]

The financial industry's position

The change in U.S. policy did not just reflect the politicization of the issue and the changing ideas of policy makers themselves. Equally important was a change in the position of private financial industry, which had resisted official regulation for many years. As the crisis intensified, leading figures in the private sector began to argue that the changes being promoted by the official sector were in the long term of material interest to the derivatives industry given the economic costs being experienced. Many saw a turning point in the industry's recognition of the case for change with the publication of an August 2008 report of the Counterparty Risk Management Policy Group III (CRMPG III): a prominent private sector group involving industry leaders, which had been involved in earlier debates. The report called for market actors to embrace a kind of "financial statesmanship" under which they accepted costly investments in infrastructure and changes in business processes and market practices in the short term in order to reap long-term gains: "Costly as these reforms will be, those costs will be minuscule compared to the hundreds of billions of dollars of write downs experienced by financial institutions in recent months to say nothing of the economic dislocations and distortions triggered by the crisis." Although it did not explicitly endorse official regulation, the report noted that the changes it recommended would fail if they were not "actively encouraged and supported by senior officials of central banks and other official institutions" (CRMPG 2008: 15, 103). The statement was a recognition of the collective action problems associated with encouraging the required scale of change using only the old self-regulatory mechanisms.

By November 2008, leading U.S. derivatives dealers appeared increasingly ready to accept mandatory regulation. Seeing which way the political wind was blowing and recognizing how the crisis highlighted the need for some reform, many in the industry sought to influence the direction of regulatory change rather than attempt to block it altogether. As one financial lobbyist put it after Geithner's proposals of May 2009, "nobody is in a 'just say no' mode. Everybody understands that we've been through a financial crisis and that change has to happen. And the only question is how the change happens" (Labaton and Calmes 2009). If the private sector needed any further reminder of the changed intellectual climate at the elite level, this was confirmed by a G30 report (Group of Thirty 2009) in January 2009 that insisted on the need for a formal system of regulation and oversight of OTC markets.

In their efforts to shape regulatory debates, the large banks involved in the CDS market on both the buy and sell sides were particularly worried about congressional proposals to prohibit unattached CDS. According to one source, approximately 80 percent of CDS trades had this quality; as one industry figure put it, "it is not an overstatement to say it [the Congressional proposal] would annihilate the CDS market" (van Duyn 2009).[9] Moving OTC trades to exchanges would also erode the high profit margins that banks earned on the transactions. One financial analyst, Christopher Whalen, went so far as to suggest that "without the excessive rents earned [from OTC activity] by JPMorgan Chase and the remaining legacy OTC dealers, the largest banks cannot survive" (quoted in Tett et al. 2009). The banks instead put their support behind CCPs, which enabled dealers to retain their central place in the market. As one private sector strategist, Brian Yelvington, put it, "a clearing organisation is better for the status quo" (quoted in Bullock and Mackenzie 2008). Two *Financial Times* reporters noted that dealers also favored the introduction of CCPs "because they anticipate that it would reduce the drain on their cash by cutting the amount of collateral they have to post overall." They continued: "instead of having to make hundreds or thousands of different collateral postings to each bilateral counterparty dealers trade with, they would need only to make a single posting to the clearing house" (Bullock and Mackenzie 2008). Bankers also noted that CCPs promised to reduce other operating costs such as settlement requirements (Alexander and Schoenholtz 2008).

Many institutional investors also supported CCPs as a tool to address counterparty risks. In a survey carried out in August 2008, 85 percent of the U.S. institutional investors surveyed saw counterparty risks in CDS markets as a serious threat and 75 percent thought CCPs would mitigate them (van Duyn 2008a). Hedge fund managers active in the CDS market, such as Jeff Kusher of BlueMountain Capital Management, also applauded the fact that CCPs and the push for standardization of contracts "would allow us to create additional transparency and liquidity in the CDS market" (quoted in van Duyn and Bullock 2008). Indeed, investor interests had pushed for greater efficiency and transparency in the dealer-dominated markets for some time and some felt that ISDA had been slow to embrace these changes in the past because it was dominated by the bank dealers "who had every incentive to keep the market opaque and bespoke, which boosted margins – and profits" (Mackenzie et al. 2009).[10] Recognizing this, U.S. regulators now pushed for investors to be better represented and, in April 2009, ISDA's CEO, Robert Pickel, noted pointedly that "the buyside will be a very significant part of what we do going forward in a more formalised manner" (quoted in Mackenzie et al. 2009).

Exchanges also had reasons to support regulation. There had long been tension and competition over derivatives market share between the New York dealers and the exchanges, with the latter "banging on the door for a piece of the over-the-counter markets" (Tett and Davies 2008; see also Tett et al. 2009). Any push by regulators to support exchange trading would benefit the latter. Interestingly, however, some representatives of the exchanges sided with the dealers in opposing congressional proposals to *force* exchange trading when the issue was debated in early 2009 hearings (Grant and Tait 2009a). As the banks are the exchanges' largest customers, perhaps they did not want to confront the banks publicly.[11] John Dizard (2008) also reports that there was some opposition to exchange trading of CDS among Chicago exchange traders because they disliked the product itself. Whatever the reason for their position, when Geithner laid out his May 2009 proposals to *encourage* exchange trading, the proposal was welcomed by many people associated with exchanges.

The exchanges have also favored the creation of CCPs. At a time when trading volume had been falling, many of them saw the clearing business as a source of new profits (e.g. Grant 2009a,b). The world's largest futures exchange, Chicago's CME, quickly began developing a CCP for CDS in partnership with the hedge fund Citadel. The electronic futures exchange, ICE, also partnered with the leading dealer banks themselves to open a CCP in March 2009 (the dealer banks had begun as early as April 2008 to develop a CCP proposal via a firm they owned, The Clearing House, which ICE then took over in October 2008).

Although favoring certain kinds of regulation, the derivatives industry also has sought to pre-empt others in the same manner as it had in the past: through self-regulatory initiatives. In particular, ISDA developed a Big Bang protocol that was implemented by more than 1,400 banks and asset managers in April 2009 and which addressed some regulators' concerns by hard-wiring a cash settlement protocol into all CDS contracts (the protocol had been developed previously to replace cumbersome physical settlement procedures at times of default), streamlining contracts for single-named CDS, and removing time lags in protection coverage from the moment of purchase (Mackenzie et al. 2009).

In the past, U.S. industry was able to stave off regulation by arguing that it would hurt the competitive position of U.S. markets and firms in the highly mobile global derivatives business. These arguments were again raised by industry and by officials during congressional hearings and broader discussions in 2008–9 (e.g. Grant and Tait 2009a). However, the political momentum behind regulation was so strong that these arguments pushed policy makers in a different direction. Instead of weakening the case for regulation, they encouraged U.S. policy makers to coordinate regulation internationally in order to maintain a level playing field for U.S. industry.[12] Hence the connection between U.S. domestic regulatory initiatives and the appearance of derivatives on the international regulatory agenda at the G20 summits and elsewhere from the fall of 2008 onwards.

Change in Europe

Why, then, did other countries endorse U.S. goals? Most G20 countries had a clear incentive to go along with the U.S. initiative. Without a significant derivatives industry in their country, international derivatives regulation posed few costs, but promised many potential gains if it addressed the negative externalities that the lack of regulation had generated for the world economy. For Europe, however, the situation was more complicated. Top European financial institutions were major players in global derivatives markets and European financial centers – above all, London – were important locations for the OTC derivatives trading. If European policy makers rejected international regulatory coordination, the unilateral tightening of regulation in the United States might pose a competitive opportunity for them to capture market share in the highly mobile global derivatives business.

European policy makers did not choose this course of action, but instead backed the international regulatory agenda for some of the same reasons as the United States. The Lehman and AIG crises in September 2008 heightened concerns within Europe about derivatives because of the exposure of European institutions to these firms. Of AIG's $446 trillion CDS contracts, $307 billion had been bought by European banks (in large part to minimize the capital they had to hold) (Sender 2009b). As the crisis politicized the question of derivatives regulation across Europe, many top European policy makers had become much more supportive of regulation than they had been in the past.

Like their U.S. counterparts, European policy makers focused most of their attention on the need for CCPs, especially for CDS products. Serious European official interest in promoting CCPs was apparent as early as July 2008, and by October the European Commission and European Central Bank (ECB) were pushing industry to build CCPs in Europe for CDS. European support for OTC derivatives regulation was then confirmed by the February 2009 de Larosière report commissioned by the European Commission. It argued that credit derivatives had played a "significant role triggering the crisis" and had helped spread exposure to U.S. subprime losses around the world (High-Level Group 2009: 10). CDS markets, it concluded, "were supposed to mitigate risk, but in fact added to it" (p. 9). The report called for the creation of at least one CCP for OTC CDS in the EU that would be regulated, and for the simplification and standardization of most OTC derivatives, as well as "appropriate risk-mitigation techniques plus transparency measures" (p. 25). Like U.S. policy makers, the report noted that strengthened derivatives markets rules "should preferably be implemented internationally" rather than just within Europe in order to avoid regulatory arbitrage and loopholes (p. 60).

The next month it was the turn of the chair of Britain's Financial Services Authority, Lord Turner, to report on the crisis and make recommendations to his government on regulatory issues. The report made clear that the crisis had prompted some profound rethinking among British officials about the benefits of financial innovation, suggesting that "some forms of financial innovation may have delivered little if any allocative efficiency benefits, while increasing aggregate intermediation margins and contributing to significantly increased systemic risk" (Financial Services Authority 2009: 108–9). The report proceeded to cite CDS markets as an example and called for tighter regulation. Although the focus was on the need for CCPs for standardized CDS contracts, the report raised questions about whether consideration should be given to the regulation of specific products such as unattached CDS as well as collateral margins in OTC derivatives contracts (in order to contain the procyclicality of that market) (Financial Services Authority 2009: 22, 24, 82, 110).

These strong criticisms of OTC derivatives highlighted the extent of the ideational shift in British official circles.[13] Not surprisingly, London financial interests involved in derivatives activity fought back. In late April, a report commissioned by the City of London Corporation reminded policy makers that Britain was the market leader in OTC derivatives trading (with 43 percent of the value traded worldwide in 2007 compared with 24 percent for the United States) and that over-regulation risked undermining London's position. The report argued that the vast bulk of OTC derivatives (e.g. interest rate and currency derivatives) had little to do with the crisis and that even CDS had been unfairly blamed: "there is very little evidence to suggest that these contributed in any significant way to the crisis"; the report blamed people rather than the product: "this was a crisis caused by people's misjudgment, not a product-led crisis" (Jones 2009: 2–3).

At the same time, the report acknowledged that the political pressure to regulate OTC derivatives was "acute in the Eurozone countries and in the US." It continued: "In accepting the inevitable additional regulation that will come, it is important that the very successful OTC Derivatives market is not crushed in the process" (Jones 2009: 2). Two regulatory proposals were singled out for particular criticism. The first was that of forcing OTC derivatives onto exchanges, a move that the report described as "extremely foolish" (Jones 2009: 2). Not surprisingly, the London-based Wholesale Market Brokers Association (WMBA) – which represents interdealer brokers – was also actively opposed to this proposal, which would undermine the core business of its members. As in the United States, this issue brought to the surface long-standing tensions between dealers/brokers and exchanges. In late January, the Secretary-General of the Federation of European Securities Exchanges, Judith Hardt (2009: 2), suggested to the de Larosière high-level group that OTC derivatives were "at the core of the crisis" and that greater exchange trading should be encouraged. The WMBA (2009) strongly objected, arguing that this move would cause "a dramatic reduction in liquidity and product flexibility in markets essential for trading and hedging," and suggested that CCPs were all that was needed.

The brokers faced opponents among not just the European exchanges but also some prominent British financial commentators such as the *Financial Times* columnist Martin Wolf, who urged the British government in May to "reject egregious special pleading from the industry." He continued:

> The sector argues that moving derivatives trading on to exchanges might damage innovation. So what? Maximising innovation is a crazy objective. As in pharmaceuticals, a trade-off exists between innovation and safety. If institutions threaten to take trading activities offshore, banking licences should be revoked.
>
> (Wolf 2009)

Other columnists of the *Financial Times* called for an outright ban on CDS (Dizard 2008).

Many London-based interests have also strongly resisted the idea that OTC derivatives in Europe must be cleared by a European CCP (e.g. Jones 2009: 2–3). In advance of the first G20 summit in November 2008, the European Commission and ECB had promoted this idea, arguing that, if CCPs did not fall under their jurisdiction, European authorities would have no ability to monitor them, request information from them, or intervene if they ran into trouble. As one European official put it, "Can we afford the luxury of having a CCP clearing the whole world, over which we have no regulatory and supervisory powers or guaranteed access to information? And what if it goes belly up?" (quoted in Grant and Tait 2009b).

The push for a European CCP also appeared to be driven by some competitive motivations: The establishment of a European CCP would ensure that some of the economic benefits of international regulatory tightening accrued to European interests. This motivation should not be surprising given the U.S.–EU struggles over the respective derivatives market share of U.S. and European exchanges earlier in the decade (Mügge 2006: 193–5). One of the firms involved in those struggles had been Eurex Clearing (jointly operated by Deutsche Börse and SIX Swiss Exchange) and it may be noteworthy that one of its board members welcomed the ECB's promotion of a European solution after a meeting in early November 2008 (Grant 2008). The other three emerging CCPs in the global derivatives market had prospects for becoming global clearers linking European and U.S. markets: the London-based LCH.Clearnet had a link to the U.S. market through its New York Stock Exchange (NYSE) connection, while both the CME and ICE soon announced plans to establish European CDS CCPs. By contrast, Eurex had no U.S. presence and its focus was more European. It may also be worth noting that the ECB invited only European banks to a meeting to discuss the European CCP proposal in February (Tait 2009a).

The clearest evidence of competitiveness concerns, however, came from an internal Banque de France memo obtained by the *Financial Times* on February 19 that revealed its support for an exclusively eurozone CCP for OTC derivatives. This idea had been broached in December by the ECB, which had noted: "given the potential systemic importance of securities clearing and settlement systems, this infrastructure should be located within the euro area" (quoted in Jones 2009: 16). The Banque de France now combined concerns about regulatory control with more mercantilist motivations vis-à-vis the London financial markets and specifically the initiative to create a London-based CCP by NYSE Liffe-LCH.Clearnet. Because the "decision-making structure" of the latter was based in London, the memo argued that this could lead to "an increase in the weight of the London financial market or the relocation of governance to the United States if the Paris financial markets do not recommend a solution." It added: "The strategic nature of this business sector means that it is important to create a pan-European clearing

house for the eurozone with sufficient critical size to face down these challenges"
(quoted in Grant 2009c).

Predictably, London financial interests – including Clearnet – strongly opposed
the idea of a mandatory eurozone CCP (e.g. Jones 2009: 2; Grant and Masters
2009). They were backed by the Turner report as well as by the British government, which explicitly rejected the idea in its response to the de Larosière report
(Financial Services Authority 2009: 83; Jones 2009: 17–18). The efforts of the
ECB and the European Commission to require at least one CCP that was located,
regulated, and supervised in the EU as a whole for CDS on European reference
entities – and indices based on these entities – was ultimately successful. This
initiative had been initially opposed by the ISDA on the grounds that the global
nature of the derivatives industry required a global CCP rather than regional
ones. In February 2009, however, it announced that nine members, along with the
European Banking Federation, had committed to use a EU-based CCP for eligible
CDS by July 31, 2009.[14] An important explanation for the turnaround appears to
have been the threat of legislative action from the European Parliament, backed
by the Commission, to impose higher capital requirements against uncleared
contracts.

The new commitment to tightening OTC derivatives regulation in Europe thus
reflected the domestic politicization of derivatives and ideational shifts among
officials, as well as some more "realist" motivations to enhance regulatory control and market share vis-à-vis other states.[15] Although the process was slower,
European policy makers had come around by mid-2009 to a similar position on
derivatives reform to their U.S. counterparts. When the European Commission
launched a formal consultation process to determine European policy in this area
in July 2009, the goals it outlined were very similar to those of U.S. policy makers,
including CCPs for OTC derivatives, central data repositories, information disclosure, more use of exchanges, and standardization. As one industry person noted at
the time of Geithner's May 2009 proposals: "I think we'll get to the same place in
Europe, but possibly over a longer timeframe and in a more piece-meal fashion"
(quoted in Tait 2009b; see also Tait 2009c). Once European policy makers were
committed to regulation, they saw the same benefits as U.S. policy makers did in
international regulatory coordination: It would help to minimize any competitive
concerns that might arise for European industry from unilateral initiatives (even
if those initiatives in some areas – such as CCPs – promised competitive gains).

Conclusion

It has been a mistake for global governance scholars not to focus more attention
on the regulation of global derivatives markets. Their complexity may be rattling,
but they are profoundly important to current debates in the field. Before the crisis,
the OTC derivatives sector provided theorists of globalization with the one of the
most extreme cases of powerful global markets largely outside official regulation.

For this reason, it has been tempting to portray their rapid growth as evidence of a broader revolution in world politics involving the rise of unaccountable transnational private power. This interpretation no longer looks so convincing. Since the start of this crisis, states have started to cooperate to rein them in through public regulation in an internationally coordinated manner. Their actions suggest that power in global governance remains firmly in the hands of public authorities working through the state system.[16]

How was this international regulatory initiative possible? More structuralist perspectives would suggest that it should have been thwarted by various factors such as the opposition of powerful private financial interests, the neoliberal ideology of influential transnational networks of elite technocrats, and/or strong international competitive deregulation pressures. We have seen how each of these factors did in fact help to explain the absence of international derivatives regulation before the current crisis. However, the more recent developments described in this paper suggest the need for a more contingent, conjunctural, and nuanced understanding of the politics of global regulation.

To begin with, private financial interests were less all-powerful, homogeneous, and anti-regulation than is often assumed. In the context of the major financial crisis, the legitimacy of private industry was seriously challenged in ways that undermined its influence over the policy process. Their dependence on state support during the crisis also forced industry leaders to recognize that moral hazard concerns would prompt policy makers to tighten regulation. Rivalries and differing interests within the private financial sector also provided regulators with opportunities to cultivate pro-change constituencies within the private sector (Mattli and Woods 2009). In addition, the crisis helped to shift the attention of some private industry leaders away from short-term-oriented opposition to regulation toward a recognition of their longer-term interest in a more stable financial system.[17]

The role of transnational networks of technocratic officials was also more complicated than sometimes portrayed. We have seen how the neoliberal orientation of these officials was not fixed and uniform; during crisis (and even before), many financial officials embraced a more skeptical view of unregulated markets and self-regulation. Indeed, it is probably the case that the transnational networks in which financial officials are embedded acted as an important channel through which new, more pro-regulatory perspectives were spread. Their autonomy from domestic politics is also easily overstated. In the context of the crisis, derivatives regulation was no longer the exclusive domain of a narrow group of experts. As one reporter put it, "'credit derivatives' almost became a household phrase" (van Duyn 2008b). The massive public bailouts of financial institutions linked to derivatives activity only contributed to the unprecedented domestic politicization of this issue within the United States and Europe, and wresting of the regulatory agenda from the technocrats.

Finally, international competitive pressures posed less of a barrier to international regulatory initiatives than is often supposed. Regulators recognized that international regulatory coordination provided a way of minimizing the negative international competitive consequences of strengthening domestic regulation (Singer 2008). Because the latter was a domestic political priority in the United States and Europe, the former quickly became a shared goal for policy makers in both regions. At the same time, we have also seen how it was not just coordination but also competition that helped to encourage regulatory strengthening. In the case of the creation of CCPs, competitive rivalries between countries – both for market share and for regulatory control – pushed regulation in a tighter rather than looser direction.

There is one area, however, where structuralist perspectives have been proven partially right. The active role of the ISDA, CRMPG III, and other industry leaders in responding collectively to the crisis highlighted the enduring importance of private rule making at the international level (Porter 2005). To be sure, since the outbreak of the crisis, this rule making took place increasingly under strong political pressure. However, its persistence in this new political environment – and the G20 leaders' continuing willingness to delegate some regulatory tasks to the private sector – suggests that international private rule making is here to stay, even if it is now taking place very much under the heavy shadow of the state.

Notes

1 I am very grateful to Dag Harald Claes and Carl Henrik Knutsen for their comments, to Stefano Pagliari for his research help and comments, and to the Social Sciences and Humanities Research Council of Canada and Trudeau Foundation for research funding.

2 I am not discussing the politics of the implementation of G20 commitments at the domestic level as this process is still ongoing.

3 The industry body, International Derivatives and Swaps Association, estimates that, if one takes into account netting of multiple trades between two counterparties and collateralization, the net mark-to-market value is closer to $4 trillion (IOSCO 2009: 26).

4 Bank for International Settlements (2009b). $25 trillion were with reporting dealers, with the remainder being with other financial institutions.

5 The Financial Stability Forum did, however, call in April 2009 for this issue to be reviewed (Financial Stability Forum 2009: 5). At their summit in Toronto in June 2010, the G20 leaders (G20 2010: 19) subsequently "agreed to pursue policy measures with respect to haircut-setting and margining practices for securities financing and OTC derivatives transactions that will reduce procyclicality and enhance financial market resilience."

6 This issue did arise in U.S. reform debates vis-à-vis commodity derivatives (Clapp and Helleiner 2010).

7 See the speculations about the case of Morgan Stanley and a Kazakhstan bank (Tett 2009), as well as that of GM restructuring (Sender 2009a).

8 Also interesting were the reported comments of Myron Scholes, the Nobel prize-winning economist who had helped pioneer the Black–Scholes formula that contributed to the growth of derivatives products. According to Das (2009), he was quoted in early March saying "[The] solution is really to blow up or burn the OTC market, the CDSs and swaps and structured products, and . . . start over."

9 Statistic from Grant and Tait (2009a).

10 See especially Whalen (2009: 3) on the long-standing dealer resistance to these and other reforms.

11 Van Duyn and Gangahar (2009) noted in May 2009: "For years, exchanges have been trying to break into the vast OTC market without upsetting their largest customers – the banks."

12 For discussions of this dynamic in the broader politics of international financial regulation, see Singer (2008).

13 The comments of other British officials provided further evidence, such as the wide-ranging critique of past regulatory approaches provided by the Executive Director, Financial Stability at the Bank of England, Andrew Haldane (2009), in an April 2009 speech, which culminated in a strong endorsement of CCPs for OTC derivatives.

14 They were Barclays Capital, Citigroup Global Markets, Credit Suisse, Deutsche Bank, Goldman Sachs, HSBC, JPMorgan, Morgan Stanley, and UBS.

15 Interestingly, a similar phenomenon was apparent in Japan, where two Japanese clearing houses began to develop CCPs for OTC derivatives as a way to boost revenue for the firms involved and help the growth of derivatives trading in Japan (Whipp 2009).

16 For this point more generally, see Pauly (2002).

17 For the tensions created by the long-term and short-term interests of capital in financial regulation, see Hawley (1984).

PART II

Domestic institutions and policies in the globalized economy

8

THE AFRICAN NEOPATRIMONIAL STATE AS A GLOBAL PROTOTYPE

Daniel C. Bach[1]

The concept of neopatrimonial rule was first applied to Africa by Jean-François Médard to account for the Cameroonian state's lack of institutionalization and "underdevelopment" (Médard 1979: 39). The lack of distinction between office and officeholder, Médard went on, is masked behind discourses, juridical norms, and institutions that nourish the illusion of a legal-bureaucratic logic. In the absence of a legitimizing ideology, the ruler owes his ability to remain in power to his capacity for transforming his monopolistic control over the state into a source of opportunities for family, friends, and clients.

Neopatrimonialism in Africa is still classically viewed as the outcome of a confusion between office and officeholder within a state endowed, at least formally, with modern institutions and bureaucratic procedures (Bach and Gazibo 2011). The introduction of "neo" as a prefix, as originally suggested by S. Eisenstadt, still means that neopatrimonialism is freed from the historical configurations with which patrimonialism had been previously associated. Unlike patrimonialism, conceived by Weber as a traditional type of authority, neopatrimonialism combines the display of legal-bureaucratic norms and structures with relations of authority based on interpersonal rather than impersonal interactions (Eisenstadt 1973: 11). This coexistence of patrimonialism with legal-bureaucratic elements begs the key question of the forms of interaction and their outcomes. Indeed, neopatrimonialism infers a "dualistic situation, in which the state is characterized by patrimonialisation, as well as by bureaucratization" (Bourmaud 1997: 62). Such dualism translates into a wide array of empirical situations as discussed below. What is ultimately at stake, however, is the state's capacity (or lack thereof) to produce public policies: Political systems in which patrimonial practices tend to be regulated should be distinguished from those in which the patrimonialization of the state has become all-encompassing, with the consequent loss of any sense of public space or public policy.

Regulated forms of neopatrimonialism

In Africa, regulated forms of neopatrimonialism have usually been associated with the introduction of a policy of ethnoregional balance. The distribution of resources and prebends by the ruler takes place on an inclusive basis. The emphasis laid on co-optation and redistribution, rather than coercion, contributes to promote a culture of mutual accommodation. The expected outcome is an increased state capacity to penetrate society and entrench its supremacy. Even though such notions as public ethics and common good may be undercut, regulated neopatrimonialism conveys its own brand of "moral economy" in so far as it favors redistribution processes that target the nation as a whole (Olivier de Sardan 1999).

The regimes of Jomo Kenyatta and Félix Houphouët-Boigny were good examples of regulated neopatrimonialism. Within the Kenyan state, impersonal rules were made to coexist with neopatrimonial practices designed to alleviate the risks that political competition might carry for the nation-state (Bourmaud 1991: 262). Synergies between presidentialism, the single-party system, and what amounted to an institutionalized system of patronage facilitated the incorporation of the periphery by the center. Similarly, in Côte d'Ivoire, the regime of Félix Houphouët-Boigny (1960–93) exemplified the combination of personal rule with regulated neopatrimonialism. Direct control was exerted over the recruitment of the political élite so as "to balance ethnic, generational and even personal rivalries" (Crook 1989: 214). The outcome was a hybrid political system in which "strong personal power . . . through patron–client relations [combined with] the use of modern bureaucratic agencies" (Crook 1989: 214). As in Kenya, the imprint of neopatrimonialism was regulated.

The 1970s were the golden age of regulated neopatrimonialism in Africa. Commodity export prices were still high, the states often had access to significant resources for redistribution, and comforting the rulers' personal power seemed compatible with ensuring state (if not nation) building. As a result, the integrative virtues of the resulting processes were often extolled.

Predatory forms of neopatrimonialism

Predatory forms of neopatrimonialism refer to systems in which personal rule and resource control have reached a paroxysmic level, with a consequent "failure of institutionalisation . . . and thus of the state" (Médard 1991: 339). The corollaries are the absence of a public space, and of any capacity to produce "public" policies. Indeed, the privatization of the public sphere is carried to such extremes that it becomes conducive to its dissolution.

The Mobutu regime (1965–97) is commonly associated with a thoroughly patrimonialized system, but this was not always so. As T. Callaghy called upon the concept of patrimonialism to account for Mobutu's political ascent in the early 1970s, the implications were radically distinct (Callaghy 1984). The author drew comparisons with the evolution of authoritarian states in Latin America, and France's absolute monarchy in the seventeenth century, before depicting the Mobutist state as an "early modern state" and an "administrative monarchy." Accordingly, Zaire's political system was ambivalently represented as "neo-traditional and patrimonial" (Callaghy 1984: 46). Interpretations of Mobutu's brand of neopatrimonial rule underwent a radical shift after 1975. Mobutu, observes René Lemarchand, differed from others on the continent because of an "unparalleled capacity to institutionalize kleptocracy at every level of the social pyramid and his unrivalled talent for transforming personal rule into a cult and political clientelism into cronyism" (Lemarchand 2003: 31; Young and Turner 1985). Casually stigmatized as arbitrary, predatory, or kleptocratic, Mobutu's Zaire has called for parallels with sultanism – the term coined by Max Weber to characterize those extreme instances in which the ruler's domination relies less upon traditional foundations than on the leader's arbitrary and uncontrolled power.

To summarize, the distinction between regulated and predatory forms of neopatrimonialism signals the two extremes of a diversity of empirical configurations. In the case of integral and predatory forms of neopatrimonialism, the ruler is the state. Conversely, regulated neopatrimonialism infers some capacity to craft "public" policies. To put it differently, an operational distinction should be drawn between patrimonial practices *within* the state and the patrimonialization of the *entire* state.

The African state as an "anti-developmental" state

The foundations of a political economy of neopatrimonialism were laid by Richard Sandbrook, who in the 1980s had undertaken to relate the private appropriation of the state's powers to the developmental failure of African states (Sandbrook 1985). The neopatrimonial state, he argued, is an archetype of the anti-developmental state, with "economic objectives [subordinated] to the short-run exigencies of political survival" for the ruler and his regime (Sandbrook 2000: 97). Göran Hyden similarly described bluntly as an "institutionalized curse" the spread of neopatrimonialism in Africa (Hyden 2000: 19). By then, the African state, stereotyped as desperately corrupt and "klepto-patrimonial" (Searle 1999: 8), provided an anti-model to the literature that, globally, attempted to conceptualize the developmental state.

The typology of Peter Evans, drawing from the experience of the first wave of emerging countries in East Asia (Japan, South Korea, and Taiwan), identified three archetypes in accordance to states' propensity to promote economic development. The model of the predatory and anti-developmental state was located in Africa, where, as in Mobutu's Zaire, "the preoccupation of the political class with rent seeking has turned the rest of society into prey" – a confirmation, Evans concluded, that "it is not bureaucracy that impedes development so much as the lack of capacity to behave like a bureaucracy" (Evans 1989: 570).

Similarly, Atul Kohli's more recent overview of development and industrialization processes in "peripheral" or "emergent" countries draws from Africa his
prototype of a highly ineffective and anti-developmental "neopatrimonial" state.
Its characteristic feature is the absence of an "effective public arena" clearly differentiated from private interests, organizations, and loyalties (Kohli 2004: 408).
Nigeria is seen by Kohli as a near-perfect example of such a prototype that is also
considered relevant to describe "almost all African states." Africa is associated
with predatory and integral forms of neopatrimonialism.

Beyond Africa . . .

In Latin America, Southeast Asia, or the Communist and post-Communist societies of Europe and Central Asia, the diffusion of the concept of neopatrimonial
rule has remained limited. Ongoing references to patrimonialism have also been
adjusted to suit specific debates, as reflected by the rich crop of lexicographic and
conceptual innovations that are presented below.

In Latin America, patrimonialism still commonly refers to the legacy of the
three centuries of Spanish and Portuguese presence (Zabludovsky 1989; Roett
1984). In the late 1950s, Richard Morse famously claimed that patrimonialism
could account for the persistence in contemporary South America of patterns
of governance that drew their roots from Spain's imperial policy (Morse 1964).
Similarly in Brazil, the state continues to be depicted as "a bureaucratic state
that traditionally has been at the service of a patrimonial order" (Roett 1984: 1;
Uricoechea 1980). Such commonly used notions as "patrimonial society," "patrimonial regime," or "patrimonial order" seek to stress the existence of continuities
that transcend regime changes or the type of elites in power.

One of the outcomes is that, in Latin America, the dividing line between
"tradition" and "traditionalism" is often blurred. References to patrimonialism
were, for instance, extended to include the return of totalitarian rule, as in Brazil,
Argentina, or Peru during the 1970s. Patrimonialism became then a metaphor
for the capture of the state by traditionalist corporate interests (Schwartman
1977). Neopatrimonialism, which Oscar Oszlak was the first to apply to Latin
America, merely referred to "contemporary cases in which personalist government turns states into the private government of those possessing the necessary
power for the exercise of political domination" (Oszlak 1986: 229). In contrast
with neopatrimonialism in Africa, personal rule was not associated with processes
of deinstitutionalization. The postulate was that a neopatrimonial regime could
even have a developmental impact if the dictator happened to be surrounded
by a "true 'Court' of 'trustworthy men' . . . who act as placemen at key institutions, and a small staff of professionals in charge of the administration of certain
large programmes (i.e. public works, industrial promotion)" (Oszlak 1986: 232).
There, as in other and more recent studies, the underlying assumption was the
lack of incompatibility between patrimonialism and the rise of a bureaucratic

and capitalist state. Latin American references to neopatrimonialism were exempt from any teleological assumption that the state was inexorably dissolving into informality.

In Africa and Latin America, the concepts of patrimonialism or neopatrimonialism have been linked to the discussion of institution and state building. In East and Southeast Asia it is the impact on the development of capitalism that provides an analytical thread. The outcome is a multiplicity of expressions designed to account for the interactions between state bureaucracies and private business – for example cronyism, oligarchic patrimonialism, predatory, rentier, and even, in the case of Malaysia, so-called *ersatz* capitalism (Yoshihara 1988; White 2004). The relationship between bureaucrats and business circles has also been central in debates on the conceptualization of the "developmental state." By contrast with the much celebrated economic performances of Japan, Taiwan, and South Korea in the 1960s, prospects for capitalist development in Malaysia, the Philippines, Indonesia, or Thailand were initially overlooked. Corruption and cronyism among rulers, bureaucrats, and big business, were considered too intense. The intimation of a thoroughly patrimonialized state conveyed by this pessimistic prognosis was eventually challenged by the economic performance of Malaysia, Indonesia, the Philippines, and Thailand in the 1990s. In Malaysia, for instance, the rise of internationally competitive forms of capitalist entrepreneurship was now treated as the counterpart of a state bureaucracy that was more regulated despite the persistence of "highly patrimonialistic relations between the state and business" (Searle 1999: 8).

In the post-Communist states of Europe, the concept of patrimonialism still bears the imprint of Weber's writings on the administrative system of Petrine Russia (Maslovski 1996: 302). Patrimonialism, as applied to Communist and post-Communist political regimes, is associated with two distinct yet closely intertwined strands of interpretations. A first type of reading stems from the analysis of patrimonialism as a historical or cultural model. Mikhail Maslovski, for instance, sees the development of patrimonialism within the Stalinist system as a "reversal" (Maslovski 1996: 302). Hans van Zon similarly depicts post-Communist Ukraine as "a patrimonial state [that] . . . furthers anti-modern tendencies in society" (van Zon 2001: 72). A second type of reading broadly coincides with what the notion of regulated neopatrimonialism stands for. The concept describes modern political systems with a capacity to produce public policies. When Yoram Gorlizski characterizes the day-to-day working of the Stalinist state as "neopatrimonial," he is insistent that he is not referring to a traditional system in which "autocratic rule [rests] on institutional confusion and disarray, but . . . [to] . . . patrimonial authority coexisting alongside quite modern and routine forms of high level decision-making" (Gorlizki 2002: 700–1).

A third type of interpretation specifically refers to situations in which patrimonialization tends to become integral. The analyses also acknowledge the influence of Africanist literature on interactions between personal rule, patronage, and the

deinstitutionalization of the state. Thus, in Ukraine, the political system dominated by Leonid Kuchma (1994–2005) has been characterized as neopatrimonial
in view of the "disintegration of the state apparatus, the capture of the state
by ruling clans [and] the spread of corrupt practices in the state bureaucracy"
(van Zon 2001: 72). Integral forms of neopatrimonialism, however, find another
almost perfect match with Islam Karimov's regime in Uzbekistan. The assimila-
tion of neopatrimonialism in the deinstitutionalization and informalization of the
post-colonial African state is echoed in this case by the "creeping capture" of
the political-administrative system inherited from the Soviet Union by networks
of patronage and private interests (Ilkhamov 2007: 75). The informalization of
interactions within the state is exacerbated by a system of personal domination
based on the conversion of clanship alliances into patronage ties and the redistribution of state resources. The related rise of a "parallel power network, matching
existing state hierarchy" (Ilkhamov 2007: 71), sketches a pattern reminiscent of
the "shadow state" of William Reno (1995: 83). In conclusion, neopatrimonialism
in Uzbekistan amounts to an almost perfect illustration of the development of
institutional underdevelopment.

Conclusion

The dissemination of the concept of neopatrimonialism in Africa has been
particularly successful. Neopatrimonialism is extensively and casually used in
studies and programs conducted under the aegis of multilateral institutions, non-
governmental organizations, "think tanks," and international donor agencies,
with the result of an association of the notion with an increasingly eclectic list of
subjects. Such a trajectory, however, has not been without a price.

The "endemic" nature (Pitcher et al. 2009) of references to neopatrimonialism has contributed to its transformation into an "elusive" notion (Erdmann and
Engel 2007), a sort of "paradigm for all African seasons" (Therkildsen 2005:
36). The outcome is a *doxa* that depicts the African state as quintessentially anti-
developmental and infers its inevitable descent into informality and capture by
criminal networks. Neopatrimonialism is, in Africa, equated to predatory and
integral forms of personal rule.

Neglected for all too long, the study of regulated or capped forms of African
neopatrimonial rule calls for fresh empirical and theoretical attention. Reasserting
the empirical relevance of regulated forms of neopatrimonialism will contribute
to restore the foundations for a truly comparative approach both within Africa
and across world regions. The developmental trajectory of the different waves
of emerging countries is a powerful reminder that neopatrimonialism – that is,
the coexistence of patrimonial and legal-rational elements with a political system
– does not predetermine outcomes. In Africa, too, states may combine neopatrimonial with "developmental" features (de Haan 2010). Monitoring processes of
regulated or capped interactions between public space and private interests should
have never ceased to call for attention.

Note

1 Emile Durkheim Centre – Comparative Political Science and Sociology, University of Bordeaux. d.bach@sciencespobordeaux.fr

9

ARE GOOD POLICIES GOOD POLITICS?

Karl Ove Moene[1]

Good policies serve economic and social improvement. Good politics serves implementation and the survival of the ruler. Do the two come together? If they do, political competition implies that the good drives out the bad. Policies that lead to good economic and social performance would also strengthen the chances of political survival of the ruler. If they don't, we may have a political version of Gresham's law, in which the bad drives out the good, and in which unfair and inefficient policies are favored in order to increase the political survival of the ruler.

Bad policies can indeed be good politics. As first pointed out by Robert Bates (1981), bad governance has been a survival tactic for the ruling elite in many African countries. Typically the incumbent undersupplies public goods. Instead he targets favors and benefits at supporters and withholds them from his opponents.[2]

But can bad policies make good politics even in well-developed democracies? If good policies serve efficiency and fairness, political competition guarantees neither. If good policies mean that one should locate the remedy as close to the problem as possible, political competition can prevent narrowly targeted remedies from being implemented – even in cases in which such policies can be both efficient and perhaps fair. Successful implementation would then be better achieved by spreading the remedies more widely across all social groups. Good politics are then best served by policies that are deemed bad by the criterion of locating the remedy where the main problem is. One example is poverty alleviation programs and welfare spending more generally. The question is what policies are most effective in fighting poverty, provided that they obtain majority support. Is it a cost-efficient policy that targets the benefits narrowly to the needy only? Or is a wider targeting, closer to universal welfare spending, that provides benefits to all, more effective? The answer depends on the power of the executive and on the inertia of the design of the program. Below I elaborate on this, building on the more formal treatment in Moene and Wallerstein (2001).[3]

The distinction between widely and narrowly targeted policies is not only relevant for redistribution of incomes from rich to poor (or vice versa). It is also important in connection with the politically determined provision of goods and services more generally. The distinction is important for any public resource allocation as long as the expected allocation affects the amount of resources to be allocated. Whereas a narrow targeting can be associated with local public goods, a wide targeting can be associated with the traditional public goods. Hence, when it comes to implementation, some of the same principles apply.

Whether the targeting is wide or narrow also plays an essential role for the stability of imperfect democracies and of authoritarian regimes. It is central to the understanding of political patron–client relationships, often denoted patrimonialism (or neopatrimonialism if it is combined with legal-bureaucratic elements as discussed in Bach's article in this volume). Used as a strategy for politicians to stay in power, patrimonialism typically targets the benefits narrowly to the supporters of the ruler. I discuss how this kind of targeting can be most profitable when the power of the patron is contested. Building on a broad survey of governance, development policies, and political power by Baland, Moene, and Robinson (2010), I emphasize how patrimonialism normally has detrimental effects on governance and economic performance, but good effects on political survival.

In all cases mentioned, the targeting of public policies is crucial for economic performance, implementation, and political survival. It is therefore essential for how policies are linked to politics. By comparing the various aspects of wide versus narrow targeting we should be able to see, I hope, how targeting may reflect the distribution of power in a way that is decisive for when good policies are good politics.

Power and political preferences

Throughout we shall be interested in how the ruler allocates economic resources and benefits to supporters and others. What targeting maximizes the political preferences of the ruler when his power is contested by challengers? We shall think of both the ruler and his challengers as political contestants who are concerned with the expected value of having their policy implemented. In this calculation each contestant's pay-off of winning and losing must be weighted by the probabilities of winning and losing. The winner of the political contest can implement his policy, but the probability of winning is affected by the policies that he chooses.

This formulation of political preferences does not only incorporate political competition. It also incorporates the possibility of opportunistic behavior. Each contestant is assumed to be willing to sacrifice some of his favored political goals in order to improve his chances of obtaining power by winning an election or another type of political contest.

A completely selfish ruler would allocate as little as possible to others – just enough to remain in power. A more ideologically motivated ruler, however, who competes against opponents who might have a somewhat different ideological orientation, may have to compromise his ideology to increase the chances of winning. This kind of opportunism implies that he lowers his ambitions of implementing a policy that is his most favored one, once in power.

The distribution of political power in society is of course not only dependent on the policies that each potential ruler suggests. Following Acemoglu and Robinson (2006b), and Max Weber long before them, one can distinguish between two components of political power: de jure and de facto political power. Here de jure political power refers to all types of power that originate from the political institutions in society. Political institutions determine the constraints on and the incentives of key actors in the political sphere. Examples of political institutions include the form of government, for example democracy versus dictatorship or autocracy, and the extent of constraints on politicians and political elites.

A group of individuals, however, may possess political power even if they are not allocated power by political institutions. They can engage in collective action, revolt, use arms, hire mercenaries, or use economically costly but largely peaceful protests in order to impose their wishes on society. This type of political power can be referred to as de facto political power.

It is the composition of de facto and de jure power in society that determines the actual power of a group determining which economic institutions and policies arise. Institutions are more persistent than policies. Those with power today can therefore take decisions not just to maximize their income today, but also to maintain their grip on power. These goals are often in contradiction. This can be for the simple reason that economic policies that increase the incomes of elites today may increase the incomes of opponents even more, thus influencing the future distribution of de facto power.

Both in democracies and in more authoritarian systems political contests affect the minimum size of the winning coalition of any ruler, or more generally the size of his supporting group. When does contested power lead to a widening and when does contested power lead to a narrowing of the favored group? I distinguish between political institutions that require equal treatment of citizens (large coalition systems) and those institutions that de facto allow unequal treatment (small coalition systems).

The first example depicts completely opportunistic politicians who are only interested in winning the executive power, but who are institutionally constrained from using grave favoritism. Do good social policies constitute good politics under these rather favorable circumstances?

How targeting affects a narrowly targeted group

By "good policy" we shall in most of this section mean the kind of policy, or social program, that reduces poverty the most. We are interested in the policy that achieves the maximum poverty alleviation when the level of support is endogenously determined through democratic elections with self-interested voters. Is it better to establish welfare policies based on a wide targeting, with participation extended to all who meet some non-income-dependent criteria such as age and sickness? Or is it better to establish a careful and narrow targeting that maximizes the impact of a given amount of tax revenues on the welfare of the poor?

These questions, addressed more formally in Moene and Wallerstein (2001), are as relevant to developing countries with a contested ruler as to developed countries with well-established democratic institutions. As mentioned, institutions may be more persistent than policies, implying that the design of the distributional program, for instance the design of the welfare state and its targeting, may be thought of as given when its funding is decided in the short run. What is the economic targeting that maximizes the political preferences of political parties or blocks in this case? The expected social utility of each party incorporates the competition from the other parties when they are adjusting their proposals in order to improve the chances of winning.

To derive the political contestants' chances of winning the policy game, we must consider the preferences of citizens. Even from a purely self-interested point of view, the reasons for supporting or opposing poverty programs are varied. The classical view is that poverty programs and welfare spending are primarily redistributive, with the rich paying taxes in excess of benefits and the poor receiving benefits in excess of tax payments. Citizens with lower incomes than the mean income in society have a redistributive motive for supporting the program (Meltzer and Richards 1981).

A second consideration stems from the incompleteness of private insurance markets. Citizens who are subject to risks that are difficult or impossible to insure privately may support welfare policies for the insurance such policies provide (Sandmo 1991; Barr 1992; Sinn 1995). Finally, there may be a deadweight cost associated with taxation and the provision of welfare benefits. To have a realistic approach we need to incorporate all three aspects. In addition it is important to embed the discussion in a set-up in which voters differ in their expected incomes and the risks they are exposed to.

Let us first consider the case of the completely opportunistic politician who cares only about winning the election. The political outcome is then best predicted as the Condorcet winner in the policy game, that is, by the political proposal that mimics the ideal policy of the median voter – here the median income earner.

Applying all this within an otherwise rather general mathematical model three results emerge (as shown in Moene and Wallerstein 2001):

1. Result I: With a wide targeting the political equilibrium outcome is a tax rate and a guaranteed income (a benefit level) that are strictly positive as long as the median voter has an income that is less or equal to the mean income in society.

   Because a policy of redistribution based on wide targeting taxes the same percentage of everybody's income and distributes these tax revenues equally to all citizens, the net impact of the policy is to redistribute income from the rich to the poor via a universal benefit. If one likes, this policy can be interpreted as a guaranteed income level, or an implicit basic income grant. Everybody with an income below the mean income benefits from the redistribution. Because the majority of the population in all known income distributions earns an income level below the mean income, the majority has a redistribution motive to support the policy. Because incomes fluctuate and are uncertain ex ante, the program also converts uncertain incomes into certain incomes, creating an additional insurance motive for supporting the policy. The net benefit from the two reasons for supporting the policy are then traded off against the possible cost in the form of a deadweight loss of financing the program.

2. Result II: With a narrow targeting to the most needy the political equilibrium outcome is a guaranteed income (a benefit level) that is basically zero as long as voters are selfish and without altruistic preferences.

   With a narrowly targeted policy the probability of receiving the benefit declines as the benefit level is reduced. There is an income threshold determined by the funding of the program, below which people receive benefits. When the benefits decline, only the most needy qualify. Hence, lowering a targeted benefit can increase the share of the electorate who would prefer the benefit to be reduced even more. In fact, when the target benefit is low enough a self-interested majority who want the spending does not exist. When benefits are narrowly targeted and voters are self-interested, a majority may simply prefer to eliminate the redistributive spending all together.

3. Result III: Including a small dose of altruism among the voters in favor of the worst off does not alter much. It implies that the guaranteed income is positive also with narrow targeting; but nevertheless the benefit level to the poor is higher with a wider targeting.

   Altruism not only works in narrowly targeted programs. It makes people more generous when voting for universal benefits as well.

All in all, result I may seem unimpressive and unimportant, but it should be contrasted with result II. Together, and combined with result III, they are suggestive for how policies can be linked to politics. The lessons can be organized into the three following groups.

Cost-efficient social arrangements can easily become politically infeasible

If true, this statement is important. In economics the search for good policies is often limited to the set of socially efficient policies. Cost-efficiency is a necessary condition for optimality. Targeted programs toward the poorest are clearly cost-efficient ways of fighting poverty. The narrow targeting implies that one can get the most out of available resources as the program allocates the entire budget to those who need support the most.

Political competition, however, does not generally reward cost-efficiency. It rewards the policy that benefits the winner, whether these benefits are cost-efficiently provided or not. As a consequence the most targeted programs need not be the ones with the greatest impact on poverty. A finer targeting may undermine political support for the required taxation and targeting can in itself create its own bureaucratic distortions.

The vanishing support for cost-efficiency has political implications. A political party that runs on a program promising generous funding of a narrowly targeted program may be bound to lose the election. There may simply be no majority support of the policy. Hence, in this case more political competition, with a commitment toward narrow targeting, implies that bad policies drive out good policies.

The ideal for many of a limited welfare state that pays benefits only to the very poor may thus be politically unsustainable in the absence of altruistic voting. Such a minimum welfare state, which is often associated with conservative politics, can be politically infeasible as long as voters behave selfishly. Ideologically a minimum welfare state should perhaps be considered conservative utopianism.

Is the low welfare spending associated with narrow targeting visible across countries? I think it is. The narrow targeting, and the high incidence of means-tested programs in the United States, are associated with low benefit levels to the worst off compared with European standards based on more universal spending (Alesina and Glaeser 2004). In addition the benefit levels in the United States seem to be more sensitive to small alterations in the level of altruism. This was evident from Ronald Reagan's storytelling about the "welfare queen" in the 1970s and from Bill Clinton's obsession to "change welfare as we know it" in the 1990s. Both led to a markable decline in the support given to single mothers.[4]

Wide targeting can in principle benefit the narrowly targeted group

These lessons basically say that less targeting of policies may result in policies that provide more to the group that now becomes less targeted. Thus to help black welfare recipients in the United States, for instance, one should target less to black welfare recipients and more to an extended group of potential welfare recipients. When the level of benefits is chosen by majority rule, a less targeted policy may result in a higher guaranteed income level for all as well as higher welfare for a majority of voters.

This lesson touches a long-standing debate regarding the relative advantages of universalistic and means-tested welfare state policies that is highly relevant in our context.

Advocates of means testing argue that universalistic programs are both expensive and inefficient. Most of the subsidies go to the better off and only a small proportion of the money reaches those who most need assistance. Advocates of universalistic programs argue that programs that spread benefits widely garner greater political support than programs whose benefits go only to a minority of the population. In addition, the supporters of universalism argue that the absence of means testing reduces administrative costs and avoids the problem of high implicit tax rates on those whose revenues are withdrawn as their income increases.

This discussion has been more active in political science and sociology than in economics; an overview of some relevant arguments from economics is surveyed by Barr (1992). My own view on this is that a traditional public economics approach would tend to recommend means testing, whereas a more modern political economy approach with endogenous implementation should be more concerned with vanishing public support for means testing, and therefore see more advantages in universalism.

Paradoxically, leakages from the poverty program to groups outside the targeted core group have sometimes been considered a politically costly misuse of resources. In line with the arguments above, however, leakages distribute the benefits more widely, implying that imperfect targeting may increase the popularity of the program and thus its expected funding in the political equilibrium.

Altruism does not necessarily imply that narrow targeting best serves the interests of the poor

This third and final group of lessons emphasizes the role of fairness norms and individual social preferences. The more people sympathize with the worst off, the more they tend to support redistribution programs in their favor. Yet it does not follow from this that such altruism makes narrow targeting the best alternative. Even when voters support narrowly targeted policies out of altruism, the poor may benefit from policy changes that lower the share of the benefits targeted to them once the impact of targeting of the political support for welfare spending is taken into account. Neither is it true that the presence of strong altruism means that targeting plays no role as people's social preferences internalize the interests of the worst off. As long as people pay some attention to their own interests – in addition to those of the worst off in society – the level of targeting is important for political support.

So, all lessons considered, are good policies good politics? As long as one is constrained within a system of a limited welfare state with narrow targeting, good welfare policies in favor of the poor are not good politics. Political competition might imply a race to the bottom via gradual tax and benefit reductions. Being committed to a design with wider targeting of, for instance, universalistic welfare spending, in contrast, can make good policies in favor of the poor a winning political strategy. Finally, in a system with no constitutional bindings, no persistence, and no commitments to a specific design, policies based on rather universal spending can be good politics. More political competition can then enhance the generosity of the policy.

On the positive side there is much to be said in favor of universalistic redistribution policies. One can emphasize their good results in poverty reductions and their implicit reluctance to divide society into contributors and benefactors. Universal insurance also fits well for small open economies, such as the Scandinavians, with a high level of income risks caused by fluctuations in the international markets (Katzenstein 1985; Rodrik 1997). They may thus be classified as typical free trade institutions. They also have low (or zero) implicit taxation of entering into active employment as most of the benefits are independent of employment status. In fact, this aspect of the policy made universal spending popular among employers. By going thorough the archives of Swedish employers Peter A. Swenson (2002) demonstrates this convincingly in his seminal book on employers against markets.

Yet, on the negative side, universalistic policies are very costly and there are strong voices today that recommend cuts in spending. Skeptics might even emphasize that universalistic spending implies that benefits are distributed in exchange for political support. As a cost-efficient policy of poverty alleviation may become politically infeasible, voters need to be "bribed." Universalistic spending could then be considered a way to bribe the majority in order to support the needy.

Targeting in regimes of personal rule

I now turn to the second example depicting more ruthless politicians. They apply more personal rule within (highly) imperfect democracies, or authoritarian regimes, like so many developing countries after independence. As indicated, I denote the regimes "patrimonial." If universalistic spending can be considered an arrangement that bribes the majority to support the needy, patrimonialism must be considered an arrangement that exploits the majority in order to bribe the minimal coalition of supporters.

Before I can discuss this claim and explore further whether good policies make good politics in this rather unfavorable case, I must briefly characterize some common features of worst-case patrimonial regimes such as Zimbabwe under Robert Mugabe, Kenya under Daniel Arap Moi, Sierra Leone under Siaka Stevens (until 1985) and subsequently Joseph Momoh, Zaire under Mobutu Sese Seko, and the Dominican Republic under Rafael Trujillo (for overviews see Meredith 2005; Turits 2003).

In these regimes the distribution of de facto power allows favoritism. Thus targeting can be used effectively by the ruler to create political support. Patrimonialism is just a style of governance in which politicians control power through a system of personal relationships. Policies and favors are distributed in exchange for political support. The exchange is structured in an attempt to maximize the control and bargaining power of those running such regimes. Accordingly, they target resources, benefits, and favors narrowly to a minimal group of supporters and withhold resources from potential challengers.

As surveyed in Baland, Moene, and Robinson (2010) patrimonialism can be viewed as an attempt to create a national political order, not by eliminating alternative sources of authority in society, but by co-opting them. It attempts to weaken potential sources of opposition or alternative identities. This leaves potential challenges simmering close to the surface, and creates its own type of fragility. Civilian control of the military seems to be inconsistent with patrimonialism, possibly because the regimes lack legitimacy and also because personalized regimes are easy for small groups of dissident soldiers to overthrow. All this exacerbates political instability.

What makes patrimonialism attractive? It is built around a small group of supporters, the winning coalition, that retains the power of the ruler. The winning coalition is drawn from a large group of potential supporters, sometimes denoted the selectorate. As stated in a influential book on the theme: "In systems characterized by small winning coalitions and large selectorates . . . supporters of the leader are particularly loyal because the risk and cost of exclusion if the challenger comes to power are high" (Bueno de Mesquita et al. 2003: 8). Hence, patrimonial systems are attractive in part because the ruler needs to bribe only a small winning coalition whose members are not much tempted to defect. They are therefore sometimes referred to as small coalition systems.

Countries with a heterogeneity of identities and where a uniform national identity is lacking seem to invite this kind of patrimonial rule. It is further encouraged in countries where there is no legitimate structure of authority. This was obviously quite common in Africa after independence when countries inherited the arbitrary boundaries created by European colonialism. Patrimonialism is a very effective way of governing a nation that can easily break up into separate parts (Herbst 2000).

To govern such countries a patrimonial ruler uses various forms of divide and rule and this strategy appears to be much more feasible in societies that have distinct allotted identities (Padro-i-Miquel 2007). In a society divided by allotted differences it is easy to conceive of a polarization between different groups that may lead people to be disposed to reject the application of universal rules, so undermining principles that would impede the creation of patrimonialism. A high level of allotted differences can generate policies and power by divide and rule that induce a high level of economic and political inequality. The system is in a sort of long-run equilibrium whenever initial allotted inequalities are maintained by the control and power generated by these inequalities.

Now, are good policies supportive for the political survival of the ruler in patrimonial regimes? Obviously not: Patrimonial rule is disastrous for economic policy and performance.

First, the form that patron–client exchanges have to take is highly inefficient. For instance, patrons find it politically desirable to use private goods that can be targeted to supporters and withheld from opponents. Public goods are not politically attractive ways to generate support and are thus heavily undersupplied. Spending on health care, infrastructure, and education would increase the incomes and welfare of most people in underdeveloped areas – including the elite (Acemoglu and Robinson 2006b). Yet such public spending can strengthen the opposition and thus undermine the ruling elite's ability to stay in power.

Second, as emphasized in Baland, Moene, and Robinson (2010: 4613):

patrimonial rulers need to make people reliant on them for their future success or failure. To do this they create insecurity and uncertainty which only they can resolve. To quote a famous example, Rafael Trujillo, who ruled the Dominican Republic for 31 years forced all politicians to write a resignation letter which he kept in his desk.

Third, property rights are insecure under patrimonial rule (Knutsen 2011). People have property only because patrons allow them to have it. Such rights are always conditional and can be withdrawn, creating terrible incentives to invest in assets. The rule of law or equality before the law is of course completely inconsistent with how clientelism is dispensed. In a patrimonial regime you have rights if you are a client of the patron and otherwise you do not. The application of uniform rules or criteria to allocate resources impedes the ability of patrons to use discretion.

Fourth, patrimonial regimes create distortions in market prices to create rents that can then be politically allocated (Bates 1981). When supply is not equal to demand, shortages emerge that can function as great political resources to those who can allocate them. This is also consistent with the empirical findings in Bueno de Mesquita et al. (2003) (especially ch. 7), demonstrating that, compared with other countries, small coalition systems have higher economic rents from illegal activities, higher black market premiums, and lower economic growth. The basic reason seems to be that leaders choose policies that enhance their survival.

The basic lesson from all this can perhaps be summed up as follows: Patrimonialism creates bad policies in the form of massive economic distortions that can constitute good politics.

Hence, it is bad policies that are good politics in patrimonial regimes. Not only that, bad policies are equilibrium outcomes in order to achieve political survival of the ruler. In other words, bad governance is the consequence of a particular strategy of rule or power consolidation. No doubt there is bureaucratic corruption in many developing countries along the lines studied in much of the literature on corruption. Yet this is of second-order importance compared with the institutionalized bad governance emanating from the state itself.

Conclusion

Today, the EU asks some of its members to cut their welfare spending to affordable levels. Similarly, developing countries are asked to reform their economic policies more generally. Serious economic reforms like these are not likely to work unless they change the political equilibrium. This is so because beneficial reforms require good policies; good polices are easily blocked if they do not serve the political survival of the incumbent government; and what serves the incumbent constitutes good politics. The polemical question is why not all countries have good governance in the first place. It cannot be because the leaders don't know what good governance is. To explain bad policies one has to understand better how authority is exercised, how the capacity to formulate policies is determined, and how governments are selected and replaced – and above all how policies are chosen in order to retain power. In other words one has to study themes both from economics and from political science. Poor governance is not exogenously assigned. It is the outcome of political decisions and reflects the political institutions and sources of power in society. Such measures are often equilibrium outcomes. Policies are chosen by those with political power and they have large impacts on the incentive structure of society. Neither economics nor political science has a satisfactory understanding of the circumstances leading to a political equilibrium that is conducive to economic growth and good performance. Governance reform is unlikely to be successful unless we understand the political forces that generate bad governance in the first place – unless we understand both political and economic processes.

Notes

1 I am grateful for comments by Jan Terje Faarlund and Carl Henrik Knutsen. The paper is part of the research activities at ESOP, a research center at the Department of Economics, University of Oslo, funded by the Research Council of Norway.
2 The work of James Robinson has also been highly influential for the understanding of the role of bad governance both in economics and in political science. See Robinson (1998) for a simple early exposition, and the many articles written jointly with Daron Acemoglu, reviewed in Baland et al. (2010).
3 There are also illuminating discussions on related issues of targeting in poverty programs in the papers by Besley and Kanbur (1993), Ravallion and Datt (1995), Gelbach and Pritchett (1997), De Donder and Hindriks (1998), van de Walle (1998), and others.
4 For a recent discussion on stereotyping in the media and the support for U.S. welfare programs, see Dyck and Hussey (2008).

10

DEMOCRACY AND ECONOMIC GROWTH

A changing relationship?

Carl Henrik Knutsen[1]

Introduction

The labeling of epochs is a popular exercise among historians and social scientists. Speaking of "the age of X" implies that X is considered not just a feature, but one of the central features of an epoch. The last three decades could be assigned different Xs. Plausible suggestions include "the age of globalization," "the age of information," or perhaps "the age of democracy" (see, for example, Fukuyama 1992). Economic indicators, such as volumes of trade and foreign direct investment (FDI), show that the international economy has become more integrated since 1980. The international political environment has also changed, especially since 1989 with the collapse of communist regimes in Eastern Europe and elsewhere, including the Soviet Union. More countries have become democratic after these events, boosting Huntington's (1991) third wave of democratization, which started in the mid-1970s. Most of the powerful global actors, including the only remaining superpower, are now democratic.

The integration of the world economy with increased trade and investment flows, as well as better opportunities for cross-border diffusion of technologies, is likely to have effects on national economic growth rates (see, for example, Romer 1990). However, whether these opportunities are properly utilized to spur national growth may be dependent on national political institutions (see, for example, Rodrik 1999). Therefore, an interesting question is: which types of political regimes can best manage the post-Cold War international political climate and a "globalized world economy" in order to generate high national economic growth? This chapter investigates the economic growth effect of democracy, and whether this effect has significantly changed in recent decades. One plausible hypothesis is that the effect of democracy on economic growth has increased over the last years, because of a likely interaction effect between national political regime type and the international political-economic context. There are at least four plausible arguments for why democracy's effect on growth may have increased in later decades: (1) democracies are better at attracting FDI than dictatorships, and the volume of global FDI has increased dramatically in the last three decades; (2) democracy provides institutions that are better able to manage external shocks to the economy, for example terms of trade shocks, and this becomes increasingly important for growth as economies become more open; (3) democracies are better able to create high productivity growth in sectors crucial to a modern knowledge economy; and (4) the international political environment has become more hostile to dictatorships after 1989, and there may be increasing economic benefits to being a poor democracy relative to a poor dictatorship, for example because of more available aid and loans.

The chapter first reviews the literature and main theoretical arguments on democracy's economic effects. Thereafter, an empirical analysis drawing on data from more than 150 countries, with time series going back to 1820 for some countries, is presented. The analysis finds that democracy has a significantly positive impact on economic growth, at least after 1980. There is also evidence that the effect has increased over the last three decades. The chapter then presents the four explanations for why the effect of democracy on growth has likely increased in the last decades.

Democracy and economic growth

Empirical relationship

Although some early studies found a negative effect of democracy on economic growth in global samples (see Przeworski and Limongi 1993 for a review), more recent statistical studies relying on better estimation techniques and more data find either no significant effect (Burkhart and Lewis-Beck 1994; Helliwell 1994; Przeworski et al. 2000), or a positive significant effect (see, for example, Leblang 1997; Baum and Lake 2003; Bueno de Mesquita et al. 2003; Doucouliagos and Ulubasoglu 2008). This chapter replicates some of the positive significant results from Knutsen (forthcoming), based on the most extensive data sample available.

The above-mentioned studies investigate the *general* impact of democracy on economic growth. However, there is another equally interesting aspect to the relationship: dictatorships show more variation in their growth performances than democracies (see, for example, Rodrik 2000; Besley and Kudamatsu 2007; Knutsen forthcoming). This is no coincidence. Power concentration in the hands of a small political elite, and the lack of other political or institutional "veto players" (Tsebelis 2002), means that the elite can more easily push through whatever policies it wants. Fewer constraints on government generate more policy variation. For example, governmental autonomy from broad population groups may be used as in Singapore or the Soviet Union of the 1930s to amass capital investment to gross domestic product (GDP) ratios above 0.4. It may, however, also provide the opportunity to realize a "Cultural Revolution" or a "Great Leap Forward," as Mao did, or to slaughter citizens with higher education or glasses, as in Pol Pot's Cambodia. How dictators use their autonomy seems to rely systematically on incentives generated by institutional and contextual factors, which determine whether it is in the self-interest of power-hungry or greedy dictators to conduct productive or destructive policies (e.g. Robinson 1998; Olson 2003; Bueno de Mesquita et al. 2003; Acemoglu and Robinson 2006a; Knutsen forthcoming). However, policy choice may also to a certain extent rely on individual-specific characteristics of the ruler (Wintrobe 1998; Jones and Olken 2005). In any case, dictatorships dominate the list of both "growth miracles" and especially "growth disasters" after World War II (Przeworski et al. 2000).

Democracy as a meta-institution

As shown above, the data suggest a higher mean and a lower variance in demo-cratic growth rates compared with dictatorial. But *why* does democracy matter for economic growth?[2] Democracy affects economic outcomes via several different channels because it is a "meta-institution" (Rodrik 2000; see also Knutsen forth-coming). That is, democracy systematically affects other institutional structures, such as those related to controlling corruption and protecting property rights, that are again vital for economic outcomes (see, for example, North 1990; Knack and Keefer 1995). Moreover, as different political regime types generate very different incentive structures for politicians in power, and also affect politician selection, politicians promote different policies under democracy and dictatorship. In democracies, it may be personally beneficial, in terms of political survival, for politicians to promote policies that increase the supply of productive public goods (Bueno de Mesquita et al. 2003). In many dictatorships, however, public goods are a waste of resources that could be used for bribing the military or other crucial supporters to avoid a coup. Thus, political regimes matter for economic outcomes because democratic politicians systematically tend to choose different economic policies from dictatorial politicians.

Furthermore, economic institutions and policies affect the more immediate sources of economic growth, namely different inputs and changes in efficiency (see, for example, Barro and Sala-i-Martin 2004). When it comes to inputs, labor, physical capital, and human capital are the three main categories specified in economic growth theory. Regarding how efficiently these inputs are combined to produce output, one may distinguish between efficiency increases stemming from changes in the economy's resource allocation (static efficiency), and efficiency increases from technological change (dynamic efficiency). To sum up, political regime type matters for economic growth, as political regimes affect the structure of economic institutions and types of policies pursued. These factors again affect accumulation of inputs or efficiency.

Democracy, dictatorship, and input accumulation

Several authors argue that autocratic regimes generate higher savings rates (see, for example, Przeworski and Limongi 1993; Knutsen forthcoming) and thus increase accumulation of physical capital. In a closed economy, savings equals investments, but empirical studies have also shown a high correlation between savings and investments in open economies (Feldstein and Horioka 1980; McGrew 2007). Thus, policies that push up savings rates, through household, business, or government saving, are likely to increase also physical capital investment as share of GDP. Examples of such policies vary from tax incentives on saving to outright bans of certain consumer products, such as tourism in South Korea under military rule (Chang 2006). Autocratic regimes are allegedly better able to promote such policies. The reason, it is argued, is their relative isolation or autonomy from the regular citizen, who under democracy is both consumer and voter. If governments are more far-sighted, and value economic growth higher than regular citizens, who prefer consumption right now, dictatorships will take tougher measures to increase savings rates than democratic governments soon up for re-election. Empirical studies do find some evidence that dictatorships have higher savings and investment rates than democracies (e.g. Tavares and Wacziarg 2001; Przeworski et al. 2000; Knutsen forthcoming).

Although dictatorships may on average save and invest more in physical capital, democracies seem to have a human capital advantage. Human capital – the skills and abilities of the workforce – is considered by many economists to be as important for income level and economic growth as physical capital (e.g. Lucas 1988; Mankiw et al. 1992). Education and health care are the most important factors affecting a population's human capital level. There are plausible theoretical arguments indicating that democracies are better at promoting policies that yield decent-quality schooling and health care for broader segments of the population (see, for example, Lake and Baum 2001; Baum and Lake 2003; Bueno de Mesquita et al. 2003; Stasavage 2005; Lindert 2005; Acemoglu and Robinson 2006b). Democratic governments are more responsive to demands from broad segments of the population, and not only to economic elites, the military, or other groups that may be especially influential under dictatorship. Education and health care for the general populace tend to be underprioritized in dictatorships. In these regimes, allocation of private benefits and handouts to a selected few supporters are often prioritized over a broad-coverage school or health-care system. Indeed, empirical evidence shows that democracy enhances human capital accumulation (Lake and Baum 2001; Bueno de Mesquita et al. 2003; Stasavage 2005; Lindert 2005), and several studies indicate that this is one of the most important channels through which democracy enhances economic growth (Baum and Lake 2003; Tavares and Wacziarg 2001; Doucouliagos and Ulubasoglu 2008). Democratic workers, because of higher human capital levels, are thus more productive than dictatorial ones. This is indicated by democratic workers' higher wages (Rodrik 1998b; Przeworski et al. 2000).

Democracy, dictatorship, and efficiency

Certain policies (e.g. micro-economic reforms and certain industrial policies) or institutional changes (strengthening of property rights, competition authorities, or institutions that control corruption) may positively improve productivity by enforcing a more efficient allocation of scarce resources. However, such policies and reforms, despite being efficiency enhancing, may be politically costly, as entrenched interest groups may lose from reform (see, for example, Hiscox 2007). Olson (1982) argues that democracies are prone to special interest group capture. This may lead to stagnation in status quo, and economic growth can be sacrificed for the protection of specific business sectors or pivotal voting blocs whose interests are not aligned with economic growth. One argument is that some autocratic regimes may be better at promoting politically painful, but ultimately efficiency-enhancing, economic reforms. These regimes are more autonomous from popular pressures, and are thus able to fend off reform opposition (Przeworski and Limongi 1993; Wade 1990; Evans 1995; Leftwich 2000).

However, as Bueno de Mesquita et al. (2003) point out, all political leaders are dependent on supporters for staying in power. Dictators may be less willing to promote efficiency-enhancing reforms if their "winning coalition" loses from reform. More generally, dictators often increase survival chances or personal wealth by promoting inefficient policies (see Robinson 1998; Bueno de Mesquita et al. 2003; Acemoglu and Robinson 2006a; Knutsen forthcoming). Rodrik (1999) presents another argument for why dictatorships may be worse at promoting efficiency-enhancing reforms: Unlike democracies, dictatorships often lack institutional frameworks that allow actors to negotiate side-payments and compensation for those that lose from reform. Thus, entrenched groups often have stronger incentives for fighting against reforms, such as land reforms or free trade reforms, under dictatorship.

However, over time, the most important source of efficiency increases, and indeed economic growth, is technological change (see, for example, Romer 1990; Helpman 2004). Knutsen (forthcoming) finds empirical evidence for the hypothesis that democracies have higher technology-induced economic growth. As Halperin and colleagues (2005: 14) argue, democracies "realize superior developmental performance because they tend to be more adaptable." In democracies, actors engage more freely and vigorously in gathering new information, debating, adjusting positions, and revising pre-existing knowledge. Civil liberties are especially relevant for these processes. Free and open debate is instrumentally important for eliminating unfounded knowledge and for opening up to new ideas (Mill 1974). This includes foreign ideas, which are essential to technological change.

Evolution in a dynamic economy is "the outcome of a constant interaction between variety and selection" (Verspagen 2005: 496). Selection reduces variety because more efficient techniques are adopted through learning or through out-competing more inefficient methods of production. In order to sustain variety, a steady introduction of novel ideas is required. Freedom of speech and open idea exchange under democracy enhance both variety and selection, as introduction of new ideas and learning processes in the economic sphere relies on possibilities for unrestricted collection and processing of information. Dictatorships often restrict such possibilities. For example, restrictions on cell phones and internet usage have been exercised in several dictatorships (e.g. Hachigian 2002). This hurts not only democracy movements, but also national economies.

To briefly sum up the arguments above, democracy may enhance growth through increasing human capital and the rate of technological change, whereas it may reduce growth through its negative effect on the savings rate, and thus on capital investment. When it comes to the propensity to generate efficiency-enhancing reforms, there are plausible arguments pointing in different directions.

However, the effect of democracy on growth may depend on contextual factors, for example global political and economic factors. The last two to three decades have seen important changes to the international economy and international political system. These changes may contribute to a changed aggregate effect of democracy on economic growth through tilting the relative importance of the various channels and mechanisms described above. For example, if human capital has become relatively more important for generating national growth in the modern, global economy, this may impact on the aggregate relationship between democracy and growth. Moreover, contextual changes may impact on democracy's ability to enhance input accumulation or efficiency through a particular channel. For example, the increasing global integration of capital markets may reduce dictatorships' advantage in physical capital accumulation, as democracies may attract FDI to compensate for lower domestic savings. In the section entitled "Why democracy's growth effect may have changed," I present four arguments that indicate a larger, positive effect of democracy in the last couple of decades compared with previous decades.

Thus, a possible *interaction effect* between the international political economic environment *and* national political regime type *on* economic growth may have altered the economic benefits of democracy over time. More precisely, there are strong reasons to believe that the economic benefits of democracy have increased since about 1980, with the specific changes that have taken place in the international political and economic context. Figure 10.1 illustrates the potential relationship.

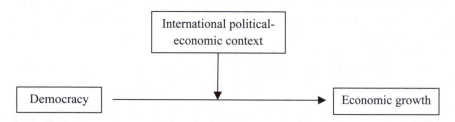

FIGURE 10.1 The contingent relationship between democracy and economic growth.

Empirical analysis

Data

In this section I test whether there is a general relationship between democracy and growth *and* whether the relationship has changed over time. I use data from more than 150 countries, with some countries having time series going all the way from the 1820s to 2003. To measure democracy I use the Polity-Index (PI) from the Polity IV data set (Marshall and Jaggers 2002). The PI goes from -10 (most dicta-torial) to 10 (most democratic). The components of the index are competitiveness of executive recruitment, openness of executive recruitment, constraints on the chief executive, competitiveness of political participation, and regulation of politi-cal participation (Marshall and Jaggers 2002: 12–15). I leave out country-years that experienced interregnum periods (Marshall and Jaggers 2002: 17). These are mainly periods of internal anarchy or civil war. I also leave out country-years that are coded as "foreign interruption," which basically is foreign occupation. GDP data and population data are gathered from Maddison (2006), and go back to 1820. The GDP data are purchasing power parity (PPP) adjusted (1990 U.S.$). Maddison's estimates contain large measurement errors.[3] Despite this, Maddison (2007: 294) claims that:

> [f]or the epoch of capitalist economic growth back to 1820, quantitative eco-nomic historians have made great progress in measuring growth performance . . . There is still a need to fill gaps and cross-check existing estimates, but the broad contours of world development in this period are not under serious challenge.

I include 832 country-years for which data on GDP per capita growth or level or population level are constructed by interpolation, assuming constant GDP per capita and population growth rates between years with recorded data (see Knutsen forthcoming).

Some descriptive statistics

The number of democracies has grown over the better part of the last two centu-ries despite some periods of setbacks, referred to by Huntington (1991) as reverse waves. Since the late 1970s, the growth in the number of democracies has acceler-ated. Notwithstanding concerns in the late 1990s that the number of democracies would regress, as many new and unstable democracies from the early 1990s were likely to face trouble, Figure 10.2 shows that the number of democracies (accord-ing to Polity) continued to grow, at least until 2004. Despite claims by journalists, academics, and others that the age of democracy is receding and that we are facing a new age of authoritarianism (e.g. Freeland 2008; Gat 2007; see even Diamond 2008), the data do not support this view. This shows the danger of generalizing

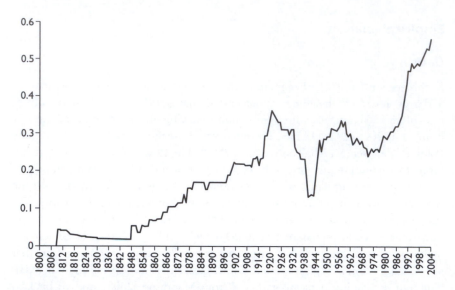

FIGURE 10.2 Relatively democratic countries (Polity-Index ≥6) as share of all countries, 1800 to 2004. Source: Marshall and Jaggers (2002).

from short-term political developments in a few cases such as Putin's Russia and Chavez' Venezuela. Even in Africa, where several analysts have predicted quite strongly that the third wave would be reversed (Bratton and van de Walle 1997), the empirical evidence seems to point in the opposite direction: There are more electoral democracies now than in the early 1990s, and even protection of civil liberties is on the increase (Lindberg 2006).

Figure 10.3 shows the smoothed three-year average GDP per capita growth rate for relatively democratic and relatively dictatorial countries from 1852 to 2003. Although there are no very clear, systematic trends easily discernible from this figure, dictatorships have, on average, very seldom outgrown democracies with a large margin. From the mid-nineteenth century onwards, democracies have on average mostly had about equal or higher growth rates than dictatorships. It is interesting for the purpose of this study to note that the period between 1980 and the mid-1990s was a period when democracies clearly outpaced dictatorships. However, to investigate whether the effect of democracy on growth increased in this period, we turn to more stringent analysis.

Regression analysis

In this section I will investigate whether the effect of democracy on growth has changed over time. However, let me first present an analysis of the (general) effect, without taking into account any potential changes over time.

The generally higher average growth rates for democracies, recorded in Figure 10.3, may be due to other factors systematically affecting both regime

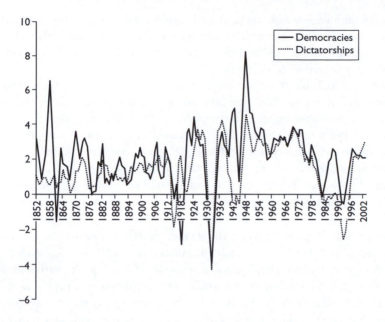

FIGURE 10.3 Three-year smoothed average GDP per capita growth for relatively democratic (Polity-Index ≥6) and relatively dictatorial (Polity-Index ≤5) countries from 1852 to 2003. Sources: Marshall and Jaggers (2002) and Maddison (2006).

type and economic growth. One should thus control for such factors. Below I use a version of ordinary least squares (OLS) with panel-corrected standard errors (see Beck and Katz 1995) that takes into account heteroskedasticity and contemporaneous correlation between panels and autocorrelation within panels (AR1). The technique allows me to base inferences on both cross-sectional and intra-national variation. The number of country-year observations utilized in this analysis supersedes that of earlier studies on the subject: There are 9,295 observations from 154 existing and previous countries, with the longest time series extending from 1822 to 2003.

Along with the PI, I enter several control variables that may affect both regime type and economic growth; I enter log of regime duration as a proxy for political stability, and the regime duration data are from Polity. Furthermore, I control for log of GDP per capita and log of population size, based on data from Maddison (2006). Moreover, I control for ethnic fractionalization, based on data from Alesina et al. (2003). These data are unfortunately time-invariant. I also enter geographical region dummies, dummies for historical colonizer, and plurality religion dummies from Knutsen (2007), to control for different political-historical, geographical, and cultural factors. The plurality religion dummies are based on relatively recent data, and are unfortunately also time-invariant. I also enter dummies for each decade (the 1990s are extended until 2003) to control for time-specific factors that may influence both regime type and economic growth; for example, the international political economic context may impact on growth rates through other channels than affecting the relationship between democracy and growth.[4] All independent variables are lagged with two years.

Column 2 in Table 10.1 shows the estimated effect of democracy on economic growth when assuming that the effect has been constant over time. The model indicates a clear positive effect of democracy. The estimated effect is around 1 percentage point extra annual GDP per capita growth when going from most dictatorial to most democratic on the PI. There is, according to these results, a substantial positive economic growth effect from democracy. In Knutsen (forthcoming) I show that this effect is quite robust to different specifications, including control for country-specific effects, non-linearity of effect, and endogeneity of democracy.

However, I still have to investigate whether the effect of democracy on growth has changed over time.[5] To test whether there has been a significant change in the effect in recent decades, I ran a new model with all of the variables in the model above, but including an interaction term consisting of a pre- or post-1990 dummy multiplied with the PI. Including this term allows me to conduct a so-called Chow-test (see, for example, Greene 2003), which tests for structural breaks in effects. If there is a significantly different effect of democracy on growth after 1990, the interaction term should be statistically significant.

The empirical picture, according to the model reported in column 3 in Table 10.1, seems to be one of continuity rather than change. There is a relatively substantial and positive growth effect of democracy, which at least has not decreased after 1990. However, there is no significant difference in the effect of democracy on growth between the pre- and post-1990 periods.

However, 1990 is an artificial breaking point, and I should thus run Chow-tests with different break points to test the robustness of the result above. I therefore tested models that use 1980 and 1985, rather than 1990, as break points. Interestingly, the results change. The "baseline" effect of PI remains positive and significant. However, there are now indications that the effect has increased in later decades: The increase in effect of democracy on growth is significant at the 10 percent level when 1985 is used as the break point, and at the 5 percent level when 1980 is used as the break point. Thus, there is some evidence for the hypothesis that democracy has had a more positive effect on growth in later decades, as the world economy has become more integrated. However, this does not mean that democracy was a drag on economic growth rates before. Democracy seems to always have had a positive effect on growth, but the effect has become stronger since around 1980. Table 10.1 shows the OLS with panel-corrected standard errors (PCSE) models, including models with Chow interaction terms. Regarding the models' control variables, we see from Table 10.1 that there are few other robust variables affecting growth than democracy. However, initially poorer countries grow faster, everything else being equal, and so do ethnically more homogeneous countries. Moreover, the Spanish colony dummy is positive and robust, whereas the indigenous plurality religion, sub-Saharan Africa, and Latin America dummies are negative and robust.

As mentioned above, the positive effect of democracy on growth in models assuming constant effect over time is very robust (see Knutsen forthcoming). However, the results for models incorporating Chow interaction terms are not robust to choice of econometric technique. Random effects and fixed effects models, which control for country-specific factors, find an insignificant *general* effect of PI at the 5 percent level, whereas the Chow terms are positive and significant even at the 0.1 percent level when 1980 and 1985 are used as structural break points.[6] Thus, when controlling for country-fixed effects, the results indicate that democracy had no significant effect on economic growth prior to the 1980s, whereas it has had a significant, positive effect thereafter. According to the point estimates from these models, the post-1980 and post-1985 effects of going from most dictatorial to most democratic on the PI are between 1.5 percent and 2 percent extra annual GDP per capita growth. Thus, more stringent models controlling for country-specific factors show solid support for the hypothesis that democracy's growth effect has increased over time.

To sum up, this analysis, conducted on the largest data set used in the literature on democracy and economic growth, shows that democracy matters for economic growth. The effect is positive, and seems to have been so since the nineteenth century if we are to believe models that allow for cross-country comparisons. However, if we believe that fixed effects models that control for country-specific characteristics are more appropriate, there is no evidence that the effect of democracy on economic growth was positive before the last three decades. But there is evidence that the effect has been significantly positive, and quite large, since 1980. There is some evidence from OLS with PCSE models that the positive effect has become stronger in the years after 1980, although the evidence of a structural break in the effect is mixed. In any case, the empirical evidence unequivocally implies that the effect of democracy on growth has been positive *at least* since 1980.

Why democracy's growth effect may have changed

Although the results above were not completely robust, the evidence is sufficiently strong to start theorizing about the underlying reasons for the likely *increase in effect* of democracy on growth since about 1980. Multiple potential explanations may be put forth to explain the results. In the following sections I propose four plausible explanations that may all have contributed to the increase in the aggregate effect of democracy on growth. I do not test these explanations' relative importance here, but leave this for future research.

Increase in foreign direct investment

As seen above, dictatorships may have higher domestic savings rates. In an open economy, there is no necessary relationship between savings and investment,

TABLE 10.1 Results from OLS PCSE analysis

Variable/model	Time-invariant effect	1990 structural break	1985 structural break	1980 structural break
	b (t-value)	b (t-value)	b (t-value)	b (t-value)
Polity	0.050*** (3.62)	0.049*** (3.24)	0.038** (2.49)	0.031* (1.96)
PolityChow		0.005 (0.13)	0.053* (1.72)	0.064** (2.30)
Ln GDP pc	−0.728*** (−3.01)	−0.730*** (−3.03)	−0.751*** (−3.12)	−0.754*** (−3.13)
Ln population	0.035 (0.58)	0.034 (0.58)	0.03 (0.50)	0.026 (0.44)
Ln regime duration	−0.044 (−0.71)	−0.044 (−0.70)	−0.036 (−0.57)	−0.032 (−0.51)
Ethnic fract.	−0.910** (−2.54)	−0.904** (−2.54)	−0.855** (−2.40)	−0.850** (−2.38)
British–American	0.089 (0.31)	0.093 (0.32)	0.151 (0.53)	0.173 (0.60)
French	−0.525* (−1.77)	−0.524* (−1.77)	−0.499* (−1.68)	−0.478 (−1.60)
Portuguese	0.81 (1.55)	0.813 (1.56)	0.861* (1.65)	0.910* (1.76)
Spanish	1.180** (2.18)	1.185** (2.19)	1.256** (2.34)	1.301** (2.43)
Belgian	−0.674 (−0.64)	−0.664 (−0.63)	−0.572 (−0.55)	−0.533 (−0.51)
Sunni	−0.915 (−1.28)	−0.91 (−1.27)	−0.865 (−1.20)	−0.813 (−1.12)
Shia	−1.972* (−1.87)	−1.969* (−1.86)	−1.895* (−1.77)	−1.832* (−1.72)
Catholic	−0.019 (−0.02)	−0.02 (−0.02)	0.004 (0.00)	0.047 (0.05)

Protestant+	−0.208 (−0.26)	−0.208 (−0.26)	−0.17 (−0.22)	−0.122 (−0.15)
Orthodox	−0.241 (−0.24)	−0.244 (−0.24)	−0.243 (−0.24)	−0.208 (−0.21)
Hindu	−0.521 (−0.59)	−0.521 (−0.59)	−0.532 (−0.60)	−0.533 (−0.60)
Buddhist+	0.888 (0.97)	0.896 (0.98)	0.968 (1.04)	0.99 (1.06)
Indigenous	−1.630** (−2.07)	−1.630** (−2.08)	−1.611** (−2.03)	−1.564** (−1.96)
E. Eur. & Sov.	−0.125 (−0.28)	−0.128 (−0.28)	−0.156 (−0.35)	−0.148 (−0.33)
S.S. Africa	−1.490** (−2.54)	−1.495*** (−2.58)	−1.529*** (−2.61)	−1.513*** (−2.58)
Asia-Pacific	−1.184 (−1.55)	−1.192 (−1.58)	−1.247* (−1.65)	−1.223 (−1.61)
MENA	0.777 (1.44)	0.777 (1.45)	0.804 (1.49)	0.836 (1.55)
Latin America	−2.124*** (−3.63)	−2.132*** (−3.67)	−2.246*** (−3.88)	−2.297*** (−3.98)
n	9,295	9,295	9,295	9,295

Notes

Decade dummies and constant omitted from table; GDP per capita growth as dependent variable.
Buddhist+, Buddhist, Confucian, and Taoist; Ln GDP pc, Ln GDP per capita; MENA, Middle East and North Africa; Protestant+, Protestant and Anglican; S.S. Africa, sub-Saharan Africa.

*$p < 0.10$; **$p < 0.05$; ***$p < 0.01$.

although the correlation has been high historically (Feldstein and Horioka 1980). With the integration of global capital markets and increased cross-border mobility of capital, the link between domestic saving and investment may be weakening (see, for example, McGrew 2007). This may also impact on the effect of democracy on growth. The expansion of global FDI flows has been tremendous since 1980, as shown in Chapter 1 in this volume. This means that countries with low savings rates, such as the United States, can presently mitigate capital scarcity more easily than before through attracting foreign capital. Foreign investors are likely to invest where expected profitability is high and risk is low (see Hveem et al. 2009), and the institutional and policy determinants that enhance FDI may not be the same as those increasing domestic saving. For example, low corruption and strong protection of property rights attract FDI (see, for example, Hveem et al. 2009; Li 2009; Blonigen 2005), and democracy, at least when consolidated, enhances both control of corruption and property rights protection (e.g. Clague et al. 2003; Rock 2009; Knutsen 2011). Thus, different studies find a positive effect of democracy on FDI (e.g. Busse and Hefeker 2007); dictatorships may force their citizens to save more, but a better investment climate in democracies attracts more FDI. The increasing total global volume of FDI, and the combination of dictatorship's savings advantage and democracy's FDI advantage, indicate that the perhaps most important growth advantage for dictatorships has been reduced over recent decades.[7] This may be a vital factor underlying the results recorded above.

Economic integration and external shocks

Democracy may improve economic performance in open economies because democracies provide institutional forums for dealing with external economic shocks. This argument is presented in detail in Rodrik (1999) and will be sketched out only cursorily here. Rodrik argues that successfully adjusting to negative external shocks (for example terms-of-trade shocks), and more generally implementing tough economic reforms and policies to reap the benefits from economic openness, require forums for negotiation and ensuring credible policies for compensating likely losers. If not, losers will fight hard to retain the status quo, and a high conflict level between different groups winning and losing from economic openness will have negative economic impacts.

Policies that compensate losers may be social welfare policies that enable different actors to take risks in the market place, and re-education programs that allow workers in inefficient sectors to retool for other jobs. Such policies are more common in democracies (see Lindert 2005). Rodrik (1999) found that democracies performed relatively well *after* the oil crisis in the early 1970s. According to Rodrik, the negotiation and compromise attributes of democracy became increasingly important as different economies opened up and the world's product and capital markets became more integrated, especially when the global economy hit hard times. The relevance of this channel, through which democracy likely enhances growth, has probably increased even further after 1989 (the last year of data used in Rodrik's regressions), as world trade and foreign direct investment have increased further in this period. In other words, the negotiation and conflict-solving properties of democracy may be one important factor for explaining the empirical results above, as these have become increasingly important as the global economy has opened up.

However, it should be noted that some dictatorial regimes, mostly in Asia, have been successful in promoting efficiency-enhancing open economy policies. Reforms that boosted certain exporting sectors were pushed through in, for example, Taiwan and South Korea (see, for example, Wade 1990; Evans 1995). The literature on Asian autocratic growth miracles discusses several explanations, ranging from state and regime autonomy, to lack of entrenched interest groups opposing reforms, to external security threats inducing reform (see Wade 1990; Evans 1995; Cho and Kim 1998; Leftwich 2000; Doner et al. 2005; Knutsen forthcoming). Thus, several authors have argued that, at least in particular instances, dictatorships are better able to make the tough political decisions necessary to take advantage of opportunities in an open, global economy.

Knowledge economy

The main sources of economic growth, at least in developed countries, may increasingly be knowledge-related factors (see, for example, Florida and Kenney 1993; OECD 1996; Houghton and Sheehan 2000). This may, for example, be due to the nature of several specific sectors that have become increasingly important (as shares of global GDP) over the last decades, such as information technology and biotechnology. Others have argued more generally that the nature of production, across the board, is changing in a direction that requires less standardization and more flexibility and expert knowledge (e.g. Hirst and Zeitlin 1997). This may imply an increasing importance of human capital, and decreasing importance of physical capital. Historically, the leader of the first industrial revolution, Great Britain, was at the time one of the laggards in education among Western European countries and settler colonies (Lindert 2005). The premium to human capital investment has likely risen over time, as production technologies have changed. There are good reasons to believe that more complex production technologies are complementary to a high human capital level (Kremer 1993). Thus, human capital formation, and perhaps also technological innovation and diffusion, may be more important as sources of growth than previously, because of the nature of modern production techniques.

If economic growth depends more and more upon diffusion of technology and the workforce's skills rather than accumulation of physical capital, this may have contributed to democracy increasing its growth advantage over time, as different studies cited above indicate democracies are better at generating human capital and technological change. The argument can be sketched out as follows:[8]

- P1: Formation of human capital and innovation and diffusion of technologies have in recent decades increased in importance as sources of economic growth.
- P2: Democracies have a "comparative advantage" in generating this type of economic growth.
- C: Democracy has in recent decades increased its effect on economic growth.

P2 is backed up by some fairly strong empirical evidence (e.g. Baum and Lake 2003; Doucouliagos and Ulubasoglu 2008; Knutsen forthcoming). However, despite much literature on the new knowledge economy (see, for example, OECD 1996; Houghton and Sheehan 2000), P1 is still an uncertain hypothesis. Physical capital still matters for transitional growth, and technological change and ideas for more efficient organization have always been important for long-term growth (see, for example, Mokyr 1990; North 1990). Thus, we may not conclude with certainty that this is the main explanation for the result recorded above.

The international political context

Fukuyama (1992) claimed that the post-Cold War era would be the era of liberal democracy and free market economies. Although Fukuyama may have exaggerated, the number of democracies (and market economies) has increased substantially since the 1980s. The Berlin Wall came down in 1989; and in 1991 so did the Soviet Union. These international political changes may also affect the linkage between democracy and economic growth, particularly for developing countries. After 1991, the world's only remaining superpower was the democratic United States. Moreover, the United States and democratic European states no longer urgently needed to ally with dictators in developing countries against the "communist threat." This was one of the main reasons why development aid and loans (both from rich nations and from important international financial institutions) to developing countries, as well as trade agreements, were increasingly conditioned on democratic practices and other domestic good governance practices (see, for example, Killick et al. 1998; Pronk 2004).

These factors may imply that, after the end of the Cold War, being a poor democracy has had some economic advantages relative to being a poor dictatorship because of the international political context. A lack of democratic institutions and practices may mean a missed opportunity to join the EU and its large market for Eastern European countries, the falling away of aid or loan opportunities for developing countries, or an economic boycott from some of the major economic powers, such as Myanmar and North Korea have experienced. These are channels through which being autocratic likely depresses economic growth. Communist dictatorships, such as Cuba and North Korea, suffered directly from the collapse of the "Second World," as their major economic partners disappeared. The Cuban and North Korean economies shrank dramatically in the 1990s. Moreover, the end of the Cold War stopped the flow of Soviet money to African authoritarian strongmen, and the United States (as well as France and Britain) was no longer willing to finance "their" corrupt authoritarian regimes either; the political gains were no longer present. This resulted in the drying up of state coffers and in some instances to the actual collapse of African states, leaving anarchy or civil war in place (Reno 1998; see also Clapham 1996). Already dismal economies such as Sierra Leone, Congo, Somalia, and Liberia deteriorated further. These factors may partially explain the result above.

However, there are also strong counterarguments to this argument. The first is that donors may apply conditionality selectively in practice, and recipients may be able to circumvent conditionality demands (see, for example, Killick et al. 1998; Pronk 2004). Moreover, many argue that foreign aid is largely ineffective in promoting economic development (see, for example, Erixon 2005; but see Riddell 2007). *If* this is true, the argument related to access to conditional aid has little relevance for democracy's increased growth advantage over time.

Conclusion

This chapter has discussed the effect of democracy on economic growth. It reviewed different general arguments on democracy's economic effects, and introduced the hypothesis that the effect of democracy on growth has increased in later decades. The chapter then tested this hypothesis, and the hypothesis of a general positive effect of democracy on growth, on a cross-section time series data set. Some of the empirical models showed a general, positive effect of democracy on growth, and there was also evidence that the effect had become stronger after 1980. The chapter also introduced four potential explanations for why the effect of democracy on growth has become more positive from the 1980s onwards. From the 1980s, there have been dramatic changes to the international political context and the international economic context, with increasing prominence of information technologies, more trade, and increased cross-border capital flows. These factors may have enhanced the aggregate, positive effect of democracy on growth.

With the rise of China, the resurgence of Russia, and the financial crisis hitting the United States and Western Europe, some analysts have now started asking whether we are leaving the era of democracy and entering a new golden age for autocracy (see, for example, Freeland 2008; Gat 2007). Others have begun asking whether the Washington Consensus is being replaced by a new Beijing Consensus (Ramo 2004). Also in the 1930s, with the Great Depression tightening its grip on Western European and North American economies, there was a debate on whether democracy (and capitalism) was incompatible with high growth rates. Several observers professed that harsher systems such as those in the Soviet Union and Germany were better at generating economic growth. A strong leader and tight governmental control over policies were seen as remedies for getting out of recession, but perhaps also for boosting long-term growth (see the examples and discussions in Hayek 1944). However, the concentration of power in Germany led that country into a devastating war that crushed the country's physical and human capital stock, and, ultimately, the Soviet command system failed economically. Here is one lesson from the debate in the 1930s: We should be wary of generalizing from some dictatorships' high short-term growth rates to the economic advantage of dictatorship. Nevertheless, this is happening today with the rise of China. As Amartya Sen (1999) pointed out more than ten years ago, the trade-off between political freedom and economic prosperity is not supported by stringent empirical evidence. To the contrary, this chapter has shown that democracy goes together with economic growth, perhaps especially in today's world.

Notes

1 Thanks to Christina Koop and Dag Harald Claes for valuable comments and suggestions. Thanks also to John Huber for valuable comments and suggestions regarding an older working paper dealing with very similar topics.
2 I have reviewed different arguments on democracy and economic growth elsewhere (Knutsen 2006, forthcoming; see also, for example, Sirowy and Inkeles 1990; Przeworski and Limongi 1993; Halperin et al. 2005).
3 See Maddison (2006: 169–228) for a description of the sources and procedures used for estimation. Unsystematic measurement errors in independent variables generate attenuation biases (Greene 2003: 83–90). If there is unsystematic measurement error in the PI, the democracy coefficient will likely be biased toward zero. The dependent variable, annual growth in GDP per capita, is likely measured with an error. If this error is unsystematic, it will be more difficult to find significant regression coefficients, for example for the PI.
4 See Knutsen (forthcoming) for a further description and justification of the choice of these control variables.
5 Indeed, a previous meta-study showed that the data sample's time span was important for determining whether a study found a positive, negative, or insignificant effect of democracy on growth (Doucouliagos and Ulubasoglu 2008). Already Przeworski and Limongi (1993) noted that more recent studies tended to find a positive significant effect of democracy on growth, whereas older studies more often found a negative effect. Przeworski and Limongi (1993), without being explicit, seem to indicate that this may be due to academic fashions and normative convictions of analysts changing over time. However, it may also be due to a real change in effect of democracy on economic growth over time, and more specifically that it has become more positive.
6 Tables with these results are available at http://folk.uio.no/carlhk/.
7 However, a high domestic savings level still means the opportunity for actors to reap benefits from investing elsewhere in the global economy. Repatriated profits may be used to further spur domestic investment, and a capital account surplus may be beneficial for countries in times of financial crisis (e.g. Stiglitz 2006).
8 One counterargument is that knowledge-driven growth is first and foremost of relevance to already rich countries. To poor countries, economic growth may still depend largely on the ability to accumulate physical capital. However, some argue that technological change is the main driving force behind growth also in poorer countries (e.g. Easterly 2001), and empirical studies indicate a vital role for human capital and technology when explaining income differences globally (e.g. Mankiw et al. 1992; Klenow and Rodriguez-Clare 1997).

11

FDI-ASSISTED INDUSTRIAL DEVELOPMENT AND EU ENLARGEMENT[1]

Rajneesh Narula and Christian Bellak

Introduction

Policy makers in most European countries consider inward foreign direct investment (FDI) as an indispensable part of their industrial development strategy. Many of the less economically developed, more "peripheral" economies of the EU-15, such as Greece, Spain, Portugal, and Ireland (referred to here as the "cohesion" countries), followed this approach. Partly as a result of their success, these policies have been pursued much more explicitly by the new member states (NMS) and those wishing to join, a large number of both groups being located in Central and Eastern Europe (CEE) (referred to in this chapter as either the accession countries or CEE countries, irrespective of their membership status). Although this chapter focuses on the accession countries as a group, we acknowledge that this classification subsumes important differences between several subgroups which are themselves made up of heterogeneous countries. Important subgroups include the twelve new member states that joined in 2004, the two new members that joined in 2008, namely Bulgaria and Romania, and other candidate countries such as Croatia or Turkey. However, our aim is to discuss the broader aspects of the role of FDI in industrial development, the principles of which, in our estimation, are broadly similar and relevant to all countries globally, although there may be differences in specific policy implementation given their specific stage of development. This chapter will discuss the costs, benefits, opportunities, and limitations of an FDI-based industrial development strategy in the accession and candidate countries.

The literature on FDI-assisted development is one that has evolved much more thoroughly in the context of developing countries (see contributions to Narula and Lall 2006 for a review). Many (but not all) of the challenges that face the peripheral economies of Europe in pursuing an FDI-based industrial policy have increasingly much in common with those that many developing countries have faced in the past, although cross-fertilization between the two literatures has been sparse.

We will attempt to raise some of these issues, framing these within the context and particular challenges that derive from EU integration. We will focus on discussing the policy issues and challenges that face accession and cohesion countries, applying lessons that by now have become mainstream in the parallel discussion of FDI-assisted development in the developing world. Our attention will primarily be on FDI in the manufacturing sector, despite the fact that a large share of FDI in the accession countries is carried out in the services sector of the countries in question. However, despite its smaller share the manufacturing sector has considerably greater economic and political significance for at least two reasons. First, the manufacturing sector tends to be regarded as more significant in terms of its potential to promote economic growth through spillovers and externalities (Narula and Dunning 2010). Second, a substantial part of the demand for services is derived demand from manufacturing activities (i.e. producer-related services such as banking, consulting, research and development [R&D], design).

This chapter discusses the policy options of cohesion, accession, and candidate countries for FDI-assisted development strategies in the light of the ongoing enlargement process of the European Union.

Some stylized facts about FDI-assisted development strategies

Although inward FDI does not represent the only option available to promote economic catching up, it may represent the most *efficient* option (Dunning and Narula 2004). FDI, however, is not a *sine qua non* for development. There are at least four main preconditions that need to be satisfied:

1. The kind of FDI being attracted must generate significant spillovers.
2. The domestic sector needs to develop the capacity to absorb these spillovers.
3. The FDI that is being attracted should be complementary to domestic industry rather than substitutory.
4. A regulatory and institutional environment must be developed in order to facilitate the integration of the foreign affiliates into the domestic economy.

These conditions tend to make FDI more sticky and sustainable in particular locations. It is true that the determinants of economic development are similar to the determinants of FDI, but this does not mean that there is a simple cause and effect between them. Particular types of FDI tend to be attracted to countries with certain levels of economic development and appropriate economic structures (Narula and Dunning 2010). However, simply to "pump" a country full of FDI will not catapult it to a higher stage of development. In other words, there are no *automatic* gains from FDI (see, for example, Mencinger 2003). For instance, FDI may not compensate for the low ratio of domestic savings in the host countries; nor do we know whether inward FDI will generate sufficient externalities.

We highlight two points about the significance and nature of the positive externalities of FDI. First, even if FDI were attracted through large subsidies it is unlikely to become embedded, or provide significant externalities and spillovers to the host economy, without the appropriate domestic absorptive capacity (Criscuolo and Narula 2008). From a developmental perspective, externalities matter only if they can be captured by other economic actors in the host economy. For externalities to be optimally utilized there needs to be an appropriate match between the nature of potential externalities and the absorptive capacities of domestic firms. It is ironic that the countries that receive the kinds of FDI that have the highest potential benefits vis-à-vis industrial development are those that already have a highly developed domestic absorptive capacity. In other words, domestic capacity – whether in the form of knowledge infrastructure or an efficient domestic industrial sector – remains a primary and crucial determinant of high-competence foreign affiliates (Radosevic 1999; UNCTAD 2005; Barnes and Lorentzen 2006). One of the most important lessons from the literature has been the emphasis on the failure by governments to promote their domestic sector when focusing on attracting multinational enterprises (MNEs) as the primary aspect of their industrial development strategy. If no viable domestic sector were to exist, by definition spillovers from FDI are largely irrelevant.[2] Even where domestic firms do exist, MNEs will not necessarily establish links with these firms – in a perfectly liberalized world in which market failures are minimized, MNEs have the capacity to bypass domestic firms completely. They can do so either by importing all their inputs, or by encouraging their captive suppliers from abroad to relocate.

Second, not all FDI is equal in the nature of the benefits it provides (Lall and Narula 2006). The quality of the spillovers that derive from an investment is associated with the scope and competence level of the subsidiary, and these are co-determined by a variety of factors (see Figure 11.1). These include internal factors of MNEs such as their internationalization strategy, the role of the new location in their global portfolio of subsidiaries, and the motivation of their investment, in addition to the available location-specific resources that can be used for that purpose (Benito et al. 2003). High competence levels require complementary assets that are non-generic in nature and are often associated with agglomeration effects, clusters, and the presence of highly specialized skills (Lall and Pietrobelli 2002). In other words, firms are constrained in their choice of location of high-competence subsidiaries by local resource availability. For instance, R&D activities tend to be concentrated in a few locations, because the appropriate specialized resources are associated with only a few locations. The embeddedness of firms is often a function of the duration of the MNEs' presence, as firms tend to build incrementally. MNEs most often rely on location advantages *that already exist* in the host economy, and deepening of embeddedness occurs generally in response to improvements of the domestic technological capacity. However, although the scope of activities undertaken by a subsidiary can be modified more or less instantly, developing

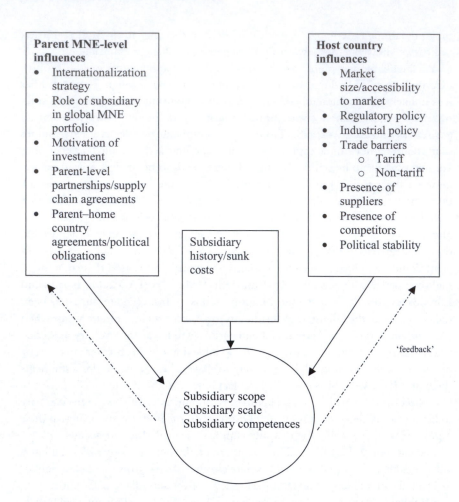

FIGURE 11.1 Determinants of the competence, scope, and scale of a foreign affiliate.

competence levels takes time. MNE investments in high value-added activities (often associated with high competence levels) have the tendency to be "sticky" (Narula and Dunning 2010).

Blomstrom and Kokko (1997) suggest that some of the host country character-istics that may influence the extent of linkages – and thereby in the longer term the extent of spillovers – are market size, local content regulations, and the size and technological capability of local firms. They argue that there is a propensity for linkages to increase over time, as the skill level of local entrepreneurs grows, new suppliers emerge, and local content increases.

In other words, government incentives and subsidies are rarely pivotal in deter-mining the scope and competence of MNEs (which normally imply higher potential for technological spillovers). MNEs do not make their proprietary assets available at the whims of governments. Instead, they tailor their investment decisions to existing market needs, and the relative quality of location advantages, but especially the skills, capabilities, and infrastructure in which the domestic economy has a comparative advantage. It is also clear that the kinds of FDI activity a country might attract (or wish to attract) are different at different stages of its industrial development (Dunning and Narula 1996b, 2004; Boudier-Bensebaa 2008). The motive of the investment is crucial in determining the extent to which linkages and externalities develop. The motive of an investment helps to determine (in conjunction with the host country-specific factors) the kind of MNE affiliate, and therefore the potential for spillovers. It is generally acknowledged that there are four main motives for foreign investment: (1) to seek natural resources; (2) to seek new markets; (3) to restructure existing foreign production through rationalization; and (4) to seek strategically related created assets (Narula and Dunning 2010). These in turn can be broadly divided into two types. The first three represent motives that are primarily asset exploiting in nature: that is, the investing company's primary purpose is to generate economic rent through the use of its existing firm-specific assets. The last is a case of asset-augmenting activity, whereby the firm wishes to acquire additional assets that protect or augment its existing created assets in some way. In general, developing countries are unlikely to attract much asset-augmenting FDI, but tend to receive FDI that is primarily resource seeking, market seeking, or efficiency seeking. Empirical evidence (e.g. Bellak et al. 2009) shows that, in the CEE countries, besides market size the level of infrastructure plays a crucial role in attracting FDI, whereas unit labor costs are comparatively less important.

The point here is that not all affiliates provide the same opportunity for spillovers. A sales office or an assembly unit may have a high turnover and employ a large staff, but the technological spillovers will be relatively fewer than, say, a manufacturing facility (see Figure 11.2). Likewise, resource-seeking activities can be capital intensive, but also provide fewer possibilities for spillovers than, say, a market-seeking type of FDI. Before economic liberalization and EU integration, MNEs responded to investment opportunities primarily by establishing truncated miniature replicas of their facilities at home, although the extent to which they were truncated varied considerably between countries. The extent of truncation was determined by a number of factors, but by far the most important determinant of truncation – and thereby the scope of activities and competence level of the subsidiary – was associated with market size, and capacity and capability of domestic industry (Dunning and Narula 2004). There is thus a hierarchy of the quality of FDI activity in Europe that reflects the stage of industrial development. At the "bottom" are countries that are at an early stage of transition (and furthest away from convergence with the EU norm, such as Romania), with a very limited domestic sector and with low domestic demand. Such countries have been host to the most truncated subsidiaries, often single-activity subsidiaries, primarily in sales and marketing, as well as natural resource extraction. The most advanced economies with domestic technological capacity (such as the core EU members) have hosted the least truncated subsidiaries, often with R&D departments. Cohesion countries (with the exception of Greece) have been in the middle.

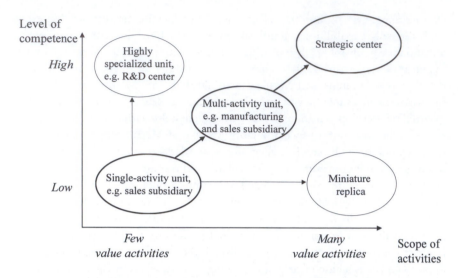

FIGURE 11.2 Different types of subsidiaries, and their relationship to scope and competence levels. Source: Benito et al. (2003).

Before globalization, MNEs were known to establish "miniature replicas" of their home country operations in foreign locations. Such miniature replica foreign subsidiaries are increasingly a concept of the past, particularly within the EU. Rationalization of activities within the single market has, in many cases, led to a downgrading of activities from truncated replica to single-activity affiliates. MNEs have taken advantage of the EU single market to rationalize production capacity in fewer locations to exploit economies of scale at the plant level, especially where local consumption patterns are not radically different to justify local capacity and where transportation costs are not prohibitive (i.e. there is a proximity–concentration trade-off). This has meant that some miniature replicas have been downgraded to sales and marketing affiliates, which can be expected to have fewer opportunities for spillovers.

The extent to which the accession countries will be able to benefit from an increase in the quality of FDI that they receive thanks to EU membership is an open question. Although there will likely be some investment in *new affiliates* resulting in new (greenfield) subsidiaries that did not exist previously,[3] there will likely also be a *downgrading of subsidiaries* (as discussed above). MNEs may divest their operations in response to better location advantages elsewhere in the EU (as Spain and Portugal are experiencing as their low-cost advantages are eroded), or reduce the intensity of operations by lowering the level of competence and/or scope of their subsidiary, and shifting from truncated replicas to single-activity affiliates. There may also be a *redistribution effect*. That is, sectors that were dominated by domestic capital are transferred to foreign ownership, particularly where domestic capitalists have failed to improve their competitive advantages to compete effectively with foreign firms. Indeed, in many of the CEE countries the share of foreign ownership in total capital stock is already typically much higher than in older EU member states, although with considerable variation across sectors.

Overestimating the effect of EU membership on FDI inflows?

Membership of the EU has two important implications with regard to FDI. First it allows countries that have small domestic markets to expand their de facto market size. Firms located in the EU have access to the entire EU. However, as the number of countries in the EU increases, this advantage is currently shared by twenty-seven member countries (and in the future possibly by the three candidate countries as of 2008 – Croatia, Former Yugoslav Republic of Macedonia, and Turkey) and even more if one includes countries that have preferential access to the single market through various lesser forms of trade agreements. Thus, this advantage has considerably less value to the accession countries than it had for the cohesion countries, and this is exacerbated by the fact that domestic firms in many of the CEE countries have little experience in dealing with competition in a market economy, thus further attenuating the benefits that derive from the competition effect.

Second, membership suggests political, economic, and legal stability. Although the absence of efficient institutions can retard the efficient accumulation and transfer of knowledge (e.g. Rodrik 1999; Rodrik et al. 2004; Meyer and Peng 2005; Asiedu 2006), EU accession countries are not competing with the least developed countries for FDI. Indeed, it is a requirement for membership that candidate countries demonstrate convergence and overlap of formal and informal institutions. This acts as a location advantage vis-à-vis non-member countries with poorly developed institutions (say, Latin America, Russia) but not necessarily so compared with non-members that demonstrate political and policy stability (for instance, some East Asian countries), or indeed relative to other long-standing EU members. Again, the greater the number of countries that are members, the less stability counts as a unique advantage to potential investors. For example, Fabry and Zeghni (2006) find that FDI in eleven former Communist countries is sensitive to *specific and local* institutional arrangements.

Given this, EU membership per se does not necessarily lead to an increase in the quality or the quantity of FDI that a country receives, and this is best illustrated by the case of Greece. In 1980, inward FDI stock per capita was U.S.$470 (all figures in current prices) compared with U.S.$315 and U.S.$137 for Portugal and Spain respectively. By 2007, FDI stock per capita in Greece had grown to only U.S.$4,740, compared with U.S.$10,750 and U.S.$12,138 for Portugal and Spain respectively.

To take just one example from the NMS for comparison, Hungary's FDI per capita in 2007 was already more than double that of Greece (U.S.$9,711). A substantial part of these flows took place *before* Hungary became an EU member in 2004. In this respect it is important to highlight that, although EU membership may help promote FDI, we argue here that the positive effect of EU membership for FDI is decreasingly important, partly because these advantages are less significant as the number of EU members increases. Furthermore, globalization and the growth of supranational agreements (particularly those associated with the World Trade Organization) mean that several of these benefits are not as unique as they once were. Firms from outside the EU are no longer "forced" into EU-based production, as tariff and non-tariff barriers are fewer. It is worth remembering that a large part of the inward FDI flows from outside the EU prior to 1992 was spurred by the fear of "Fortress Europe." These fears have largely proven to be unfounded. Finally, the growth of peripheral trade and investment agreements with non-EU members also may impact on the effects of EU membership.

The point here is that the benefits that accrued from EU membership to the countries that joined earlier are substantially attenuated for later entrants to the EU because of globalization. First, the benefits are reduced because global financial, political, and economic liberalization that forms a large part of the globalization process has "leveled the playing field" in lowering the risk associated with trade and investment in most parts of the world (Narula 2003). With growing technological convergence, increasing homogeneity of consumption patterns, and improved communication and transportation facilities these factors have reduced the costs associated with supplying EU markets from East Asia or the Americas.

Thus, many of the new entrants to the EU are faced with increased competition for FDI not just from other European countries but also from other parts of the world, most notably Asia. The total flows of FDI are not fixed and thus *in principle* countries need not compete for FDI, as the volume of FDI depends on the level of domestic investment in the home countries. Therefore, FDI need not be a zero-sum game. Nonetheless, particularly when host countries are at a similar level of development, substitution effects may occur and hence they de facto compete for a limited amount of FDI.

The empirical evidence on the effects of EU membership and the shift of FDI from the cohesion countries to the NMS by and large confirms our skeptical view of FDI flows to the cohesion and accession countries. *Ex ante studies* on the effects of EU membership on the shift of FDI not unexpectedly have found a wide range of effects. These studies are mainly simulations based on theoretical models. From as early as the mid-1990s, Lankes and Venables (1996), Baldwin et al. (1997), Brenton and DiMauro (1999), Pfaffermayr et al. (2001), and Galego et al. (2004) examined various aspects of the shift of FDI from the periphery to the CEE countries. Other papers (e.g. Goerg and Greenaway 2002) examined the FDI potential of the CEE countries upon accession. Altomonte and Guagliano (2003) go beyond the cohesion countries and examine the potential of the CEE countries compared with the Mediterranean region, which can be considered as a competitor location. Clausing and Dorobantu (2005) found significant effects of key European Union announcements regarding the accession process. Garmel et al. (2008) in a growth model predict that three-quarters of capital in the NMS will ultimately be acquired by investors from the "core" member states in the long run.

Ex post studies have generally found some, but no dramatic, shift of FDI (see, for example, Buch et al. 2003; Meyer and Jensen 2003; Kalotay 2006).

This increased competition for FDI challenges both the cohesion countries and the CEE countries. Many (but not all) of these countries have sought to compete globally on the basis of two primary location advantages: low labor costs and EU membership. As we have discussed above, EU membership is not as much of an advantage in a liberalized, stable, and shrinking world where distance does not form as much of a barrier to trade and investment as it once did. For similar reasons, the low-cost advantage of these countries has also been dissipated in many cases, particularly as a result of productivity gains in China and other Asian economies (Kalotay 2004). Spain and Portugal have experienced some displacement of FDI or lost sequential FDI because they have not been able to develop location advantages in knowledge- and capital-intensive activities to compensate for the rising labor costs that have eroded their industrial base in low value-adding activities. This development has also been observed in CEE countries, where already some production activities have been shifted "further East."

FDI and the cohesion countries: policy implications

In light of the empirical evidence discussed in the previous section, in the cases of Spain, Portugal, and Ireland we expect to see some level of displacement to the new members in industries in which:

1. Low-cost labor remains the primary reason for location and the MNE subsidiary has not expanded its original low value-adding activities toward knowledge-intensive areas in which the domestic economy has a competitive advantage.
2. The MNE subsidiary is not embedded through important linkages to other firms in the host economy. On the contrary, when the MNE subsidiary is located close to an important customer or supplier, and proximity is important (e.g. because of just-in-time delivery), it is unlikely that the firm will relocate.
3. The sunk costs of an FDI in the host economy are low.
4. Productivity gains have overcome disadvantages associated with rising labor costs.
5. Skill levels are not particularly high and thus employees are easy to substitute,[4] as in these cases (tacit) know-how hardly limits the slicing of the value-chain.

In other words, the most obvious long-term solution for cohesion countries is to improve their location advantages in other areas, toward more science-based technological sectors. Ireland has succeeded in doing so with its focus on the ICT sectors (Barry 2004), although Portugal and Spain have so far failed to make significant moves toward more science-based sectors. Beyond the fact that science-based sectors and knowledge-intensive activities fit the current comparative advantage of these countries much better, they are also less footloose. This is partly because these sectors tend to rely on location-specific and location-bound assets that are less easily substitutable.

Disinvestments in the cohesion countries are of course not happening suddenly, because although these countries do rely on cheap factor inputs they are also capital intensive. They are also less footloose partly because they are in industries in which these host countries are firmly established locations within the major MNEs' global production networks. In each of these locations the MNE affiliates are well embedded in the local economy, and the specialized infrastructure to support this sector is well developed.

It is not immediately obvious that when MNEs begin to disinvest from the cohesion countries this will automatically result in increased investments in the accession countries in the same industries. In the automobile industry, for instance, the efficiency of a new greenfield plant tends to require a relatively large minimum efficiency scale. MNEs are reluctant therefore to start out in greenfield sites, which is a further deterrent to setting up new investments in the CEE countries. Except where strong domestic sectors and specialized knowledge-based clusters exist – whether public or private – the CEE countries are unlikely to receive major inflows of FDI that are intended to supply the EU as a single market.

The lesson here for most peripheral countries is very much the same as one that development policy experts (see, for example, Rodrik 1999; Lall 1997a, 2004; Haque 2007) have been arguing for the developing countries: Dependence on static and generic location advantages – whether drawing from the development of institutions, infrastructure, stability, or low-cost labor – is necessarily short term and short-sighted. The last two decades of increasing liberalization, falling transportation and communication costs, and investment in knowledge-based activities in East Asia has meant that the peripheral EU countries are no longer as attractive (although it should be noted that the lack of strong intellectual property rights enforcement in some Asian countries does provide a small window of opportunity). It is axiomatic that, as industrial development takes place, the comparative advantage of these countries needs to shift away from low value-adding activities to higher value-adding activities, which are necessarily science based.

It is only in those sectors in which "specialized" location advantages associated with higher value added exist that host countries can benefit significantly from MNE activity in the long run. This requires a considerable amount of government interaction and investment into tangible and intangible infrastructure. As countries reach a threshold level of technological capabilities, governments need to provide more active support through macro-organizational policies. This implies developing and fostering specific industries and technological trajectories, such that the location advantages they offer are less "generic" and more specific, highly immobile, and such that they encourage mobile investments to be locked into these assets. Many of the CEE countries have the basis for creating such science-based location advantages. For instance, Poland has strengths in certain natural and life sciences, as does Hungary in electro-mechanical sectors. The Czech Republic has opted to focus on the automotive sector, given the existence of large automotive plants, while the Slovak Republic has attracted a number of greenfield automotive plants. Of course, adapting to such challenges is not costless from three points of view. First, countries need considerable resources to invest in such vertical industrial policy actions. Second, they require considerable political will and discipline, because other industries will necessarily need to be "wound down." Third, fostering new sectors requires major institutional change. Innovation systems and firms designed, developed, and ingrained within central-planning models and their associated institutional arrangements do not function effectively in a market economy (Narula and Jormanainen 2008). Such radical systemic change requires resources and an effective period of transition given the inertia associated with formal and informal institutions.

There are two points of caution that need to be raised here. First, in pursuing such a strategy, the peripheral EU countries face competition not just from Asia, but also from the "core" economies of the EU that have systematically developed strengths in technology-intensive sectors over decades, and can often outcompete weaker, peripheral economies in terms of resources, incentives, and opportunities. Nonetheless, there are several niches and gaps in the technological competences of core countries that can be effectively exploited by the peripheral economies.

Second, such a strategy requires systematic long-term investment, in terms of both building up the appropriate public infrastructure, and promoting domestic capacity in both supplier and related activities. Many of the CEE countries have well-trained and skilled workforces. However, the availability of a large stock of suitably qualified workers does not in itself result in efficient absorption of knowledge, or its efficient use in industrial development; the much lower level of relevant infrastructure (Bellak et al. 2008) may especially deter FDI. Rather, this requires the presence of institutions and economic actors within the industry, which defines the stock of knowledge in a given location, and the efficient use of markets and hierarchies, be they intra-firm, intra-industry, or intra-country. This knowledge is not costless, and must be accumulated over time. Important externalities arise that impinge on the ease of diffusion and efficiency of absorption and utilization of external knowledge (Criscuolo and Narula 2008).

Industrial policy in which certain industries are selected for rapid growth by focused investments through intensive development of created assets can and does accelerate economic development. The examples of both the more advanced industrializing countries (such as the Asian newly industrializing countries) and emerging economies such as Malaysia and Brazil illustrate this. Attracting specialized FDI to a particular sector can alter the sequence of industrial upgrading (Williamson and Hu 1994), because specialized FDI may help improve the created assets associated within a sector (say consumer electronics production). Created assets in this sector may have significant knowledge flow externalities in another sector (say micro-electronics design), which in turn may represent significant input to a third sector (say software development). However, this assumes the presence of a virtuous circle, and the development of appropriate clusters.

Specifically, for the CEE countries it is argued that both proactive and reactive policies are needed to achieve sustainability of FDI. Proactive policies are geared to attract FDI and affect the sustainability through sectoral targeting. Reactive policies aim at making FDI more sustainable through three distinct policy channels, namely through strengthening comparative advantage; enabling firms to benefit from economies of scale; and supporting agglomeration forces. In this respect, emphasis should be put on providing specific bundles of location factors as public goods for closely defined value-added activities of the MNE (Bellak and Leibrecht 2007: 234).

There is empirical evidence that a clear gap exists between "old" and "new" member states' policies to attract additional FDI (Bellak et al. 2008). The older member states gained most by focusing on infrastructure and R&D policies. "New" member states' policies have tended to focus on reducing the share of low-skilled workers (e.g. by encouraging firms to restructure production and increase capital intensity) and a reduction of labor costs through a decrease in non-wage-labor costs. The fact that different policy areas are relevant in the two groups of countries opens the possibility for focused policy approaches geared to the needs of individual sectors.

FDI-assisted growth requires the capacity to be a "strategic follower" (Ramos 2000). This requires a systematic understanding of what technological capabilities need to be developed or enhanced, and to seek to actively coordinate potential users with sources of the appropriate technologies. Asian governments such as China, Taiwan, and Korea that have pursued such a strategy successively have actively sought to identify, acquire, and transfer technologies, with government agencies acting as market makers. Left to their own means, firms have a tendency to be risk averse, and to avoid the financial and technological risk of upgrading their technological assets as long as these continue to provide a reasonable rate of return. This tendency to focus on short-term gains and to minimize risk is not unique to firms of any given nationality. Many governments recognize this problem, and seek to overcome or at least reduce the perceived risk levels by providing subsidized loans and other incentives to domestic firms that restructure their existing operations by adopting new technologies in the products and processes that promote international best practice.

The countries with the most successful technological upgrading – Korea, Taiwan, and to a lesser extent Brazil – allocated subsidies in what Amsden and Hikino (2000) and Amsden (2001) call a "reciprocal control mechanism." That is, incentives and subsidies to upgrade technologically, promote local content, expand exports, or reduce import dependence were subject to performance standards that were actively monitored, and in Amsden's (2001) words were "redistributive in nature and results-oriented" and acted to prevent government failure.

To be sure, upgrading of the technological capabilities of domestic firms can no longer be pursued in quite the same way in a globalized world. International competition is a given, and there is likely to be no return to the infant industry model (except for few particular industries). Although a number of CEE countries have had considerable investment in R&D, a majority of the formal R&D

efforts have been conducted by state-owned enterprises and the non-firm sector. Although the state must necessarily remain a significant investor in innovation, these policies need to be orchestrated with the private firm sector, whether domestic or foreign. Given that the CEE countries prior to their EU membership have to accept the *acquis communautaire*, discrimination between domestic and foreign firms is no longer possible as stated in the competition policy regulations of the EU.

Market forces cannot substitute for the role of governments in developing and promoting a proactive industrial policy (Lall 1996, 1997a,b, 2003). Firms necessarily take a shorter-term, profit-maximizing view because they are largely risk averse. MNEs and unrestrained flows of inward FDI may well lead to an increase in productivity and exports, but they do not necessarily result in increased competitiveness of the domestic sector or increased industrial capacity, which ultimately determines economic growth in the long run. FDI per se does not provide growth opportunities unless a domestic industrial sector exists that has the necessary technological capacity to profit from the externalities from MNE activity. Yet, as there are only very few domestic firms left in some industries in the CEE countries, this possibility of growth may be limited. This is also well illustrated by the inability of many Asian countries that have relied on a passive FDI-dependent strategy to upgrade their industrial development. It should be remembered that unrestrained FDI inflows often results in "crowding out" of the domestic sector. FDI and domestic capabilities and a domestic sector need to be concatenated and properly phased if positive results are to be achieved. The lesson here is not that the role of government should be substituted by the market, but that markets and governments each perform important complementary functions.

The lessons of developing countries cannot be applied without some modification to understanding the impact of FDI on the development strategies of the NMS and the cohesion countries. As we have emphasized here, there are additional layers of complexity that derive from "deep" integration within such a powerful economic and political bloc. However, these are – by and large – positive, in the sense that "insider" status within the EU provides a considerable boost to the location advantages of these countries, even if they are less significant than in previous rounds of EU expansion. The largest challenge is that of institutional restructuring, and the move – especially for the CEE countries – away from national champions and state ownership of key sectors, and state-defined priorities, which has been achieved in the CEE economies to different degrees, partly as a result of specific funds made available to these countries by the European Commission. On the other hand, these countries are also limited by EU policies, particularly those associated with regulation, competition, and state aid.

Specific challenges for the accession countries

Many of the new and accession member states have yet to confront the difficulty of embedding inward FDI into domestic economic and innovation systems and here is where the challenge lies. One of the challenges in creating embeddedness is associated with matching the industrial structure and comparative advantage of the region[5] with the kinds of FDI that are being attracted. As highlighted in the previous sections, benefits from FDI are maximized when the kinds of investment projects being attracted are matched with the potential clusters of domestic competitiveness that the MNEs may be able to tap into.

In the case of the accession countries, many have well-developed components of science and technology systems. Some are even endowed with considerable capacity in high value-adding activities such as R&D, software development, and design. This has been used as a basis to attract and embed highly specialized, high-competence MNE facilities.[6] Nonetheless, one of the considerable disadvantages that these countries face is the challenge of dismantling centrally planned innovation systems, which are driven primarily by planners and bureaucrats rather than by demand conditions and the specific needs of firms. Such restructuring has to deal with considerable inertia in the institutional arrangements (Narula and Jormanainen 2008), which is often difficult to overcome.

Ceteris paribus, foreign affiliates interact with knowledge organizations such as local universities and public research institutes that undertake basic or applied research, produce R&D manpower, and provide technical services to firms (see UNCTAD 2005: ch. VII). Foreign affiliates may cooperate with these institutions, for example by providing financial support and conducting joint research projects. Such collaboration can also help R&D by other enterprises, by raising the research capabilities of knowledge institutions, bringing them into contact with industrial work, and promoting spin-offs. At the same time, however, MNEs may also be locked into existing supplier relationships, partnerships, and R&D networks in other locations and may be reluctant to seek to establish new associations with as-yet unproven local suppliers and universities. Indeed, as MNEs increasingly seek to rationalize their activities, decisions about local linkages are not always made at the subsidiary level, but sometimes at the headquarters level, by comparing the various options available to the MNE globally. Thus governments need to create incentives for the MNE to consider local partners, and not expect these to happen "naturally." Because EU member states cannot discriminate by nationality of ownership, in circumstances in which domestic firms are not present, linkages between foreign affiliates and other foreign firms (but located and engaged in economic activity in the same host location) may represent the sole available mode of industrial upgrading and capability development in the CEE countries. As long as industrial and technological upgrading happens and spills over to more than one firm, it does not matter who the beneficiary is, as long as it serves to further embed the MNE affiliate in the host country.

Often there may not be domestic firms and organizations that properly match the potential needs of the MNE, and this also requires government intervention. At one level, projects need to be led by investment by the government, by establishing science and technology incubators for small groups of industry-facing researchers who help bridge the research undertaken in public institutes to the commercial needs of MNE affiliates. It is important that the focus of these incubators is on the collaboration with MNE affiliates, and the provision of the infrastructure and environment to foster competitive R&D. At another level, it may also be necessary to create (and encourage the creation of) new, more nimble and entrepreneurial smaller firms, and not attempt to force a "fit" between the older, large, and former state-owned enterprises whose competences do not properly match the needs of the MNE affiliates. In the case of the accession countries, there has been a historical trend to focus on large firms, and the absence of special treatment for start-up firms and small and medium-sized enterprises means that the bureaucratic red tape prevents the establishment of such a policy.

The challenges that the accession countries face vis-à-vis developing countries are plainly easier in many ways, because EU membership does provide the accession countries with important location advantages. They have access to a much larger and more affluent market; valuable resources are made available by the EU to improve their basic infrastructure; they are obliged to converge their institutional arrangements to the EU standard; they are protected by EU regulation and laws; and they have the political and economic clout of the EU in the areas of competition policy, trade policy, and so forth. However, they are also in the "home region" of some of the world's largest MNEs, and thus face greater and immediate competition, and cannot afford to be passive.

Notes

1 This chapter is a revised version of a paper previously published in 2009 in *Transnational Corporations*, 18: 69–89. We gratefully acknowledge permission from UNCTAD.
2 Empirical evidence for the CEE countries is provided by Konings (2001) and Nicolini and Resmini (2006).
3 A relevant question that arises is this: Will there also be an increase in FDI relative to the counterfactual of no membership? A study by Benito et al. (2003) compares MNE subsidiaries in Norway, Denmark, and Finland. They find that Norwegian affiliates tend to be less well developed in terms of scale and scope and these effects remain strong even when controlling for other potentially influential factors. The findings indicate that being on the "outside" of the EU may indeed carry the price of becoming less attractive to MNE activity.
4 The EU KLEMS database, http://www.euklems.net/index.html, has detailed accounts for high, medium and low skilled by industry for a large range of countries and for long time periods.
5 Again, it should be noted that we do not aim to address issues of particular countries, but rather try to provide a sketch of the broader aspects.
6 Kokko and Kravtsova (2007) provide case studies on these aspects.

12

JAPAN

Dealing with global forces: multilateralism, regionalism, bilateralism

T. J. Pempel

Helge Hveem has, over the course of a lifetime of scholarship, addressed a multitude of issues. However, three threads strike me as running consistently through the vast majority of his work: political economy, regionalism, and the complexities of any state's adjustment to global pressures (e.g. Hveem 1999, 2002; Hveem and Nordhaug 2002, inter alia). This chapter endeavors to address these key issues through an examination of Japan's post-Cold War engagement with the complex processes of multilateralism, regionalism, and bilateralism. In the course of developing my argument about how Japan has mixed and matched these complex approaches to its foreign political economic policies, I think the reader will see important echoes of Hveem's concerns. Even more specifically, I believe it will show the underlying correctness of his claims that adjustment to global processes continues to show the critical nature of choice and agency, and the growing importance of both multilateralism and regionalism as driving norms and concrete institutional processes.

Japan provides a tantalizing case. Readers not familiar with its post-war place in the global political community should know that, following its disastrous adventure with expansion and its loss in World War II, its close bilateral security alliance with the United States allowed it to focus its national policy attentions on achieving the high economic growth that allowed it to grow at roughly double the Organisation for Economic Co-operation and Development (OECD) averages from 1952 to 1990 and to achieve exceptionally high levels of business sophistication in many of its firms. As its products gained ever larger shares of global exports, its share of world gross domestic product (GDP) soared from about 7 percent in 1970 to 18 percent in the early 1990s. Japan's rapid rise was subsequently mirrored by the equally exceptional growth of almost all of the rest of Asia during the late 1980s and early 1990s.

Although most of Asia continues to show incredible levels of economic dynamism, even during the period since the global meltdown of 2008–9, Japan has been the major exception. A classic asset bubble popped in Japan during the early 1990s and since then the country's once staggering growth has stagnated. Nothing indicates that stagnation more than the fact that its share of world GDP has now returned to roughly the same level as the country enjoyed thirty years ago.

In the early post-war years, Japan was an ardent joiner of virtually all multilateral institutions generated by the Western powers – the United Nations, the World Bank, the International Monetary Fund (IMF), and others. All could be seen as embodiments of U.S.-driven bodies aimed, in John Ikenberry's (2001) words, at "locking in" a pro-U.S. global order (pp. 3–20).

Today however, many puzzles surround Japan's behavior toward more recent efforts at multilateral cooperation. On the one hand, Japan was an ardent supporter of the Kyoto Protocol ratified in 2002, the International Criminal Court, the cultural diversity treaty built around UNESCO, and the International Agreement to Ban Anti-Personnel Landmines adopted by the UN General Assembly on December 10, 1996. In all such cases, Japan worked closely with the EU, Canada, and other powers to create new regimes that expanded *multilateralism* into new areas despite resistance from the United States. These actions also benefited from widespread domestic support that grew out of the agendas of national and global non-governmental organizations (NGOs). The combination put strong pressure on Japan's political elites to reshape the country's national agenda. Such experiences suggest Japan's collaboration in multilateral efforts toward a growing degree of concordance among the EU, Japan, and Canada that favors cross-national citizen participation in the creation of international institutions or protocols establishing seminal standards for global cooperation. The evidence supports arguments about causation resting more heavily on considerations that were both "normative" and involved "political leadership" rather than those driven by "competition" with the United States. Yet, at times, these new multilateral commitments can also be interpreted as congruent with hypotheses about creating a counterweight to U.S. power, as all of these regimes went forward in the face of strong opposition by the American government, although there is little evidence that these actions were driven by any conscious Japanese efforts to compete with or balance against the United States in any generic sense. In addition, cooperation among these middle powers created global public goods and helped to reshape existing national identities, even when doing so conflicted with domestic political pressures and national economic interests.

Yet offsetting any quick conclusion that Japan has embraced a new multilateralism or is seeking to generate new global norms or take a position of global leadership by itself or in conjunction with the EU is the fact that Japan has also been exceptionally active in the International Whaling Commission (IWC), where, isolated with Norway and Iceland, it has resolutely opposed efforts to ban commercial whaling, despite overwhelmingly contradictory global norms. Indeed, in the June 2006 meetings, Japan actively encouraged a number of land-locked countries to join the IWC in hopes of bolstering numerical support for Japan's position.[1] Additionally, Japan, as David Leheny (2006) demonstrates so vividly, has formally embraced various global norms such as those concerning the banning of child prostitution and child pornography as well as those against international terrorism but domestic implementation has often involved turning the norms on their head and using them as cudgels against largely unrelated domestic political targets. In such cases, domestic political pressures blatantly trump multilateralism, global norms, and middle power concordance; on such occasions, Japan shows itself willing to follow an explicitly *unilateral* course of action.

Equally important is the fact that Japan has shown a special interest in advancing multilateralism and new regimes within its immediate geographical neighborhood. *Regionalism* has been an important subcategory of Japan's multilateralist impulse. Japan has, for example, moved independently of Canada and Europe, although often with the support of Australia and South Korea, to foster a variety of regionally specific East Asian institutions such as the Asia-Pacific Economic Cooperation (APEC) forum and the ASEAN Regional Forum (ARF). Japan has also been active in the multilateral Six Party Talks on the North Korean nuclear problem as well as the Proliferation Security Initiative (PSI). However, unlike instances noted above, such as Kyoto, or the ban on landmines, none of these Asian institutions poses challenges to U.S. hegemony. To the contrary, each explicitly included the United States, the first two as a result of Japan's active solicitations for the United States to behave more multilaterally, and the latter two as outgrowths of direct U.S. solicitations. All therefore worked in congruence with, rather than in opposition to, U.S. policy objectives.

At the same time some of Japan's Asian activities, particularly those since the economic crisis of 1997–8, have in fact challenged U.S. interests. Most notably, Japan's proposal for an Asian Monetary Fund (AMF) at the time of the Asian economic crisis was presented as a unilateral action independent of the IMF. Blistering U.S. opposition made clear how direct a challenge it presented to U.S. economic dominance, and Japan quickly withdrew its proposal. However, Japan subsequently supported the Chiang Mai Initiative with its series of intra-Asian currency swaps, the Asian bond market, and more recently the East Asia Summit (EAS) launched in December 2005. All involved exclusively East Asian memberships devoid of the United States. In several cases there was a clear collective Asian agenda, often pressed by China, of keeping the United States out. Also, when Japan operates from a "competitive" standpoint, most typically within the Asian region, the object of Japan's competition is most frequently China, not the United States. Thus, in the EAS, which has thus far excluded the United States, Japan tempered the kinds of collective anti-U.S. bias shown in the Chiang Mai Initiative (CMI) or the bond initiative by teaming up with other pro-U.S. Asia-Pacific allies including Australia, New Zealand, and India as potential counterweights to China and as presumed supporters of broad global goals not at odds with U.S. preferences.

In sum, Japan's regional actions in Asia, compared with its more global behaviors, offer far more evidence of a willingness to exert political leadership and to foster Asian regional linkages that are more in accord with Japan's perceived normative interests. In the Asian context, Japan has more often operated from explicitly competitive motivations, but from a competition directed against a presumably rising China, rather than the already dominant United States.

Overall, Japan's actions have less often involved clear-cut choices among multilateralism, regionalism, or unilateralism as strategies in themselves. Indeed, on occasion, Japanese policy retains a dollop of bilateralism, as was seen most notably in Japan's pursuit of various preferential trade agreements with Singapore, Mexico, Malaysia, the Philippines, and Thailand, as well as Japan's extensive deepening of its bilateral security ties to the United States, particularly under the Koizumi administration (Pempel and Urata 2005; Pempel 2007).

In short, Japanese policy makers have mixed and matched their specific approaches to these alternative options depending on the particular issue involved. Ideally, Japanese leaders have sought constantly to achieve policy solutions that ensure domestic political gains, retain close ties with the United States, demonstrate regional leadership in Asia, and show Japan to be a good global citizen to the largest possible audience of international actors. Rarely has the government been able to achieve that ideal mix; coordination has been complex; trade-offs have been inevitable. Cumulatively, however, from an institutional standpoint Japan has retained considerable "forum flexibility," opting in different instances to create, oppose, or utilize different institutional formats in the pursuit of alternative policy objectives. At the same time, within the context of Japan's political history, recent activities suggest far more *multilateralism* and *regionalism* than was the case a decade or two ago.

Japan's behavior thus contrasts to some extent with that of other mid-level powers, particularly Canada, as well as most members of the European Union, which show far stronger normative predispositions to multilateralism as a tactic in itself. Multilateralism, the actions of these countries suggest, will foster greater levels of global cooperation, socializing nation-states into "cooperative behaviors," and as a consequence provide the most promising avenue along which to pursue their own long-term national (but also regional and global) interests. This has *not* been Japan's position. Instead, Japan has followed a more mixed array of institutional strategies in dealing with its distinct problems in diverse functional areas.

At the same time, Japan's behavior, as the evidence below will demonstrate, pursues a far from random walk along a miscellany of institutional paths. Three overview hypotheses drive this paper:

1. Japan is typically eager to provide active support to multinational organizations, particularly when doing so enjoys support from powerful domestic actors, but the country is far more reluctant to do so when such actions require major compromises of the interests of powerful domestic constituencies.
2. As a supplement to its global multilateral endeavors, Japan has been especially active in fostering new institutions within East Asia. Much of this involves efforts to counter China's rising regional influence. However, equally, Japan's

efforts allow it to demonstrate regional leadership on non-strategic issues in areas such as the environment and finance.

3. Japan is quite prepared to provide active support to multinational organizations, even opposing the United States on specific matters, so long as doing so does not compromise its close security ties with the United States. It faces far more of a dilemma when multilateralism clashes with pro-U.S. bilateralism.

Beneath all three premises is an important chronological shift: Japan has become increasingly active in pursuit of new multilateral institutions since the 1980s and with accelerating interest since the early years of this century. Moreover, as will be shown below, Japan's political leaders have become more willing to press for Japan's adherence to new global norms, often against counter pressures from bureaucratic or interest group demands. Rather political leaders increasingly respond to pressures from the Japanese public and global NGOs.

To appreciate how different Japan's recent approach to multilateralism really is, it is well to highlight the earlier pattern by which Japan long operated. Only then will it be possible to appreciate Japan's new, but far from universal, role in global institution building.

The Cold War pattern: multilateralism compatible with U.S. bilateralism and domestic politics

Reversing its relative international isolation in the years before World War II, Japan became an active petitioner for multilateral membership in virtually all post-war institutions, including the United Nations, the General Agreement on Tariffs and Trade (GATT), the IMF, the World Bank, the World Health Organization (WHO), and a host of other bodies. Accepted into all, Japan, for the bulk of the post-war period, sought to prove itself a good global citizen by close adherence to their institutional norms. Indeed, from the time of its admission to the United Nations in 1956, Japan's Ministry of Foreign Affairs has rather consistently declared "UN compatibility" to be one of three central pillars in Japanese foreign policy.

Such Japanese multilateralism rarely involved opposition to the United States. Quite the contrary: These early post-war institutions were core elements in what Ikenberry and Mastanduno (2003: 7) have labeled the "dense set of international and intergovernmental institutions" through which America exercised its post-war foreign policies and advanced its Cold War strategies. Post-war U.S. strategy involved reassuring its allies by binding itself to a complicated set of institutional rules that set broad standards for global economics and security. Japan's participation in such multilateral bodies was a logical extension of its bilateral alliance with the United States. In no way did Japan's early multilateralism require any serious challenges to U.S. hegemony, the surrender of domestic interests supporting the dominant political coalition, or adherence to a network of contested global norms.

Until the end of the Cold War, in accord with the Yoshida Doctrine (Kosaka 1968; Pyle 1992), the combination of multilateralism and U.S.-oriented bilateralism harmonized well for Japanese foreign policy in both security and economics (Krauss and Pempel 2004). Under the bargain, Japan remained content to allow the United States to carry the lion's share of the military responsibilities for the defense of Japan as well as the preponderant flexing of military muscle in or around Asia. In exchange, Japan concentrated on high economic growth at home, aided by favorable access for its exports to the U.S. market. In the process, Japan was able to portray itself as a good global citizen, active in multilateral institutions and adherent to their norms.

This particular blend of close U.S. ties and generic multilateralism resonated well with domestic Japanese political conditions. The government was constrained at home by an ambiguously pacifist constitution, a public skeptical about military means to secure peace, and opposition parties hostile to the U.S.–Japan Security Treaty and desirous of restrictions on Japan's own Self-Defense Forces. By fits and starts, old taboos eroded, and by the early 1980s Japanese public opinion had come to tolerate and eventually to offer positive support for the overall U.S.–Japan security relationship. Far more enthusiasm was consistently forthcoming in public opinion surveys for Japanese multilateralism, the ideals of which were seen as unassailable and the domestic costs of which were minimal.

With limited exceptions, Japanese politics and foreign policy, until roughly the end of the Cold War, consequently faced few hard choices among multilateralism, U.S. bilateralism, and domestic politics. This all changed with the end of the Cold War, Japan's growing involvement in East Asia, a "regime shift" within Japan (Pempel 1998; Vogel 2006; Green 2001; Pyle 2007, inter alia), and, finally, U.S. moves, particularly under the Bush administration, to break with past American multilateralism in a disastrous lurch toward unilateralism and preventive war. In response to this complex mix of circumstances, Japan moved more conspicuously to embrace a less U.S.-centric multilateralism and a more autonomous Asian regionalism – particularly when this involved few sacrifices of powerful domestic interests or challenges to security ties to the United States. In these situations, Japan shifted its foreign policies "beyond bilateralism" (Krauss and Pempel 2004). Nevertheless, as Michael Green (2001: 193) has aptly phrased it, "The multilateral impulse has been strong in Japan's post-war foreign policy thinking, but in practice it has often been elusive."

Japan's new multilateralism

As early as the 1980s, Japan began taking a more active role in international organizations by, among other things, increasing its funding for the United Nations, becoming more active in UNICEF, signing on to the Convention on International Trade in Endangered Species (CITES), taking on and then expanding its role in peacekeeping operations, and helping to create APEC. Japan's leadership, with what was then its tremendous economic success, and particularly with the explosive if short-lived burst of growth in the late 1980s, sought to create new global and regional roles for Japan, particularly those congruent with its enhanced economic and technological status. This effort has largely continued through the 1990s to the present.

Since the mid-1990s, Japan has been even more overt in taking an active leadership role in the creation of new multilateral institutions and regimes. Yet with the Bush administration's rejection of most forms of multilateralism, Japan has on numerous occasions been forced to choose between newer versions of multilateralism and long-standing ties to the United States. However, from within Japan at least, any appearance of a new balancing against America has been the result largely of America's new unilateralism rather than of any Japanese desire to create a series of multilateral counterweights to U.S. hegemony.

It was Bush administration policies that took the United States out of multilateral bargains previously entered into by that country and these were partly responsible for the appearance that Japan, and other mid-level powers, were "going it alone." Thus, soon after the Bush administration came to power it broke with fifty years of U.S. multilateralism by explicitly renouncing a host of long-standing and relatively new global agreements, from the anti-ballistic missiles (ABM) treaty to the Kyoto Accord to the Convention Against Small Arms, the Biological Weapons Convention, the Chemical Weapons Convention, the International Court of Justice, and many others (Daadler and Lindsey 2003: 13; Ikenberry 2001; Pempel 2008; Walt 2005: 97). In virtually all cases, the U.S. government had been a proponent of these regimes prior to Bush. Nevertheless, Japan, like many other countries, chose to continue the pursuit of these and newer multilateral institutions rather than opting, as it might once have done, to abandon them to adhere more faithfully to American's foreign policy path.

Thus, Japan has been an active advocate for a number of the new institutions and it has continued its vigorous support of most of them even in the face of U.S. abandonment. This was certainly true with the development and advance of the Kyoto Protocol, which Japan and its leaders saw as a signature effort to advance its national identity as an industrial country that had already become something of a "green superpower" through anti-pollution efforts tracing to policy changes in the 1970s (McKean 1977, 1981; Schreurs 2002; Ohta 2007). Kyoto also provided Japan with an economic opportunity to export pollution control equipment, an area in which it enjoyed a comparative advantage, as well as to provide technical assistance to polluting countries, particularly within the Asian region. Importantly, Japan has shifted the terms of much of its overseas development assistance, including aid to China, into areas designed to generate environmental improvements in developing countries (Hook et al. 2001: 322). Thus, Japan quite self-consciously finalized ratification of Kyoto on June 4, 2002, and it came into effect in February 2005. Moreover, despite huge technical problems in meeting its commitments to reduce emissions in many categories, the Japanese government has remained committed to the protocol's ultimate implementation (Ohta 2007).

Moreover, Japan made serious diplomatic efforts to encourage the Bush administration not to abandon Kyoto; Japan was hardly anxious to see Kyoto become an anti-U.S. institution. Thus, in April 2001, Foreign Minister Kono Yohei telephoned U.S. Secretary of State Colin Powell and expressed "disappointment" with the U.S. decision that President George W. Bush said he took in order "not (to) do anything that harms our economy." At the same time, a Japanese government delegation headed by Senior Vice Foreign Minister Araki Kiyohiro traveled to Washington and appealed to Bush to continue to cooperate in global efforts to enforce the Kyoto treaty. However, U.S. Environmental Protection Agency administrator Christine Whitman rejected the Japanese demands, reiterating claims that Washington would seek a global warming treaty that has reduction commitments not only from industrialized countries but from developing ones too (Kakuchi 2001).

Japan has also been anxious to promote global efforts associated with disarmament and non-proliferation. Such efforts resonate effectively with Japan's domestic population. They also offer the country a unique and ongoing opportunity to distance itself from its aggressive past history. Japan was thus an early advocate of the global ban on landmines as well as efforts to control conventional arms (the latter through the U.N. Register of Conventional Arms, established in 1992). A task force of four Japanese ministries was created in 2002 to investigate new technologies to clear landmines (Hughes 2004: 200). Japan also entered the Convention on the Prohibition of Chemical Weapons in April 1997. The country destroyed its own stockpile of 1 million landmines in February 2003 and provides landmine clearance in countries such as Afghanistan. It also carries out a small-arms collection project in Cambodia and has been working closely with Europe in support of the ABM and non-proliferation norms. In the words of Hook et al. (2001: 328):

> In the post-Cold War world, Japan is demonstrating signs of having emerged from the cocoon of the Yoshida Doctrine, and is developing cautiously a degree of international leadership. It is adjusting its previous emphasis on bilateral relations, especially with the United States, and supplementing it with multilateral relations and the development of a greater emphasis on human contributions.

Japan's performance with regard to the International Criminal Court (ICC) has been somewhat more uneven. Along with 119 other states, Japan voted in favor of the Rome Statute in July 1998; but it was slow to ratify the treaty. The Ministry of Foreign Affairs continued to maintain that ratification could not occur until Japan passed domestic legislation that would deal with complicated issues such as treatment of prisoners of war and the role of the Japanese Self-Defense Forces. As late as April 2002 Justice Minister Moriyama expressed government concerns that the ICC might undermine Japanese sovereignty – an argument that resonated with American opposition to the ICC (Gould 2002). However, global and Japanese NGOs such as Human Rights Watch and Amnesty International pressed hard for Japan's accession. Moreover, China was opposed to the ICC, thereby affording Japan an excellent opportunity to enter a multilateral commitment that would outflank its Asian rival (Lu and Wang 2005). Thus, in December

2006 Prime Minister Abe announced that Japan would sign on to the ICC as of 2007.

The above examples show that in a number of cases Japan was willing to embrace new institutions that were highly responsive to domestic and international public opinion and that allowed Japan to underscore its identity as a "peaceful nation." However, several, particularly the ICC, also showed that Japanese actions were simultaneously congruent with using such institutions as elements of realpolitik, although not as a balancer against the United States, but rather against China.

Quite a different causal mode operated in regard to the Cartegena Biosafety Protocol of 2000 and genetically modified organisms (GMOs). As with so many of the other new multilateral institutions, the United States was reluctant to join. In this case, the United States aligned itself with a coalition of agricultural exporting countries called the Miami Group (United States, Canada, Australia, Chile, Argentina, and Uruguay) to stress their claims that Cartegena stood in opposition to free trade. A so-called "Like Minded Group" of developing countries focused on gaining individual rights to oppose any import of GMOs. The EU position fell between those of the two previous groups while Japan formed an odd coalition with Mexico, Norway, Singapore, South Korea, and Switzerland, among others (Andree 2005; Newell and MacKenzie n.d.). Following the initiative of Japan, this group sought to bridge the gaps between the other negotiating blocs by proposing agreement on a so-called "precautionary principle" consistent with earlier WTO agreements. The EU found this principle acceptable and Japan, the European Commission, and all EU states either have ratified or are in the process of ratifying the protocol. The protocol came into effect in September 2003.

Japan's position reflected an effort to respond to the country's strong consumer groups and their collective aversion to genetically modified organisms. According to one public opinion poll taken by the Japanese government in 2000, 96.3 percent of those surveyed were either very (60.1 percent) or moderately (36.2 percent) worried about GM foods (as quoted by Maclachlan 2006: 250). The Japanese anti-GMO movement has sought a complete ban on all imports of GMOs; they successfully joined forces with both environmental and farming groups in an effort to create GMO-free zones, encourage organic farming, and discover instances in which imported GMOs have caused problems. Seeking to respond to such pressures but to avoid instituting a general ban on GMO imports that would spark a trade conflict with the United States, the Japanese government has been strict in shutting out any imports, such as StarLink Corn, that raised serious safety risks. Of course the government was exceptionally tough in its ban on U.S. beef when dangers arose concerning mad cow disease. Importantly, Cartegena also affords Japan an alternative international regime through which to pursue issues that might otherwise have gone to the WTO, where U.S. preponderance is much greater. Cartegena represents one more instance of Japan's option to go "forum shopping."

Also worth noting from a policy-making standpoint is the fact that, on numerous occasions, when negotiations were stuck, or when domestic political differences threatened to derail the country's forward momentum, top Japanese leaders intervened to commit the nation fully to the new regimes. Thus, well into 1997, as Japan continued to debate whether the country needed to retain landmines as a deterrent to attacks, Prime Minister Hashimoto reversed his previous opposition and pushed the ban forward. The Ottawa Protocol was signed by Japan on December 3, 1997, and ratified on September 30, 1998. Similarly, Prime Minister Takeshita was a key proponent of environmental safety and the Kyoto Accord. Indeed, given the times, he was able to parlay environmental aid and active support for the environment into political capital in ways that participating in peacekeeping operations would have made more difficult. And finally, Prime Minister Obuchi was a strong proponent of the ban on landmines and in favor of the ICC.

What is clear from the above cases is that Japan has indeed been multilaterally active, pushing hard for a number of the new global institutions. Its motivations have, as is true of most complex cases, been complex. However, weighing heavily has been its effort to stake out a new leadership role congruent with its status as a mid-level industrial power. In most cases, doing so has resonated well at home. Peace, environmental cleanliness, and safe foods are hard to oppose. In this sense Japan has often led but in ways that have hardly been normatively disinterested. Japan's efforts have in some instances put it on opposite sides from the United States. In the past, Japan might not have been willing to take the risk of upsetting American policy makers, but clearly in the recent instances noted above Japan has been willing to join with other mid-level powers to press forward their collective agendas despite American abdication. Importantly, however, the challenges to the United States have been both multilateral (rather than unilaterally Japanese) and largely marginal to U.S. autonomy, particularly within the security arena. As will become clear in the final section, Japan has shown far greater reluctance to break with the United States in that vital area of bilateral cooperation. Before exploring that trade-off, however, it is valuable to explore Japan's role within the Asian region, where many of its actions have been similar to those taken on a global scale.

The regional variant

Japan's new multilateralism has been particularly in evidence within East Asia. As Figure 12.1 makes clear, Japan's economy has become increasingly dependent on Asian markets, increasingly those of China, largely at the expense of its earlier dependence on the United States. For Japan to give enhanced focus to East Asia is a logical consequence.

By far the most prominent of Japan's efforts at regional institution creation was APEC. Japan, along with Australia, was an active proponent of APEC as an Asia-Pacific ministerial forum designed to advance economic liberalization, trade facilitation, and economic and technical cooperation throughout the region. For Japan it was important that APEC, unlike proposals for more "closed" regional

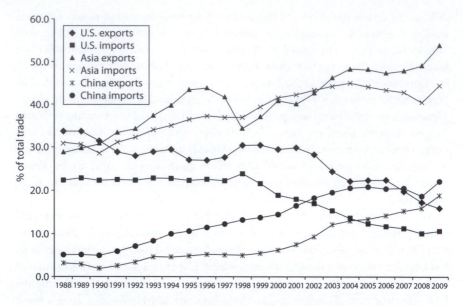

FIGURE 12.1 Japanese trade levels 1988–2009. Source: Prepared from Ministry of Finance trade statistics. Available at http://www.jetro.go.jp/en/reports/ statistics (accessed May 24, 2010).

bodies, was explicitly "Asia-Pacific" in character and included the United States, Canada, Australia, and New Zealand as members. APEC's first meeting was held in Canberra in November 1989 just days before the Berlin Wall came down (Green 2001: 208–11; Ashizawa 2004: 250–1). For much of the 1990s – largely until the crisis of 1997–8 – both the U.S. and Japanese governments collaborated actively with the other APEC member economies in laying the groundwork for a variety of policies designed to enhance regional economic cooperation.

Japan also played a key role in forming the ASEAN Regional Forum. Initially skeptical of any proposed regional security framework when ARF was first proposed in the late 1980s and fearful that such an arrangement might undercut their bilateral security alliance, Japan, in the summer of 1991, officially shifted its position in favor of Foreign Minister Nakayama proposing that the ASEAN Post Ministerial Conference take on new functions "to improve the sense of security" among members (Ashizawa 2004: 251). Although initially greeted with skepticism from the United States and ASEAN, the Japanese proposal gained traction among ASEAN members by early 1992 and, under prodding by the Ministry of Foreign Affairs, with the new Clinton administration in July 1993. The latter officially endorsed the proposal, declaring that "a multilateral forum for security consultations" was one of the ten major goals for U.S. policy in the Asia-Pacific region (Ashizawa 2004: 252). Over time ARF moved to institute a sequence of confidence-building measures, although it continues to remain far from a "security community" (Acharya 1991, 2001).

Both APEC and ARF enjoyed enthusiastic support from Japan and at least luke-warm support from the United States. Initial American skepticism waned during the 1990s as both bodies provided regional forums that advanced policy issues important to America. Of particular interest were APEC's Bogor Declaration (1994) and Osaka Declaration (1995), committing all members to trade barrier reductions. These goals were especially significant following the collapse of the Uruguay Round of GATT talks in 1990. They also served as a shot across the bow of an increasingly introspective European Union that seemed hesitant to continue global approaches to trade liberalization.

Both institutions eventually had to confront diminished credibility, however. The Asian economic crisis deflated APEC's stature, even though APEC had never claimed a mandate as an instrument of financial rescue. Even more damaging was the fact that, in the aftermath of 9/11, the Bush administration sought to shift APEC's orientation from economics to support for the so-called "global war on terror." However, Japan also drove its own nail into the APEC coffin by refus-ing to collaborate with Early Voluntary Sector Liberalization (EVSL) efforts. The EVSL initiatives, as Green (2001: 212) has stated, led to a confrontation between "the US results-oriented approach and Japan's process-oriented approach." Ultimately, Japan stood alone in its defiance of demands for tariff liberalization in such domestically sensitive areas as wood products and fish (Krauss 2004). With this important failure to move forward on sectoral liberalization, APEC became effectively moribund (Ravenhill 2000; Webber 2001), although it may gain some revitalization as a result of President Obama's decision to host the 2011 APEC meeting in his home state of Hawaii. ARF, as well, lost support, particularly from the United States, which under the Bush administration was far more skeptical about multilateral approaches to security than the previous administration. Indeed, in 2005 Secretary of State Condoleezza Rice did not even show up for the ARF meetings. Again, the Obama administration has moved to rectify such actions by creating an ambassador to ASEAN, by signing ASEAN's Treaty of Amity and Cooperation (TAC), and by Secretary of State Clinton's regular attendance at ARF meetings, all measures applauded by Japan's government.

During the financial crisis of 1997–8, Japan sought – in a unilateral action seen by the United States and the IMF as a challenge – to create an Asian Monetary Fund that would provide needed liquidity to the crisis-affected countries. This pro-posal was quickly shot down by the United States and the IMF as well as by China. Yet the crisis and the terms of IMF "conditionalities" spurred a widespread con-viction across much of Asia, led often by Japan, that regional financial solutions could serve as an alternative and moreover that the global financial architecture needed to be reconfigured to take greater account of the growing financial power of Asian economies. (It is worth noting that the IMF is engaged in precisely such a reallocation of its internal voting rights.)

The first collective regional response to this mix of incentives came with the Chiang Mai Initiative of May 6, 2000. CMI came about as the result of a Japanese proposal to create an extensive network of currency swaps among the ten ASEAN countries (ASA) as well as a network of bilateral swap arrangements (BSA) among the ASEAN countries, China, Japan, and the Republic of Korea (ROK). Japan, in the words of Amyx (2006: 4), "played the role of arbitrator as countries in the region negotiated the general terms for the swap arrangements."

When the CMI originally came into effect, considerable stress was placed on the limited amounts of money involved in the swaps, as well as on the requirement that most swaps be congruent with IMF regulations. Yet by early 2005 some sixteen bilateral swap agreements had been organized under CMI totaling $39 billion. Then at the eighth meeting of finance ministers of the APT (ASEAN Plus Three) in Kuala Lumpur on May 5, 2005, the APT agreed to double the amounts in existing swap arrangements, raising the total to $80 billion. Then, the finance ministers meeting on May 5, 2007, went much further when they agreed "in principle" to multilateralize the CMI through a reserve pool and a single contractual agreement for the drawing of funds. Such an arrangement took effect in 2010 and has moved CMI to a more comprehensive reserve pool with a single contractual agreement that centralizes and multilateralizes the entire arrangement as CMIM (Chiang Mai Initiative Multilateralisation). Of special interest is the fact that China, Korea, and Japan – as the three largest potential contributors – were able to agree on a formula that muffled any rivalries between Japan and China. Japan's financial stake amounts to 32 percent of the total while the contribution of China plus Hong Kong also equals 32 percent. Thus, Japan is the "single largest single contributor" while at the same time the People's Republic of China (including Hong Kong) and Japan are the "largest co-equal contributors."[2] Current arrangements are still a long way from providing any explicit challenge to the IMF, but they indicate a growing capacity for Asia as a region to provide a partial alternative to unbridled dependence on the IMF and its policy views.

A particularly strong advocate of the increases was Kuroda Haruhiko, head of the Asia Development Bank (ADB) and an original proponent of the Japanese proposal for an AMF in 1997. In April 2005 he created the Office for Regional Economic Integration and appointed Kawai Masahiro, a well-known proponent of regional monetary union, as its head. Kuroda's actions were in keeping with Japanese efforts to foster a yen-denominated version of the AMF and thereby to blunt the rising economic influence of China (*Asia Pacific Bulletin*, May 13, 2005). Kuroda, Kawai, and the ADB, in conjunction with many Asian governments, have been important forces pushing for greater Asian financial cohesion.

The more advanced economies in Asia have also moved to develop Asian bond markets. Here too Japan has been an active leader. The bond markets would provide an additional mechanism of regional financial stability and reduce Asian dependence on the U.S. dollar for financial reserves, currency baskets, and international transactions. Japan's Ministry of Finance and the Japan Bank for International Cooperation (JBIC) have been in the forefront of efforts to reduce impediments to its functioning in an effort to allow smooth and rapid issuance of local currency bonds (details in Pempel 2007).

Both the currency swaps and the bond market serve more as indicators of intentions than of deep and powerful integration. Many steps remain before either will emerge as an active and dynamic element in the regional political economy. In particular, it seems clear that Japan is following up its unsuccessful efforts to create an Asian Monetary Fund at the time of the Asian crisis. Although the current measures are hardly defined as potential counters to the United States as well as U.S. influence in global money markets and in the IMF, they certainly are institutionally independent of both. Moreover, they offer the promise of longer-term balancing against global U.S. financial heft. As Katada (2004: 178) has suggested, Japan, with its regional financial efforts, is pursuing a "counterweight strategy," challenging and attempting to modify the dominant U.S.-led international financial system. The new bodies will not necessarily become *alternatives* to the current system, but they provide at least an additional forum in which Japanese influence will be greater and one through which it can pursue its goals, giving it both a counterweight to the United States as well as an opportunity to "forum shop."

Potentially of great interest is a mini-lateral body that has spun off from the ASEAN Plus Three. In 2008, the "plus three" nations, Japan, China, and Korea, met separately in Fukuoka, Japan, in a bigger power effort to resolve a variety of common issues. Two subsequent meetings in Beijing and Jeju, Korea, during the following years have led to a trilateral commitment to establish a secretariat and to work toward a common investment treaty and a free trade treaty. The three leaders' meetings are now being supplemented by an increasing number of lower-level dialogues among other officials and by efforts to find multilateral solutions to a host of common problems. Tellingly, these meetings have shown considerable independence from broader global bodies and from the oversights of the United States, reinforcing suggestions that many Japanese multilateral actions are driven by self-interest and enhanced self-confidence about moving independently of the United States.

The final institutional body worth mentioning is the East Asia Summit. EAS first met on December 14, 2005, and it held a second meeting in January 2007. In attendance at both were leaders from sixteen countries: the ten ASEAN members, the additional "three" from the APT – China, Japan, and the Republic of Korea – plus Australia, New Zealand, and India.

EAS emerged in response to the proposal of the East Asia Vision Group (EAVG) chaired by former Korean Prime Minister, Kim Dae-jung. It was one of nine specific proposals put forward by EAVG. Japan declared itself an enthusiastic supporter and promised to contribute proactively to its success, despite warnings from former U.S. Deputy Secretary of State Richard Armitage (*Asahi Shimbun* 2005) that the United States thought the EAS a poor idea, and despite the fact that the United States would not be a participant.

An important characteristic of EAS is its broadened membership, which reaches beyond the thirteen APT members to include Australia, New Zealand, and India. Japan played a continuous behind-the-scenes role in this broadening, despite Chinese reluctance. For Japan, the new members add a core constituency more likely to support overall Japanese goals for the region than those in the ASEAN Plus Three, particularly those linked to democracy and security cooperation with the United States. Although the meetings so far have been more show than substance, and it is not clear just how large a role EAS will eventually play as a regional institution, this presents one more case in which Japan has been active in support of regional institution building, in this case in the area of financial cooperation. Interestingly, as part of the Obama administration's efforts to "re-engage" with Asian regionalism, the United States announced in 2010 that it planned to attend the 2011 EAS meeting in Jakarta (along with Russia) as an observer, suggesting perhaps a renewed overlap between the United States and Japan in their approaches to Asian multilateralism.

Japanese security: tightening the bilateral embrace

Although the Cold War ended in Europe with the collapse of the Soviet Union and its Eastern European allies, powerful Cold War residues remained in Asia, most notably in the bifurcated Korean peninsula, the cross-Straits relationship between Taiwan and China, and a host of unresolved territorial disputes. Japan has nevertheless gone through substantial changes in its security policies (Green 2001; Hughes 2004; Pempel 2007, inter alia). Despite its reorientation, and despite all of the evidence that Japan is increasingly concerned about taking greater leadership on a host of global issues along with Europe, Japan's bilateral security ties with the United States have, if anything, been bolstered, not weakened, often at the expense of any broader multilateralism.

Within Japan, any enhanced embrace of multilateralism has continued to be balanced off by the overwhelming desire to maintain close security relations with the United States. The security alliance appeared to be adrift in the early 1990s, but spurred by the Assistant Secretary of Defense for International Security Affairs, Joseph S. Nye, and boosted by Japan's own concerns over warming bilateral ties between the United States and China, Japan and the United States reaffirmed their bilateral security relationship in a set of revised and considerably widened guidelines for defense cooperation agreed to in 1997 and subsequently modified in 1999.

Indeed, serious domestic pressures continued to mount among defense hawks for Japan to take a more positive global role and thus to become a "normal" nation. Hence, Japan responded to Bush's shift toward unilateralism, preventive attacks, and demands to be "with us or against us" by enthusiastically tightening its security embrace of the United States. This Japanese shift was particularly clear in both Afghanistan and Iraq. With the domestic political left having self-destructed, the Koizumi government faced little parliamentary opposition in altering a series of security laws, first to allow Japanese Maritime Self-Defense Forces to support U.S. military actions in Afghanistan, and then to commit Ground Self-Defense Forces to the "coalition of the willing" in Iraq, the latter marking the first time

Japanese ground troops were sent abroad during active hostilities and without the patina of U.N. sanctions (Pempel 2007).

Japan also tightened its embrace of the United States with its new National Defense Planning Outline (NDPO) of December 2004 (Fouse 2005; Pempel 2007). The NDPO abandoned prior ambiguities by explicitly identifying China and North Korea as potential security concerns. The NDPO also called for policy changes to deal with both ballistic missile and guerrilla attacks in addition to the traditional focus on invasion threats involving Japanese airspace and territorial waters. Japan's security interests were overtly expanded from defense of the home islands to include international security, international peacekeeping, and counter-terrorism as key targets of Japan's overall national defense strategy. To meet the newly characterized threats, Japan, it was argued, needed a bolstered multifunc-tional military capability with a centralized Self-Defense Force command and a rapid reaction force.

Japan as well joined the United States in joint development of a ballistic missile defense system, and following the July 4, 2006, missile tests by the Democratic People's Republic of Korea (DPRK) it advanced the purchase timetable for the relevant weapons. In all of these ways, Japan demonstrated a singular willingness to reinforce pre-existing bilateral mechanisms so as to enhance its security ties with the United States. Such actions were in sharp distinction to Japan's multilateral institution building in so many other areas. Indeed, although Japan has acceded to the ban on land mines and has destroyed its own stockpile, it has said little about the U.S. maintenance of land mines on U.S. bases within the country (Landmine Monitor Report 1999).

At the same time, Japan's security ties with the United States have not been exclusively bilateral. Both the Six Party Talks and the Proliferation Security Initiative provide instances of Japanese security multilateralism in the Asian region. However, in both of those multilateral processes, Japan and the United States have rarely strayed far from one another.

The Six Party Talks (involving the United States, Japan, China, ROK, Russia, and the DPRK) began in Beijing in August 2003 in an effort to resolve the growing threat of a nuclear North Korea. These talks, although regional in membership, nonetheless saw Japan and the United States in virtual lockstep on most issues. Indeed, for much of the negotiation, the United States was the only country of the six to support Japan's continued insistence in linking the so-called abductees issue to denuclearization. (The United States continued to be a nominal supporter of Japan's claims, but the staggering electoral defeat of Prime Minister Abe in the House of Councillors elections in July 2007, the rapid moves by the DPRK to shut down its Yongbyon facilities, and Japan's unwillingness to participate in economic assistance to the DPRK all combined to leave Japan more isolated from 2007 until 2009 than at any previous time.) However, it is also worth noting that former Prime Minister Koizumi was apparently quite effective in pressing President Bush to abandon his initial absolutist support for "regime change" and to adopt a more flexible negotiating position following the stalled situation in 2003. (Japan and the

United States, along with South Korea, have reforged their close ties regarding the DPRK since the second nuclear test by the DPRK in early 2009, the election of Lee Myong-bok in Korea, the sinking of the ROK's corvette, the *Cheonan* – purportedly by the DPRK – and the much harder DPRK line taken since 2008.)

The Proliferation Security Initiative is also multilateral, involving as it does seventeen countries cooperating for pre-emptive interdiction of aircraft or ships suspected of transporting weapons of mass destruction or otherwise presumed to be a security risk. Japan was one of eleven charter members of the PSI in May 2003. The initiative is designed to create a cooperative network focused on reducing the spread of weapons of mass destruction. As early as June 2003, Japan used the PSI to change its policy in regard to the ferries operating from North Korea. Nearly 2,000 inspectors went to the port of Niigata to check for customs and immigration violations, infectious diseases, and safety violations on the North Korean vessel *Man Gyong Bong-92*. North Korea responded by immediately ceasing all ferries traveling between the two countries and canceled a port visit by an unnamed vessel believed to be involved in espionage. The Japanese policy appears to be part of a larger strategy to involve regional actors in policing North Korean exports.

Japan also hosted its first PSI Maritime Interdiction Exercise off the coast of Sagami Bay and off the Port of Yokosuka from October 25 to October 27, 2004. Eleven of those exercises have been conducted in various regions of the world. Again, although nominally multilateral, the PSI is a U.S.-generated institution and Japan's participation represents less a measure of free-floating multilateralism and more a willingness to multilateralize its bilateral security links with the United States.

Additionally, and with particular vigor under the Obama administration, Japan and the United States have cooperated in expanding their bilateral security ties in two separate directions: first, trilateralizing previously bilateral links among Japan, Australia, and the United States; and, second, in a similar trilateralization of U.S., ROK, and Japan ties.

Finally, as but one brief indicator of the tightening of ties between Japan and the United States consider Figure 12.2. This measures the percentage of times that Japanese voting in the U.N. General Assembly matched U.S. voting. Following a high of 70 percent in 1977, the overlap in voting slipped consistently until roughly the end of the Cold War. In the early 1990s it rose steadily but then began to drop again with the early years of the Bush administration. However, in the following two years, at the height of U.S. unilateralism, Japan was once again voting more closely with the United States.

The central point here is clear. Japan has taken several important steps to advance multilateralism in cooperation with the other mid-level powers as well as moving to enhance regionalism within the Asia-Pacific. Some, such as the ARF, even involved security. When the Bush administration opted for a new U.S. unilateralism, Japan chose unmistakably to reinforce its ties to the United States, at least in the area of defense and security, in ways that have recommitted it to bilateralism

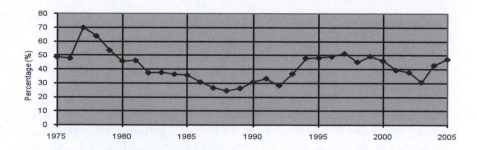

FIGURE 12.2 Japanese coincidence in voting with the United States in the UN General Assembly.

over multilateralism. That proclivity for hugging the United States closely on security was more recently demonstrated by Prime Minister Hatoyama's reversal of his campaign pledge to end or reduce the U.S. military presence on Okinawa. Under withering U.S. criticisms he finally agreed to implement a 2006 bilateral agreement on re-basing Futenma to another area of Okinawa, a move that contributed substantially to Hatoyama's subsequent resignation but an issue that, as of this writing, has yet to be satisfactorily resolved by the two countries.

Conclusion

In the last decade plus, Japan has become a far more active multilateralist than it was in the previous forty years. It has been an active creator and sustainer of a host of new multilateral institutions, particularly within the Asian region and particularly in the areas of economics and trade as well as in environmental technology – all of which are comparative strengths for the country and all of which have been welcomed by Japan's Asian neighbors as ways to foster closer regional connections. Japan does especially well when it emerges as a strong proponent of new institutions, regimes, and norms that allow it to advance its image as "non-military" and "peaceful."

In a host of its non-Asian, global endeavors Japan has often emerged as a close ally of the European Union and Canada. In such areas Japanese multilateralism has been heavily normative and has shown clear political leadership. Such global efforts complement Japanese leadership in its Asian regional efforts. To the extent that national competition, as opposed to regional solidarity, has motivated Japanese policy makers, it has been competition with China in Asia, rather than with the United States globally, that has driven Japanese behavior.

At the same time, certain of Japan's activities have gone forward without active assistance from the other middle powers. In particular, Japan's option to "go multilateral" has played out on the East Asian regional stage and not just in the global theater. Some of these efforts have been similar to Japan's global efforts at redefinition of national identities and the provision of global public goods.

However, Japan's actions in East Asia have also been motivated at least in part by regional strategic considerations and the effort to show itself to be at least as good a "global citizen" as China. To date, although most of its Asian neighbors are reluctant to bandwagon against China, they welcome Japanese efforts to be an active counterweight to Chinese influences in emerging regional bodies.

Furthermore, Japan benefits from the rising number of multilateral and regional institutions by acquiring multiple forums within which to "shop" for policy solutions addressing specific problems. If the WTO poses problems, Cartegena may provide a better alternative. Similarly, if the IMF or the global bond market poses difficulties, then CMI or the Asian bond market may prove to be better tracks. In the search for multiple forums within which to advance its national interests Japan is perhaps no different from other mid-level powers, although European powers seem far more likely to seek regional coordination in advance than does Japan with its Asian neighbors. Through it all, by becoming a more active multilateralist, Japan raises its overall stature with most other countries, always seeking (however unrealistically) to enhance its chances of gaining a permanent seat on the UN Security Council.

At the same time, Japan's shift toward multilateralism and East Asian regionalism has, in the last five or six years, continued to be counterbalanced by a reinvigoration of its bilateral ties to the United States, most especially in the area of security. In this complex mixture, it is difficult not to conclude that Japanese multilateralism has been quite selective and generally in tune with the country's perceived national interest and with the pressures exercised by its domestic politics. Clearly, Japan is a long way from being a committed multilateralist and instead balances bilateralism, multilateralism, and regionalism in its efforts to interact in the most nationally expeditious way on the global stage.

Notes

1 See http://www.iwcoffice.org/commission/iwcmain.htm (accessed January 19, 2011).
2 See http://www.rttnews.com/Content/AsianEconomicNews.aspx?Node=B2&id=1249386 (accessed January 24, 2011).

13

INDUSTRIAL POLICY IN AN INTEGRATED WORLD ECONOMY

The South Korean paradox

Chung-in Moon and Dae-yeob Yoon

Introduction

South Korea was one of the poorest countries in the world in the early 1960s, with its per capita income being less than U.S.$100. Poverty and underdevelopment followed by Japanese colonial rule, national division, and the Korean War were seen as its destiny. Within less than four decades, however, South Korea became a member of the Organisation for Economic Co-operation and Development (OECD) by graduating from the status of developing country and emerged as one of the powerhouses of the world economy. Central to the amazing transformation was the timely adoption of an export-led industrialization that was backed up by an assertive industrial policy. The South Korean government selected strategic industrial sectors with greater forward and backward linkage effects and orchestrated their promotion through the strategic allocation of resources. Despite its temporary setbacks in the late 1970s, the big push through heavy chemical industrialization paved the way to an impressive take-off of the South Korean economy.

However, the magic of this industrial policy did not last long as it encountered three profound challenges. The first challenge was democratization. The democratic opening and expansion of civil society since 1987, an outcome of rapid industrialization, fundamentally delimited the scope of economic policy maneuver by the state. The second came from the outside. Rectification of the Uruguay Round and new membership at the OECD no longer allowed South Korea to enjoy the old benefits of trade protectionism and industrial policy. The third challenge emerged in the wake of an acute economic crisis during 1997–8 that resulted partly from a deeper integration into the world economy. The International Monetary Fund (IMF)'s neoliberal prescriptions involving structural adjustment radically realigned the institutional and political foundation of industrial policy. These challenges notwithstanding, the South Korean economy bounced back in the first decade of the twenty-first century. Its growth rate was restored, and exports have been on the rise. Remarkable is the structure of its economic performance. South Korea is currently leading the world in the areas of such high value-added, cutting-edge sectors as semi-conductors, consumer electronics, shipbuilding, and automobiles. Such a remarkable comeback was not an outcome solely of spontaneous market forces. New patterns of industrial policy wrapped in R&D investments and science and technology policy have contributed to reversing the downward trend.

Against this backdrop, our paper explores the dynamics of economic transformation in South Korea through the analysis of its industrial policy. The first section presents a brief analytical discussion on the ideas of developmental state and industrial policy in the South Korean context. The second examines a historical overview of correlates of development strategy, industrial policy, and economic performance in South Korea. The third section traces how democratization and globalization have affected the evolving nature of industrial policy. The fourth delineates new patterns of industrial policy that were responsible for the economic reversal. Finally, the concluding section suggests some theoretical and comparative implications.

The developmental state and industrial policy: some analytical notes

Determinants of economic success in South Korea have long been subject to hot scholarly debates. Neoclassical economists have attributed South Korea's economic success to the interplay of an open economy, market-conforming government policies, and assertive entrepreneurship by the private sector (Balassa et al. 1981; Hughes 1988; Krueger 1990; World Bank 1993). According to this view, South Korean economic performance can be seen not as a miracle, but as a natural and spontaneous outcome of the application of classical economic principles. South Korea sought an aggressive economic liberalization through a sequence of macro-economic stabilization, liberalization, and export-led growth industrialization that not only reduced static inefficiencies arising from resource misallocation and waste, but also enhanced learning, technological change, and economic growth. Its market-based economic system was less prone to wasteful rent-seeking activities and was more flexible in dealing with the transmission of external shocks (Rodrik 2010; Haque 2007; Noland and Pack 2003). Also, neoclassical economists believed that optimum industrial upgrading and changes in production structure had occurred rather automatically when the South Korean government got prices and institutions right (Wade 2010).

However, the neoclassical account presents a rather simplistic view. South Korea's economic transformation was not a product solely of the workings of the invisible hand of the market. The "visible hand" of the state played the crucial role in shaping its economic miracle. The South Korean state was not a minimalist state envisioned by neoclassical economists that would simply guarantee the existence of a free and competitive market or serve as a passive and neutral container of contending social and political interests. It had clearly defined developmental goals and undertook an extensive strategic intervention in the economy through plan rationale, industrial targeting, and mobilization and selective allocation of resources in strategic sectors in order to achieve such goals. The state virtually dictated the nature and direction of market forces in order to achieve its objectives by effectively utilizing the reservoir of available policy instruments (Magaziner and Hout 1980; Johnson 1982; Reich 1982; Dore 1986; Jones and Il 1980; Amsden 1985, 1989; Chang 1993, 1994; Evans 1995; Wade 1990; Haggard and Moon 1983; Haggard 1990).

Industrial policy was an important tool for the interventionist state (Moon and Lim 2001: 194–7). Chalmers Johnson defined industrial policy as "coordinated government activities to leverage upward the productivity and competitiveness of the whole economy and of particular industries in it" (Johnson 1984: 8). It can be seen as "the infusion of goal oriented, strategic thinking into public economic policy," which grew out of a changing concept of comparative advantage (Johnson 1984: 8). In a similar vein, Noland and Pack (2003: 10) regard industrial policy as "an effort by a government to alter the sectoral structure of production toward sectors it believes offer greater prospects for accelerated growth than would be generated by typical process of industrial evolution according to static comparative advantage." Thus, industrial policy is concerned with a mix of public policies to "promote competitiveness through structural adjustment" (Commission of the European Communities 2007) or "to maximize its potential to contribute to economic growth while minimizing the risks that it will generate waste and rent-seeking" (Rodrik 2004: 3). In view of the above, industrial policy comprises a wide range of policies involving banking and financing, taxation, competition, trade and investment, science and technology, regulation, labor and wage, and administrative incentives.

Industrial policy per se does not assure anything, however. Its performance should be measured by the degree of efficiency, coherence, and consistence in its policy formulation, as well as by the degree of effectiveness in its implementation. Despite some drawbacks such as overinvestment and surplus capacity in the late 1970s, it is generally known that the South Korean government was able to formulate efficient and coherent industrial policies and to implement them in a consistent and effective way (Amsden 1989; Wade 1990). Such policy performance has been attributed to the developmental nature of the state, which was rather unique to South Korea (Moon and Prasad 1994).

First, executive dominance mattered. The executive leadership prevailed over the legislative and judiciary branches. Former president Park Chung-hee was the paramount leader in steering industrial policy. Second, vertical executive–bureaucratic ties were also conducive to the successful performance of industrial policy in which executive leadership effectively utilized bureaucrats as agents of industrial transformation through control and coordination. Third, bureaucrats showed an unusually high degree of unity of purpose for modernization and development, defying inertia-driven interagency turf fighting. It was also known that a tough recruitment process and meritocracy were able to produce top-notch technocrats. Fourth, the economic policy decision-making process was relatively insulated from contending social and political pressures, partly because of the authoritarian mode of governance. Also, concentration of policy instruments in the government ensured speedy and effective policy management. Finally, the state and society were constantly interconnected through a myriad of formal and informal networks. In this sense, state–society networks have been based on a vertical hierarchy that enabled the state to dictate to society. However, such a hierarchy has been complemented by horizontal ties formed through formal (e.g. examination council) and informal organic (e.g. family, school, regional) networks. Vertical command and discipline were matched with horizontal consultation and consensus through shared corporate goals, and enhancing trust and the exchange of knowledge essential for economic performance (Moon and Lim 2001; Evans 1995; Fukuyama 1995).

However, the developmental state described above did not last long. Democratization, globalization, and the acute economic crisis in 1997 have fundamentally altered the landscape of state structure and the policy-making and management system. Executive dominance was undercut by the empowerment of the legislative branch and the penetration of social and political pressures, especially those associated with electoral cycles. Whereas presidential control and coordination over bureaucrats have become weakened, the unity of purpose among them waned. The process of democratic consolidation and globalization profoundly eroded the shield of insulation surrounding the policy-making process. Formal and informal networks between the state and social constituents were broken in the aftermath of the 1997 economic crisis (Moon and Rhyu 2002). The changing contour of the state led to shifting industrial policy.

Industrial policy and the South Korean economic miracle: historical overview

Initial conditions for South Korea's economic development were miserable. After thirty-six years of Japanese colonial rule, Korea achieved national independence in 1945, but it was soon divided into two halves. Worse was the outbreak of the Korean War, which lasted for three years from 1950 to 1953, leaving behind enormous destruction. Per capita income in 1953 was $67, current account deficits were $67.5 million, and rampant post-war inflation and a high unemployment rate haunted the South Korean economy. More critically, South Korea could not survive without American assistance.

The dismal economic performance notwithstanding, the Rhee Syngman government initiated an import substitution industrialization (ISI) strategy for major non-durable consumer goods such as textiles, sugar, and food processing starting in the mid-1950s. However, the ISI strategy was abruptly halted as the First Republic was overthrown by the April 19 Student Revolution in 1960. Moreover, the strategy distorted the allocation of resources through political-economic collusion and rent-seeking behavior. In addition, chronic inflation, structural unemployment, and pervasive corruption posed major obstacles to economic reconstruction (Moon and Lim 2001: 198). Political characteristics in the 1950s were inimical to overall development planning. The government was poorly insulated from the demands of the private sector, having been penetrated by patron–client networks. Economic bureaucracy was subject to political interference from both the executive and the ruling party. The last years of the Rhee administration witnessed some innovation within the economic bureaucracy, but these innovations took place in a larger political context that blocked reform (Haggard and Moon 1993: 64). Social and political instabilities ensued through acute economic crises and ultimately led to two major regime changes in 1960 and 1961.

The Second Republic created by the Student Revolution in 1960 was short-lived. It fell prey to a military coup by then Major General Park Chung-hee. After nineteen months of military interregnum, Park became the leader of the Third Republic by winning the 1963 presidential election. He undertook comprehensive economic policy reforms: devaluation, tax, and interest rate reforms, an opening to foreign capital, and a drive to expand exports. Export promotion policies constituted the central part of the new policy initiative under the slogan "Export Number One" (Haggard et al. 1991). The Park government delicately linked the export promotion strategy to an assertive industrial policy. A wide range of incentives were provided in this regard: tax holidays to exporters, preferential allocation of credits to the export sector, exemption of tariffs on raw material and intermediate goods for export, the establishment of export-processing zones for foreign investors as well as of the industrial complex for domestic manufacturers, and the provision of information infrastructure through the establishment of the Korea Trade Promotion Agency (KOTRA).

This labor-intensive export promotion strategy was orchestrated under the philosophy of "guided capitalism." Although the principle of free enterprise and respect for the freedom and initiative of private enterprise were observed, the South Korean government either directly participated in or indirectly rendered "administrative guidance" to the basic industries and other important fields (Amsden 1989; Wade 1990). Such an arrangement was possible because of the rise of the developmental state. The military coup of May 16, 1961, broke the political networks of the Rhee period by centralizing power in the executive leadership. Even after the transition to a nominally democratic system in 1964, the new political structure resulted in a high degree of executive independence from the demands of both legislators and interest groups. Equally important was the overall restructuring of business–state relations. A new alliance with the private sector was forged during the early 1960s in which opportunities for rent seeking were considerably curtailed. Finally, the centralization of political authority was matched by a centralization of economic decision making in the Economic Planning Board, and the Ministry of Commerce and Industry was empowered as the central coordinator of the industrial policy (Haggard et al. 1991: 857).

After six years of labor-intensive export industrialization, the Park government initiated an ambitious campaign in 1971 known as the Heavy and Chemical Industry (HCI) drive. Six industries, namely the steel, automobile, electronics, shipbuilding, petrochemical, and non-ferrous special metal industries, were designated as strategic sectors (World Bank 1993; Amsden 1989; Wade 1990; Moon and Lim 2001: 199; Leipziger and Thomas 1993: 15). The "big push" toward heavy industrialization, which defined the nature and direction of economic development in South Korea between 1972 and 1979, was initiated in a larger political context. "Industrial deepening" through the promotion of heavy and chemical industries was designed to resolve several problems simultaneously. Nominally speaking, heavy chemical industrialization was seen as a new engine of rapid economic growth and export expansion that could reverse the eroding international competitiveness, while effectively coping with growing U.S. protectionism on light, labor-intensive manufactured goods. More critically, the drive was the political leadership's choice to accelerate military self-reliance by promoting defense industrialization amidst waning American security commitment and the growing military provocation of North Korea. The six strategic sectors were closely related to defense industrial capability. Finally, the big push was believed to facilitate the legitimization of Park's authoritarian *Yushin* regime through impressive economic performance (Haggard and Moon 1983: 76; Kim 2005).

The formulation and implementation of the heavy chemical industrialization plan epitomized the very strength of the Korean state. Planning was highly centralized in the Blue House and the Ministry of Commerce and Industry, bypassing the more orthodox Economic Planning Board. President Park's obsession with defense industrialization and thereby the big push minimized bureaucratic feuds. Moreover, the government had centralized control over the policy instruments required to implement its designs, despite some initial skepticism from the private sector. From 1977 to 1979, 80 percent of total investment in manufacturing went into the heavy and chemical industries, largely in the form of "policy loans" from the state-owned banking system. At the broader political level, the new authoritarian structures of the *Yushin* Constitution precluded legislative scrutiny (Haggard and Moon 1990: 217).

The Park government pursued heavy chemical industrialization by enacting six promotional laws. They included laws on industrial machinery (1967), shipbuilding (1967), electronics (1969), steel (1970), and petrochemicals (1970). In accordance with the promotional laws, the government steered heavy chemical industrialization through directed, subsidized credit, selective protection, regulations affecting industrial entry, and direct government involvement in industrial decision making. The National Investment Fund (NIF) was created in 1974 to finance the HCI drive. It was funded by the compulsory deposit of savings by all managers of pensions, savings, postal savings accounts, and life insurance. Policy loan, the directed credit instrument of government, rose from an already high 41 percent of total domestic credit in 1975 to 51 percent in 1978 (Kim and Leipziger 1993: 22). And the HCI was driven by the second phase of ISI in which restricted import of machinery rose from 34 percent of the total in 1968 to 61 percent in 1978; iron and steel rose from 28 percent to 75 percent (Kim and Leipziger 1993: 22). In addition, those firms that were engaged in the heavy chemical industry with forward and backward linkages with the defense industry were given lucrative tax incentives, free plant sites, and even the supply of qualified manpower (Moon 1991). In this process, the Park government controlled the credit system to provide strategic industries with access to substantially subsidized bank loans. These included the power to impose ceilings on the aggregate outstanding volume of loans for each banking institution, to approve in advance individual loan applications made to banks in excess of specified amounts in periods of pronounced monetary expansion, and to establish general guidelines on the efficient allocation of bank funds. The Korean government dictated who could and could not obtain loans (Lee and Jung 2000: 11–12).

The heavy chemical industrial drive, which not only disregarded inflationary consequences but also was littered with overinvestment and surplus capacity, encountered a devastating setback in 1979. Growth rates that had averaged almost 10 percent a year between 1962 and 1978 fell to just over 2 percent between 1979 and 1981, with a particularly sharp contraction of the economy in 1980. At the same time, inflation rose to 26 percent from an annual average of 16 percent between 1962 and 1978. Exports fell from a 27 percent average annual rate of real growth between 1962 and 1978 to 7.5 percent between 1979 and 1982. The current account deficit widened from $1.1 billion in 1978 to $4.4 billion in 1981. In addition to domestic economic mismanagement, external economic conditions were not favorable. Whereas the second oil shock worsened Korea's terms of trade and balance of payments, rising interest rates deepened the country's debt-service burden. The assassination of President Park in 1979 created immense political uncertainty (Haggard and Moon 1990).

The Chun Doo-hwan government, which seized political power through a mutiny and a military coup in December 1979 in the wake of the assassination of Park by his trusted aide on October 27, 1979, undertook the extensive neoliberal reform measures to stabilize the macro-economy, solve mounting financial problems in major industries, and establish new directions for industrial policy under pressures from the IMF. Realizing that the economic downfall in 1979–80 was a result of mismanaged industrial policy, the new government attempted to make a fundamental break with the style of economic management of the past by emphasizing comparative advantage rather than industrial targeting and import substitution, while fostering the transition toward an economy led by the private sector with a general reduction of state intervention and wider play for market forces (Haggard and Moon 1990: 219). As part of this effort, the government introduced an industrial rationalization plan to realign the heavy chemical sector through merger, phase out, and consolidation. Its past preferences for heavy industry firms were reversed by reserving credit for small and medium firms. At the same time, the government sold the commercial banks to private shareholders, although it continued to exercise significant influence over banking decisions.

Also, the scope of interest rate subsidies for particular borrowers was substantially reduced (Kim and Leipziger 1993: 23).

The penalty of success? Democratization, globalization, and limits to industrial policy

The Chun government's neoliberal reform proved to be successful. By 1985, South Korea enjoyed record-breaking economic success by overcoming the downturn, which was in turn followed by two major trends, democratization and globalization. These two trends had profound implications for industrial policy in South Korea. Whereas forces of democratization fundamentally weakened the power of the developmental state, globalization and increased compliance with norms, principles, rules, and procedures of liberal international economic order gradually deprived the South Korean state of policy tools to steer industrial policy.

South Korea underwent a dramatic democratic transition in 1987. As Chun's term was nearing its end in 1987, the opposition circle comprising college students, workers, and dissidents staged massive street demonstrations calling for constitutional amendment that would allow the direct election of a president. Chun was desperate to preserve the existing constitution so that his hand-picked successor Roh Tae-woo could become the next president through an indirect election. Street demonstrations became intensified, and confrontation between the Chun regime and its opponents deepened. A critical moment came. The middle class, which used to remain silent in favor of political and social stability, began to exert pressure on Chun by joining the street demonstrations. Facing immense pressures, Chun accommodated the citizens' demand for constitutional amendment. His successor Roh won the presidential election in December 1987 as a result of the three-way split in the opposition camp. Nevertheless, the overall political landscape was significantly altered.

The democratic change empowered the legislative branch, while limiting executive power. President Roh could no longer prevail over the ruling party and the legislative branch. Legislative check and balance became all the more pronounced. Along with this, executive leadership over bureaucrats was also severely damaged. Unlike during the Park and Chun regimes, bureaucrats did not comply with presidential orders blindly. As vertical presidential control over bureaucrats became troublesome, horizontal unity among bureaucrats was also on the wane, intensifying interagency conflicts. More importantly, the Economic Planning Board, the powerful superministry, was dissolved, and the Ministry of Commerce and Industry could not enjoy its old power and influence as the principal agent of industrial policy. More emphasis was given to welfare and education, whereas public policies related to growth did not get attention from the president. Equally critical were the changing relationships between the state and civil society. The state could no longer dictate to the private sector, and labor became a significant actor after the democratic transition. In addition, NGOs have become influential in shaping the public arena (Moon and Rhyu 2002).

The expansion of business conglomerates known as *chaebol* deserves special attention in this context (Moon 1994). Park Chung-hee was instrumental in creating *chaebols* as agents of rapid industrialization. However, after the democratic transition in 1987, the state began to lose its tight grip over big business. It was an inevitable outcome of changing policy environments. Whereas government regulation, especially in the areas of environmental and competition policy, was strengthened, traditional incentives such as preferential financing, tax and tariff holidays, and subsidies began to disappear. Equally critical was the relative weight of the private sector. The South Korean government depended heavily on big business for its economic and export performance. As of 1985, 72.2 percent of South Korea's exports came from big business. As Table 13.1 shows, big business accounted for 68.0 percent of manufacturing output and 72.2 percent of total exports in 1985 (Table 13.1).

Another example can be found in the changing composition of R&D investment. During the period of the active developmental state (1970–80), the government share of R&D investment accounted for more than 50 percent (61.9 percent during 1970–5, 52.5 percent during 1976–80), but this figure has declined markedly to 20.3 percent during 1991–2000 and 27 percent during 1996–2008). Meanwhile, the private sector has accounted for over 70 percent since 1986 (STEPI 2009). The new business environment fundamentally delimited the scope and effectiveness of industrial policy.

Forces of globalization posed additional limits to the conduct of industrial policy. In the first half of the 1990s, South Korea undertook two major measures to foster its integration into the global economy. One was the ratification of the Uruguay Round, and the other was the admission to the OECD through which South Korea graduated from the status of developing country. Both measures had profound implications for the conduct of industrial policy, severely undercutting its institutional foundation. The advent of the World Trade Organization (WTO) system forced South Korea to further dismantle barriers to trade, especially non-tariff ones that served as a valuable instrument of industrial policy. Increased restrictions on trade-related subsidies, restrictive import licensing, and the import diversification program virtually deprived the South Korean government of its

TABLE 13.1 Manufacturing output and exports of big, and small and medium business (percent)

		1985	1990	1995	2000	2005
Small and medium business	Output	32.0	42.6	46.6	47.3	47.8
	Export	27.8	42.1	41.8	36.9	32.4
Big business	Output	68.0	57.4	53.4	52.7	52.2
	Export	72.2	57.9	58.2	63.1	67.6

Source: Korea Federation of Small and Medium Business statistics. Available at http://www.kbiz.or.kr (accessed January 19, 2011).

crucial tools to implement industrial policy. Bilateral pressures from the United States further delimited the scope of industrial policy maneuver (Ahn 2008: 6; Go 2005). Admission to the OECD also narrowed the scope of its industrial policy. As with the WTO, the OECD urged South Korea to comply with tougher restrictions on industrial subsidies. It also called for the relaxation of regulations in the industrial, banking and financial, and service sectors. The OECD's request for higher standards in labor management relations such as the protection of regular workers meant that South Korea faced much tougher challenges of spontaneous globalization.

Facing this new internal and external environment, the Kim Young Sam government initiated the *segyehwa* (globalization) campaign (Moon 1995; Moon and Mo 1999; Sechuwi 1995, 1996, 1998; Kim 2000).[1] The move reflected a major shift in the thinking of economic management from a defensive, mercantilist adaptation to external changes to a positive accommodation of outside stimuli. Globalization was more than a political slogan or an administrative guide for economic management. It has evolved into a new hegemonic ideology replacing the old developmentalism. The *segyehwa* campaign set South Korea's ascension to a first-rate state in the twenty-first century as its principal goal, and identified productivity, flexibility, and fairness and autonomy as new guiding principles for national economic management. Its target was not limited to the economic domain, but extended to entire segments of society ranging from education, law, and foreign policy to politics, culture, environment, and the quality of life.

South Korea's ratification of the Uruguay Round and admission to the OECD were parts of this globalization campaign. Economic liberalization under Kim was quite extensive in scope and ambitious in its implementation plans. Another related move was deregulation. South Korea began to realize negative aspects of the government's strategic intervention in the economic domain, which in the past was considered a major source of international competitiveness. However, strategic intervention was correlated with mounting regulations, undermining its international competitiveness. Deregulating economic life and correcting government failures were singled out as a major target of globalization. Finally, rationalization constituted another important component of globalization. State intervention was gradually replaced by market principles. Institutional reforms aimed at rationalization and accountability were undertaken virtually in all sectors of the state and society. Globalization became a new, omnipotent ideological tool of governance in the new era (Sechuwi 1998).

The Kim Young Sam government's portrait of *segyehwa* as "the shortcut to a first-class country in the twenty-first century" proved to be false even before reaching the new century. A major setback to *segyehwa* took place during his tenure. The sudden collapse of the Korean economy in November 1997 alarmed the entire world. After a series of financial and foreign exchange crises, the Kim Young Sam government filed for national economic bankruptcy by asking the IMF for $57 billion in bail-out funds on December 3, 1997. The myth of the Korean economic miracle was shattered, and national shame prevailed. During Kim Young Sam's term in office, South Korea's foreign debts increased from $43.9 billion to $160.7 billion in 1996 and $153 billion in 1997, while foreign reserve assets dwindled from $20.2 billion in 1993 to $12.4 billion in 1997. At the peak of the currency crisis, foreign reserves held by the central bank were less than $8 billion, spreading the fear of default. With foreign reserves being depleted, the Korean currency rapidly depreciated. In 1993, the won/dollar exchange rate was 808.1 won, but the Korean won devalued by almost two times by the end of 1997, posting an exchange rate of 1,415 won/dollar. At one point, the exchange rate reached 2,000 won/dollar (Moon and Mo 2000).

More troublesome was the private sector. A sharp increase in non-performing loans literally paralyzed the banking and financial sector, precipitating a credit crunch, corporate bankruptcies, and the financial crisis. Non-performing loans accounted for 6.8 percent of total bank loans as of the end of September 1997. The stock price index immediately reflected failures of the corporate as well as the banking and financial sector. The average annual stock price index was 808.1 in 1993 and 1,027.4 in 1994. However, it continued to slide down throughout 1995 and 1996, falling to 375 by the end of 1997, the lowest since the opening of the securities markets. Falling stock prices amidst rapid currency devaluation drastically reduced the value of Korean firms' assets. According to an analysis by the *Financial Times* in 1997, the total assets of all 653 Korean firms listed on the Korean Securities Exchange Market were estimated to be worth only 66.3 trillion Korean won, which was the equivalent to the assets held by one European company, ING Group, a Dutch banking and financial firm ranked as the seventieth largest firm in the world (*Financial Times* 1997).

What went wrong? The genesis of the Korean economic crisis can be attributed to the interplay of domestic mismanagement and external financial volatility (Moon and Mo 2000: 14–24). Beneath the "healthy fundamentals" of its macro-economy, its micro-economic foundations had slid into deep trouble. Declining international competitiveness, dismal corporate performance and bankruptcies, mounting non-performing loans and the paralysis of the banking and financial sectors, and extensive government failures had all contributed to the downfall of the Korean economy. However, equally critical was its unprepared integration into the global economy through hasty globalization. The premature opening of capital markets made the South Korean economy extremely vulnerable to the transmission of external financial instabilities.

Adaptation and finding institutional niches: a new industrial policy initiative

The 1997 financial crisis and subsequent mandates of structural adjustment as IMF conditionalities brought about major changes in the institutional landscape of the South Korean economy. Flexible labor markets, removal of moral hazards through the radical liberalization and rationalization of the banking and financial sector, corporate restructuring toward a greater accountability, transparency, and international competitiveness, and liberalization of trade and foreign investment constituted the core elements of the IMF reform mandates (Moon and Mo 2000: 25–34). Industrial policy, which was once touted as the paramount hero of economic transformation in South Korea, was all of a sudden accused of being the primary cause of economic disaster. It was pointed out that excessive state intervention through industrial policy bred a milieu conducive to reckless corporate expansion with borrowed money that eventually created a snowballing effect of non-performing loans by major business conglomerates in South Korea. In fact, the assertive pursuit of industrial policy was responsible for creating the myth of "too big to fall." Both the financial crisis and structural adjustment resulted in tremendous trauma for the Korean people.

However, South Korea made an amazing comeback. As Table 13.2 shows, Korea's GDP growth rate returned to a 4–5 percent level during the early 2000s, one of the highest among OECD countries. Since 2000 balance of payments has begun to show a surplus. By 2005, South Korea also emerged as the eleventh largest economy in the world. In 2010 the size of its foreign reserve assets exceeded $300 billion. It is remarkable that its economic comeback has been closely associated with the revitalization of the manufacturing sector. Even without any explicit industrial policy, the South Korean manufacturing sector has been resuscitated. As Figure 13.1 reveals, the share of manufactured goods in South Korea's GDP hovered around the 30 percent level between 1995 and 2007, which is much higher than in Germany, Japan, the United States, and France. Another striking

TABLE 13.2 Economics indicators after the economic crisis

Economic indicator	2000	2005	2006	2007	2008	2009
Balance of CA (U.S. dollars, billions)	12.3	15.0	5.4	5.9	−5.8	42.7
Balance of trade (U.S. dollars, billions)	11.8	23.2	16.1	14.6	−13.3	38.8
Exports (U.S. dollars, billions)	172.3	284.4	325.5	371.5	422	361.6
Imports (U.S. dollars, billions)	160.5	261.2	309.4	356.8	435.3	322.8
Unemployment rate (%)	4.4	3.7	3.5	3.3	3.2	3.6
GDP growth rate (%)	8.5	4.0	5.2	5.1	2.3	0.2
Foreign reserve (U.S. dollars, billions)	96.2	210.4	239.0	262.2	201.2	270.0
Market capitalization (Korean won, trillions)	217.1	726.0	776.7	1051.9	623.1	974.0
Stock market index (KOSPI)	504.62	1,379	1,434	1,897	1,124	1,683

Source: Bank of Korea Economic Statistics Systems. Available at http://ecos.bok.or.kr (accessed January 25, 2011).

Note
CA, current account; KOSPI, Korea Composite Stock Price Index.

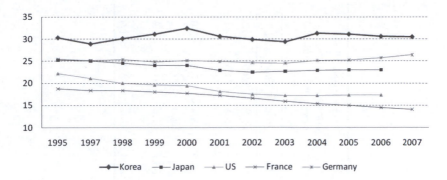

FIGURE 13.1 Share of manufacturing output in GDP. Source: *OECE Factbook*, 2009. Available at http://www.oecd-ilibrary.org/economics/oecd-factbook-2009_factbook-2009-en (accessed January 25, 2011).

aspect is a sharp increase in exports of high value-added manufactured goods. The relative share of high-value manufactured goods such as semi-conductors, electronic components, automobiles, communication equipment, shipbuilding, and petrochemical products rose from 38 percent in 1995 to 60 percent in 2008 (KIET 2009).

Table 13.3 presents some comparative indicators of industrial performance between South Korea, the United States, Japan, Taiwan, the United Kingdom, and Germany. South Korea outperformed other competitors in several categories. For example, South Korea's manufactured exports per capita rose by more than four times, from $1,455 in 1990 to $5,766 in 2005, the highest among the six countries. The share of manufactured exports in total exports was 97.9 percent in 2005, again the highest. All of the countries except for South Korea showed a decline in the share of medium/high technology production in manufacturing value added from 1990 to 2005. The figure for South Korea increased from 55.1 percent in 1990 to 60.3 percent in 2005. South Korea also showed the best performance in the share of medium/high technology exports in manufacturing exports in 2005. All of these figures imply that South Korea has been moving into constant industrial and technological upgrading and deepening.

How could such performance be possible? An OECD document makes an interesting statement on correlates of industrial policy and economic performance in South Korea:

> It is fair to say that since the 1980s, Korea has not adopted a national champion promoting strategy and so its leading exporters in shipbuilding, automobiles, and electronics sectors have gotten on their feet without government assistance to survive fierce competition at home and abroad and become the world leaders.

(OECD 2009c: 126)

TABLE 13.3 Indicators of industrial performance

Country and indicator	Manufacturing value added per capita ($)			Manufactured exports per capita ($)			Share of manufactured exports in total exports (%)			Share of medium/high technology production in manufacturing value added (%)			Share of medium/high technology exports in manufacturing exports (%)		
	1990	2000	2005	1990	2000	2005	1990	2000	2005	1990	2000	2005	1990	2000	2005
Korea	2,237	2,855	3,827	1,455	3,582	5,766	96.2	97.8	97.9	55.1	53.7	60.3	52.9	69.6	75.1
United States	4,325	5,414	5,528	1,181	2,480	2,707	81.1	89.7	88.7	63.0	57.0	55.7	73.4	74.5	72.1
Japan	9,696	8,130	8,474	2,263	3,598	4,387	97.5	95.2	94.2	66.5	54.2	56.9	83.9	85.2	82.0
Taiwan	2,842	3,426	4,144	3,148	6,494	8,053	95.8	97.5	96.8	52.2	49.4	49.4	51.6	71.3	70.2
United Kingdom	3,807	3,921	3,707	2,655	3,978	5,464	82.4	84.0	85.6	60.0	48.1	56.1	67.3	67.9	65.4
Germany	6,871	4,770	5,179	4,665	5,914	10,900	93.2	88.5	92.0	66.5	61.0	61.1	68.7	72.2	71.9

Sources: UNIDO (2005, 2009).

The statement implies that South Korean firms have been performing better even without the government's industrial policy support. The OECD attributes the South Korean success to a low general tax level for all companies, removal of unnecessary administrative burdens on firms, a flexible labor market, provision of training and education to the unemployed, and the promotion of non-sector-specific research and development (OECD 2009c: 16). The OECD observation makes sense, but it comes short of unraveling the real dynamics of economic dynamism in the post-industrial policy period. Although the South Korean government could not undertake the old type of assertive industrial policy, it has undertaken prudent and quite extensive industrial promotional policies that are characterized mostly by non-sector-specific R&D support as well as other measures congruent with OECD/WTO compliance.

Let's take an example of the Kim Dae-jung government. Having suffered from the acute financial crisis in 1997–8, the Kim government was desperate to come up with a new policy initiative that could vitalize the stagnant economy. Promotion of venture industry became the core of its new industrial policy drive. The Kim government believed that the promotion of venture industry could achieve three goals simultaneously, namely proactive structural adjustment of Korean industry in favor of small and medium-sized industries, the development of new technology, and the alleviation of unemployment through new job creation. The new policy initiative reflected the dominant social mood of the time, which was critical of big business, emphasized the importance of information and communication, and realized the mandate of transition to a new knowledge economy. In order to support the venture industry, the Kim government enacted a special law concerning the promotion of venture firms and established a committee for the vitalization of the venture industry in 1999 in which the Minister of Industry and Resources was appointed as chairman, and the head of the Small and Medium Business Agency as vice-chairman. The Kim Dae-jung government allocated a total of 1.92 trillion Korean won to 8,000 venture firms as seed money (Chang 2005: 33). The venture industry initiative was not as successful as the Kim Dae-jung government envisaged. Massive government financial support of venture firms led to the problem of moral hazards. Nevertheless, some venture firms flourished with greater forward and backward linkages to high-tech industries such as IT and biogenetics.

The Roh Moo-hyun government also conducted an industrial policy in the disguised form of R&D and science and technology policy. The Roh government designated ten fields as the engine of next-generation growth. They were digital TV/broadcasting, display, intelligent robots, future automobiles, next-generation semi-conductors, next-generation mobile communication, intelligent home networking, digital contents/software solutions, next-generation batteries, and biomedicine. As part of efforts to promote these ten sectors, the Special Committee for the Promotion of Next Generation Growth Engine was established under the Committee on Science and Technology chaired by the president. In addition, a division of labor was made in which the private sector would lead digital TV, display, intelligent home networking, next-generation semi-conductors, and mobile communication, whereas the government would take the initiative in biomedicine and internal organs. The remainder (i.e. digital contents, software solutions, next-generation batteries, intelligent robots, and future automobiles) were to be co-developed through the cooperation of the government and the private sector (STEPI 2005). The Roh government invested a total of 2.056 trillion Korean won for the promotion of ten sectors (NABO 2010: 8).

The Lee Myung-bak government, which was inaugurated in February 2008, had a more ambitious plan to promote cutting-edge technologies. It identified twenty-two sectors in six fields (energy/environment, transportation, new information technology, new fusion industry, bio, and knowledge service) as new engines of growth: twelve more items were added to the existing ones (Planning Committee on New Growth Engine 2008). In November, 2010, the Lee government further narrowed the new growth engines to five areas as the feasibility of the original plan was questioned. They are green transportation, system semi-conductors, energy efficiency maximization through smart grid, thin film solar batteries, and natural biomedicine. A total of 700 billion Korean won was allocated for the promotion of these technological sectors (Sung-hoon 2010).

What is interesting is that the new pattern of industrial policy primarily involves the creation of R&D infrastructure. Table 13.4 offers interesting data in this regard. State-led R&D projects for which the annual allocation of the government budget exceeds more than 10 billion Korean won, such as the Industrial Complex Innovation Cluster project, Parts and Components Competitiveness

TABLE 13.4 Major state-led R&D projects in the 2000s

Project	Agency in charge	Start date	2009 budget (100 million Korean won)
Industrial Complex Innovation Cluster project	MOKE	2005	688
Parts and Components Competitiveness enhancing project	MOKE	2001	3,187
Technology transfer	MOKE, SMBA	2004	990
Northeast R&D Hub Creation	MEST	2002	283
Next Generation Core Environment Technology	MOE	2003	1,003
Agro-Bio Engineering Technology Project	RDA	2001	423
Total			6,574

Source: Ministry of Knowledge Economy (2010).

Note
MOKE, Ministry of Knowledge Economy; SMBA, Small and Medium Business Administration; MEST, Ministry of Education, Science and Technology; MOE, Ministry of Energy; RDA, Rural Development Administration.

enhancing project, transfer of advanced technology, and Northeast R&D Hub Creation, are closely related to the creation of R&D infrastructure. This can be sharply contrasted with industry- and sector-specific state intervention. The trend is further evidenced by the enactment of legislative bills. Most of the industry-specific promotion laws (e.g. machine industry 1967, shipbuilding industry 1967, electronic industry 1969, textile industry modernization 1969, steel industry 1970, petrochemical industry and non-ferrous metal industry 1971) were phased out. Although the Special Law for the Promotion of Venture Firms and the Special Law on the Promotion of Parts and Components Manufacturing Firms were enacted in 1997 and 2001, they were also phased out. Thus it can be said that industry-specific promotional policies are no longer in existence.

As Figure 13.2 demonstrates, the ratio of R&D investment in South Korea's GDP rose from 0.38 percent in 1970 to 3.37 percent in 2008, almost a ten-fold increase. And a great proportion of South Korea's R&D went to product development. In 2005, for example, 50.2 percent of total R&D was allocated for product development, whereas basic research and applied research accounted for 24.2 percent and 25.6 percent respectively. This allocation pattern contrasts sharply with that of the United States in which only 11.1 percent was allocated for product development, while 45.9 percent was allocated for basic research and 43 percent for applied research (KISTEP 2007; Ahn 2008: 65). Another interesting pattern is that the overall R&D investment has been led by the private sector. As Table 13.5 shows, the composition of R&D financial sources has changed from the government to the private sector. During the period of the developmental state (1970–80), more than 55 percent of the R&D fund came from the government, whereas the private sector accounted for 45 percent. However, since 2001, more than 70 percent of the R&D fund has come from the private sector.

Apart from the R&D policy, the South Korean government has employed a wide range of new industrial policies to enhance its international competitiveness.

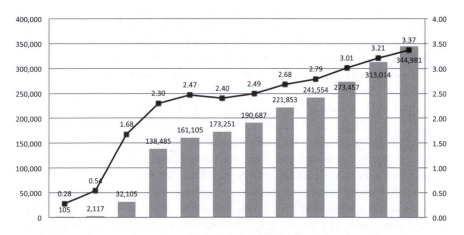

FIGURE 13.2 R&D investment in South Korea, 1970–2009. Source: STEPI (2009).

TABLE 13.5 Composition of R&D investments by agents and financial sources (percent)

	Agents			Financial sources		
	Public	University	Private firms	Public sector	Private sector	Foreign sector
1970–5	66.0	5.1	28.9	61.9	29.9	8.3
1976–80	58.4	8.7	33.4	52.5	46.5	1.0
1981–5	33.6	11.0	55.2	30.0	69.3	0.7
1986–90	20.5	9.5	69.9	18.0	82.0	0.1
1991–5	20.5	7.2	72.3	20.3	79.6	0.2
1996–2000	16.8	10.9	72.3	28.4	71.5	0.1
2001–8	13.4	10.3	76.2	(26.8)	(72.9)	(0.3)

Source: KISTEP (2009).

Note
The numbers in parentheses indicate 2008 statistics.

Although it cannot adopt an old style of overt "tax holidays," private firms' investments in research and human development, productivity enhancement, environment and occupational safety, and energy efficiency have been reciprocated with corresponding tax credits by the South Korean government. Such tax credit practices have been much more diverse and generous than in other OECD member countries (Kim et al. 2008: 27). The old practice of preferential financing for strategic sectors is no longer available, but the South Korean government has utilized state-owned special purpose banks (e.g. the Korea Development Bank and the Korea Industrial Bank) and public funds such as the Fund for Technology Guarantee and the Fund for Credit Guarantee as new vehicles of financial support for the promotion of strategic industries, R&D, small and medium-sized firms, and equipment investment. These special purpose banks and funds have been financed through the issuance of bonds. In the case of the Korea Development Bank, its development financing bond accounted for 5 percent of GDP in 2009 (Yong Hyo 2009). Moreover, the South Korean government has relaxed the loan to deposit ratio in order to ensure a more flexible lending. Whereas the ratio for commercial banks was 112 percent, those for the Korea Development Bank and the Korea Industrial Bank were 418 percent and 266 percent, respectively, in 2009 (*Money Today* 2010). As this practice received criticism from abroad, the South Korean government decided to establish the Korea Finance Corporation, while privatizing the Korea Development Bank in 2009. Also, in addition to the Korea Credit Guarantee Fund and the Fund for Technology Credit Guarantee, the South Korean government currently operates several funds related to the promotion of science and technology, nuclear research and development, the enhancement of the information and communication industry, the promotion of small and medium-sized industry and industrial technology infrastructure, and export insurance. Therefore, a new form of industrial policy is still being widely practiced in South Korea.

The Office of the United States Trade Representative (USTR) has criticized these practices through its annual National Trade Estimates on Foreign Trade Barriers. It has come up with several observations regarding South Korea's unfair trade practices. For example, it points out that export credit and insurance schemes below market rates, concessional tax and duty provisions, and export-processing zones have become other forms of non-tariff barriers (Bora et al. 2000). It also raised a question about government procurement and technology standard policy by arguing that:

> As part of its Voice over Internet Protocol (VoIP) plan, the Korean government considered mandating that government agencies purchase equipment that contains encryption technology based on a Korean encryption standard called "ARIA," despite the availability and wide use of international standards for encryption of VoIP.
>
> (USTR 2010: 231)

A critique over banking and financial policy also draws our attention:

> Korea adopted a holding company system in October 2009 and divided the Korean Development Bank (KDB) into two new companies: (1) KDB; and (2) the Korea Finance Corporation (KFC). While still government-owned, the KDB is to operate as a commercial bank under this restructuring plan and the KFC will operate as a policy lending bank.
>
> (USTR 2010: 232)

South Korea's competition policy has also been subject to grievances:

> Korea currently prohibits foreign satellite service providers from selling services (e.g., transmission capacity) directly to end users without going through a company established in Korea. Given investment restrictions in place, and the fact that establishing a local presence may not make economic sense, this prohibition significantly restricts the ability of foreign satellite service providers to compete in the Korean market.
>
> (USTR 2010: 234)

An examination of industrial policy since 1998 reveals that the South Korean government has not adopted the old pattern of assertive industrial policy. Nevertheless, it does not mean the end of state intervention. On the contrary, the South Korean government has been carving out new institutional niches that do not violate codes of fair trade practices mandated by the WTO/OECD. Non-sector-specific science and technology policy and flexible utilization of R&D investment policy belong in these new niches. In some cases, as USTR critiques draw to our attention, the South Korean government seems to be still engaged in industrial policy rather similar to old practices. As long as South Korea pursues an export-led growth strategy, it is likely to rely on the innovative application of some form of industrial policy in order to enhance the international competitiveness of its economy.

Conclusion

Industrial policy is at the heart of South Korea's economic transformation. Its economic miracle would not have been possible without the developmental state and its active intervention in the market through industrial policy. Nevertheless, economic success through industrial policy fostered its own demise. Whereas democratic opening and consolidation eroded the foundation of the developmental state that was crucial for making successful industrial policy, forces of globalization and further integration in the global economy fostered the process of its dismantling. The old pattern of industrial policy is not possible, but the South Korean government has resurrected it in new forms of R&D and science and technology policy.

In the wake of the global financial crisis and the impending surge of new technologies, the role of industrial policy – promoting some sectors or products ahead of others – is again drawing attention from policy circles and scholars. As Robert Wade (2010: 150) has suggested, developing country governments and firms might have to be prepared to push back against the shrinking latitude for industrial policy instruments allowed in international trade and investment agreements. Rodrik (2010) even declared that industrial policy is back. By arguing that successful economies have always relied on government policies that promote growth by accelerating structural transformation, he underscores three principles. First, industrial policy is a state of mind rather than a list of specific policies. Its successful practitioners understand that it is more important to create a climate of collaboration between government and the private sector than to provide financial incentives. Second, industrial policy needs to rely on both carrot and stick. Given its risks and the gap between its social and private benefits, innovation requires rents – returns above what competitive markets provide. Finally, industrial policy's practitioners need to bear in mind that it aims to serve society at large, not the bureaucrats who administer it or the businesses that receive the incentives.

Even the World Bank, which was somewhat skeptical of the effectiveness of industrial policy within the framework of the so-called Washington Consensus, echoes a fresh new view on its relevance. Lin (2009: 4), Senior Vice-President and Chief Economist of the World Bank, states that:

> at each given stage of development, the market is the best mechanism for effective resource allocation. However, economic development as the dynamic process of moving from one stage to the next requires industrial upgrading and corresponding improvements in hard and soft infrastructures. The

industrial upgrading is an innovation. The pioneer firms in the upgrading process generate non-rivalry, public knowledge to other firms in the economy. The improvements of infrastructures have large externalities to firms' transaction costs and returns to capital investment. Thus, the government should play an active, facilitating role in the industrial upgrading and in the improvements of infrastructures.

Déjà vu? We do not think South Korea can re-adopt the previous pattern of industrial policy. However, the South Korean state cannot stay idle. It will intervene in the market, cooperate with the private sector, and come up with promotional policies through knowledge generation and pooling in order to cope with infinite competition in the globalized economy.

Note

1 The Roh government initially undertook a campaign for internationalization. The Kim Young Sam government, however, changed it into the globalization campaign. For the analytical and policy differences between the two campaigns, see Moon (1995).

PART III

Corporate strategies in the globalized economy

14

CRISIS . . . WHAT CRISIS? (REVISITED)

Exploring multinational enterprises' responsiveness to the financial crisis

Rob van Tulder[1]

Introduction

Can and do multinational enterprises (MNEs) contribute to solving societal problems – some of them of their own making? This contribution assesses the strategies developed by MNEs on two related phenomena: globalization and corporate responsibilities on the one hand, and the global financial crisis on the other hand. It makes a conceptual contribution by classifying societal (or non-market) strategies of MNEs as passive or active, and an empirical contribution by applying this classification to the strategies of a sample of the world's 100 largest MNEs toward the global financial crisis.

This paper proceeds as follows. The next section discusses the nature of the present stage of globalization and its underlying mechanisms. To what extent is globalization surrounded (or triggered) by crises? The following section explains why the most important actors in globalization can be considered MNEs, not only because they face the biggest influence of globalization, but also because they are in fact the prime carriers of globalization, thus directly contributing to its present rather ambiguous shape. The next section builds on previous research on variation in corporate social responsibility (CSR) strategies of the 100 largest multinationals in the first six years of the twenty-first century (cf. van Tulder 2010; see http://www.erim.nl/scope), which creates the "baseline" or "benchmark" with which actual strategies of these same firms can be compared. This makes it possible, next, to investigate whether the basic position of corporations in 2006 toward CSR influenced their approach toward the first shocks of the financial crisis at the end of 2008.

The following section zooms in on a subgroup ($n = 61$) of the original sample of the 100 largest firms: a combination of the largest financial and non-financial corporations. The financial corporations have been most involved in (responsible for?) the proliferation of the financial crisis, so one can expect them to experience the strongest urge to become active in creating solutions. Do companies with a more active stance toward societal problems prove less susceptible to the financial crisis? Is there a relationship between internationalization and decreases in stock prices and can this also explain a company's initial attitude toward the financial crisis?

Data-gathering limitations – at the time of writing financial annual reports for 2009 were not yet available – meant that it was only possible to consider the direct response to the crisis, which shows a more intuitive and perhaps less (rationally) elaborate attitude. The initial responses of a public enterprise, however, very often "frame" later more elaborate – ex post rationalized – responses. In the words of behavioral economists Thaler and Sunstein (2009: 81), they represent a *choice architecture* (or Nudge) that strongly influences the mindset on future approaches. The present study, therefore, could have predictive value, although this is certainly not its primary aim.

"Globalization" equals "crisis"?

"Globalization" as a process of international economic and societal change is not new. It has come in waves and creates sizable tensions. At the moment we are, on most accounts, in the middle of a third wave of globalization, which started in 1989 with the fall of the Berlin Wall. Earlier waves of globalization were related to industrial revolutions in Europe and the formation of colonial empires. This more formal form of globalization has been qualified by some as even more pervasive because it resulted also in a share of trade and foreign investment volumes compared with global domestic product that surpassed even present levels (cf. Maddison 1991; Ruigrok and van Tulder 1995). The present wave of globalization is built on less formal institutions, which therefore create different kinds of tensions. Initially, the third wave represented to many the victory of capitalism as the dominant and most obvious *modus operandi* for economies or even the "end of history" according to philosopher Fukuyama (cf. van Tulder with van der Zwart 2006). Globalization optimists proclaimed plan economics dead and market economics the leading paradigm for future progress and prosperity. As a consequence, all countries were expected to become more open in order to profit from the gains of increased mobility of goods, services, people, and capital. However, this optimism has been challenged by at least two major forces: one from "without" and one from "within."

First, the existence and success of political-economic models that defied some of the basics of capitalism – often in competition with the leading economies themselves – challenges the traditional book recipes for growth. The Chinese political and economic model challenges the idea heralded by Armatya Sen (1999) that economic growth should always be combined with political democratization, while the strategies of leading Chinese (state-owned) companies defied the idea that internationalization is primarily the area of publicly traded companies (multinationals). Other new contenders – particularly from so-called BRIC countries:

Brazil, Russia, India, and China – show that economic success need not always be built on economic and political "openness" (Rodrik 1999) nor on fully developed liberal market economies. One size does not fit all, and as a consequence public policy in the age of globalization (Hveem and Nordhaug 2002) is surrounded by growing controversy and ambiguity. For instance, the principles of the Washington Consensus – introduced by the Bretton Woods institutions to steer aid and growth programs – have been seriously debated and practically abandoned.

Second, globalization has been accompanied by considerable and sustained crises. Some crises (food, poverty) affected developing countries in particular. Other crises (ecology) have also had major repercussions for the developed world. Do we witness mere incidents, logical transition pains, or structural/systemic problems? Some even claimed that crises and shocks have regularly been created in order to enable particular interest groups to press for further and pervasive change in a particular direction – the rise of so-called "disaster capitalism" (Klein 2007). The most recent, most vicious, and systemic crisis in this context is arguably the crisis of the financial system, resulting in global recession. The global (credit/mortgage) crisis commenced in October 2008 and was precipitated by a long sequence of smaller national crises such as the peso/ruble/real crisis, the savings and loans crisis in the United States, the Asia currency crisis – some observers counted as many as 150 financial crises since 1989. The liberalization of the financial markets has been one of the strongest forces in support of globalization. This long sequence of financial crises, therefore, alludes to major governance and regulatory deficiencies across and within borders.

The sources of the 2008 financial crisis can be attributed to the irresponsible behavior of banks and consumers, but also to failing regulation, whether in the hands of governments or the sector itself. Regulatory voids appeared in particular for new financial products or techniques such as derivatives or securitization. Products were primarily (cf. McDonald 2009) created to evade or frustrate effective regulation – not for the sake of innovation. The trade-off between "risk" (creating uncertainty) and "responsibility" (managing uncertainty) became settled in favor of the risk takers.[2] The financial crisis has shown that even the most sophisticated risk management models – at least according to the sector itself – did not function properly. An alternative approach is required to prepare for uncertainty. Could this be based on a redefinition of the firm's responsibilities and a different attitude toward the root causes of the crisis? Crises are enhanced by denial of their seriousness or lack of acceptance of one's own responsibilities, which hampers effective and timely measures. Denial can come from the participants themselves ("crisis . . . what crisis?") or from influential commentators such as the development economist André Gunder Frank or the British rockband Supertramp, who used the phrase as the title of an influential column and a protest song, respectively, in the 1970s.

These inside and outside forces put mounting pressure especially on multilateral organizations in all areas related to globalization, such as trade, intellectual property rights protection (cf. Hveem 2008a), investment, climate change, and poverty alleviation. How to make "globalization good" has become a relevant theme (Dunning 2003), accompanied by an increased search for corporations behaving "responsibly" and "ethically." There remain, however many routes and recipes toward prosperity and growth (cf. Rodrik 2007a), with serious trade-offs between liberalization – as a precondition for releasing the beneficial forces of globalization – and regulation – as a guarantee for managing the destructive forces of globalization.

Some have even argued that the actual process of globalization has to fear more from its supporters than from its critics. The latter will help to make globalization more sophisticated and thus sustainable, whereas the former are not interested in dealing with the obvious side effects of globalization, which seriously threaten its sustainability. The consequence of the present shape of globalization has been that rivalry between countries has increased, which has put multilateral institutions even further under pressure. The trade talks under the auspices of the World Trade Organization have encountered great difficulties, as has been the case with efforts to come to global solutions to climate change. No international investment regime exists and – despite major efforts to rule out tax harbors following the 9/11 terrorist attack on the Twin Towers in New York – international tax harmonization is still under way. The global financial crisis has prompted surprising new coalitions amongst the G20 group of governments, some new financial regulation by European governments, but no sustainable and legitimate solutions yet.

MNEs as carriers of the third wave of globalization

At the governmental (formal) level of international governance and institutions, globalization therefore remains poorly regulated. Does this also apply to the informal institutional level of governance through multinational enterprises? The role of multinational corporations as creators of formal and informal institutions around the world has seriously increased in the third wave of globalization, not least because the growth of foreign direct investment (FDI) rather than trade has shaped the present era of globalization. FDI flows and stock are the macro-economic expression of the micro-economic strategies of multinational enterprises. Figure 14.1 illustrates that, since 1980, the growth of trade (exports) outpaced that of global domestic products, which made trade in the 1980s the leading factor of internationalization. Since 1990, however, the growth of FDI dominates that of trade, making multinational enterprises the leading carrier of globalization in the modern era. There are indications that comparable processes appeared in earlier waves of globalization (cf. Ruigrok and van Tulder 1995). FDI flows are dominated by often comparatively small numbers of multinationals (cf. van Tulder with van der Zwart 2006), which makes FDI and therefore globalization a relatively small numbers game.

Despite their limited numbers, the decisions made by the largest multinationals create the – often informal – institutions that shape the nature and direction of globalization. The transnational networks created by multinational enterprises

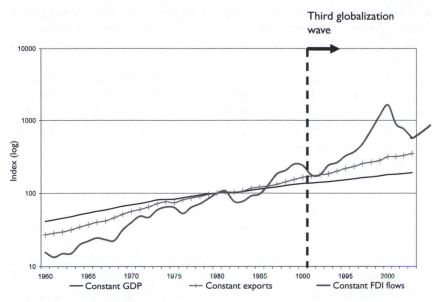

FIGURE 14.1 The third globalization wave (global domestic products, trade, and FDI). Source: GDP, exports from World Development Indicators, World Bank, 2010, available at http://data.worldbank.org/indicator (accessed January 26, 2011); direct investment flows compiled from IFS database, International Monetary Fund, 2010, available at http://www.imfstatistics.org/imf/about.asp (accessed January 26, 2011).

represent an important political force (Hveem 2007b). Therefore, the question becomes relevant of what kind of approaches these companies have adopted vis-à-vis some of the destabilizing societal challenges that have appeared in the third wave of globalization. Do multinationals take an inactive or an active approach and is this affected by their national or industry origins? Do corporate leaders deny the problems at hand, or do they search for solutions and if so what solutions do they propose (either individually or as a group)? How do they frame the problem? In this area, hardly any systematic research has been carried out, so any type of research is bound to be exploratory.

Making globalization good: multinationals and responsibilities

In assessing the strategies of firms toward societal problems, leading scholars have taken either a stakeholder- or a resource-based view of the firm (cf. van Tulder et al. 2009). Firms in interaction with societal stakeholders – represented by non-governmental organizations (NGOs) as well as governments – in the first approach face the extrinsic tension between a defensive (reactive) and an accommodative/preventive (proactive) strategy. A resource-based view of the firm adds "intrinsic" motivations to the stakeholder view. Depending on their capabilities and own ambitions, managers face the tension between an inactive or an active attitude. Two types of trade-offs exist: extrinsic (reactive vs. proactive) and intrinsic (inactive vs. active). Both represent the more fundamental trade-off between "risk" (inactive/reactive) and "responsibility" (active/proactive). This leads to four specific CSR approaches, with different levels of awareness of responsibility, with different procedural attributes, and in which the very CSR abbreviation also has four different meanings.

1. An *inactive* approach reflects the classical notion of Milton Friedman that the only responsibility companies (can) have is to generate profits. This is a fundamentally inward-looking (inside-in) business perspective, aimed at efficiency, and thus can be dubbed "corporate *self* responsibility." It also tends to be linked to a state of denial of corporate responsibilities toward societal problems.
2. A *reactive* or defensive approach shares a focus on efficiency but with particular attention to not making any mistakes ("don't do anything wrong") and minimizing risk. This requires an outside-in orientation. CSR translates into corporate social *responsiveness.*
3. An *active* approach to CSR is explicitly inspired by ethical values and virtues (or "positive duties") of the entrepreneurs themselves. Such entrepreneurs are strongly outward oriented (inside-out) and they adopt a "positive duty" approach. They are set on doing "the right thing." CSR in this approach gets its most well-known connotation – that of corporate *social* responsibility – in which a corporation tries to look for solutions to societal problems, but primarily within its own confines.
4. A *proactive* CSR approach materializes when an entrepreneur involves external stakeholders, right at the beginning of an issue's life cycle. This proactive CSR approach is characterized by *interactive* business practices, in which an inside-out and an outside-in orientation complement each other. In moral philosophy, this approach has also been referred to as "discourse ethics" and can be referred to as corporate *societal* responsibility (Andriof and McIntosh 2001). This shifts the issue of CSR from a largely instrumental, managerial, and negative-duty approach to one aimed at managing strategic networks in which public and private parties have a role and firms actively strike partnerships with non-governmental organizations to come up with more structural and longer-term solutions to societal problems, which represents a largely "positive-duty" approach.

Figure 14.2 summarizes some of the patterns that have evolved between multinationals that operate in different regional and regulatory settings (see van Tulder and Fortanier 2009; Annex 1 gives more detailed observations per company

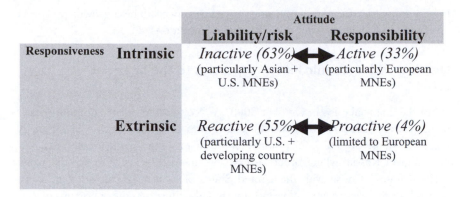

FIGURE 14.2 CSR approaches of the largest Fortune 100 corporations. Sources: van Tulder (2010); van Tulder et al. (2009).

for a subsample of sixty-one firms that will be used in the second part of this contribution).

At the moment most big multinational corporations face a transition period in which they are "somewhere in between" different positions. This represents the different trade-offs these firms and their leaders experience. In particular, country of origin effects are strong. European corporations have adopted the most active CSR approaches, whereas Asian firms have been most inactive. Firms such as Nestlé and Shell, for instance, have taken initiatives that also include a large number of partnerships with NGOs. The corporatist European tradition, of institutionalized negotiations with trade unions and governments, proves helpful in this respect. An inactive approach is understandable, in particular for the five Chinese companies that are included in the sample, as the leading paradigm for national development is still economic growth, which requires that companies concentrate on growth without reference to wider social and ecological dimensions. American firms remain relatively stuck in a reactive strategy. This has been particularly because of the legal system – or CSR regime – in which they operate (cf. van Tulder with van der Zwart 2006).

Sector effects have been strongly mitigated by these influences, but the most active firms can be found in the non-financial sectors of oil/petroleum, food, utilities, and to a lesser extent the car industry. In the banking industry primarily European firms have tried to adopt a more active societal stance. The bulk of the firms, in sum, still remain relatively passive in their societal strategies, but a trend toward more active (non-reactive) strategies has nevertheless been observable over the last ten years. General economic conditions have been particularly supportive for this. One can interpret the early twenty-first century as a period of relative unchallenged growth for multinational enterprises. Steady growth – in particular because of the emerging markets and steadily growing stock prices – after the early collapse due to the dot-com bubble – provided the leading multinationals in general with sufficiently optimistic growth prospects. These growth prospects applied to both financial and non-financial corporations.

Dealing with systemic flaws: responses to the financial crisis

Enter the financial crisis in October 2008 – a "colossal failure of common sense" in the characterization of an insider at Lehman Brothers (McDonald 2009). A typical response of denial, for instance in the first months of the credit crisis, can be found in Russia, where broadcasters were instructed never to use the word "crisis," unless it dealt with the United States of America. This not only is an example of an inactive or reactive attitude, but also illustrates the opportunism that is triggered by crises related to the process of globalization (see " 'Globalization' equals 'crisis'?," above). Annex 1 shows a subsample of sixty-one multinational enterprises that were studied in more detail for their immediate response to the financial crisis. The general attitude of MNEs toward the shock of a (nascent) systemic crisis can be read in their first financial reports that appeared in the course of April–June of 2009. How do firms "frame" the crisis? Do they identify it as a "crisis" or something else? What strategic consequences do they draw from the crisis: an inactive approach toward the causes of the crisis, some small alterations, or important changes that require not only an active approach, but also new rules of the game?

This section looks at the general response of leading MNEs, but also tries to come up with some exploratory observations on influencing factors. Strategic indicators that are taken as possible influencing factors include, first, the degree of internationalization. This is measured as the Transnationality Index (TNI), which is a weighted ratio of the degree of internationalization of sales/employment/ assets of these firms (cf. UNCTAD 2009). A second factor can be found in the extent to which these firms were hit by the financial crisis. This is measured by the drop in stock price they experienced between September 2008 – just before the crisis – and the end of March 2009 – the moment most of these companies had to draft their annual reports. The stock prices are indexed for December 2006, at a time when there was no serious threat to the financial system. Figure 14.3 illustrates this by considering the fluctuations along three intimately related indices: Dow Jones, Standard and Poor, and Nasdaq. The baseline defined at 0 percent on (1) December 29, 2006, is reached again on (2) September 26, 2008, after which the bottom of the crisis is reached on (3) March 27, 2009.

A third factor that will be explored are the previously built-up CSR strategies of companies. This in itself – as explained in the section "MNEs as carriers of the third wave of globalization," above – is the result of country-of-origin and sector effects, which will not be dealt with in this contribution (see van Tulder 2010). What will be elaborated is whether corporate statements or "narratives" on the financial crisis can be classified in the same manner as their CSR strategies.

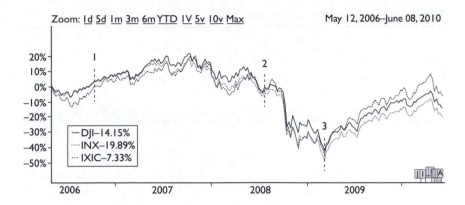

FIGURE 14.3 Key dates in the financial crisis.

The particular framing of the crisis in a more or less active manner – including a particular trade-off between risk and responsibility – is bound to be influenced by the built-up position of the corporation in the area of CSR. Does an active approach toward CSR also trigger a more active approach toward the crisis and is this influenced by the degree to which these companies were hit by the financial crisis?

Framing: the general response

Political leaders, finance ministers, and central bank presidents are always extremely cautious in denominating a "crisis" as a "crisis" – even when it has already materialized. Using synonymous concepts such as "recession" is even more dangerous for fear of creating a self-fulfilling prophecy and triggering multiplier effects – through which "recession" automatically turns into "depression." Well-functioning financial markets are strongly influenced by trust and other non-tangible subjective categories, and so perceptions and framing are extremely important. On the other hand, business leaders face the dilemma much earlier than politicians of warning shareholders of the nascent crisis, which makes the choice they face between reassurance/denial and trust a somewhat different trade-off. A business leader who denies a problem that is already there probably loses more credibility (directly mirrored by a drop in market capitalization) than a regulator and politician. Sometimes, proclaiming a "recession" proves an even stronger statement than noticing that there is a crisis going on. This is an interesting line of further research.

For this study, the following exploratory approach was chosen. Annual reports from 2006 and 2008 (issued in April–June 2009) were scanned for the use of eight different words. It can be assumed that the stronger the wording, the bigger probably is the influence of the crisis on the corporation (Table 14.1).

TABLE 14.1 Framing the crisis: key terms

	Key terms
Strong statements	Recession, downturn, crisis
Moderate statements	Slowdown, severe economic condition, severe economic environment
Weak statements	Challenging year for the company, challenging economy

Tables 14.2 and 14.3 show the averages per company for two different sectors, non-financials and financials respectively, whilst also distinguishing between "big league" and "major league" multinationals, and between European, Asian, and North American multinationals (if applicable) for the years 2006 and 2008. What becomes immediately clear is the stronger framing of almost all companies in 2008 compared with 2006. Although in 2006 most companies marginally referred to some challenging conditions, the word "crisis" does not really appear. This drastically changes by the end of 2008. Most non-financial companies refer to the (financial) crisis, but have difficulty in assessing the extent to which this is related to their own sector and might result in a slowdown, a downturn, or even an outright recession. In particular, the utilities and automotive sectors directly identified the seriousness of the financial crisis for their sectors, which illustrates the extreme degree of "financialization" of these sectors. Firms such as General Motors had become primarily profitable – and therefore financially vulnerable – because of their credit activities. The crisis was directly linked to bad house mortgages, which makes the link with utilities most obvious. Both sectors had already shown a bigger sense for increasingly difficult environmental conditions.

The actual crisis had been anticipated by the management of some corporations. For the financials, the anticipated effect has been stronger. Already in 2006 some reference was made to crisis and recession, which was often related to worsening conditions and the first acknowledgement of a slowdown in the sector. In both sectors, the biggest firms (the "major league" MNEs) as a group have on average been more explicit in their negative assessments.[3] This shows perhaps also a bigger awareness of these firms of their vulnerability to macro-economic fluctuations. Whether it is proof of a bigger awareness of their own responsibilities for the outbreak of crises could be a topic for further research.

Regional patterns exist as well, with European multinationals being most concerned, negative, and explicit, and American firms – certainly in the non-financial sector – remaining relatively silent about the causes as well as the consequences of the crisis. Asian MNEs are on average somewhere in between the United States and Europe. Firms acknowledge the possibility of a recession at a much lower level. American financials are more inclined to consider the crisis as a "challenging" environment and even opt for the possibility of a downturn or recession than to frame the raised problems (for which they in many accounts should be considered primarily responsible) as a "crisis." Again, this is proof of the influence

TABLE 14.2 Average framing (2006–8), non-financials (n = 43)

		Key terms (averages)							
		Crisis	Recession	Downturn	Slowdown	Condition***	Environment	Challenging	Economy****
Totals	2006	0.0	0.1	0.3	0.4	1.0	1.2	0.7	0.6
	2008	8.6	1.8	3.0	1.4	5.1	4.3	1.8	3.5
Big league MNEs (n = 32)*	2006	0.0	0.1	0.3	0.4	0.9	1.1	0.7	0.5
	2008	6.9	1.3	2.8	1.4	5.2	4.0	1.9	3.2
Major league MNEs (n = 11)**	2006	0.0	0.2	0.5	0.5	1.4	1.5	0.5	0.8
	2008	12.8	3.3	3.3	1.3	4.8	5.2	1.7	4.3
Europe (n = 18)	2006	0.1	0.1	0.4	0.6	1.2	1.8	0.7	0.8
	2008	18.1	3.3	5.4	2.2	6.7	6.0	2.2	5.3
Asia (n = 10)	2006	0.0	0.2	0.2	0.3	1.0	1.4	1.0	0.4
	2008	2.6	0.3	1.3	1.0	3.3	2.9	1.6	1.4
N. America (n = 15)	2006	0.0	0.1	0.3	0.3	0.8	0.5	0.4	0.4
	2008	1.3	1.1	1.2	0.7	4.4	3.3	1.6	2.7
Food and retail (n = 9)	2006	0.1	0.1	0.3	0.3	0.2	0.6	1.0	0.3
	2008	4.0	1.1	1.9	0.8	4.0	5.3	2.1	1.7
Extractive (n = 12)	2006	0.0	0.1	0.3	0.2	0.9	0.8	0.3	0.2
	2008	4.2	2.1	3.6	0.9	6.6	2.8	1.9	2.4
ICT (n = 12)	2006	0.0	0.0	0.5	0.2	1.2	1.3	0.5	0.3
	2008	3.6	0.3	1.8	0.8	3.1	4.3	1.2	2.3

TABLE 14.2 continued

| | | Key terms (averages) | | | | | | | |
		Crisis	Recession	Downturn	Slowdown	Condition***	Environment	Challenging	Economy****
Utilities (n = 4)	2006	0.0	0.3	0.0	1.5	1.5	2.0	0.5	2.3
	2008	30.5	4.0	7.3	4.8	7.0	4.5	3.3	10.5
Automotive (n = 6)	2006	0.0	0.5	0.3	0.8	1.8	2.5	1.3	1.2
	2008	20.0	3.8	2.8	2.2	6.7	5.8	1.7	6.2

Notes
Revenues: *$50–100 billion; **$100–500 billion (2006).
***In expressions such as "severe economic condition" or "difficult financial condition."
****In expressions such as "challenging economy" or "severe economy."

TABLE 14.3 Average framing (2006–8), financials (n = 12)

		Key terms (averages)							
		Crisis	Recession	Downturn	Slowdown	Condition***	Environment	Challenging	Economy****
Totals	2006	0.5	0.3	0.3	1.6	2.4	2.0	1.8	0.7
	2008	33.2	5.8	6.8	2.8	27.3	15.0	5.3	8.3
Big league MNEs (n = 7)*	2006	0.7	0.4	0.4	2.0	2.7	1.4	1.0	0.6
	2008	31.4	7.0	5.9	4.1	33.9	16.6	4.9	11.1
Major league MNEs (n = 5)**	2006	0.2	0.2	0.2	1.0	2.0	2.8	2.8	0.8
	2008	35.6	4.0	8.0	1.0	18.2	12.8	5.8	4.4
Europe (n = 8)	2006	0.8	0.4	0.5	2.4	3.1	2.5	1.8	0.6
	2008	40.1	5.8	6.4	3.1	26.0	10.9	5.3	7.6
United States (n = 4)	2006	0.0	0.3	0.0	0.0	1.0	1.0	1.8	0.8
	2008	19.3	5.8	7.5	2.3	30.0	23.3	5.3	9.8

Notes
Revenues: *$50–100 billion; **$100–500 billion (2006).
***In expressions such as "severe economic condition" or "difficult financial condition."
****In expressions such as "challenging economy" or "severe economy."

of the American institutional system or CSR regime, which gives strong negative incentives for firms to move beyond denial and what is minimally needed in terms of liability in order to take a more active responsibility.

Positioning as factor: internationalization and sensitivity to the crisis

One explanation for the globalization of the mortgage crisis in the United States is related to the extensive internationalization of the financial sector itself. The financial tool of securitization has been linked to the possibility for firms to repackage and spin off risks to other – preferably international – partners. The more international banks are, the more they have been inclined to engage in this mechanism, in particular the American banks. One might expect therefore a positive link between internationalization and the drop in stock prices. For non-financial firms, the exact operation of this mechanism is less obvious. A high degree of internationalization could moderate the risk as experienced by the collapse of stock markets.

Figure 14.4 differentiates between the samples of financials and non-financials and shows that there has been a modest but positive correlation – although not statistically significant – between degree of internationalization for financials and decrease in stock price during the month immediately following the crisis. This is all the more remarkable because a number of the financials (UBS, AIG, Citigroup, ING) had already experienced a considerable drop in their stock prices in the December 2006–September 2008 period (Annex 1). On average the drop in stock price has been considerably lower for the non-financial MNEs than for the financial MNEs. An interesting area for further research in this context could be the extent to which the internationalization of financial institutions has been a factor in the willingness of national authorities to save them. Bank of America, for instance, which has been one of the least international banks in the sample, experienced a big drop in its stock prices, and has become one of the prime targets for the U.S. government's rescue plan. Does the moral hazard problem differ for "national champions"? For non-financials there is not even a moderate correlation.

Corporate narratives

To identify the nature of the strategy chosen by MNEs, we can consider in more detail the "narratives" that were formulated by companies in their annual reports. We try to interpret these narratives as more or less active in (1) understanding the causes of the crisis, (2) addressing companies' own responsibilities, and (3) delineating particular strategies to recover from the crisis. A number of representative quotes are used to illustrate particular strategies. They more or less speak for themselves, and so the comments and interpretation are kept to a minimum. The financial and non-financial sectors will be separately addressed.

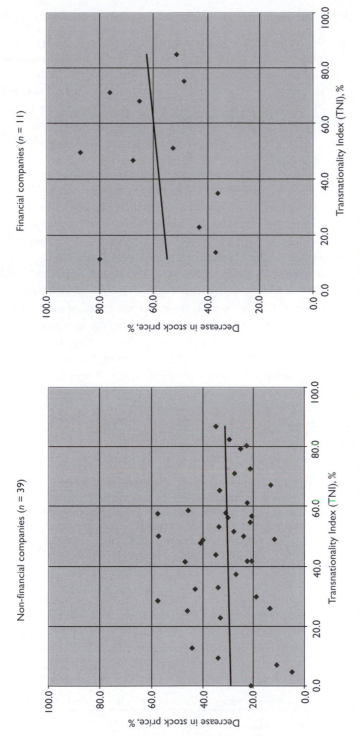

FIGURE 14.4 Relationship between internationalization and changing stock prices (September 2008–March 2009).

Inactive responses

A number of non-financial MNEs (around ten in the sample) can be classified as inactive. They either consider themselves not part of the crisis or reiterate their confidence in a continuation of their previous strategies (see Table 14.4). The corporations that did not issue any statements on the crisis were also amongst the ones with the lowest drop in share prices. Most of the inactive firms originate in the United States and in sectors such as oil and food.

Reactive approaches

The majority of non-financial MNEs take a reactive approach to the crisis. They underline the seriousness of the crisis, and search for answers within their own business environment. No comments are made that new institutions are required or drastically new operating practices need to be developed (see Table 14.5). The framing of corporations here is interesting, as can be illustrated by the quote from the Chinese state-owned oil company Sinopec. It favors a "proactive" approach, which nevertheless should largely be classified as "reactive," as it only specifies the corporate strategy in its direct market environment, taking advantage of the weakness of its competitors. Comparable statements are made by other East Asian companies (in particular from China and South Korea) that have suffered less from stock price declines and have a tradition of putting market shares and economic growth above profitability and shareholder value. "Coming out of the crisis stronger" represents an absolute and a relative statement, but both dimensions largely represent a "resource-based" view of the firm. Other similar expressions refer to, for instance, structural reform (Hitachi), yet not for the industry or the regulatory environment but for the internal operations of the company. In the banking industry a comparable and explicit mix-up between a proactive and a

TABLE 14.4 Inactive approaches to the financial crisis: non-financials (2009)

Chevron	"While times are challenging, the people of Chevron have their eyes fixed on the horizon. That's where growth will take hold. And when it does, the world will need all the energy it can get."
DaimlerChrysler	"The best remedy in these hard times is strong products and pioneering technologies. We have both." "This economic situation is unusual, but so is our determination. We will stay on track."
Conoco	"We remain confident of our ability to maintain current levels of production while fully replacing reserves over the long term."
Total	"We are confident in the Group's ability to weather the storm without revising its strategy."
IBM, Kroger	No major statements (limited drop in share prices 1996–7)

Sources: quotes from 2009 annual reports of individual companies.

TABLE 14.5 Reactive approaches to the crisis: non-financials (2009)

Toyota	"These challenging times are particularly well suited to the development of strong human resources. There is a phrase that says, 'The strongest grass is revealed after swift wind.' I believe that the experience of overcoming tough challenges is essential to developing a corporate structure that is strong and flexible enough to adapt to change."
Sinopec	"In 2009, the Company will proactively respond to the influence of international financial crisis, take the market opportunity and adjust its operation strategies to expand resources, expand market, improve management, and reduce cost, in order to fulfill the full year targets."
Hitachi	"In response to these challenges we have pushed ahead with a series of structural reforms with a view of growing our business and becoming a truly global company."
Metro Group	"Although the effects of the global financial crisis on sales, procurement, currency and refinancing markets are difficult to gauge, we are determined to continue to strengthen our position as a leading international retailing group." "Nonetheless, we feel well prepared for a deteriorating market environment with our price-aggressive sales brands Metro Cash & Carry and Media Markt and Saturn." "we want to serve our customers even better this year and strengthen our market position."
E.ON	"2008 made it abundantly clear that we must redouble our efforts if we want to maintain our position as a leading player." "We now need to work just as hard to further improve our performance and competitiveness – all the more so as our markets become more difficult." "We need to focus on leveraging our strengths so that we can better realize." "The current financial and economic crisis makes it essential that we make better use of our resources and our potential." "I am convinced that we'll succeed and that E.ON can confidently face the challenges of the future."
Statoil	"With a strong balance sheet and a flexible and robust portfolio, StatoilHydro is well positioned to manage through the global economic downturn, but we have to adapt to the new realities. We have made firm plans to respond to both upsides and downsides, and are prepared to act quickly to changing conditions." "A downturn also represents an opportunity for improvements. We seek to reduce our own costs, improve quality and processes and work with our suppliers to bring industry costs down to more sustainable levels."
LG	"The volatility and uncertainty in the financial markets are unprecedented. Never before in LG Electronics' history have we witnessed such rapid deterioration and retrenchment in major markets. However, regardless of whether or not countries emerge from recession in 2009 or 2010 or even 2011, we will take a longer-term view of our priorities. I believe that we need to stay even more focused on the six strategic pillars laid out before to guide our innovation."

Sources: quotes from 2009 annual reports of individual companies.

reactive strategy can be found with BNP Paribas (see Table 14.7). The French bank officially aims for a "proactive approach," which in practice, however, boils down to reiterating its core businesses already decided earlier and a strict cost-cutting strategy. This almost touches upon an "inactive" strategy portrayed as "proactive."

Active responses

At least two non-financial companies were identified that have been trying to address the financial crisis in a more active manner. In practice – as illustrated by Electricité de France and General Electric (see Table 14.6) – this implies, first, that the management of the company reiterates its societal mission toward external as well as internal stakeholders; and, second, the corporation provides an analysis of the changes at hand and makes some proposals on how to deal with them. The search for new opportunities is framed in a "reset world," for which the company, however, does not give major details on how it wants to contribute.

Financial services

The statements of the financial services firms show that many of them are still in a reactive mode immediately following the crisis. Efficiency measures – such as simplifying the organization, cutting down on overheads, and creating coherence – are proposed to reduce risk and limit speculation, but hardly any statement is made on firms' own responsibilities. The crisis is caused by others. The CEO tries to boost the morale of the employees, for instance that the company has repeatedly weathered this kind of storm in the past. This applies in particular to North American banks. The more active statements come primarily from

TABLE 14.6 Active statements: non-financials (2009)

Electricité de France	"Against a backdrop of global economic crisis, EDF Group senior management will reiterate its commitment to sustainable development and to addressing the three primary challenges." "EDF is keeping its eye on the long term in spite of the current crisis." "We must not allow the global recession to bring our initiatives to a halt."
General Electric	"The current crisis offers the challenge of our lifetime . . . The global economy, and capitalism, will be 'reset' in several important ways. The interaction between government and business will change forever. In a reset economy, the government will be a regulator; and also an industry policy champion, a financier, and a key partner. The financial industry will radically restructure. There will be less leverage, fewer competitors, and a fundamental repricing of risk. It will remain an important industry, just different. Successful companies won't just 'hunker down'; they will seek out the new opportunities in a reset world."

Sources: quotes from 2009 annual reports of individual companies.

European banks. They stress the need for new rules of the game, and link this to a renewed sense of responsibility. Whereas the inactive or reactive banks stress risk, the active banks stress responsibility (in a variety of ways). Additionally the more active banks also spend more energy searching for the causes of the crisis, which makes it consequently easier to legitimize the strategic changes as proposed in the annual reports. Active banks address much more their "stakeholders" and society at large, whereas in/reactive banks primarily address their "shareholders." It seems that the more companies are affected by the financial crisis (measured by a drop in share prices), the more they are inclined to look for a more active strategy. Examples are UBS and Credit Agricole. Interestingly enough, both companies in the past had been relatively inactive in their CSR strategies. General Electric presents another example of this type of mechanism (Table 14.6); because of its sizable financial activities, this company could have been classified as a "financial" as well.

Table 14.7 provides somewhat longer quotes from the industry itself. The more active approaches are often also accompanied by a more elaborate vision on the position and the responsibility of the bank in the economy. HBSC provides perhaps the clearest example of how corporations can productively "frame" their approach to the crisis: first, by providing their own analysis of the causes of the crisis; second, by identifying the role and responsibilities of the banking industry in this crisis, as well as the role played by others – without becoming too defensive or apologetic; and, third, by delineating ways out of the crisis – without denying that a systemic crisis requires a redesign of the regulatory framework. The two other exemplary active responses provide other interesting quotes along comparable lines.

CSR attitude and crisis proneness

In sum, the narratives show relatively inactive (48 percent) and reactive (43 percent) immediate responses to the financial crisis. Only a few companies immediately responded to the financial crisis with an active attitude (6 percent). None could be classified as proactive. A proactive approach would include a specification of the way that the company would like to implement (active) ideas in collaboration/ partnership with direct and indirect stakeholders. This addition would make the statement an ideal-type "sustainable corporate story." The more sophisticated the "story" of a corporation is, the more it receives a "moral authority" in a particular issue, which as a consequence increases its "license to operate" and its overall legitimacy (cf. Schultz et al. 2000).

This finding seems to support earlier skepticism as to the potential contribution of MNEs to the build-up of new institutions that could increase the social potential of globalization (cf. Frynas 2008). The lack of proactive responses, however, should not come as a major surprise. The exact consequences and repercussions of the crisis were largely unclear. Statements had to be issued immediately after the actual outbreak of the crisis. A proactive strategy is always part of a bargaining

TABLE 14.7 Financial services and the crisis (2009)

Inactive	Fortis	"We believe [. . .] it is time now to look forward and to seize this opportunity to build for the future." "While none of us know today how quickly the economy will recover – or indeed how long it will take for confidence to return to the markets – we can assure you that we are wasting no time in exploring every opportunity available to us to create value and a return for shareholders." "The financial difficulties of a number of large U.S. and UK financials, emanating from the bankruptcy of Lehman Brothers in the United States, had a severe impact on the financial markets, financials in general and Fortis in particular, leading to a new wave of speculation and negative rumours."
Reactive	ING	"As the increased complexity of the financial services industry has been a major cause of the crisis, going back to the basics of finance is inevitable." "While drawing lessons from the crisis . . . we will focus on fewer, coherent and strong businesses. Also, we will simplify the organisation, improve the fundamentals of our business and invest in improving commercial processes." "ING is confronting the crisis head-on by putting customers first, preserving a strong capital position, further mitigating risks and lowering costs." "Active repositioning of its product portfolio was at the core of ING's response to changing customer needs due to the economic downturn." "We are steering the business through these turbulent times, focusing on today's priorities with the discipline that these exceptional times require." "The financial crisis has demonstrated the importance of having a robust risk management organisation in place. The lessons learned in this crisis will contribute to this continuous process."
	Citigroup	"The environment in 2008 was significantly more challenging than expected. [. . .] It is our commitment to Citi's customers, shareholders, and employees to create solutions that mitigate the impact of these difficult times. With the top team in the industry, we will succeed. I have no illusions about the impact of the severe financial turmoil. But I have no doubt that with continued hard work, Citi will again be at its best in these difficult times and beyond. [. . .] Throughout 2008, in the midst of a global economic downturn and global financial crisis, we remained focused on Getting Fit. We have made and continue to make significant progress in strengthening Citi's capital and structural liquidity; reducing the balance sheet, expenses and headcount; and decreasing risk across the organization."

BNP Paribas	"We will [. . .] take a proactive approach by implementing the action plans for each of our core businesses as announced upon publication of our 2008 results. In all our businesses, customer service, risk control, capital and liquidity management and cost discipline will remain our key priorities." "More than ever before, our goal is to consolidate on the leading position forged by BNP Paribas, the bank for a changing world, in a European and world banking industry in the throes of far-reaching change."
Bank of America	"The opportunity we have in 2009 is to increase customer loyalty for the future as we help customers work through hard economic times." "The industry that emerges from this crisis will look much different. Credit markets will feature simpler, more transparent products." "Despite a year with no shortage of bad news, I maintain a positive and optimistic outlook for our future." "2008 was one of the most challenging years in our company's history. 2009 will be a great challenge as well. But this is not the first time this company has faced and successfully managed through economic or business crises. We have a 225-year history of persevering during hard times, and positioning ourselves to be even stronger when economic growth returns. [. . .] Despite all this change – and, in some ways, encouraged by it – we remain committed to our core vision for this company." "Our industry as a whole did a poor job on that front in the lead-up to our current crisis. We all have learned – or relearned – hard lessons."
Active Crédit Agricole	"For us, the main conclusion is that we need a new international framework for banking and finance. In addition, the crisis has given us a stronger sense of our responsibility as a bank, of our obligation to look at the long-term consequences of our business and financial decisions." "Crédit Agricole S.A. strengthens its senior management organisational structure to adapt to the new global financial environment and to prepare for a post-crisis era. Crédit Agricole, France's biggest bank and the leading provider of funds within the French economy, will be at the forefront for the French government plan to support the economy." "Of course, the banking landscape is undergoing a dramatic shift. The role of governments and the extent of their involvement in regulating and supporting the banking industry have been completely redefined." "The French government's plan was more of a way to help the banks to support lending than a bailout. Naturally, Crédit Agricole backed this plan, in keeping with its position as the leading financial partner to the French economy. With its extremely solid financial position, our Group has the wherewithal to fulfil its role during the difficult times we face while actively preparing for the post-crisis period."

TABLE 14.7 Continued

HSBC

"The causes of the crisis are complex and interrelated. But we can clearly see that a number of different factors contributed: First, the global financial imbalances that arose from the accelerating global economic shift toward emerging markets. Second, cheap credit. Third, securitisation based on overly complex product structures. And finally, excessive gearing. The result has been unprecedented stress in the financial system, and it has led to a major breakdown in trust." "The banking industry has done many things wrong. Inappropriate products were sold inappropriately by many. Compensation practices ran out of control and perverse incentives led to dangerous outcomes. There is genuine and widespread anger that the contributors to the crisis were in some cases amongst the biggest beneficiaries of the system. Underlying all these events is a question about the culture and ethics of the industry. The industry needs to recover a sense of what is right and suitable as a key impulse for doing business." "One of the consequences of the crisis – and rightly – is that we are going to see a fundamental re-evaluation of the rules and regulations that govern our business. But we should remember that no amount of rules and regulations will be sufficient if the culture does not encourage people to do the right thing. It is the responsibility of Boards to supervise and management to embed a sustainable culture into the very fibre of the organisation. For HSBC, there is nothing more important." "We are living through a genuinely global crisis; it cannot be solved by one nation alone. Governments need to work together with our industry to tackle the root causes of the crisis, while maintaining the open, globalized markets that have helped spread prosperity in the last two decades. Protectionism, both in trade and in capital flows, is a threat and in all its forms must be resisted." "Our strategy has been tested and remains intact." "We remain confident that HSBC is well-placed in today's environment and that our strength leads to opportunity."

UBS

"We will continue to make changes in 2009, including the implementation of a new compensation model for senior executives that aligns compensation with the creation of sustainable results for shareholders." "The crisis faced by the financial services industry made it difficult for the firm to do as much as it would have liked to fulfill its stakeholder expectations. Still, as can be seen from the examples given below – from anti-money laundering to community development and human rights to protecting the environment – UBS continued with a wide range of important and effective corporate responsibility-related activities during 2008. Even in difficult times, UBS remains convinced that corporate responsibility makes good business sense." "UBS has crafted its business strategy to benefit from one underlying global trend: the growth of wealth. Despite the current financial crisis, the firm believes that over the long term wealth creation will continue to be a prominent characteristic of the world economy. UBS's three core businesses of wealth management, asset management and investment banking are geared to take advantage of this trend."

Sources: quotes from 2009 annual reports of individual companies.

game, and so the active strategies of the five corporations illustrated (of which four are strongly involved in financial services) can also be interpreted as the first step in a complex bargaining process. The initial positions, however, in this bargaining process are clear.

The number of firms that consider the crisis as a step up to a more systemic change in the global economy remains still quite limited. This finding implies that a more fundamental discussion on the nature of globalization and how to make it more sustainable (see "MNEs as carriers of the third wave of globalization," above) cannot be expected to be initiated by the multinational enterprises alone. The early phase of the global crisis has not yet proven to trigger major corporate initiatives as the corporate narratives illustrate.

Their previous stance on CSR – as an indication of their general approach toward society – provides part of the explanation for this finding. In the section " 'Globalization' equals 'crisis'?" it was illustrated that on average firms have a relatively inactive/reactive approach toward CSR, with some exceptions, in particular from Europe. A first simple statistical analysis of the possible correlation between CSR approaches and stock price decreases shows, however, that a more active CSR approach does not necessarily contribute to lower decreases in stock prices (Annex 1 contains the basic data). A more active CSR strategy cannot prevent a public company from being affected by the immediate effects of a financial crisis. But can it contribute to the formulation of more active responses? The above narratives were taken as a first indication of a company's attitude toward the crisis. In Annex 1 these are summarized and superimposed on the CSR approaches of these companies. In 62 percent of cases, the established CSR strategy functions as a rough predictor of the corporate attitude/narrative toward the financial crisis. One-third choose the lower (passive) end of their CSR approach; one-sixth choose the higher (more active) end. This subgroup on average faces relatively small drops in stock prices, with the exception of some of the banks, for example Bank of America, which however reiterated its already inactive CSR stance in its initial response to the crisis.

Perhaps the most interesting subgroup is represented by the companies that – under the influence of the financial crisis – have adopted more active attitudes than we would have expected from their previous CSR approach. One-fifth of all the companies in the sample chose this stance. Primarily banks and insurers adopted this strategy, but none really jumped to a radical new position. Most of these companies were badly affected by the financial crisis in their market capitalization.

A less active stance than might have been expected on the basis of their CSR policies is adopted by one-sixth of the companies. This includes a small number of banks (BNP, ING) and a variety of other corporations (BP, DaimlerChrysler, Total, Carrefour, Tesco, Altria, Sony), primarily from Europe, that also might be considered less "responsible" for (banks) or affected by (petroleum, food, retail) the crisis. A notable exception is Citigroup, which has taken a remarkably passive stance, but is generally considered to be one of the root causes of the financial crisis by (illegally) taking over an insurance company, which prompted the Clinton administration in 1998 to liberalize banking regulation that had been in force since the financial crisis of the 1930s (and for good reasons; see McDonald 2009).

Conclusion: globalization saved?

The exploratory research on which this contribution reports is far from finished. The statistical tests can be improved, the period under consideration expanded, the number of firms broadened, the indicators and narratives made conceptually more sophisticated. What is needed is a follow-up study of corporate attitudes after the immediate post-crisis period. The documentation of initial responses to the crisis, however, tells a clear story about the likelihood that companies in the future can help build appropriate (informal) institutions to make globalization "good" and autonomously help structurally overcome inherent crises.

This study found a prevalence of relatively inactive and reactive approaches toward globalization and the financial crisis. The determinants of these approaches can be found in national regulation, sector origins, degrees of internationalization, and/or previously implemented CSR strategies. If the process of successful globalization depends on the strategies of leading corporations (as the section "MNEs as carriers of the third wave of globalization" suggests), it is far from saved.

This study, however, also documented a number of mechanisms that can help in a more active (and sometimes even proactive) approach of MNEs toward globalization: (1) previous active CSR strategies prove a (moderate) predictor of a more active stance; (2) internationalization is a positive force for higher awareness of the uncertainty surrounding globalization and could lead to a greater interest in more sophisticated regulatory regimes; and (3) European MNEs generally tend to adopt a more active stance not only in their own responses to mitigating negative aspects of globalization, but also in how to make globalization as a system more sustainable.

This paper has identified a number of interesting corporate cases and corporate leaders that might be studied in more detail. The paper has hinted at the importance of "framing" and "awareness" – as behavioral attributes – in making change actually happen or stall (because of denial). The behavioral dimension needs to be further explored by studying the actual actions of the leaders (CEOs) of these MNEs combined with the question of what leadership in a complex world looks like. More and more leadership studies describe the birth of new types of leadership, which are referred to as "transformational," "servant," or "collaborative." One characteristic of this type of leadership is that no leader of major corporations can develop sound business strategies without a longer-term vision on sustainability. Even Jack Welch, proclaimed "manager of the century" as former CEO of General Electric, had to admit in the course of the financial crisis that going only for profit maximization and "shareholder value" was a bad idea. It might have prompted his successors – as illustrated in this paper – to take a more active stance in the financial crisis. One other characteristic of the new type of corporate leadership is the search for cross-sector partnering with leaders of civil society and governments – the proactive approach delineated in this paper. A research agenda on how corporations can contribute to making globalization sustainable should therefore also include the development of new (business) models for making these "partnering" initiatives effective. To facilitate these processes, a Partnerships Resource Centre for sustainable development was founded in the Netherlands (http://www.erim.nl/partnerships).

The approach taken in this paper remains exploratory, multilevel, international, and multidisciplinary, which undoubtedly is in the spirit of and contributes to the legacy of Helge Hveem.

Notes

1 Professor of International Business, Department of Business-Society Management, Rotterdam School of Management, Erasmus University. Excellent and timely research support by Ecaterina Demcencov is gratefully acknowledged.
2 A comparable – in hindsight badly judged – trade-off in favor of the risk takers was made by BP in its Mexican Gulf operations. After the biggest oil spill in U.S. history in early 2010, it was found not only that oil companies had successfully lobbied for diminished safety regulation, but also that the company itself had economized on its risk and safety procedures in order to increase short-term profits and return on investments. The reputational and actual damages of approximately U.S.$20 billion, as well as lower share prices, further illustrates the bad judgment of the corporate risk takers even on economic grounds.
3 If the median instead of the average value is taken for the non-financials, scores change slightly in favor of the "big league MNEs." For the other MNEs the overall patterns are largely the same. Using the median instead of the average would have stressed that in 2006 hardly any company had any major score on crisis-related terms.

Annex 1 overleaf

ANNEX 1: Sample companies – basic descriptives (2006–9)

Fortune global rank (2006)	Company	Sector	Country	Sales/revenues 2005 ($ millions)	Sales/revenues 2008 ($ millions)	TNI[a] (%)	Stock price (Dec 2006[b]=100%) Sept 2008[c]	March 2009[d]	CSR approach (shaded); crisis approach (X) Inactive	Reactive	Active	Proactive
1	Exxon Mobil	Petroleum refining	USA	339,938.0	442,851.0	67.1	105%	91%				
2	Wal-Mart Stores	General merchandisers	USA	315,654.0	405,607.0	26.0	131%	114%				
3	Royal Dutch Shell	Petroleum refining	NLD	306,731.0	458,361.0	71.1	90%	65%				
4	BP	Petroleum refining	GBR	267,600.0	367,053.0	79.4	81%	61%	X			
5	General Motors	Motor vehicles and parts	USA	192,604.0	148,979.0	42.9	N/A	N/A				
6	Chevron	Petroleum refining	USA	189,481.0	263,159.0	56.8	118%	94%				
7	DaimlerChrysler	Motor vehicles and parts	DEU	186,106.3	140,328.0	29.9	68%	55%	X			
8	Toyota Motor	Motor vehicles and parts	JAP	185,805.0	204,352.0	51.6	68%	49%		X		
9	Ford Motor	Motor vehicles and parts	USA	177,210.0	146,277.0	47.6	64%	38%				
10	ConocoPhillips	Petroleum refining	USA	166,683.0	230,764.0	41.4	106%	56%				
11	General Electric	Diversified	USA	157,153.0	183,207.0	50.1	68%	29%			X	
12	Total	Petroleum refining	FRA	152,360.7	234,674.0	72.5	90%	71%	X			
13	ING Group	Bank insurance	NLD	138,235.3	226,577.0	71.0	59%	14%	X			

#	Company	Industry	Country							
14	Citigroup	Banks: commercial and savings	USA	131,045.0	112,372.0	49.4^c	36%	5%		X
17	Volkswagen	Motor vehicles and parts	DEU	118,376.6	166,579.0	57.6	183%	78%		
18	Fortis	Banks: commercial and savings	BEL	112,351.4	N/A	23.5	N/A	N/A		
19	Crédit Agricole	Banks: commercial and savings	FRA	110,764.6	103,582.0	34.9	45%	29%	X	
20	American Intl. Group	Insurance: P & C (stock)	USA	108,905.0	96,004.00	46.6	4%	1%	X	
22	Siemens	Electronics, electrical equipment	DEU	100,098.7	123,595.0	65.3	89%	59%		
23	Sinopec	Petroleum refining	CHN	98,784.9	207,814.0	N/A	47%	55%	X	
24	Nippon T&T	Telecommunications	JAP	94,869.3	103,684.0	N/A	93%	79%		
25	Carrefour	Food and drug stores	FRA	94,454.5	129,134.0	61.1	82%	63%		X
26	HSBC Holdings	Banks: commercial and savings	GBR	93,494.0	142,049.0	68.1	89%	31%		
27	ENI	Petroleum Refining	ITA	92,603.3	159,348.0	49.0	76%	67%		
29	IBM	Computers, office equipment	USA	91,134.0	103,630.0	54.7	123%	97%		
30	McKesson	Wholesalers (health care)	USA	88,050.0	10,632.0	9.4	109%	72%		
31	Honda Motor	Motor vehicles and parts	JAP	87,510.7	99,652.0	80.3	81%	63%		
33	Hewlett-Packard	Computers, office equipment	USA	86,696.0	118,364.0	56.3	116%	81%		

ANNEX 1 continued

Fortune global rank (2006)	Company	Sector	Country	Sales/revenues 2005 ($ millions)	2008 ($ millions)	TNI[a] (%)	Stock price (Dec 2006=100%) Sept 2008[c]	March 2009[d]	CSR approach (shaded); crisis approach (X) Inactive	Reactive	Active	Proactive
34	BNP Paribas	Banks: commercial and savings	FRA	85,687.2	136,096.0	51.0	83%	39%	X			■
36	UBS	Banks: commercial and savings	CHE	84,707.6	59,882.0	84.8	35%	17%	■	X		
37	Bank of America Corp.	Banks: commercial and savings	USA	83,980.0	113,106.0	11.5	69%	14%	■			
38	Hitachi	Electronics, electrical equipment	JAP	83,596.3	99,544.0	28.5	112%	47%	■	X		
39	China Nat. Petroleum	Petroleum refining	CHN	83,556.5	181,123.0	4.4	N/A	N/A	■			
40	Pemex	Mining, crude oil production	MEX	83,381.7	119,235.0	48.5[f]	N/A	N/A	■			
41	Nissan Motor	Motor vehicles and parts	JAP	83,273.8	83,982.0	58.5	58%	31%	■		X	
43	Home Depot	Specialist retailers	USA	81,511.0	71,288.0	7.0	66%	59%	■	X		
44	Valero Energy	Petroleum refining	USA	81,362.0	118,298.0	12.6	67%	37%	■			
45	J.P. Morgan Chase	Banks: commercial and savings	USA	79,902.0	101,491.0	22.9	100%	57%	■			
46	Samsung Electronics	Electronics, electrical equipment	KOR	78,716.6	110,350.0	45.4	N/A	N/A	■	X	X	

47	Matsushita Electric Ind. (Panasonic)	Electronics, electrical equipment	JAP	78,557.7	77,200.00	43.7	90%	58%	
48	Deutsche Bank	Banks: commercial and savings	DEU	76,227.6	81,360.0	75.2	62%	32%	
49	HBOS	Banks: commercial and savings	GBR	75,798.8	62,400.0	13.8	62%	39%	
50	Verizon Comm.	Telecommunications	USA	75,111.9	97,354.0	4.6	86%	82%	
51	Cardinal Health	Wholesalers (health care)	IRL	74,915.1	91,091.0	86.8	77%	50%	
53	Nestlé	Food consumer products	CHE	74,658.6	101,565.0	74.9	N/A	N/A	
54	Deutsche Telekom	Telecommunications	DEU	74,061.8	90,260.0	41.8	87%	67%	
55	Metro Group	Food and drug stores	DEU	72,814.3	101,217.0	53.2	76%	50%	
59	Tesco	Food and drug stores	GBR	71,127.6	94,300.0	32.8	85%	56%	X
60	Peugeot	Motor vehicles and parts	FRA	69,915.4	79,560.0	N/A	61%	31%	
61	U.S. Postal Service	Mail, package and freight delivery	USA	69,907.0	74,932.0	N/A	N/A	N/A	X
62	Altria Group	Food and tobacco	USA	69,148.0	23,600.00	41.8	105%	84%	X
64	E.ON	Energy	DEU	66,313.2	127,278.0	48.8	34%	21%	
65	Sony	Electronics, electrical equipment	JAP	66,025.6	76,945.0	57.9	76%	52%	X
66	Vodafone	Telecommunications	GBR	65,314.2	69,138.0	82.4	84%	59%	

Fortune global rank (2006)	Company	Sector	Country	Sales/revenues		TNI^a (%)	Stock price (Dec 2006=100%)		CSR approach (shaded); crisis approach (X)			
				2005 ($ millions)	2008 ($ millions)		Sept 2008^c	March 2009^d	Inactive	Reactive	Active	Proactive
68	Électricité de France	Electric and gas utilities	FRA	63,434.1	94,084.0	32.4	94%	54%		■	■	■
70	Statoil	Mining, crude oil production	NOR	61,032.7	116,211.0	37.3	96%	70%		■	■	■
71	France Télécom	Telecommunications	FRA	60,932.9	78,290.0	49.9	107%	81%		■	■	■
72	LG	Electronics, electrical equipment	KOR	60,574.1	82,082.0	49.2	N/A	N/A	■	X		
73	Kroger	Food and drug stores	USA	60,552.9	76,000.0	N/A	121%	96%	■	■		
75	Deutsche Post	Mail, package and freight delivery	DEU	59,989.8	98,708.0	25.1	68%	36%			■	■
77	Marathon Oil	Petroleum refining	USA	58,958.0	73,504.0	22.7	88%	59%	■			

Notes

a TNI, the Transnationality Index, is calculated as the average of the following three ratios: foreign assets to total assets, foreign sales to total sales, and foreign employment to total employment.

b Closing stock price of December 29, 2006, is considered to be the base value (100%).

c Closing stock price of September 26, 2008, is considered.

d Closing stock price of March 27, 2009, is considered.

e Because of incomplete data, the Transnationality Index for this company is calculated as the average of the following two ratios: foreign assets to total assets and foreign sales to total sales.

f Because of incomplete data, the Transnationality Index for this company has been estimated solely from the following ratio: foreign sales to total sales.

15

NON-TRIAD MULTINATIONAL ENTERPRISES AND GLOBAL ECONOMIC INSTITUTIONS[1]

Andreas Nölke

Non-triad multinational enterprises: definition and scope

During the last years, we have witnessed a surge in multinational enterprises (MNEs) from outside the traditional triad (Japan, North America, and Western Europe). This development has become one of the most interesting topics in the study of North–South relations in the international political economy, a study that has been pioneered by scholars such as Helge Hveem. In contrast to earlier times, foreign direct investment (FDI) is no longer an activity of triad enterprises alone. More and more, companies from the former periphery are expanding, increasingly also by acquiring assets within the triad.

As of 2010, five of the top fifteen largest global companies as established within the FT Global 500 are based outside the triad, notably from China and Brazil (Table 15.1). Other non-triad multinational enterprises (NTMNEs) come from Russia (Gazprom, no. 33), South Korea (Samsung, no. 43), Saudi Arabia (Saudi Basic Industries, no. 66), India (Reliance, no. 68), Mexico (AMX, no. 126), Taiwan (Taiwan Semiconductor Manufacturing, no. 133), and Singapore (Singapore Telecom, no. 200). Most of these companies have expanded strongly over the last few years, also reflected by the fact that, out of the seventy-nine newcomers on the FT list, only forty-one are from the triad, with as many as thirty-six from outside the triad (including an increasing number of companies from Turkey, South Africa, Qatar, Indonesia, and Malaysia), bringing the total number of non-triad companies in the 2010 FT Top 500 to 124.

In a more comprehensive perspective, the *World Investment Report 2010* notes that "while more than 90 percent of all TNCs [transnational companies] were headquartered in developed countries in the early 1990s, parent TNCs from developing and transition economies accounted for more than a quarter of the 82,000 TNCs (28 percent) worldwide in 2008" (UNCTAD 2010: 17). Remarkably,

TABLE 15.1 The top fifteen of the *FT* Global 500

Global rank 2010	Global rank 2009	Company	Country
1	2	PetroChina	China
2	1	Exxon Mobil	US
3	6	Microsoft	US
4	4	Industrial & Commercial Bank of China	China
5	33	Apple	US
6	19	BHP Billiton	Australia/UK
7	3	Wal-Mart Stores	US
8	12	Berkshire Hathaway	US
9	23	General Electric	US
10	5	China Mobile	China
11	13	China Construction Bank	China
12	15	Nestlé	Switzerland
13	17	Petrobras	Brazil
14	10	Procter & Gamble	US
15	8	Johnson & Johnson	US

Source: Financial Times, market values at March 31, 2010.

the recent financial crisis supported rather than limited this process. Although the crisis has slowed down the NTMNE expansion, many non-triad economies appear to have been able to weather this downturn in a better fashion than those of the triad countries. Thus, the contraction of foreign direct investment from outside the triad was less severe than from within the triad, enabling developing and transition economies to increase their share as sources of FDI from 19 percent in 2008 to 25 percent in 2009 (UNCTAD 2010: 6).

A breakdown of sectors demonstrates that fossil fuels clearly are among the most typical focus of NTMNEs, as indicated by the leading role of companies such as PetroChina or Petrobras (see also the contribution by Dag Harald Claes in this volume). Other important sectors include basic materials, banking, and telecoms, in particular for their home country's neighbourhood. Chinese and Indian MNEs, however, not only have involved themselves in nearly every sector, but also are increasingly becoming involved in more innovative industries, which allows them to move up quite quickly on global value chains. In this context, they have also acquired numerous companies in the triad. Although most of these companies are rather small, some are quite prominent. Among the most well-known examples are the Mittal/Arcelor takeover, the Dubai bid for U.S. port authorities, the Lenovo acquisition of IBM's personal computing division, and Tata Motors acquisition of Britain's famous Jaguar and Land Rover brands. Although these acquisitions have raised considerable concerns within the affected economies, the focus of this contribution is on a more indirect and structural implication of the rise of NTMNEs, that is, their role as transnational actors in shaping global economic institutions.

Global economic institutions such as the World Trade Organization (WTO) not only provide important political frameworks for MNEs and their transnational production systems, but also are important focal points for their political activities (Hveem 2007b). Over the last decades, most triad MNEs have transcended their traditional limitation for lobbying on the national level, and have begun to involve themselves directly within global economic regulations, either by acting as transnational lobbies, or by setting up rules themselves, within transnational private self-governance or public–private partnerships (Fuchs 2005; Ougaard and Leander 2010). Obviously we need to know whether NTMNEs are any different. How do NTMNEs behave with regard to global economic institutions? Are they present and do they articulate their preferences at global negotiations? Do they challenge the rules that have been established by and for their counterparts from the triad?

The next section demonstrates that the behavior of NTMNEs with regard to global economic institutions is still rather low-key. This observation stands in marked contrast to the rather noisy statements of some non-triad governments, for example with regard to WTO negotiations or global currency questions. To solve this puzzle, this paper puts forward two complementary hypotheses. One of these hypotheses looks at the *substance* of global economic rules and compares these rules with the domestic regulatory environment of NTMNEs (see "NTMNEs and substantial issues in global economic institutions"). From this perspective, conflicts between NTMNEs and global economic institutions are rather rare, given the lack of binding global rules in those cases in which preferences of non-triad enterprises and international institutions diverge. The second hypothesis looks at the *mode* of global economic regulation, in particular at the division of responsibilities between companies and governments in rule setting (see "NTMNEs and the mode of global economic institutions," below). From this perspective, the low-key approach of NTMNEs might be explained by the closer collaboration between these companies and their home governments. Correspondingly, they are less relevant as transnational actors in global economic institutions given that their preferences are mainly articulated through governmental channels.

Because of the very early explorative stage of research on non-triad multinational enterprises and their involvement in global economic institutions we cannot yet test these hypotheses in any meaningful way. Still, I will provide some empirical illustrations, mainly based on companies from Brazil and India.[2] These countries serve as rather hard cases for our hypotheses, given the obviously close character of state–business relations in former communist countries such as China and Russia. It would be hardly surprising if companies based in non-democratic political regimes or from economies dominated by state ownership refrained from transnational lobbying and rather preferred to act through governmental channels. The same observation for rather liberal countries such as Brazil and India, in contrast, is more decisive. Similarly, one might expect that the differences in the substance of economic regulations are more severe if companies from former communist countries are confronted with the existing global regulations.

The puzzle: a low degree of visibility of non-triad companies in global economic institutions

The role of business as transnational actor in global economic institutions has received ample attention during the last years, including its role as an independent pressure group in global negotiations (Braithwaite and Drahos 2000; May 2006; Sell 1998, 2003), its ability for self-regulation in transnational private authority (Cutler et al. 1999; Hall and Biersteker 2002; Graz and Nölke 2008), and its more structural power in global commodity chains (Strange 1988; Gereffi and Korzeniewicz 1994; Hveem 2007b; see also the contribution by Rob van Tulder in this volume). Nearly all of these surveys, however, focus on business from the Organisation for Economic Co-operation and Development (OECD) world, most notably the European Union and the United States. Studying the role of companies from outside the triad, however, is not only relevant from an academic perspective. European policy makers have already dubbed the rise of NTMNEs as the "second wave of globalization" and have identified a third challenge to European business (after the American and Japanese ones during earlier decades). However, also from a non-European perspective important issues are at stake. Arguably, a great share of global income differences between the triad and other regions can be attributed to the dominant role of triad MNEs in the global economy. This dominance is based not only on market shares, but also on the dominance of triad interests in global economic governance arrangements, governing how the value added within global value chains is attributed to the different parties involved (e.g. by setting service or product standards or by regulating intellectual property rights [IPR]). How will this be affected by a rise of NTMNEs? Will the established arrangements (e.g. in competition policy or IPR) be utilized to limit the further ascent of non-triad multinationals? Or will the rise of NTMNEs lead to more egalitarian, just, and democratic patterns within global economic institutions?

Existing literature hardly addresses these questions. Because of the recent character of the rise of NTMNEs, there is hardly any empirical evidence on the activities of NTMNEs within global economic institutions. This is also demonstrated by taking a closer look at those research efforts that have studied the role of southern actors in global economic institutions in a systematic manner (see also the contribution by Morten Ougaard in this volume), namely by looking at negotiations over AIDS/Trade-Related Aspects of International Property Rights (TRIPS) and other WTO issues, or over climate change.

Given the crucial importance of the AIDS problematique for many countries of the global South, one would assume that southern MNEs would play a very prominent role within international negotiations on related topics, such as the agreement on TRIPS in the context of the establishment of the World Trade Organization. Their role should be particularly pertinent because of the specific structure of competition in global pharmaceutical markets, with a prominent role of triad producers of expensive and new AIDS treatments (anti-retrovirals or ARVs) and an equally prominent role of southern producers in the market for generics. Admittedly, the original TRIPS agreement had been negotiated before the rise of NTMNEs as documented above, but later modifications of this agreement should have been an obvious focus of NTMNE lobbying at the WTO. Indeed, the changes to Article 31 of the TRIPS agreement approved in December 2005, allowing countries unable to produce low-cost generic medicines themselves to issue compulsory licenses for production in a foreign country, marked the first time that a core agreement of the organization had been amended, and consti-tuted a major victory for the South in global health governance (Wogart et al 2008: 13). Although Brazilian companies became involved in this struggle by start-ing the production of ARVs in the late 1990s, and Indian producers of low-cost ARVs have substantially contributed to reducing the costs of treating AIDS, no NTMNE has become involved in the very public struggle around these issues, in marked contrast to, for example, the governments of Brazil and South Africa (Wogart 2006).

A major study of the implications of the rise of China and India for diverse global economic governance arrangements leads to a similar evaluation. A detailed survey of the participation of Chinese actors in diverse issues of global economic governance, such as the WTO and the regulation of development assis-tance, does not mention MNEs as actors at all (Kaplinsky and Messner 2008). The same applies to the case of climate policy. Compared with the massive lob-bying of triad MNEs in settings such as the Bali conference, a detailed survey of the politics of Chinese participation in these negotiations does not mention MNEs as actors or lobbyists at all, in marked contrast to the multiple bureaucratic bodies involved (Scholz 2008). Even in the context of ecological and food safety standards, an issue area that is dominated by self-regulation schemes organized by MNEs and non-governmental organizations, the participation of China is top-down and government controlled. Although China is one of the largest producers of organic agricultural products in the world, it stubbornly refuses to participate in the established private schemes and prefers to set up its own state-directed cer-tification system, Green Food (Basu and Grote 2006), in marked contrast to the strong participation by Western MNEs in various forms of transnational private self-regulation.

In conclusion, the existing literature indicates an era in which non-triad governments, such as China, Brazil, and India, are increasing their presence in current global economic institutions, but MNEs from these countries remain rather low-key. Surprisingly, and in contrast to their rapid growth, these compa-nies have hardly begun to get involved in current global economic institutions, either as lobbyists, or as self-regulators. This is in marked contrast not only to the role of European, U.S., and Japanese MNEs within these institutions, but also to the ever-increasing role of their own, non-triad governments, for example in the context of WTO negotiations, the G20, or the reform of the International Monetary Fund.

In order to explain the so-far relatively limited role of NTMNEs as transnational actors in global economic institutions, we need to distinguish between the substantial content and the mode of interest representation within global economic institutions (Nölke et al. 2007). The *substantial content* refers to the issues at stake, that is, the specific design of accounting standards or labor regulations. The *mode* refers to the way that these substantial issues are decided upon, that is, within private self-regulation, in public–private policy networks, or within intergovernmental regulations.

As demonstrated above, we do not yet know much about the preferences of NTMNEs regarding the substantial content of global economic regulations, because of a lack of clear articulations. To make up for this limitation, I will look at the domestic political and economic institutions supporting the rise of NTMNEs. The basic assumption is not only that NTMNEs will tend to protect these institutions when dealing with global economic institutions, but also that it is these domestic institutions which will shape the interests and strategies that NTMNEs pursue regarding global business regulation. If we compare the substantial focus of global economic regulations with the outline of domestic institutions in the home economies of NTMNEs, we can identify numerous potential areas of conflict (Nölke and Taylor 2010). However, most of these global economic regulations are not strictly binding, therefore reducing the need of NTMNEs to act as transnational lobbyists or self-regulators.

At the heart of the argument regarding the mode of interest representation is the assumption that NTMNEs are much more closely linked with their national governments than their triad counterparts. Accordingly, there has been a lack of investment on their part in global economic institutions as they have often relied on the representation of their interests through their national governments. Correspondingly, the growing importance of NTMNEs within the global economy might have substantial repercussions for the future of some of these institutions, by redirecting them to the more government-centric pattern of the past.

As discussed above, it is not yet possible to test these hypotheses in any comprehensive fashion. The same is true for alternative explanations. One alternative explanation for the different behavior of triad and non-triad MNEs might be the fact that the former have made participation in global economic institutions a habit, that is, they have built up the adequate organizational structures and expertise. Arguably, the rise of NTMNEs is too recent to allow them to fully articulate their preferences on global economic institutions and to explore their ability to influence these institutions through transnational channels. Consequently, non-triad MNEs will more or less automatically follow suit in the years to come. However, it is too soon to test this argument in any meaningful way. Alternatively, it could be argued that the degree to which MNEs deem it necessary to involve themselves directly in global negotiations is related to the degree of preference divergence from their national governments, irrespective of their character as triad or non-triad MNEs. In this line of argument, we should see a decrease in participation if a new government is more attentive to a particular MNE's interests.[3] Given the broad character of the argument, however, the current study does not look at issues between individual governments and MNEs, but rather focuses on broad, structural patterns, that is, the general correspondence between the basic features of NTMNEs and current global economic regulation.

NTMNEs and substantial issues in global economic institutions: some differences in the regulation of capitalism

In the absence of direct empirical evidence on NTMNEs' preferences on global regulatory issues, I take a more indirect approach in order to formulate theoretically grounded expectations. To do so, I assume that the differences between the national business systems in which triad and non-triad MNEs are rooted inform their substantial preferences on global economic institutions. Given that the rise of NTMNEs has been supported by certain domestic institutions, it is reasonable to expect that these companies will lean on these institutions when developing their preferences on global economic order (see Woll 2005 for a similar perspective on Western MNEs). The identification of the relevant institutions is based on a comparative capitalism framework that highlights the existence of multiple types of capitalism, against the "one size fits all" logic of (U.S.) economic liberalism (Hall and Soskice 2001; Jackson and Deeg 2006).

Basic assumptions shared across the various strings of the comparative capitalism perspective include the following: "that capitalism is a socially embedded construction; that models of capitalism are distinguished one from the other by their underlying institutional configurations; and that modes of capitalist organisation are crucial in determining relative levels of economic performance" (Phillips 2004a: 9). For my purposes, the most important analytical contribution of the comparative capitalism perspective is the identification and elaboration of various core institutional domains within modern capitalism, including the financial system, corporate governance, industrial relations, skill creation, and the various mechanisms for the transfer of innovations throughout a specific capitalist formation. In the following I use the institutional spheres identified by the comparative capitalism approach as a heuristic device in order to identify the institutional circumstances and corresponding preferences of NTMNEs, contrast these preferences with the existing global governance institutions (as mainly shaped by the preferences and practices of triad MNEs), and chart the corresponding future conflict potential.[4]

As discussed above, I will focus on MNEs from Brazil and India for illustrations and anecdotal evidence, backed up by some more general literature (Goldstein 2007) to increase external validity. Although there are of course considerable differences between companies from Brazil, Russia, China, India, Singapore,

Taiwan, Mexico, Turkey, South Africa, Qatar, Indonesia, and Malaysia, I am arguing that – at a high level of aggregation – they share important common traits that set them apart from the liberal Anglo-Saxon principles dominating current international institutions, as demonstrated below.[5] In terms of global business regulation I will focus on those institutions that are affecting all companies alike, thereby neglecting regulations that are focused on specific sectors such as nuclear energy, telecommunications, drugs, etc. These general regulations refer to property, financial regulations, corporate governance, competition policy, and labor standards.[6] In each regulatory field I will select one issue for more intense scrutiny to increase the degree of precision in the discussion.

Financial regulation: accounting

The most important issue area in which business activism is influencing the globalization of financial regulation is accounting (Braithwaite and Drahos 2000: 121). Global standards are set by the International Accounting Standards Board (IASB), based in London. Besides being accepted within more than 100 countries (with the notable exception of the United States), IASB standards are also supported by most global institutions such as the International Monetary Fund and the World Bank. In terms of substance, the IASB leans strongly toward the perspective of Anglo-Saxon standards in financial market regulation, that is, it takes on an investor perspective and asks for a maximum degree of transparency, for example in order to force companies to make use of hidden reserves for more profitable purposes, to the advantage of their shareholders (Perry and Nölke 2006; Nölke and Perry 2007).

In contrast to triad multinationals, most NTMNEs are less dependent on international capital markets. Instead, they rely on internally generated funds or long-term bank loans. Correspondingly, they are less pressed to look for short-term shareholder value. This allows NTMNEs to build up a reserve of slack resources as a financial cushion in case of unforeseen crises in turbulent markets, an obvious advantage during the recent subprime crisis. Accordingly, Brazilian MNEs weathered the crisis very well (Ocampo 2009: 19; Grün 2010: 14). Given the rather different outlook of IASB-sponsored accounting standards, however, we may expect an increasing number of conflicts over these issues, similar to those witnessed between the IASB and German small-scale enterprises (Nölke and Perry 2007). For the time being, however, most of these conflicts are not being played out in the open. In the case of accounting regulation this means that NTMNEs do not oppose the dominant global regulation (e.g. by lobbying within the IASB, or not adopting IASB rules at all), but rather only selectively implement IASB standards.

Corporate governance: protection of minority shareholders

Corporate governance issues are not regulated by a powerful global regime such as, for example, the World Trade Organization. Instead, these issues are quite loosely institutionalized. Most regulations are in the form of voluntary codes, such as those issued by the OECD as well as by numerous private bodies. The substantial thrust of these regulations is geared toward the protection of minority shareholders, including institutional investors (Overbeek et al. 2007). Minority shareholders require a maximum degree of transparency (as in accounting standards), and an active market for corporate control, in order to trade their assets at favorable conditions.

NTMNEs, in contrast, typically are not dominated by dispersed shareholders and the organized forces of global capital markets (mutual funds, pension funds, investment banks, hedge funds, etc.), but rather are family owned or state controlled. Family and state ownership might even be counted among the "distinguishing features" of NTMNEs (Goldstein 2007: 148). Thus, most Indian multinationals are dominated by a blockholder, usually the founding family (Allen et al. 2006: 21). Important Brazilian MNEs such as Embraer or Petrobras have substantial or even dominating state ownership. Even if NTMNEs are listed on their home markets' exchanges, in most of these enterprises strategic investors (not dispersed minority shareholders) play a key role. Although making some limited overtures to the demands of international investors, this NTMNE feature is maintained:

> Family-controlled companies, the typical business arrangement of the Brazilian bourgeoisie, fell from 23 to 17 units of the 100 largest between 1990 and 1997. Meanwhile, a new mode of local bourgeoisie organization, dominant minority property (companies whose controllers hold between 20 and 50 percent of the voting shares, with the remainder being offered to the public) increased from 5 to 23 of the largest 100 companies. This shift reflected the legal changes made to attract international investors.
>
> (Abu-El-Haj 2007: 106)

Similar to the issue area of corporate finance, one might expect a similar opposition against a too-forceful export of financial market-driven Anglo-Saxon corporate governance standards on the global plane, as the focus of these standards on minority shareholder protection would clash with the interests of strategic investors, the state, or founding families governing NTMNEs. Still, given that international corporate governance standards such as the OECD guidelines so far are of a voluntary character, it is not necessary for NTMNEs to get involved in transnational activism against these standards.

Labor standards: corporate social responsibility

Similar to the case of corporate governance, labor standards are not regulated by a powerful global regime or organization. The International Labour Organization, in spite of its rather "sophisticated dialogic machinery for securing compliance" (Braithwaite and Drahos 2000: 239), has only rather limited means to enforce its codes within its member countries. Instead, the most meaningful global labor standards are being developed in the context of cooperation by NGOs and enterprises on standards for corporate social responsibility (CSR; see also the contribution of Rob van Tulder to this volume). Triad MNEs are leading forces in this process, for example in the context of the UN-sponsored "Global Compact."

Again, global labor standards tend to run counter to the business models of most NTMNEs that are inter alia based on lower wages and more flexible labor contracts than in the triad. Low wages in Brazil and India are made bearable by the existence of a large informal sector that provides cheap goods and services. Although there are fairly stringent Indian labor laws on paper, enforcement of these regulations is quite limited (Sharma 2006). Correspondingly, NTMNEs are opposing proposals for comprehensively enforced global labor standards, in order not to lose their cost advantage. The same is mostly true for institutions propagating corporate social responsibility. For example, NTMNEs are clearly underrepresented in the ranks of companies supporting the Global Compact. However, a few NTMNEs (including Brazilian ones) find it useful to engage with CSR initiatives, in particular if they own a brand name that can easily be identified (and boycotted) by Western CSR-conscious consumers (Araya 2006: 33; Goldstein 2007: 135). In any case, the rather loose regulation of labor standards by the International Labour Organization and by the various schemes for corporate social responsibility do not provide a strong incentive for NTMNEs to develop activities for influencing these standards as transnational actors.

Property rights: intellectual property

Intellectual property rights are regulated on the global level mainly in the context of two institutions, the World Intellectual Property Organization (WIPO) and the World Trade Organization, through the Agreement of Trade-Related Intellectual Property Rights (TRIPS). Whereas the work of the latter is mainly in the field of patent registration as well as in the technical support of its members in order to handle the international intellectual property support system, the former has been initiated and promoted by large triad MNEs in order to enforce their property rights (Hveem 2008b: 1).

Not surprisingly, the global regulation of intellectual property rights is one of the fields in which global economic regulations may disaffect the growth process of NTMNEs by making a soft patent system and reverse engineering increasingly difficult. Correspondingly, intellectual property rights regulation is a core area of contestation between triad and non-triad governments (Sell 1998, 2003; see also the AIDS case documented above). So far, NTMNEs have frequently been able to subvert IPR regulation because of weak enforcement. However, this is becoming increasingly difficult because of the inclusion of IPR issues in bilateral or regional preferential trade agreements (Hveem 2008b). On the other side, as more and more NTMNEs move up global value chains (such as the Brazilian airplane producer Embraer or Indian IT and pharmaceutical companies) they increasingly develop an interest in the protection of their own IPR, thereby reducing their inclination to mobilize as a transnational lobby against the current IPR regime.

Competition policy: anti-trust

Competition policy is not (yet) regulated by a powerful global regime, but there has been a strong increase in activities to institutionalize it more thoroughly globally, based inter alia on an increasingly dense interaction between the EU and U.S. competition authorities, the transfer of competition policies and institutions into the national framework of countries outside the triad (Braithwaite and Drahos 2000: 190), and its inclusion in bi- and multilateral trade agreements. These activities are loosely coordinated at the OECD and, more recently, the International Competition Network (ICN).

Even leaving the contentious issue of state subsidies aside (but see the following section), there are considerable opportunities for conflicts between the emerging international competition regime and NTMNEs. In terms of anti-trust, two practices are paramount. On the one side, NTMNEs prefer rather lax policies on interfirm cooperation (partnerships, joint ventures), given their reliance on this cooperation for the acquisition of technology from more advanced companies. On the other side, many NTMNEs have grown up as a result of a generous policy for the protection of national champions, as indicated, for example, by the importance of the temporary monopoly in Mexican telecommunications for the rise of TelMex, but also for the oligopolies that are typical in many sectors of the Brazilian economy that are dominated by the national elite (Abu-El-Haj 2007: 100). So far, however, the inclination of NTMNEs to mobilize against global competition rules has been moderated by the fact that these rules are not yet binding (except for the extraterritorial reach of certain EU and U.S. decisions) and certainly not implemented in any comprehensive fashion. Moreover, some NTMNEs are increasingly developing an interest in liberal competition policies on the global level as a result of their growing desire to acquire companies (brands, technologies, and marketing channels) within the triad.

In conclusion, I have identified numerous areas of potential conflict between non-triad MNEs and global economic institutions. At the same time, I have noted that most of these conflicts do not have to be played out in the open, given the rather open, voluntary character of most global regulations. From this angle, we may explain the limited presence of NTMNEs as transnational actors in global economic institutions at least in part by their capacity for avoiding the implementation of these regulations.

NTMNEs and the mode of global economic institutions: toward neomercantilism

In their comprehensive survey of the implications of the rise of India and China for global economic governance, Kaplinsky and Messner (2008: 198) do not identify any meaningful role for MNEs as actors within these arrangements. Still, they give us a clue to why this is the case by highlighting the "different combinations of state and capitalist development compared with the industrialized world." In particular, Chinese MNEs have very strong linkages with public authorities and therefore do not need to participate in global economic governance arrangements on their own. As discussed below, this close relationship between state and MNEs is a general tendency of NTMNEs, also in more liberal countries such as Brazil and India. One factor that has repeatedly set NTMNEs apart from other MNEs is the crucial role of the state and of public policies in their rising importance, a factor that tends to be undervalued in many discussions about globalization (Hveem and Nordhaug 2002).

Studies on the participation of various social actors in transnational policy networks have demonstrated that those actors that are used to cooperating very closely with the state on the domestic level, such as labor unions, tend to follow the same pattern regarding their involvement in international institutions, that is, they mainly express their preferences through their national governments and do not invest heavily in transnational associations. In contrast, those social interests that are used to operating at a somewhat greater distance from the state, such as non-governmental organizations and (triad) multinational enterprises, are better organized at the transnational plane and participate actively in transnational policy networks and transnational private self-regulation (Nölke 2004; Graz and Nölke 2008). Non-triad multinational enterprises tend toward the former, given their particularly close relationship with the state.

Although a particularly close relationship between enterprises and the state is quite obvious in former communist countries such as China or Russia, we also find this relationship for MNEs from Brazil and India. There are abundant examples of close collaboration between the state and Brazilian MNEs. These MNEs can frequently make use of some kind of direct or indirect state financing, including fiscal incentives, financial guarantees, and credits from state-owned banks. This allows them to obtain access to financial resources that are on comparatively favorable terms and less volatile (at least during difficult conditions) than those that rely on stock market capital. Of particular importance in this context is the support by the national development bank BNDES (Banco Nacional de Desenvolvimento Econômico e Social), contributing to the "thick ties between the traditional oligarchy and the state" (Phillips 2004b: 55) that are so typical of Brazil. Moreover, most Brazilian multinationals do not directly go global, but rather transnationalize their activities in the region first. Correspondingly, there is a very close relationship with public authorities with regard to the negotiation of regional trade and FDI agreements (Bull and McNeill 2007).

Similarly, support by the state and its public policies have been a crucial factor contributing to the rise of Indian MNEs, as can be witnessed with regard to financial support, innovation, and competition policies as well as inward and outward investment regulation. These business-friendly policies are based on very dense networks between government officials and managers of Indian MNEs (Taylor and Nölke 2010). On a more fundamental level, the whole history of expansion of Indian multinationals during the last two decades is directly based on government decisions. This pertains both to the surge of outward foreign direct investment after the post-1991 liberalizations, and also to the sector focus of Indian multinationals on generic pharmaceuticals and IT software services, sectors that were protected and supported by various governmental regulations (Taylor and Nölke 2010).

In light of this, we can thus highlight that the state and its public policies are more important for NTMNEs than for multinationals based in Western Europe, the United States, or Japan. Correspondingly, it is hardly surprising that non-triad MNEs are far more likely to work hand in hand with their national governments regarding the articulation of their interests within global economic institutions. Compared with the strongly independent role of Western MNEs during the last decades, the rise in NTMNEs may well lead to a more mercantilist pattern of global economic politics. As a consequence, the role of public–private partnerships such as the Global Compact may stagnate in the near future. As indicated in the section on NTMNEs and substantial issues in global economic institutions, this does not necessarily mean that we will witness increasing contestation about these institutions. It seems more likely, rather, that the global share of companies that consistently follow the rules of these schemes will decrease in the years to come, because of the rising importance of NTMNEs and their less stringent implementation of the corresponding standards. At the same time, we are witnessing an increasing degree of distrust in the private self-regulation of global business, as demonstrated by the increasing public oversight of rating agencies or the decision of the G20 to install a monitoring board as a public oversight of the activities of the IASB (Nölke 2009).

Conclusion and perspectives

The point of departure for this contribution was the minimal participation of NTMNEs as transnational actors in global economic institutions, compared with their strongly rising importance as a source of foreign direct investment. This observation is even more puzzling if we take the potential conflicts between the domestic institutional settings of NTMNEs and the substantial content of global economic regulations into account. However, many global economic institutions in fields such as corporate governance or industrial relations are not strictly binding, therefore reducing the potential for conflict and transnational mobilization. More importantly, I have demonstrated that NTMNEs operate in closer collaboration with national governments than triad MNEs. Correspondingly, they are more inclined to further their interests through governmental channels, rather than by transnational participation in global economic institutions.

These findings set NTMNEs somewhat apart from most of their triad counter-parts. Arguably many smaller triad companies rely on their governments in order to further their interests in global negotiations and the same argument might be made for MNEs from triad countries with very close government–business relation-ships such as France. Still, most triad MNEs, in particular those of Anglo-Saxon origins (but also German and Japanese ones), clearly have made it their habit to participate in global economic governance arrangements themselves, either as lobbyists during the negotiation of global agreements or as participants in private self-regulation. In all of these cases, the substance of business preferences and the mode of participation in global economic institutions appear to be interrelated – preferences for liberal regulations go hand in hand with a rather independent role for business as a transnational lobbying power and self-regulator, whereas a strong background in state support seems to be linked to a preference for global business regulation in intergovernmental settings.

Taken together, these observations allow us to expect a less liberal and more mercantilist form of global economic order in the near future, both regarding the substance and the mode of international institutions. In terms of substance, NTMNEs might lean away from more stringent, thoroughly enforced regulations along a market-based, Anglo-Saxon model. In terms of mode of governance, NTMNEs seem to be less inclined to participate within the various schemes of transnational private governance and transnational lobbying than their triad counterparts. However, it is yet too early to make firm judgments on these issues. We have also seen a few instances in which NTMNE preferences converged on those of their triad counterparts, for example with regard to intellectual property rights or corporate social responsibility, and more convergence might follow suit in the field of financial regulation and corporate governance should NTMNEs increasingly mobilize resources in global financial markets. Moreover, NTMNEs might simply need time to set up organizations and networks for transnational activities. Thus, we might witness more NTMNE participation in and conflicts with international institutions in the long run. For the next years, however, the prospect for more stringent global business regulation along neoliberal lines (e.g. better protection for minority shareholders or stricter rules on state subsidies) seems bleak, given the rising importance and the divergent preferences of non-triad multinational enterprises.

Notes

1 I am very much indebted to Heather Taylor for intense research collaboration on this topic. Work on this contribution has been supported by a research stay at the Max Planck Institute for the Study of Societies in 2008/9.
2 For a more detailed survey of Indian multinationals see Taylor and Nölke (2010); on Brazil see Nölke (2011).
3 I owe these points to the editors of this volume.

4 I exclude skill formation from this analysis, as this sphere is hardly affected by comprehensive global regulation.
5 Arguably, Japanese and German MNEs in the past shared some common features with current NTMNEs. Most of the major stock exchange-listed companies in Japan and Germany, however, have switched to an outlook that is very similar to that of their U.S. counterparts.
6 The choice of institutions is based on the comprehensive overview by Braithwaite and Drahos (2000); the case for environmental regulation is excluded but should be rather similar to the issue of labor standards as discussed in the relevant section.

16

STATES AND FIRMS IN THE INTERNATIONAL OIL MARKET

Dag Harald Claes

In Chapter 14, Rob van Tulder provides a general discussion of the present global structures of multinational enterprises (MNEs), the key role of foreign direct investment (FDI), and variations in MNEs' strategies for corporate social responsibility (CSR). In Chapter 15, Andreas Nölke discussed the role and strategies of a particular group of MNEs, namely those emerging from non-triad countries. In this chapter the role of MNEs will be discussed from a third angle: how the role of MNEs in the global oil industry varies over time, in particular how changes in the relationship between MNEs and governments have influenced the governance structure of this important industry.

Energy is an important input factor in most industries, a prerequisite for modern transportation and vital for almost all kinds of human activities and general welfare. This has motivated political interference in energy industries at the local, national, regional, and international levels. Prospects of shortages or shutdowns in the supply of oil have caused oil-consuming countries, in particular the United States, to use foreign diplomacy, economic bargaining, and military force to regain security in oil supplies (Klare 2004: 26–74). Such cases of political interference gain high public attention. They also have implications for the analytical approach to the oil industry: "Oil, unlike other commodities, has a universality of significance which in the real world places limits on the application of economic rationale to the evolution of the industry" (Odell 1996: 38). In this chapter the discussion of the nexus between politics and economics in the oil industry will focus on how states and firms interact in the governance of the global oil industry, how this relationship has changed over time, and what consequences these changes have had on the industry and the global economy in general.

The triangular diplomacy

According to Susan Strange, energy is a topic in need of "some analytical framework for relating the impact of states' actions on the markets for various sources of energy, with the impact of these markets on the policies and actions, and indeed the economic development and national security of the states" (Strange 1988: 191). One such approach is found in her book co-authored with John Stopford, *Rival States, Rival Firms*. Their starting point is how:

> The upheavals of the international political economy during the last decade have altered, irreversibly we believe, the relationship among states and multinational enterprises . . . As a result, firms have become more involved with governments and governments have come to recognize their increased dependence on the scarce resources controlled by firms.
>
> (Stopford and Strange 1991: 1)

A core element of their approach is what they call the triangular diplomacy, suggesting that there is a dynamic interaction between three different relationships: (1) between governments; (2) between companies; and (3) between governments and companies (see Figure 16.1).

There are conflicting and cooperative aspects within all these three relationships. This is particularly prominent on the seller side of a market, regardless of whether the sellers are governments or companies, as sellers in a market can "simultaneously compete for market shares, face product prices as collective goods (externality), and stand a chance of increasing cost-efficiency by coordinating R&D or production or distribution activities (synergy)" (Underdal 1987: 175). This aspect becomes particularly important in the international oil market, where the concentration on the seller side is high, with ten to fifteen important exporting countries and a similar number of important companies, and there are virtually billions of consumers.

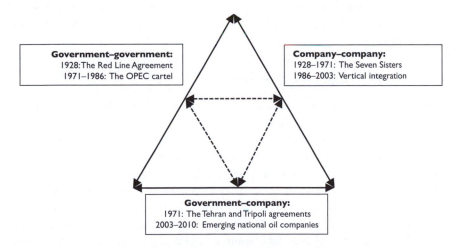

FIGURE 16.1 The triangular diplomacy of international oil.

In addition, cooperation and conflicts in the oil industry play themselves out in both a vertical and a horizontal market structure. The vertical structure is the stages of refinement of the product from raw materials to the final product sold to the end user or consumer. In the vertical structure market power arises as actors are able to control other actors' outlets or access to the goods traded at the various stages of the product chain. In the oil industry we usually call exploration and production of crude oil the *upstream* segment of the market, and transportation, refining, marketing, and sales as the *downstream* segment. The horizontal structure is the relationship between companies in the various stages of the vertical structure. In the horizontal structure market power arises as actors are able to form monopolies, oligopolies, or various forms of cartelization of the market. The horizontal structure forms the basis for the exercise of market power by coherent action by a group of actors that might lead to the realization of monopoly profit.

One fundamental feature of the oil industry is that the upstream segment, exploration and production of crude oil, can take place only where the oil resources are located. Oil, as with natural resources in general, has a surplus value after all costs and normal returns have been accounted for, called the resource rent. The access to natural resources is usually controlled by governments. A special relationship emerges between companies that have capital and technological know-how but seek opportunities for foreign direct investment in the upstream segment of the oil industry and host governments that control the ownership of oil resources but seek revenues from extraction of the resources. Initially the companies have the upper hand as they can choose where to go, but once they have made a substantial amount of investments they are hostages in the hands of the government. The companies' investments are sunk costs and the government can impose additional conditions on the companies and increase taxation without risking the companies leaving the country. This phenomenon was named the obsolescing bargain by Raymond Vernon (1971: 46–59). The relative power of governments and companies in the oil industry has varied over time; thus, the relevance of the obsolescing bargain has also changed. Vivoda (2008) argues that its relevance has increased in recent decades.

Changes in oil market governance

The history of the international oil market suggests that different actors have dominated the market at various times, based on market power resources, but also on constellations of collusion among market actors. In this section six key factors in the development of the governance of the global oil market are outlined. Some of them are specific historical events, whereas others represent changes in more structural features of the market. However, all of them relate to the three categories of relationships outlined by Stopford and Strange (1991), as illustrated in Figure 16.1. Although within its limits, the chapter is inspired by what Bates et al. (1998: 10) call an *analytic narrative* approach as "it pays close attention to stories, accounts and context . . . [but also] extracts explicit and formal lines of reasoning, which facilitate both exposition and explanation."

1928: government–government relations: the Red Line Agreement

After World War I the lack of access to foreign oil supplies was regarded as a serious challenge for the United States. Even more important was a particular change in the United Kingdom. As part of the naval arms race with Germany prior to World War I the British First Lord of the Admiralty, Winston Churchill, took the decision to switch from coal- to oil-fired naval vessels. This had two major implications: first, the oil market became an international market, as the oil used in these vessels was located in the Middle East; second, it became highly politicized because of the immediate security importance of the oil resources for warfare.

The most promising area to look for new oil resources was the Middle East. The British had made Mesopotamia a British mandate under the League of Nations. According to the San Remo Agreement France got 25 percent of the oil from Mesopotamia. The vehicle for oil development remained the British Turkish Petroleum Company; access seemed closed to U.S. interests. However, with the breakdown of the Ottoman Empire, the status of the Turkish Petroleum Company concession was unclear. The U.S. government seized the opportunity and invoked "the open door policy," which had three elements: that the nationals of all nations be subject, in all mandated territories, to equal treatment in law, that no economic concessions in any mandated region be so large as to be exclusive, and that no monopolistic concession relating to any commodity be granted (FTC 1952: 51).

The U.S. government argued that the war had been won by the Allied Powers fighting together. Consequently, any benefit should be available to all Allied Powers. The United States also claimed that:

> the San Remo agreement discriminated against the rights of American nationals, that no rights in Iraq were vested in the Turkish Petroleum Co., and that no valid concessions could come into existence through the government of the people of the territory.
>
> (FTC 1952: 51–2)

The British government argued that British nationals had "acquired rights." The fact that the United States had been an Allied Power gave it no right to trespass upon such rights.[1]

After year-long negotiations, the United States, the United Kingdom, and France reached a compromise in 1928. The American companies got one-fourth of the Iraq Petroleum Company (IPC, formerly the Turkish Petroleum Company) concession. The companies and authorities also agreed to the so-called self-denying clause of 1914 stating that all parties should work jointly – and only jointly – in the region (Yergin 1991: 204). The region included the Arabian peninsula (except Kuwait), Iraq, and Turkey. This was the so-called *Red Line Agreement* (Yergin 1991: 203–6). In the areas inside the red line, the companies would pursue joint concessions. As soon as the U.S. companies were included in the agreement, the open door policy was abandoned and the door was shut to any new company, U.S. based or not (Anderson 1981: 19). Although the private international oil companies (IOCs) were important players, and to some extent pushed the governments into the Middle East, the governments of the United States, the United Kingdom, and France took the leading role in defining the rules of the energy game in the area. Furthermore, the policy process was one of interstate bargaining. Thus, this phase was dominated by the government–government dimension.

1928–71: company–company relations: the Seven Sisters

By 1928 more than 50 percent of oil production outside the United States was controlled by Exxon, Shell, and British Petroleum (BP). These companies took their cooperation one step further when they met secretly and worked out a market-sharing deal, the so-called "as is agreement" (Yergin 1991: 260–5). This was an agreement to keep the respective percentage market shares of sales in various markets and thus not challenge each other's positions. Another important point in the agreement was the "Gulf plus pricing system," according to which crude was to be priced as if produced in the Mexican Gulf regardless of actual origin. Later the companies also agreed to control production. Most of the other U.S. companies joined the agreement. The various agreements covered operations in all countries except the United States and the Soviet Union. By the end of the 1920s, the companies had set up agreements governing their interrelations in the whole production chain.

After World War II the international oil market was totally dominated by seven companies, popularly known as the "Seven Sisters."[2] The Seven Sisters accounted for virtually all of the oil produced outside the United States and Russia. They were integrated companies in the sense that they controlled the entire production chain from exploration to sale of the refined products. As of 1953 these companies controlled 95.8 percent of the reserves, 90.2 percent of the production, 75.6 percent of the refining capacity, and 74.3 percent of the product sales outside the United States and communist bloc (Schneider 1983: 40). This created a stable structure as long as the oil market did not expand:

> Only a few firms were capable of the risky search for oil in remote often harsh places. In each consuming country, refining and marketing was a small industry, protected by distance and government, making entry difficult and unprofitable. Production was too risky without an assured outlet, known as "finding a home for the crude." Refining was too risky without an assured

supply of crude. Hence in each country the few sellers were confronted by few buyers, and neither side wished to be at the mercy of the other. The obvious solution was vertical integration.

(Adelman 1995: 44)

The integrated structure created high barriers to entry for other oil companies, also called the newcomers.

The Sisters informally organized their operations in the Middle East through a consortium in which all the major companies were engaged in at least two countries (see Table 16.1). In this way, the Sisters stood stronger against possible regulation by the producing countries, as none of them was totally dependent on the will of one government only. If the government of a producing country should put pressure on one of the Sisters in order to increase taxes or introduce less favorable conditions, this company could increase its operation in another country. The other Sisters would compensate the company under governmental pressure. This solidarity between the Sisters made it hard for governments of producing states to increase their control and revenues from oil production within their own territories. The Sisters were able to recreate on the international scene some of the features of the logic behind the strategy of Standard Oil in the U.S. market seventy years earlier, a position that had been broken by anti-trust legislation.[3] The Sisters' tacit cooperation in the Middle East would clearly have been illegal in the United States (Odell 1986: 16). This totally dominant position of the Sisters is an extreme case of how cooperation among MNEs can define the rules of the game in a vital economic sector.

TABLE 16.1 Ownership shares in Middle East production distributed by companies in 1972 (percent)

Company	Iran	Iraq	S. Arabia	Kuwait
Exxon	7	11.875	30	
Texaco	7		30	
SoCal	7		30	
Mobil	7	11.875	10	
Gulf	7			50
BP	40	23.75		50
Shell	14	23.75		
CFP	6	23.75		
Iricon	5			
Gulbenkian		5		

Source: MNC Hearings (1974: part 5, p. 289).

1971: government–company relations: the Tehran and Tripoli agreements

There is a widespread belief that the decisive change in the oil market appeared in 1973 when the Arab oil producers initiated an embargo toward the United States in order to make the United States change its support for Israel in the ongoing Arab–Israeli War. This is a misconception. The decisive change took place two years earlier in 1971 with the Tehran and Tripoli agreements between the international oil companies (IOCs) and members of the Organization of the Petroleum Exporting Countries (OPEC). The background for these events and the formation of OPEC itself lies in changes in market conditions. The 1950s were a time of rapid growth in demand. However, production capacity grew even more rapidly. As there was nothing holding this oil from the market, the official or so-called "posted" prices were undermined by competitive discounting. This created a dilemma for the companies' relations with the host governments, as it was the posted price that was the basis for the producer countries' taxes and royalties. Both in 1959 and 1960 the international oil companies cut the posted prices. This angered the oil-producing governments and triggered the establishment of OPEC in September 1960.

After the 1956 Suez crisis and the 1967 Arab–Israeli War, North African oil exploration was intensified. The North African production had an important advantage over that in the Persian Gulf in that the oil did not have to be transported through the conflict area around the Gulf and the Suez Canal. As the Libyan oil contained less sulfur than most Gulf oil, it was cheaper to refine and could therefore be priced higher than the heavier crudes of the Gulf region. "Because of these advantages, Libya received the highest per barrel payments of any Arab government, but most observers still considered Libyan oil underpriced" (Schneider 1983: 140). Furthermore, Libya was not part of the Sisters' cooperation, as other independent U.S. and European oil companies (called the newcomers) had almost 52 percent of the Libyan oil production. This, together with a new radical regime, meant that the road was open for a confrontation with the oil companies. On September 13, 1969, a coup d'état took place in Libya; two weeks later, Muammar al-Qadhafi became president. On January 20, 1970, the new oil minister, Ezzedine Mabrouk, told the oil companies operating in Libya that the government wanted negotiations about a price rise as soon as possible. The Libyan authorities' strategy was to negotiate with the companies individually, not as a bloc. By playing the independent Occidental and the multinationals against each other, Libya managed to raise posted prices and the government take thereof. Libya was in a somewhat different position from most other OPEC countries.

After the Libyan affair, Iran and Venezuela increased their share of profits and a "game of leapfrog began" (Yergin 1991: 580). After some internal differences, the companies united in a common front and sought to negotiate with OPEC in two rounds of negotiations: one with the Gulf exporters and one with the Mediterranean exporters. It should be noted that the market structure had not changed; there was no scarcity caused by underlying changes in the relationship between supply and demand: "From early 1971 to nearly the end of 1972, prices increased despite continuing substantial excess supply" (Adelman 1995: 93).

On February 14, 1971, the so-called Tehran agreement between the international oil companies and the OPEC members exporting through the Persian Gulf was signed. On April 2, 1971, a similar agreement was signed for the OPEC members exporting through the Mediterranean. The agreements covered tax and price increases, inflation compensation, and a fixing of such rates for future years. The effects of the agreements were a 21 percent price increase for Saudi Arabian crude (from $1.80 to $2.18) and an increase in revenue of 38.9 percent. What was more important, however, was the fact that the producer countries had now gained firmer control over the price setting.

> Even as late as a few months ago, the very idea of the producing countries of the Gulf achieving an across-the-board price increase . . . [as] agreed upon in Tehran on the 14 February would have seemed almost inconceivable . . . This victory – and victory it certainly was – was mainly due to two factors: firstly the unprecedented degree of unity shown by the OPEC member countries; and secondly the great skill and nerve of the three-man ministerial committee which negotiated the deal on behalf of the Gulf States.
>
> (Adelman 1995: 80)

By these agreements the distribution of market power in the international oil market had changed dramatically:

> Unilateral tax increases were not new. Before Tripoli and Tehran, the OPEC nations had exerted defensive market power. Their excise taxes had put a floor of tax-plus-cost under the price. But raising taxes in concert, to raise the worldwide price floor, was indeed new.
>
> (Adelman 1995: 80)

The outcome of the Tehran–Tripoli negotiations was the result of a combination of lack of unity among the IOCs and a newfound unity among the OPEC members. One could argue that both factors were necessary, but neither of them alone was sufficient to explain the events of 1971. A unified OPEC strategy would not have succeeded unless the companies' unity had begun to crack, as in the Libyan case. The lack of unity among the companies would have meant nothing unless the OPEC members had gained some ability to act in concord. This case belongs to the government–company dimension of Stopford and Strange (1991), but the relationship was one of conflict not cooperation.

1971–86: government–government relations: the OPEC cartel

After 1971 the role of the IOCs in governing the international oil market diminished. A new group of companies emerged, the national oil companies (NOCs). In 1972 the Iranian state-owned company NIOC took control of Iranian oil production. In Saudi Arabia oil production was controlled solely by the American companies, organized in the consortium Aramco (Arabian American Oil Co.). Saudi Arabia gradually took control over Aramco in the 1970s.[4] Iraq nationalized IPC (the Iraq Petroleum Company) in 1972, and Kuwait was assigned 60 percent of the interests in KOC (the Kuwait Oil Company) in 1974. Qatar and Abu Dhabi followed the Kuwaiti model. By the mid-1970s most of the OPEC members had de facto nationalized their oil industry. In the 1970s the NOCs could be regarded as only part of the public policy of the oil producer governments and not as actors with independent aims and interests:

> The NOCs were initially created as instruments of government policy, whose aim was primarily to assert sovereign rights over national resources. In a context of resource nationalism, they were to give the state control over the pace of exploitation and the pricing of its finite resources. NOCs also ensured that the state received an equitable share of profits.
>
> (Marcel 2006: 8)

The NOCs were confined to operating the extraction of national energy resources. None of them had ambitions outside their own country.

More important for the governance of the oil market was the intergovernmental cooperation among the member countries of OPEC. The price and production policies of the OPEC members invoke a perspective combining cartel theory and the theory of collective action (Claes 2001). In strict economic terms, the OPEC countries have behaved cooperatively since 1971 to the present, as the price of oil has been substantially above its production costs. Some degree of market control has been exercised, and it has been beneficial to the oil producers. During the 1970s, OPEC as an organization played a minor role; however, the behavior of the OPEC members did cause substantial price increases and, in fact, changed the structure and market power relations in the international oil market.

In 1982, Saudi Arabia took on a "benevolent hegemony strategy," characterized by behavior as a swing producer, leaving room for the smaller members to exploit the big one. The weakening of the market, that is, reduced consumption and increased production by non-OPEC producers, made the hegemonic role increasingly costly. This caused Saudi Arabia to change its market strategy in 1985 in order to regain market share. Subsequently, the Saudi strategy became more of a coercive hegemonic power. By changing its strategy from trying to sustain prices by cutting production, Saudi Arabia tried to regain its market share by flooding the market with oil and thus instigated a price war with other producers. Toward the other OPEC members the aim was to force them to cooperate by cutting their production. Toward the new oil producers outside the organization the aim was to force these producers out of business, in particular as they generally had higher production costs than the OPEC countries (Claes 2001: 281–97).

The consuming countries tried to counter the market power of OPEC by creating the International Energy Agency (IEA) in 1974. The core aim of the IEA was inter alia to handle future oil supply disruptions using an emergency oil crisis management system, originally triggered by a 7 percent reduction in daily oil supplies, but in 1979 a more flexible system of crisis cooperation was adopted, and this was used again in the Gulf War in 1991 and following Hurricane Katrina in 2005. The IEA has become a vital institution for providing information on international energy and its agenda-setting role has increased in recent years. However, as a market-governing institution it is safe to conclude that the IEA "has limited authority in rule creation and enforcement" (Kohl 2010: 198), although the organization might contribute to coordinated consumer behavior by other means, such as information and statements regarding the market situation and proposals for joint action by the member states. The OPEC cartel had a similar market control to the Sisters, and the benefit of a dominant position in the upstream sector was transferred from the big private oil companies to the treasure chest of oil-producing countries.

Already in the late 1970s some initiatives were taken in order to create a dialogue between oil producers and consuming countries. Norway, as a newborn oil exporter with close political ties with the United States, made some diplomatic efforts under the slogan "global energy order" (Bergesen 1982: 112). In 1991 a gathering of ministers from both oil-producing and oil-consuming countries met in Paris. Such meetings have continued every two years and grown into a semi-formal organization called the International Energy Forum, which today has a permanent secretariat in Riyadh (Lesage et al. 2010: 61–3).

1986–2003: company–company relations: vertical integration

As outlined in the introduction to this chapter there are two dimensions of the market structure: horizontal and vertical. So far I have mainly focused on the horizontal structure in the crude oil market, that is, the upstream segment. The OPEC countries dominated the upstream segment from the 1970s. However, the IOCs still controlled the downstream segment of the market, such as refineries, marketing, and product sales. From the early 1980s some of the major oil-exporting countries have made downstream investments in Western Europe and the United States, gaining partial or total control over companies that can refine and distribute part of their crude oil exports in the main consuming countries, with the aim of securing outlets for sales and thereby more stable revenues in an increasingly volatile market. These exporters also bought tankers, harbor and storage facilities, and petrochemical plants in consuming countries. Among the largest downstream investors were Kuwait, Venezuela, Saudi Arabia, Libya, and

Norway. By 1990 Kuwait and Venezuela had refining capacity (domestic and foreign) covering 90–100 percent of their production capacity; the corresponding figure for Saudi Arabia was about 50 percent (Finon 1991: 264). The pace of downstream integration slowed during the 1990s (Hamm 1994: 186). This might be explained by the weakened financial position of several oil producers as the price level lowered. With the OPEC countries taking control over crude production the IOCs tried to develop alternatives to the OPEC crude, such as in Alaska and the North Sea.

The decline in refining and distribution margins in the late 1970s and early 1980s lead to a wave of closures, modernizations, and takeovers, especially in the United States. During this period of painful restructuring, independents and majors were competing for a limited volume of known reserves that more than tripled the median transaction value for reserves in place in the United States (Smith et al. 1986). Much of this wave of reserve purchases and oil company mergers and acquisitions was financed through debt. Thus it came as no surprise that, as soon as spot prices began to show the first indications of decline, companies with financial difficulties tried to resell the same reserves bought some years before. Numerous properties changed hands repeatedly in a short period. In a similar way, refiners who had upgraded their facilities at high costs in the late 1970s became caught in an economic squeeze in the mid-1980s. Refinery upgrades were based on the belief that the wide price spread between heavy and light crudes that had existed in the 1970s would continue. It actually narrowed, from $8.5 per barrel in 1982 to $4 per barrel in 1984. Costly revamping to feed heavy crude proved to be a bad investment in a business already beset by marginal economics. In several cases banks helped companies resist selling upstream and downstream properties by restructuring loans and advancing some loan forgiveness, but the price decline in 1986 forced many companies to divest in order to fulfill debt obligations. This reduced the number of oil companies and improved the position of those that were able to react quickly to changes in crude supply and product demand.

In the upstream segment of the market there were similar problems. Between 1985 and 1987 the seven largest majors replaced only 40 percent of oil consumed in the United States and 59 percent outside the United States through new discoveries, extensions, and improved recovery rates in existing fields. When revisions of oil reserves and purchases are taken into account, the majors' replacement was still 11 percent short compared with production. The majors – primarily Exxon, Shell, and BP – purchased reserves from smaller companies that were either cutting back their oil activity or dropping out of the industry completely, but the majors were still "crude short," even if they were better off in this regard than some of their smaller competitors. The companies seemed to be preparing for a more competitive environment, in which increased size is perceived as necessary in order to take higher risks in upstream investments. For the OPEC countries the key problem was the ability, or rather lack of ability, to finance the necessary investments in their existing production facilities, on their own. As most OPEC countries produced close to capacity, increase in production capacity would imply new investments. The financial reserves of the OPEC countries were no longer what they were in the heyday of high oil prices. By 1990 virtually all OPEC countries were in need of more financing, more technology, and more organization (Finon 1991: 263). Many OPEC countries revised their policies and opened up for production-sharing agreements with foreign firms.

During the 1990s a new order emerged in the international oil market, based on a convergence of interests between the international oil companies providing technology and financial resources for exploration and production and producing countries controlling the access to the resources. The large oil exporters searched for secure outlets for their crude oil in order to protect themselves against future market volatility. Downstream integration – in one way or another – is an expression of a risk-averse attitude on their part, which is understandable given their experience in the oil market during the 1980s. Companies with financial difficulties need new investments – for example in their refineries – whereas crude-short companies are interested in arrangements improving their access to oil reserves. For the majors, joint ventures with NOCs from the OPEC countries provide protection against future scarcity, which was the companies' nightmare of the 1970s. This has opened the way for the companies' return to the upstream market, and subsequently partly reverses the structural change of the 1970s.

Whereas the 1950s and 1960s were dominated entirely by the major IOCs, the upstream section of the market in the 1970s was taken over by the main oil-producing countries. These were first of all the OPEC members, but other producing countries also reserved a large share of the upstream sector for national oil companies, as in Mexico (PEMEX), the United Kingdom (BP), and Norway (Statoil). Most NOCs were established by oil-producing countries as part of nationalization of their respective industries in the early 1970s. Some of them control enormous oil reserves. The Saudi Aramco holds ten times the reserves of Exxon. The NOCs of Venezuela, Iran, and Iraq have been important actors in the international oil industry for more than three decades. Many European consuming countries also established national oil companies with the objective of controlling the downstream segment of their national oil industry. Some of these consumer NOCs also engaged in upstream activities in other countries, such as the Italian ENI. Some producer NOCs, such as the Norwegian Statoil, have also been engaged in exploration and production outside the home country for a few decades, but the main picture has been that NOCs have been confined to serve as an essential part of public administration in the domestic oil industry, without international ambitions. This has changed dramatically. Furthermore a new type of NOC has entered the global energy scene.

2003–10: government–company relations: emerging national oil companies

During the last decade new NOCs from China, India, Malaysia, Brazil, and Russia have entered the international oil industry, competing with the IOCs for upstream contracts. This has made the category of NOCs more heterogeneous. Modifying the typology suggested in Quilés and Guillet (2006), Claes and Hveem (2009: 4–5) suggest that three different types of state-controlled oil companies may be identified according to two dimensions, *the type and extent of state control* of the company and the company *strategy*:

1. national companies under total state control, producing mostly at home and thus being mostly export oriented in their strategy; examples are ARAMCO (Saudi Arabia), PDVSA (Venezuela), NIOC (Iran), and PEMEX (Mexico);
2. national companies under state control, but with a strategy of increasing foreign production as they represent import-dependent countries; key examples are the Chinese companies Sinopec, CNOOC, and CNPC;
3. state-controlled companies that primarily follow a commercial and global strategy whether as exporters or importers; examples are ONGC (India), Petrobras (Brazil), Petronas (Malaysia), and Statoil (Norway).

Many of these companies have grown fast in terms of turnover, they invest aggressively in expansion, and they do it in particular abroad. And as in most of the cases their home base is a BRIC[5] country. They are also perceived as being associated with the emerging geopolitical powers of the world, pushing a new world order, and are thus named emerging national oil companies (ENOCs). The ENOCs are regarded as less efficient than the IOCs:

> Many of these companies have been found to be inefficient, with relatively low investments rates. They tend to exploit oil reserves for short-term gain, possibly damaging oilfields, reducing the longer term production potential . . . The potential supply constraint related to the inefficient operations of the national oil companies may be a destabilizing factor in the world oil market.
>
> (Pirog 2007: summary)

Furthermore, it is argued that ENOCs' behavior is infused with politics: "At worst, the business of pumping and selling oil is entirely subsumed by politics."[6] This creates an unfair competitive situation for the IOCs: "International companies face intense pressure from shareholders to maximize profits. National oil companies, however, often do not have the same profit needs and in some cases [have] been willing to plunk down more money and accept lower returns."[7]

In particular, the increased international operations of the Chinese oil companies have attracted public attention in the West. In 2005 the CNOOC bid for Unocal, a California-based exploring and marketing company, resulted in high-level political reactions. Following a vote in the U.S. House of Representatives, the bid was referred to President George W. Bush for review of its implications for national security. CNOOC withdrew its bid. It did, however, succeed in making fairly large investments in Australia and Canada, in addition to investments in several transition or developing countries. In particular, the Chinese oil companies' investments in Africa have created political overtones in the West. Compared with the commercial asset value of investments in Africa, Chinese ENOC investments are just 8 percent of the combined value of IOC investments, and only 3 percent of all companies' investments in African oil (Downs 2007: 44). The production of the Chinese ENOCs in Africa was about 267,000 barrels per day in 2006, compared with 4.1 million per day produced by Algerian Sonatrach, the biggest company in Africa (in volume terms). Sudan is the most important operating country for the Chinese ENOCs in Africa; 81 percent of the 267,000 barrels per day are produced in Sudan. CNPC's investments in upstream activities in Sudan are the company's largest investment abroad (UNCTAD 2007: 118). In 2006 less than half of this production reached China; most of it is sold on the international market. This is probably a result of the high price in the international market (Downs 2007: 45), and this indicates that the Chinese ENOCs may be making market decisions based on commercial motives. Kong (2010: 158) concludes that "Chinese NOCs will be run like a commercial international oil company that follows market principles." However, as the commercial logic of the Chinese companies is not focused on short-term returns and shareholder values, they are able to pursue long-term industrial interests. Without reference to shareholders' alternative investment options, the companies can also enter into projects that IOCs would regard as too risky. If this is the case, the role of the Chinese companies could be regarded as serving the interests of consuming countries as they would bring to the market oil that would otherwise not be produced and marketed.

In Russia Vladimir Putin increased state control over the petroleum sector, pushing a merger of gas and oil producers and exercising effective management control over companies in which the state is the principal shareholder, as in the case of Gazprom, or actively supports the company, as in the case of Lukoil (Boussena and Locatelli 2006). The Russian state has also introduced a tougher tax regime for foreign companies operating Russian petroleum resources. Venezuela, under President Hugo Chávez, and Bolivia are two other cases that have followed the same pattern. Bolivia nationalized its gas industry and Venezuela reduced the agreed share of foreign companies in the development of the oilfields in the Orinoco basin. Not accepting the new conditions, the two U.S. companies ExxonMobil and ConocoPhillips abandoned their operations. In particular ConocoPhillips was negatively affected as its Venezuelan investments constituted approximately 10 percent of its total reserve holdings.

The IEA *World Energy Outlook* of 2008 painted a rather bleak picture regarding the future for long-term oil supplies following the role of the ENOCs:

> The national oil companies in the leading resource-holding countries are increasingly taking on the task of developing new fields themselves . . . The increasing ambitions of the national companies reflect a trend in emerging economies towards greater direct state control over natural resources, a phenomenon commonly referred to as "resource nationalism" . . . There are concerns that the national companies may, in general, be less willing than

the international companies to develop and produce remaining oil and gas reserves on the scale required to meet global demand.

(IEA 2008: 334)

Although there are some cases of renationalization in the oil industry, one should, for several reasons, be cautious in interpreting this as a general new trend. First, one could question the idea that NOCs are less willing to develop and produce oil than IOCs. Why should state-owned companies be less interested in making money than private firms? Also, governments benefit from richness, possibly even more so than private shareholders, as a government's existence can depend on income from oil production (Crystal 1990; Selvik and Stenslie 2011). Second, "resource nationalism has not challenged the free international trade in crude oil: in fact, it has diversified the crude market and made it more competitive . . . than during the period of control by the 'Seven sisters'" (Mitchell 2007: 85).

Third, one could argue that rather than being a new trend it is a correction of a previous anomaly:

In all these cases, the terms for foreign companies were negotiated in the 1990s during a period when the host countries' governments were politically and economically exceptionally weak. One could argue that the terms granted then were unsustainably good for the foreign investors during the current period of high oil and gas prices.

(Mitchell 2007: 93)

Fourth, the rules of the WTO apply in principle to oil and gas trade; China, India, Saudi Arabia, the Gulf states, and all other OPEC members, except Iran and Algeria, are members of the WTO. Fifth, the combined production of crude by CNOOC, CNPC, Sinopec, Lukoil, Petronas, Petrobras, and Indian ONGC was a little more than the total production of ConocoPhillips, one of the Big Five, in 2005 (UNCTAD 2007: 116). In a survey of the fifty largest upstream oil and gas companies conducted in preparation for the 2008 edition of *World Energy Outlook* the IEA found that in the period 2000–7 60 percent of all upstream investments had been conducted by private companies. Their plans for the period 2008–12 suggest that this distribution will be about the same (IEA 2008: 305–6).

Finally, the international oil industry has become increasingly technology driven. The IOCs are still the technological spearheads of the industry. State-controlled companies have contributed relatively little to exploration since the mid-1990s. World investments in exploration doubled from 1995 to 2005 to reach U.S.$225 billion. The Big Five contributed 22 percent, OPEC national companies 7 percent, and the other national and state companies of producer countries 24 percent of this total (Quilés and Guillet 2006: 79). This is another indication that the NOCs represent a dynamic source of investments in the industry besides the Big Five and "junior" companies (which account for the remaining 47% of exploration investments). Table 16.2 shows how investments in exploration and production in

TABLE 16.2 Upstream investments in the oil and gas industries, 2010

Rank	Company	Home country	$ billion	% change 2009/10
1	ExxonMobil	US	27.5	33
2	Petrobras	Brazil	23.8	29
3	PetroChina	China	23.1	22
4	Shell	UK/Netherlands	19.4	−5
5	ChevronTexaco	US	17.3	−1
6	Pemex	Mexico	16.0	−4
7	Total	France	14.0	2
8	ENI	Italy	13.8	5
9	BP	UK	13.0	−12
10	Gazprom	Russia	12.9	13
11	Statoil	Norway	11.1	−6
12	ConocoPhillips	US	9.7	9
13	Sinopec	China	8.2	9
14	CNOOC	China	7.8	22
15	Rosneft	Russia	6.5	11
16	BG	UK	6.2	41
17	Lukoil	Russia	5.5	17
18	Apache	US	4.7	49
19	Devon	US	4.7	12
20	Chesapeake	US	4.5	−7
21	Anadarko	US	4.5	12
22	Suncor	Canada	4.5	8
23	EnCana	US	4.4	19
24	Occidental	US	3.6	21
25	Repsol	Spain	3.4	36
Subtotal 25			270.0	10
World			468.1	9

Source: IEA (2010: 136), based on company reports and announcements, and IEA analysis.

the oil and gas industries are made by companies from all around the globe, inside and outside of OPEC and from developed and emerging economies alike.

The complexity of the set of actors has increased, and the number of agreements and cooperative arrangements among different types of companies have increased dramatically. We are facing a new and far more complex oil industry structure.

A new complex global oil industry structure

Some analysts draw pessimistic conclusions based on the renewed market power of the NOCs:

> If an increasing proportion of global oil and gas resources are under the control of NOC's, it is reasonable to expect that an increasing majority of oil and gas developments will be driven with political objectives in mind. Relative to a commercial outcome, this will result in inefficiencies in the production of revenues, which can manifest through lower levels of production, and higher prices, than would otherwise occur.
>
> (Eller et al. 2007: 33–4)

However, along several dimensions the nature, behavior, and roles of NOCs are very different today from the situation in the 1970s. First, although the NOCs of the 1970s were almost totally oriented toward the domestic oil industry, several of today's NOCs are going abroad, in line with the claims by Stopford and Strange (1991). There they face other NOCs on the opposite side of the negotiation table. Marcel (2006: 218) finds that Middle East NOCs distrust other NOCs and do not find them attractive partners, as they complement their own strengths and assets to a lesser extent than IOCs. Nevertheless various alliances between NOCs are emerging, something that did not happen in the old structure. One illustration is how "Sonatrach, Statoil, Petrobras and Saudi Aramco are active participants and organizers of the NOC Forum, which . . . has brought CEOs of national oil companies [together] to share ideas on how to develop NOCs' core competences" (Marcel 2006: 220). Second, the oil industry has become more fragmented during the last three decades, as oil companies have outsourced several engineering and technological services. Thus NOCs can acquire technology from other sources than the IOCs (UNCTAD 2007: 118). Third, various forms of contractual relations between oil-producing governments and IOCs have emerged (Likosky 2009). Consequently, the IOCs have re-entered exploration and production in many of the oil-producing countries that they were kicked out of in the 1970s. Fourth, the wide variety of alliances between NOCs and IOCs have become the order of the day. This will potentially influence the operations and behavior of NOCs in a commercial direction. Marcel (2006: 209) observes "an increased blurring of differences between NOCs and IOCs."

Thus the set of influential actors in the oil industry has increased, and the structure has become more complex. It is unlikely that this "network" structure will imply a shutout of the traditional IOCs. However, their role is changing, and will continue to do so in partnerships with NOCs of both producing and consuming countries. In most cases producing governments are also likely to welcome the IOCs as partners in the development of their energy resources. After a period of transition such a structure could possibly be as stable as both the era of the Sisters and the OPEC era. However, it will not give a single group of actors the kind of market power that has characterized the previous periods.

In the 1970s and 1980s the structure of the international oil market was described as a "trilateral oligopoly" among the three parties: (1) oil-consuming countries; (2) oil-producing countries; and (3) the private international oil companies (Adelman 1977; Roncaglia 1985). Today the structure of the global oil industry can be described as a pentangle of interrelated actors cutting across the government–company and the IOC–NOC dimensions (Figure 16.2).

As the number of dyadic relations is given by the following formula:

$$n(n-1)/2,$$

increasing the number of groups of actors from three to five increases the number of dyadic relationships from three to ten. In addition there are several formal and informal alliances among actors in the five groups leading to a potential total of fifteen cells of various forms of interactions, although not all of these constellations are empirically interesting (Table 16.3).

At face value this increased complexity implies weaker governance and increased instability, which potentially can result in increased conflict among both companies and countries. To avoid this "policy-makers need to adapt and strengthen the institutional architecture of international oil and gas relations" (Goldthau and Witte 2009: 390; see also Goldthau and Witte 2010). Since oil trade has become globalized and the interdependence among the actors has increased, political institutions should also be renewed. Neglecting the role of commercial actors in the governance structures of the oil market would be a great mistake. As pointed out by Keohane and Underdal (Chapter 3 in this volume) one essential

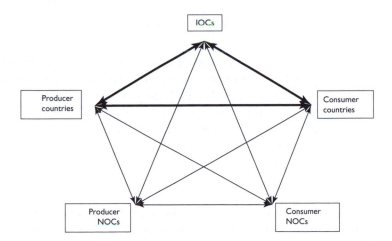

FIGURE 16.2 The governance structure of the global oil industry. Note: Old structure indicated by thick lines.

TABLE 16.3 Various alliances among actors in the global oil market

	IOCs	Producer countries	Consumer countries	Producer NOCs	Consumer NOCs
IOCs	Seven Sisters	Concessions for exploration and production (E&P)	Private downstream activities in refining and product sales	Production-sharing agreements (PSAs)	Minimal activity
Producer countries		OPEC	International Energy Forum	State ownership of E&P in domestic oil provinces, e.g. NOCs in OPEC countries	Upstream investments, e.g. Chinese companies' E&P in Sudan
Consumer countries			International Energy Agency	Foreign NOCs' downstream investments abroad, e.g. Kuwait's investments in U.S. refining	State ownership of domestic downstream activities, e.g. ENI in Italy
Producer NOCs				The NOC Forum	NOC alliances in upstream investments abroad, e.g. Statoil and Sinochem in Brazil
Consumer NOCs					Minimal activity

feature of international governance today is that "many of the most important institutions . . . are not built around formal organizations but constitute networks with regular patterns of interaction." This, indeed, applies to the international oil market. These patterns of interaction cut across the NOC–IOC divide, and include both governments and companies. Although several international governmental organizations address energy issues (Lesage et al. 2010), analysts of global energy industries should not repeat the mistakes of the past, pointed out more than thirty years ago:

> The tendency to overlook or underestimate the interests and influence of the large transnational corporations and "their" home governments has been strong, not only in the case of crude oil, but in the case of primary commodities and raw materials in general.
>
> (Hveem 1978: 11)

Notes

1 The term "acquired rights" referred to the rights held by the Turkish Petroleum Company and the rights promised to that company by the Ottoman Grand Vizier, as evidenced by his letter of June 28, 1914, to the British and German ambassadors (FTC 1952: 51–2).

2 The name "Seven Sisters" was phrased by Enrico Mattei, the director of ENI, the Italian national oil company, and later used by Anthony Sampson as the title of his book about the big oil companies (Sampson 1975).

3 In 1890 the U.S. Congress passed the Sherman Antitrust Act with the aim of restricting monopolistic and anti-competitive market behavior of large corporations. In 1906 the U.S. administration prosecuted Standard Oil for violation of the Sherman Act. In 1911 the U.S. Supreme Court rejected the company's final appeal and Standard Oil was broken up into thirty-four different companies (Yergin 1991: 106–10).

4 The Saudi Arabian case evolved in three stages: in 1973 the government acquired a 25 percent share of the Arabian American Oil Company (Aramco) from the U.S. owners; in 1974 the government increased its share to 60 percent; and in 1980 it finally acquired full control of the company, transforming a previous IOC into a NOC. It was not until 1988 that the company elected a Saudi Arabian chairman.

5 Acronym used to represent the emerging economic powers Brazil, Russia, India, and China.

6 Leader in *The Economist* (2006), August 10.

7 Justin Blum (2005) in *The Washington Post*, August 3.

REFERENCES

Abdelal, R., Blyth, M., and Parsons, C. (2010) 'Re-constructing IPE: Some conclusions drawn from a crisis', in R. Abdelal, M. Blyth, and C. Parsons (eds.) *Constructing the international economy*, Ithaca, NY: Cornell University Press.

Abu-El-Haj, J. (2007) 'From interdependence to neo-mercantilism: Brazilian capitalism in the age of globalization', *Latin American Perspectives*, 34, 5: 92–114.

Acemoglu, D. and Robinson, J. A. (2006a) 'Economic backwardness in political perspective', *American Political Science Review*, 100, 1: 115–31.

—— (2006b) *Economic origins of dictatorship and democracy*, New York: Cambridge University Press.

Acemoglu, D., Johnson, S., and Robinson, J. A. (2001) 'The colonial origins of comparative development: An empirical investigation', *American Economic Review*, 91, 5: 1369–1401.

Acharya, A. (1991) 'The Association of Southeast Asian Nations: "Security community" or "defence community?"', *Pacific Affairs*, 64, 2: 159–78.

—— (2001) *Constructing a security community in Southeast Asia: ASEAN and the problem of regional order*, London: Routledge.

Adelman, I. (2001) 'Fallacies in development theory and their implications for policy', in G. M. Meier and J. E. Stiglitz (eds.) *Frontiers of development economics: The future in perspective*, New York: Oxford University Press.

Adelman, M. A. (1977) 'Producers, consumers, and multinationals: Problems in analyzing a non-competitive market', Working Paper MIT-EL 77–038WP (World Oil Project), Cambridge, MA: MIT Energy Laboratory.

—— (1995) *The genie out of the bottle – world oil since 1970*, Cambridge, MA: MIT Press.

Adler, E. and Pouliot, V. (2008) 'The practice turn in international relations: Introduction and framework', paper presented at the Munck Centre for International Affairs conference on The Practice Turn in International Affairs, University of Toronto, Canada, November 2008.

Ahn, D. K. (2008) *Jungbu Yeonku Gaebal Jiwon WTO Gubeom Juchoksung Yeonku* [*Essay on contradictory of Korean government's R&D support against WTO*], Seoul: KOTEF.

Alesina, A. and Glaeser, E. L. (2004) *Fighting poverty in the US and Europe*, Oxford: Oxford University Press.

Alesina, A., Devleeschauwer, A., Easterly, W., Kurlat, S., and Wacziarg, R. (2003) 'Fractionalization', *Journal of Economic Growth*, 8, 2: 155–94.

Alexander, L. and Schoenholtz, K. (2008) 'Centralised counterparties could lessen systemic risk', *Financial Times*, June 5. Available at http://www.ft.com/cms/29d1f72a-329a-11d d-9b87-0000779fd2ac.html (accessed January 19, 2011).

Allen, F., Rajesh, C., De, S., Qian, J., and Qian, M. (2006) 'Financing firms in India', EFA Zurich Meetings. Available at http://ssrn.com/abstract=898066 (accessed January 19, 2011).

Alter, K. J. and Meunier S. (2009) 'The politics of international regime complexity', *Perspectives on Politics*, 7, 1: 13–24.

Altomonte, C. and Guagliano, C. (2003) 'Comparative study of FDI in Central and Eastern Europe and the Mediterranean', *Economic Systems*, 27, 2: 223–46.

Amsden, A. (1985) 'The state and Taiwan's economic development', in P. B. Evans, D. Rueschemeyer, and T. Skocpol (eds.) *Bringing the state back in*, Cambridge, UK: Cambridge University Press.

—— (1989) *Asia's next giant: South Korea and late industrialization*, New York: Oxford University Press.

—— (2001) *The rise of the "the rest,"* Oxford: Oxford University Press.

Amsden, A. and Hikino, T. (2000) 'The bark is worse than the bite: New WTO law and late industrialisation', *Annals of the American Academy of Political & Social Sciences*, 570, 1: 104–14.

Amsden, A. and Chu, W.-W. (2003) *Beyond late development: Taiwan's upgrading policies*, Cambridge, MA: MIT Press.

Amyx, J. (2006) 'Regional financial cooperation in East Asia since the Asian financial crisis', draft paper for the Conference on the Political Economy of East Asia Ten Years after the Crisis, Canberra, Australia, July 21.

Anderson, I. H. (1981) *Aramco, the United States, and Saudi Arabia: A study of the dynamics of foreign oil policy, 1933–1950*, Princeton, NJ: Princeton University Press.

Andree, P. (2005) 'The Cartegena Protocol on biosafety and shifts in the discourse of pre-caution', *Global Environmental Politics*, 5, 4: 25–46.

Andriof, J. and McIntosh, M. (eds.) (2001) *Perspectives on corporate citizenship*, Sheffield: Greenleaf Publishing.

Araya, M. (2006) 'Exploring terra incognita: Non-financial reporting in corporate Latin America', *Journal of Corporate Citizenship*, 21: 25–38.

Asahi Shimbun (2005) 'Armitage warns against East Asia Summit', May 2, p. 1.

Ashizawa K. P. (2004) 'Japan, the United States, and multilateral institution building in the Asia-Pacific', in E. J. Krauss and T. J. Pempel (eds.) *Beyond bilateralism: U.S.–Japan relations in the New Asia-Pacific*, Stanford, CA: Stanford University Press.

Asiedu, E. (2006) 'Foreign direct investment in Africa: The role of natural resources, market size, government policy, institutions and political instability', *World Economy*, 29, 1: 63–77.

Avant, D., Finnemore, M., and Sell, S. K. (2010) 'Who governs the globe?', in D. Avant, M. Finnemore, and S. K. Sell (eds.) *Who governs the globe*, Cambrige, MA: Cambridge University Press.

Bach, D. (ed.) (1999) *Regionalisation in Africa: Integration and disintegration*, Oxford: James Currey.

Bach, D. and Gazibo, M (eds.) (2011) *L'Etat neopatrimonial: Genèse et trajectoires contemporaines*, Ottawa: Presses de l'Université d'Ottawa.

Bairoch, P. (1993) *Economics and world history: Myths and paradoxes*, Chicago: Chicago University Press.

Baker, A. (2005) *The Group of Seven finance ministries, central banks, and global financial governance*, London: Routledge.

Baland, J.-M., Moene, K. O., and Robinson, J. A. (2010) 'Governance and development', in D. Rodrik and M. Rosenzweig (eds.) *Handbook in development economics, vol. 5*, Amsterdam: North Holland.

Balassa, B. (1981) *The newly industrializing countries in the world economy*, New York: Pergamon.

Baldwin, D. A. (1993) *Neorealism and neoliberalism: The contemporary debate*, New York: Columbia University Press.

Baldwin, R., François, J. F., and Portes, R. (1997) 'The costs and benefits of Eastern enlargement: The impact on the EU and Central Europe', *Economic Policy*, 12, 24: 125–76.

Bank for International Settlements (BIS) (2009a) *79th Annual Report*, Basle: BIS.

—— (2009b) *OTC derivatives market activity for the second half of 2008*, Basle: BIS.

—— (2010a) *80th Annual Report*, Basle: BIS.

—— (2010b) *BIS Quarterly Review*, Basle: BIS.

Barnes, J. and Lorentzen, J. (2006) 'Learning, upgrading, and innovation in the South African automotive industry', in R. Narula and S. Lall (eds.) *Understanding FDI-assisted development*, London: Routledge.

Barr, N. (1992) 'Economic theory and the welfare state: A survey and interpretation', *Journal of Economic Literature*, 30, 2: 741–803.

Barrett, S. (2007) *Why cooperate? The incentive to supply global public goods*, Oxford: Oxford University Press.

Barro, R. J. and Sala-i-Martin, X. (2004) *Economic growth*, Cambridge, MA: MIT Press.

Barry, F. (2004) 'Prospects for Ireland in an enlarged EU', *The World Economy*, 27, 6: 829–52.

Barth, J., Caprio, G., and Levine, R. (2006) *Rethinking bank regulation: Till angels govern*, New York: Cambridge University Press.

Basu, A. K. and Grote, U. (2006) 'China as standard-setter: The examples of GM-cotton and ecological and food safety standards', paper presented at the Seventh Annual Global Development Conference Pre-Conference Workshop on Asian and Other Drivers of Global Change, St Petersburg, January 18–19, 2006.

Bates, R. H. (1981) *Markets and states in tropical Africa*, Berkeley: University of California Press.

Bates, R. H., Greif, A., and Jean-Laurent M. L. (1998) *Analytical narratives*, Princeton, NJ: Princeton University Press.

Baum, M. A. and Lake, D. A. (2003) 'The political economy of growth: Democracy and human capital', *American Journal of Political Science*, 47, 2: 333–47.

Beck, N. and Katz, J. N. (1995) 'What to do (and not to do) with time-series cross-section data', *American Political Science Review*, 89, 3: 634–47.

Beckert, J. (2002) *Beyond the market: The social foundations of economic efficiency*, Princeton, NJ: Princeton University Press.

Bellak, C. and Leibrecht, M. (2007) 'How to make FDI in Central and Eastern European countries sustainable', in K. Liebscher, J. Christl, P. Mooslechner, and D. Ritzberger-Grünwald (eds.) *Foreign direct investment in Europe: A changing landscape*, London: Edward Elgar.

Bellak, C., Leibrecht, M., and Stehrer, R. (2008) 'The role of public policy in closing foreign direct investment gaps: An empirical analysis', WIIW Working Papers 48, Vienna: Vienna Institute for International Economic Studies.

Bellak, C., Damijan, J., and Leibrecht, M. (2009) 'Infrastructure endowment and corporate income taxes as determinants of foreign direct investment in Central and Eastern European countries', *The World Economy*, 32, 2: 267–90.

Benito, G., Grogaard, B., and Narula, R. (2003) 'Environmental influences on MNE sub-sidiary roles: Economic integration and the Nordic countries', *Journal of International Business Studies*, 34, 5: 443–56.

Bergesen, H. O. (1982) 'Not valid for oil: The petroleum dilemma in Norwegian foreign policy', *Cooperation and Conflict*, 17, 2: 105–16.

Bernstein, S., Lebow, R. N., Stein, J. G., and Weber, S. (2000) 'God gave physics the easy problems: Adapting social science to an unpredictable world', *European Journal of International Relations*, 6, 1: 43–76.

Besley, T. and Kanbur, R. (1993) 'The principles of targeting', in M. Lipton and J. van der Gaag (eds.) *Including the poor*, Washington, DC: World Bank.

Besley, T. and Kudamatsu, M. (2007) 'Making autocracy work', DEDPS Working Paper No. 48, London: London School of Economics.

Best, J. (2004) 'Hollowing out Keynesian norms: How the search for a technical fix under-mined the Bretton Woods regime', *International Studies Review*, 30, 3: 383–404.

Bhagwati, J. (ed.) (1977) *The new international economic order: The North–South debate*, Cambridge, MA: MIT Press.

—— (1998) 'The capital myth: The difference between trade in widgets and dollars', *Foreign Affairs*, 7, 3: 7–12.

—— (2003) *Free trade today*, Princeton, NJ: Princeton University Press.

Blomstrom, M. and Kokko, A. (1997) 'How foreign investment affects host countries', Policy Research Working Paper, Washington, DC: World Bank.

Blonigen, B. A. (2005) 'A review of the empirical literature on FDI determinants', *Atlantic Economic Journal*, 33, 4: 383–403.

Blum, J. (2005) 'National oill firms take bigger role: Governments hold most of world's reserves', *The Washington Post*, August 3, p. D01.

Blyth, M. (2006) 'Great punctuations: Prediction, randomness, and the evolution of com-parative political science', *American Political Science Review*, 100, 4: 493–8.

Boix, C. (2003) *Democracy and redistribution*, New York: Cambridge University Press.

Boli, J. and Thomas, G. M. (1999) 'INGOs and the organization of world culture', in J. Boli and G. M. Thomas (eds.) *Constructing world culture: International nongovernmental organizations since 1875*, Stanford, CA: Stanford University Press.

Boli, J., Lola, T. A., and Loftin, T. (1999) 'National participation in world-polity organiza-tion', in J. Boli and G. M. Thomas (eds.) *Constructing world culture: International nongovern-mental organizations since 1875*, Stanford, CA: Stanford University Press.

Bora, B., Lloyd, P. J., and Pangestu, M. (2000) *Industrial policy and the WTO*, New York: United Nations.

Bordo, M., Eichengreen, B., Klingebiel, D., and Martinez-Peria, M. (2001) 'Is the crisis problem growing more severe?', *Economic Policy*, 16, 32: 51–82.

Boudier-Bensebaa, F. (2008) 'FDI-assisted development in the light of the investment development path paradigm: Evidence from Central and Eastern European countries', *Transnational Corporations*, 17, 1: 37–67.

Bourmaud, D. (1991) 'L'état centrifuge au Kenya', in J.-F. Médard (ed.) *États d'Afrique Noire: Formation, mecanismes et crise*, Paris: Karthala.

—— (1997) *La politique en Afrique*, Paris: Montchrestien.

Boussena, S. and Locatelli, C. (2006) 'Le nouveau role de l'etat dans l'industrie petroliere en Russie: Le prive en tutelle?', *MEDenergie*, 20: 32–8.

Brainard, L. (1997) 'An empirical assessment of the proximity–concentration tradeoff between multinational sales and trade', *American Economic Review*, 87, 4: 520–44.

Braithwaite, J. and Drahos, P. (2000) *Global business regulation*, Cambridge, UK: Cambridge University Press.

Bratton, M. and van de Walle, N. (1997) *Democratic experiments in Africa: Regime transitions in comparative perspective*, Cambridge, UK: Cambridge University Press.

Breitmeier, H., Underdal, A., and Young, O. R. (forthcoming) 'The effectiveness of international environmental regimes: Comparing and contrasting findings from quantitative research', *International Studies Review*.

Brenton, P. and DiMauro, F. (1999) 'The potential magnitude and impact of FDI flows to CEECs', *Journal of Economic Integration*, 14, 1: 59–74.

Buch, C. M., Kokta, R. M., and Piazolo, D. (2003) 'Foreign direct investment in Europe: Is there redirection from the South to the East?', *Journal of Comparative Economics*, 31, 1: 94–109.

Buchanan, A. B. and Keohane, R. O. (2006) 'The legitimacy of global governance institutions', *Ethics and International Affairs*, 20, 4: 405–37.

Bueno de Mesquita, B., Smith, A., Siverson, R. M., and Morrow, J. D. (2003) *The logic of political survival*, Cambridge, MA: MIT Press.

Bull, B. and McNeill, D. (2007) *Development issues in global governance: Public–private partnerships and market multilateralism*, London: Routledge.

Bull, H. (1977) *The anarchical society: A study of order in world politics*, New York: Columbia University Press.

Bullock, N. and Mackenzie, M. (2008) 'A clearer picture set to emerge of state of credit derivatives', *Financial Times*, July 31. Available at http://www.ft.com/cms/082d9d5 2-5e98-11dd-b354-000077b07658.html (accessed January 19, 2011).

Burkhart, R. E. and Lewis-Beck, M. S. (1994) 'Comparative democracy: The economic development thesis', *American Political Science Review*, 88, 4: 903–10.

Busse, M. (2004) 'Transnational corporations and repression of political rights and civil liberties: An empirical analysis', *Kyklos*, 57, 1: 45–65.

Busse, M. and Hefeker, C. (2007) 'Political risk, institutions and foreign direct investment', *European Journal of Political Economy*, 23, 2: 397–415.

Calhoun, C. (2009) 'Social science for public knowledge', Social Science Research Council. Available at http://publicsphere.ssrc.org/calhoun-social-science-for-public-knowledge/ (accessed December 4, 2009).

Callaghy, T. M. (1984) *The state–society struggle: Zaire in comparative perspective*, New York: Columbia University Press.

Campanella, E. (2010) 'The Triffin dilemma again', *Economics: The Open-Access, Open Assessment E-Journal*, 4, 2010–25. Available at http://www.economics-ejournal.org/ economics/journalarticles/2010–25/view (accessed October 11, 2010).

Campbell, I. (2004) 'Retreat from globalization', *The National Interest*, 75, Spring 2004: 111–17.

Cerny, P. G. (ed.) (1993) *Finance and world politics: Markets, regimes, and states in the post-hegemonic era*, Cheltenham: Edward Elgar.

—— (1996) 'International finance and the erosion of state policy capacity', in P. Gummet (ed.) *Globalisation and public policy*, Cheltenham: Edward Elgar.

Chan, S. (2008) *China, the U.S., and the power-transition theory*, London: Routledge.

Chang, H.-J. (1993) 'Political economy of industrial policy in Korea', *Cambridge Journal of Economics*, 17, 2: 131–57.

—— (1994) *Political economy of industrial policy*, London: Macmillan.

—— (2002) *Kicking away the ladder: Development strategy in historical perspective*, London: Anthem Press.

—— (2003) 'Kicking away the ladder: Infant industry promotion in historical perspective', *Oxford Development Studies*, 31, 1: 21–32.

—— (2005) 'Kim Dae-jung Jungbuei Venture Giup Jiwonjungcheck Gochal [Venture business policy under Kim Dae-jung government: Resurrection of old industrial policy or catalystic role of government?]', *Korea Journal of Public Administration*, 39, 3: 21–41.

—— (2006) *The East Asian development experience: The miracle, the crisis and the future*, London: Zed Books.

Cho, H. M. and Kim, E. M. (1998) 'State autonomy and its social conditions for economic development in South Korea and Taiwan', in E. M. Kim (ed.) *The four Asian tigers: Economic development and the global political economy*, San Diego: Academic Press.

Chorev, N. (2005) 'The institutional project of neo-liberal globalism: The case of the WTO', *Theory and Society*, 34, 3: 317–55.

Chung, J. (2009) 'CFTC nominee vows to fight futures speculation', *Financial Times*, February 25. Available at http://www.ft.com/cms/3a1ae18c-02dd-11de-b58b-000077b07658.html (accessed January 19, 2011).

Claes, D. H. (2001) *The politics of oil-producer cooperation*, Boulder, CO: Westview Press.

Claes, D. H. and Hveem, H. (2009) 'Emerging national oil companies: Challengers or partners?', paper presented at the 50th Annual Convention of the International Studies Association, New York, February 2009.

Claes, D. H., Hveem, H., and Tranøy, B. S. (2006) *Økonomisk globalisering og politisk styring*, Oslo: Universitetsforlaget.

Claessens, S., Underhill, G. R. D., and Zhang, X. (2008) 'The political economy of Basel II: The costs for poor countries', *The World Economy*, 31, 3: 313–44.

Clague, C., Keefer, P., Knack, S., and Olson, M. (2003) 'Property and contract rights in autocracies and democracies', in S. Knack (ed.) *Democracy, governance and growth*, Ann Arbor: University of Michigan Press.

Clapham, C. (1996) *Africa and the international system: The politics of state survival*, Cambridge, UK: Cambridge University Press.

Clapp, J. and Helleiner, E. (2010) 'Troubled futures? The global food crisis and the politics of agricultural derivatives regulation', *Review of International Political Economy*. Available at http://www.informaworld.com/smpp/content~db=all~content=a929157857~frm =abslink (accessed January 19, 2011).

Clausing, K. A. and Dorobantu, C. L. (2005) 'Re-entering Europe: Does European Union candidacy boost foreign direct investment?', *Economics of Transition*, 13, 1: 77–103.

Coase, R. (1937) 'The nature of the firm', *Economica New Series*, 4, 16: 386–405.

Cohen, B. J. (1982) 'Balance of payments financing: Evolution of a regime', *International Organization*, 36, 2, 457–78.

—— (1993) 'The triad and the unholy trinity', in R. Higgott, R. Leaver, and J. Ravenhill (eds.) *Pacific economic relations in the 1990s*, Boulder, CO: Lynne Rienner.

—— (1996) 'Phoenix risen: The resurrection of global finance', *World Politics*, 48, 2: 268–96.

—— (2007) 'The transatlantic divide: Why are American and British IPE so different?', *Review of International Political Economy*, 14, 2: 197–219.

—— (2008a) *International political economy: An intellectual history*, Princeton, NJ: Princeton University Press.

—— (2008b) 'The transatlantic divide: A rejoinder', *Review of International Political Economy*, 15, 1: 30–4.

Coleman, J. S. (1973) *The mathematics of collective action*, London: Heinemann.

Coleman, W. D. (1996) *Financial services, globalisation, and domestic policy change*, Basingstoke: Macmillan.

—— (2003) 'Governing global finance: Financial derivatives, liberal states and transformative capacity', in L. Weiss (ed.) *States in the global economy*, Cambridge, UK: Cambridge University Press.

Colgan, J., Keohane, R. O., and van de Graaf, T. (2010) 'Institutional change in the energy regime complex', unpublished paper.

Commission of the European Communities (2007) 'Mid-term review of industrial policy: A contribution to the EU's Growth and Jobs Strategy', Commision Staff Working Document. Available at http://ec.europa.eu/enterprise/policies/industrial-competitiveness/files/industry/doc/sec_2007_917_en.pdf (accessed February 17, 2011).

Cooper, R. (1968) *The economics of interdependence: Economic policy in the Atlantic community*, New York: McGraw Hill.

Cox, C. (2008) 'Opening remarks at SEC Roundtable on modernizing the Securities and Exchange Commission's disclosure system', October 8, SEC. Available at http://www.sec.gov/news/speech/2008/spch100808cc.htm (accessed January 19, 2011).

Cox, R. W. (1987) *Production, power, and world order*, New York: Columbia University Press.

Cox, R. W. and Jacobson, H. K. (1973) *The anatomy of influence*, New Haven, CT: Yale University Press.

Criscuolo, P. and Narula, R. (2008) 'A novel approach to national technological accumulation and absorptive capacity: Aggregating Cohen and Levinthal', *European Journal of Development Research*, 20, 1: 56–73.

CRMPG (2008) 'Containing systemic risk: The road to reform'. Available at http://www.crmpolicygroup.org (accessed August 6, 2008).

Crook, R. C. (1989) 'Patrimonialism, administrative effectiveness and economic development in Côte d'Ivoire', *African Affairs*, 88, 351: 205–28.

Crystal, J. (1990) *Oil and politics in the Gulf: Rulers and merchants in Kuwait and Qatar*, Cambridge, UK: Cambridge University Press.

Cutler, A. C., Haufler, V., and Porter, T. (eds.) (1999) *Private authority and international affairs*, Albany: State University of New York Press.

Daadler, I. and Lindsey, J. M. (2003) *America unbound: The Bush revolution in foreign policy*, Washington, DC: Brookings Institution.

Das, S. (2006) *Traders, guns and money*, Harlow: Pearson Education.

—— (2009) 'CDS markets: Through the looking glass', *RGE Monitor*, March 23. Available at http://www.roubini.com/financemarkets-monitor/256113/cds_markets_through_the_looking_glass (accessed January 19, 2011).

Davidson, D. (1974) 'On the very idea of a conceptual scheme', *Proceedings & Addresses of the American Philosophical Association*, 47: 5–20.

DeBurca, G. (2010) 'The EU in the negotiation of the UN Disability Convention', *E.L. Review*, 35, 2: 175–96.

De Donder, P. and Hindriks, J. (1998) 'The political economy of targeting', *Public Choice*, 95, 1–2: 177–200.

de Haan, L. J. (2010) 'Perspectives on African studies and development in sub-Saharan Africa', *Africa Spectrum*, 45, 1: 95–116.

Demetriades, P. and Hussain, K. (1996) 'Does financial development cause economic growth?', *Journal of Development Economics*, 51, 2: 387–411.

Deutsch. K. W. (1957) *Political community and the North-Atlantic area*, Princeton, NJ: Princeton University Press.

Dewan, T. and Shepsle, K. A. (2008a) 'Recent economic perspective on political economy, Part I', *British Journal of Political Science*, 38, 2: 363–82.

—— (2008b) 'Recent economic perspective on political economy, Part II', *British Journal of Political Science*, 38, 3: 543–64.

Diamond, L. (2008) *The spirit of democracy*, New York: Times Books.

Dicken, P. (2003) *Global shift: Reshaping the global economic map in the 21st century*, 4th edn, London: Sage.

Dinallo, E. (2009) 'We modernized ourselves into this Ice Age', *Financial Times*, March 31. Available at http://www.ft.com/cms/3b94938c-1d59-11de-9eb3-00144feabdc0.html (accessed January 19, 2011).

Dizard, J. (2008) 'Put the credit default swaps market out of its misery', *Financial Times*, December 9. Available at http://www.ft.com/cms/8979777c-c591-11dd-b51 6-000077b07658.html (accessed January 19, 2011).

Doner, R. F., Ritchie, B. K., and Slater, D. (2005) 'Systemic vulnerability and the origins of developmental states: Northeast and Southeast Asia in comparative perspective', *International Organization*, 59, 2: 327–61.

Dore, R. P. (1986) *Flexible rigidities: Industrial policy and structural adjustment in the Japanese economy 1970–1980*, London: Athlone Press.

Doucouliagos, H. and Ulubasoglu, M. A. (2008) 'Democracy and economic growth: A meta-analysis', *American Journal of Political Science*, 52, 1: 61–83.

Downs, E. S. (2007) 'The fact and fiction of Sino-African energy relations', *China Security*, 3, 3: 42–68.

Drezner, D. W. (2009a) 'Bad debts: Assessing China's financial influence in great power politics', *International Security*, 34, 2: 7–45.

—— (2009b) 'The power and peril of international regime complexity', *Perspectives on Politics*, 7, 1: 65–70.

Dunning, J. H. (1980) 'Toward an eclectic theory of international production: Some empirical tests', *Journal of International Business Studies*, 11, 1: 9–31.

—— (1981a) 'Explaining outward direct investment of developing countries: In support of the eclectic theory of international production', in K. Kumar and M. G. McLeod (eds.) *Multinationals from developing countries*, Lexington, MD: Lexington Books.

—— (1981b) 'Explaining the international direct investment position of countries: Towards a dynamic or development approach', *Weltwirtschaflliches Archiv*, 117, 1: 30–64.

—— (ed.) (2003) *Making globalization good: The moral challenges of global capitalism*, Oxford: Oxford University Press

Dunning, J. H. and Narula, R. (1996a) 'The investment development path revisited: Some emerging issues', in J. W. Dunning and R. Narula (eds.) *Foreign direct investment and governments*, London: Routledge.

—— (eds.) (1996b) *Foreign direct investment and governments: Catalysts for economic restructuring*, London: Routledge.

—— (2004) *Multinational and industrial competitiveness: A new agenda*, Cheltenham: Edward Elgar.

Dunning, J. H. and Lundan, S. M. (2008) *Multinational enterprises and the global economy*, 2nd edn, Cheltenham: Edward Elgar.

Dyck, J. J. and Hussey, L. S. (2008) 'The end of welfare as we know it? Durable attitudes in a changing information environment', *Public Opinion Quarterly*, 72, 4: 589–618.

Easterly, W. (2001) *The elusive quest for growth: Economists' adventures and misadventures in the tropics*, Cambridge, MA: MIT Press.

Easton, D. (1953) *The political system: An inquiry into the state of political science*, New York: Alfred E. Knopf.

The Economist (2006) 'Really big oil: Sluggish behemoths control virtually all the world's oil; they should be privatised', August 10, leader.

—— (2008) 'Finance and economics: But will it work? Rescuing the banks', October 18. Available at http://www.economist.com/node/12432432 (accessed January 19, 2011).

—— (2010) 'Emergency repairs', May 13. Available at http://www.economist.com/node/16106575 (accessed January 19, 2011).

Edwards, S. (1993) 'Openness, trade liberalization, and growth in developing countries', *Journal of Economic Literature*, 31, 3: 1358–93.

Eichengreen, B. and Hausmann, R. (eds.) (2005) *Other people's money: Debt denomination and financial instability in emerging market economies*, Chicago: University of Chicago Press.

Eisenstadt, S. N. (1973) *Traditional patrimonialism and modern neo-patrimonialism*, Beverly Hills, CA: Sage.

Eller, S. L., Hartley, P., and Medlock III, K. B. (2007) 'Empirical evidence on the operational efficiency of national oil companies', report from the James A. Baker Institute for Public Policy, Rice University, March 2007, Houston, TX: Rice University.

Erdmann, G. and Engel, U. (2007) 'Neopatrimonialism reconsidered: Critical review and elaboration of an elusive concept', *Commonwealth & Comparative Politics*, 45, 1: 95–119.

Erixon, F. (2005) *Aid and development: Will it work this time?*, Islington: International Policy Centre.

Esping-Andersen, G. (1990) *The three worlds of welfare capitalism*, Cambridge, UK: Polity Press.

Evans, P. B. (1989) 'Predatory, developmental and other apparatuses: A comparative analysis of the Third World state', *Sociological Forum*, 4, 4: 561–82.

—— (1995) *Embedded autonomy: State and industrial transformation*, Princeton, NJ: Princeton University Press.

Fabry, N. and Zeghni, S. (2006) 'How former communist countries of Europe may attract inward foreign direct investment? A matter of institutions', *Communist and Post-Communist Studies*, 39, 2: 201–19.

Feenstra, R. C. (2004) *Advanced international trade: Theory and evidence*, Princeton, NJ: Princeton University Press.

Feldstein, M. (1997) 'The political economy of the European Economic and Monetary Union: Political sources of an economic liability', *Journal of Economic Perspectives*, 11, 4: 23–42.

—— (2000) 'The European Central Bank and the euro: The first year', NBER Working Paper No. 7517, February, Cambridge, MA: National Bureau of Economic Research.

Feldstein, M. and Horioka, C. (1980) 'Domestic saving and international capital flows', *Economic Journal*, 90, 358: 314–29.

Feyerabend, P. (1962) 'Explanation, reduction and empiricism', in H. Feigl and G. Maxwell (eds.) *Minnesota studies in the philosophy of science, vol. 3*, Minneapolis: University of Minnesota Press.

Financial Services Authority (UK) (2009) *The Turner Review: A regulatory response to the global banking crisis*, London: Financial Services Authority.

Financial Stability Forum (2009) 'Report of the Financial Stability Forum on addressing procyclicality in the financial system', April 2, Basel: Financial Stability Board.

Financial Times (1997) 'A wounded tiger reluctant to change its stripe', December 29.

Findlay, R. and O'Rourke, K. H. (2007) *Power and plenty: Trade, war and the world economy in the second millennium*, Princeton, NJ: Princeton University Press.

Finon, D. (1991) 'The prospects for a New International Petroleum Order', *Energy Studies Review*, 3, 3: 260–76.

Florida, R. and Kenney, M. (1993) 'The new age of capitalism', *Futures*, 25, 6: 637–51.

Flyvbjerg, B. (2001) *Making social science matter*, New York: Cambridge University Press.

Fouse, D. (2005) 'Japan's FY 2005 National Defense Program Outline: New concepts, old compromises', *The Asia Pacific Center for Security Studies*, 4, 3: 1–4.

Freeland, C. (2008) 'The new age of authoritarianism', *Financial Times*, November 8. Available at http://www.ft.com/cms/4bd4868e-6806-11dd-8d3b-0000779fd18c.html (accessed January 19, 2011).

Frieden, J. and Martin, L. (2002) 'International political economy: The state of the sub-discipline', in I. Katznelson and H. Milner (eds.) *Political science: The state of the discipline*, New York: W. W. Norton.

Frieden, J. A., Lake, D. A., and Broz, J. L. (2009) *International political economy: Perspectives on global power and wealth*, 5th edn, New York: W. W. Norton.

Frynas, J. (2008) 'Corporate social responsibility and international development: Critical assessment', *Corporate Governance*, 16, 4: 274–81.

FTC (1952) 'The International Petroleum Cartel', staff report to the Federal Trade Commission, Washington, DC: U.S. Senate.

Fuchs, D. (2005) *Understanding business power*, Baden Baden: Nomos.

Fukuyama, F. (1992) *The end of history and the last man*, New York: Free Press.

—— (1995) *Trust: The social virtues and the creation of prosperity*, New York: Free Press.

G20 (2008) 'Declaration of the summit on financial markets and the world economy', Washington, DC. Available at http://www.g20.org/Documents/g20_summit_declaration.pdf (accessed November 15, 2008).

—— (2009a) 'Declaration on strengthening the financial system', London. Available at http://www.g20.org/Documents/Fin_Deps_Fin_Reg_Annex_020409_-_1615_final.pdf (accessed April 2, 2009).

—— (2009b) 'Leaders' statement', The Pittsburgh Summit, September 24–5. Available at http://www.pittsburghsummit.gov/mediacenter/129639.htm (accessed January 19, 2011).

—— (2010) The G20 Toronto Summit Declaration, June 26–7. Available at http://www.g20.org/Documents/g20_declaration_en.pdf (accessed January 19, 2011).

G20 Working Group 1 (2009) 'Enhancing sound regulation and strengthening transparency', March 25, London: G20.

Galbraith, J. K. (1993) *A short history of financial euphoria*, New York: Penguin.

—— (1995) *Money: Whence it came, where it went*, London: Penguin.

Galego, A., Vieira, C., and Vieira I. (2004) 'The CEEC as FDI attractors: A menace to the EU periphery?', *Emerging Markets Finance and Trade*, 40, 5: 74–91.

Gapper, J. (2009) 'Volcker sets his sights on Goldman', FT.Com/Gapperblog. Available at http://blogs.ft.com/gapperblog/2009/03/the-glass-steagall-act-revisited-by-paul-volcker/ (accessed March 6, 2009).

Garmel, K., Maliar, L., and Maliar, S. (2008) 'EU eastern enlargement and foreign investment: Implications from a neoclassical growth model', *Journal of Comparative Economics*, 36, 2: 307–25.

Gat, A. (2007) 'The return of authoritarian great powers', *Foreign Affairs*, 86, 4: 59–70.

Gelbach, J. and Pritchett, L. (1997) 'Indicator targeting in a political equilibrium: Leakier can be better', Policy Research Working Paper 1523, Washington, DC: World Bank.

Gereffi, G. and Korzeniewicz, M. (eds.) (1994) *Commodity chains and global capitalism*, Westport, CT: Greenwood Press.

Gerth, J. and O'Harrow, R. (2009) 'As crisis loomed, Geithner pressed but fell short', *The Washington Post*, April 2. Available at http://www.washingtonpost.com/wp-dyn/content/article/2009/04/02/AR2009040203227.html (accessed January 19, 2011).

Gilpin, R. (1975) *U.S. power and the multinational corporation: The political economy of foreign direct investment*, New York: Basic Books.

—— (1981) *War and change in world politics*, Cambridge, UK: Cambridge University Press.

—— (1987) *The political economy of international relations*, Princeton, NJ: Princeton University Press.

—— (2001) *Global political economy: Understanding the international economic order*, Princeton, NJ: Princeton University Press.

Go, J. S. (2005) 'WTO Chejehaesu Kookga R&D Jungcheck Unyoung Bangan [National R&D Policy under WTO system]', *Korea Industrial Economy and Trade*, December: 51–62.

Goerg, H. and Greenaway, D. (2002) 'Is there a potential for increases in FDI for Central and Eastern European countries following EU accession?', in H. Heinz and R. E. Lipsey (eds.) *Foreign direct investment in the real and financial sector of industrial countries*, Berlin: Springer.

Goffman, E. (1959) *The presentation of self in everyday life*, Garden City, NY: Doubleday Anchor.

Goldstein, A. (2007) *Multinational companies from emerging economies*, New York: Palgrave Macmillan.

Goldthau, A. and Witte, J. M. (2009) 'Back to the future or forward to the past? Strengthening markets and rules for effective global energy governance', *International Affairs*, 85, 2: 373–90.

—— (eds.) (2010) *Global energy governance: The new rules of the game*, Washington, DC: Brookings Institution Press.

Gorlizki, Y. (2002) 'Ordinary Stalinism: The Council of Ministers and the Soviet neopatrimonial state, 1946–1953', *Journal of Modern History*, 74, 4: 699–736.

Gould, B. (2002) 'Ratifying the Rome Statute: Japan and the International Criminal Court', *Hurights Osaka*. Available at http://www.hurights.or.jp/asia-pacific/no_29/05japanandicc.htm (accessed November 29, 2010).

Gourevitch, P. (1978) 'The second image reversed: International sources of domestic politics', *International Organization*, 32, 4: 881–912.

Grant, J. (2008) 'ECB backs central clearance for CDS', *Financial Times*, November 4. Available at http://www.ft.com/cms/d7422b9a-a9dd-11dd-9586-000077b07658.html (accessed February 17, 2011).

—— (2009a) 'Case for change heard loud and clear', *Financial Times*, February 9. Available at http://www.ft.com/cms/9f68719a-f648-11dd-a9ed-0000779fd2ac.html (accessed January 19, 2011).

—— (2009b) 'Battle shapes up for credit derivatives clearing', *Financial Times*, March 17. Available at http://www.ft.com/cms/4e5d9304-125c-11de-b816-0000779fd2ac.html (accessed January 19, 2011).

—— (2009c) 'Banque de France in CDS clearing plea', *Financial Times*, February 17. Available at http://www.ft.com/cms/1fe35486-fe26-11dd-932e-000077b07658.html (accessed January 19, 2011).

Grant, J. and Masters, B. (2009) 'Brokers set out to fight backlash against OTC trade', *Financial Times*, April 28. Available at http://www.ft.com/cms/719789ce-338b-11de-8f1b-00144feabdc0.html (accessed January 19, 2011).

Grant, J. and Tait, N. (2009a) 'Plea for dialogue on regulation of financial sector', *Financial Times*, February 4. Available at http://www.ft.com/cms/582c40a0-e111-11dd-b0e8-000077b07658.html (accessed January 19, 2011).

—— (2009b) 'European CDS clearing hits hurdle', *Financial Times*, January 13. Available at http://www.ft.com/cms/194b175c-f25b-11dd-9678-0000779fd2ac.html (accessed January 19, 2011).

Graz, J.-C. and Nölke, A. (eds.) (2008) *Transnational private governance and its limits*, London: Routledge.

Green, J. (2010) 'Private actors, public goods: Private authority in global environmental politics', PhD dissertation, Woodrow Wilson School of Public and International Affairs, Princeton University, June 2010.

Green, M. J. (2001) *Japan's reluctant realism: Foreign policy challenges in an era of uncertainty*, New York: Palgrave.

Greene, W. H. (2003) *Econometric analysis*, 5th edn, Upper Saddle River, NJ: Prentice Hall.

Greif, A. (1993) 'Contract enforceability and economic institutions in early trade', *American Economic Review*, 83, 3: 525–48.

Group of Thirty (2009) *Financial reform: A framework for stability*, New York: Group of Thirty.

Grün, R. (2010) 'For a Brazilian sociology of finance', *Economic Sociology: The European Electronic Newsletter*, 11, 2: 10–15.

Guttman, R. (2009) 'Asset bubbles, debt deflation, and global imbalances', *International Journal of Political Economy*, 38, 2: 46–69.

Haas, E. B. (1958) *The uniting of Europe: Political, social and economic forces, 1950–1957*, Stanford, CA: Stanford University Press.

—— (1964) *Beyond the nation-state: Functionalism and international organization*, Stanford, CA: Stanford University Press.

Haas, P. M. and Haas, E. B. (2009) 'Pragmatic constructivism and the study of international institutions', in H. Bauer and E. Brighi (eds.) *Pragmatism in international relations*, New York: Routledge.

Haas, R. N. (2008) 'The age of nonpolarity: What will follow U.S. dominance', *Foreign Affairs*, 87, 3: 44–56.

Hachigian, N. (2002) 'The internet and power in one-party East Asian states', *The Washington Quarterly*, 25, 3: 41–58.

Haggard, S. (1990) *Pathways from the periphery: The politics of growth in the newly industrializing countries*, Ithaca, NY: Cornell University Press.

Haggard, S. and Moon, C. (1983) 'The South Korean state in the international economy: Liberal, dependent, or mercantile?', in J. G. Ruggie (ed.) *The antinomies of interdependence: National welfare and the international division of labor*, New York: Columbia University Press.

—— (1990) 'Institutions and economic policy: Theory and a Korean case study', *World Politics*, 17, 2: 210–37.

—— (1993) 'The state, politics, and economic development in post-war South Korea', in Hagen Koo (ed.) *The state, society and economics in contemporary Korea*, Ithaca, NY: Cornell University Press.

Haggard, S., Kim, B., and Moon, C. (1991) 'The transition to export-led growth in Korea, 1954–1966', *Journal of Asian Studies*, 50, 4: 850–73.

Haldane, A. (2009) 'Rethinking the financial network', speech delivered at the Financial Student Association, Amsterdam, April.

Hall, P. A. (2003) 'Adapting methodology to ontology in comparative politics', in J. Mahoney and D. Rueschemeyer (eds.) *Comparative historical analysis in the social sciences*, New York: Cambridge University Press.

Hall, P. A. and Soskice, D. (2001) 'An introduction to varieties of capitalism', in P. A. Hall and D. Soskice (eds.) *Varieties of capitalism: The institutional foundations of comparative advantage*, Oxford: University Press.

Hall, R. and Biersteker, T. (eds.) (2002) *The emergence of private authority in global governance*, Cambridge, UK: Cambridge University Press.

Halperin, M. H., Siegle, J. T., and Weinstein, M. M. (2005) *The democracy advantage: How democracies promote prosperity and peace*, New York: Routledge.

Hamm, K. (1994) 'The refining industry in the North Atlantic', *The Energy Journal*, 15: 179–93.

Hansen, H. K. and Salskov-Iversen D. (eds.) (2008) *Critical perspectives on private authority in global politics*, Basingstoke: Palgrave Macmillan.

Haque, I. (2007) 'Rethinking industrial policy', G-24 Discussion Paper Series, No. 183, Geneva: UNCTAD.

Hardt, J. (2009). Letter to Mr. de Larosière: Submission to the High-Level Group on Cross-Border Financial Supervision, January 30. Available at http://www.fese.be/_mdb/posdocs/FESE%20inpute%20high%20level%20group.pdf (accessed January 20, 2011).

Hasenclever, A., Mayer, P., and Rittberger, V. (1997) *Theories of international regimes*, Cambridge, UK: Cambridge University Press.

Hawley, J. (1984) 'Protecting capital from itself', *International Organization*, 38, 1: 131–65.

Hayek, F. A. von (1944) *The road to serfdom*, Chicago: University of Chicago Press.

Held, D., McGrew, A., Gloldblatt, D., and Perraton, J. (1999) *Global transformations: Politics, economics and culture*, Cambridge, UK: Cambridge University Press.

Helleiner, E. (1994) *States and the re-emergence of global finance: From Bretton Woods to the 1990s*, Ithaca, NY: Cornell University Press.

Helliwell, J. F. (1994) 'Empirical linkages between democracy and economic growth', *British Journal of Political Science*, 24, 2: 225–48.

Helpman, E. (2004) *The mystery of economic growth*, Cambridge, MA: Belknap Press of Harvard University Press.

—— (2006) 'Trade, FDI, and the organization of firms', *Journal of Economic Literature*, 44, 3: 589–630.

Heradstveit, D. and Hveem, H. (eds.) (2004) *Oil in the Gulf: Obstacles to democracy and development*, Aldershot: Ashgate.

Herbst, J. I. (2000) *States and social power in Africa: Comparative lessons in authority and control*, Princeton, NJ; Princeton University Press.

Higgott, R. and Watson, M. (2008) 'All at sea in a barbed wire canoe: Professor Cohen's transatlantic voyage in IPE', *Review of International Political Economy*, 15, 1: 1–17.

High-Level Group on Financial Supervision in the EU (2009) 'Report', Brussels: European Union.

Hirschman, A. O. (1970) 'The search for paradigms as a hindrance to understanding', *World Politics*, 22, 3: 329–43.

Hirsh, M. and Thomas, E. (2009) 'The reeducation of Larry Summers', *Newsweek*, February 21. Available at http://www.newsweek.com/2009/02/20/the-reeducation-of-larry-summers.html (accessed January 20, 2011).

Hirst, P. and Zeitlin, J. (1997) 'Flexible specialization: Theory and evidence in the analysis of industrial change', in J. R. Hollingsworth and R. Boyer (eds.) *Contemporary capitalism: The embeddedness of institutions*, Cambridge, UK: Cambridge University Press.

Hiscox, M. J. (2007) 'The domestic sources of foreign economic policies', in J. Ravenhill (ed.) *Global political economy*, Oxford: Oxford University Press.

Hobson, J. M. and Seabrooke, L. (eds.) (2007) *Everyday politics of the world economy*, Cambridge, UK: Cambridge University Press.

Hoffmann, S. (1961) 'International systems and international law', *World Politics*, 14, 1: 205–37.

—— (1966) 'Obstinate or obsolete? The fate of the nation-state and the case of Western Europe', *Daedalus*, 95, 3: 862–915.

Hook, G. D., Gibson, J., Hughes, C. W., and Dobson, H. (2001) *Japan's international relations: Politics, economics and security*, London: Routledge.

Houghton, J. and Sheehan, P. (2000) 'A primer on the knowledge economy', paper, Melbourne: Center for Strategic Economic Studies, Victoria University.

Hughes, C. W. (2004) *Japan's security agenda: Military, economic, and environmental dimensions*, Boulder, CO: Lynn Rienner.

Hughes, H. (ed.) (1988) *Archiving industrialization in East Asia*, Cambridge, UK: Cambridge University Press.

Hummels, D., Ishii, J., and Yi, K. M. (2001) 'The nature and growth of vertical specialization in world trade', *Journal of International Economics*, 54, 1: 75–96.

Huntington, S. P. (1991) *The third wave: Democratization in the late twentieth century*, Oklahoma: University of Oklahoma Press.

Hveem, H. (1977) *The political economy of Third World producer associations*, Oslo: Universitetsforlaget.

—— (1978) *The political economy of Third World producer associations*, Oslo: Universitetsforlaget.

—— (1982) 'Selective dissociation in the technology sector', in J. G. Ruggie (ed.) *The antinomies of interdependence*, New York: Columbia University Press.

—— (1994) *Internasjonalisering og politikk. Norsk utenriksøkonomi i et tilpasningsperspektiv*, Oslo: Tano.

—— (1996) *Makt og velferd: Teorier i internasjonal politisk økonomi*, Oslo: Universitetsforlaget.

—— (1999) 'Explaining the regional phenomenon in an era of globalization', in R. Stubbs and G. R. D. Underhill (eds.) (1999) *Political economy and the changing global order*, 2nd edn, Oxford: Oxford University Press.

—— (2002) 'Globalisation, governance and development: A political economy perspective', *European Journal of Development Research*, 14, 1: 219–43.

—— (2006) 'Explaining the regional phenomenon in an era of globalization', in R. Stubbs and G. Underhill (eds.) *Political economy and the changing international order*, 3rd edn, Oxford: Oxford University Press.

—— (2007a) 'Institutions, power, and knowledge: Bargaining over the WTO TRIPS Agreement', paper presented at the GARNET JERP 5.3.6 workshop on FDI-Led Innovation, Transfer and Dissemination of Knowledge, and their Multilateral and Regional Regulation, Oslo, Voksenåsen, May 3–5, 2007.

—— (2007b) 'The politics of transnational production systems: A political economy perspective', paper presented at the GARNET General Conference and Tenth Anniversary Conference of the Centre for the Study of Globalisation and Regionalisation, Warwick University, September 18–20, 2007.

—— (2008a) 'Contested multilateralism: EU, the TRIPS Agreement and global governance', Annual Conference of GARNET Network of Excellence (EU), September 16–20, 2008.

—— (2008b) 'Knowledge, intellectual property rights and equity: The WTO's TRIPS Agreement and EU policy', GARNET Policy Brief No. 3. Available at http://www.garnet-eu.org/fileadmin/documents/policy_briefs/TRIPS%202007%20Policy%20Update.pdf (accessed January 19, 2011).

—— (2009) 'Pluralist IPE: A view from outside the "schools"', *New Political Economy*, 14, 3: 367–76.

Hveem, H. and Nordhaug, K. (eds.) (2002) *Public policy in the age of globalisation*, Cheltenham: Palgrave Macmillan.

Hveem, H. and Iapadre, L. (2011) *Global governance of knowledge: Education, research, innovation and international cooperation*, London: Routledge.

Hveem, H. and Knutsen, C. H. (2011). 'Co-operation on knowledge activities', in H. Hveem and L. Iapadre (eds.) *The global governance of knowledge: Education, research, innovation and international cooperation*, London: Routledge.

Hveem, H., Knutsen, C. H., and Rygh, A. (2009) 'Foreign direct investment and political systems in host countries: The case of Norway', Working Paper, Oslo: Department of Political Science, University of Oslo.

Hyden, G. (2000) 'The governance challenge in Africa', in G. Hyden, D. Olowu Dele, and H. W. O. Okoth-Ogendo (eds.) *African perspectives on governance*, Trenton, NJ: Africa World Press.

IEA (2008) *World energy outlook*, Paris: International Energy Agency.

—— (2010) *World energy outlook*, Paris: International Energy Agency.

IIF (Institute for International Finance) (2006) 'Principles for stable capital flows and fair debt restructuring in emerging markets: Report on implementation by the Principles Consultative Group', September, Washington, DC: IIF.

Ikenberry, G. J. (2001) *After victory: Institutions, strategic restraint, and the building of order after major wars*, Princeton, NJ: Princeton University Press.

—— (2008) 'The rise of China and the future of the West', *Foreign Affairs*, 87, 1: 23–37.

—— (2010) 'The liberal international order and its discontents', *Millennium*, 38, 2: 509–21.

Ikenberry, G. J. and Mastanduno, M. (eds.) (2003) *International relations theory and the Asia-Pacific*, New York: Columbia University Press.

Ilkhamov, A. (2007) 'Neopatrimonialism, interest groups and patronage networks: The impasses of the governance system in Uzbekistan', *Central Asian Survey*, 26, 1: 65–84.

International Monetary Fund (IMF) (2009) 'Greece: IMF country report for the 2009 Article IV Consultation', IMF Country Report 09/244, Washington, DC: IMF.

IOSCO (2009) 'Unregulated financial markets and products, report of the Technical Committee of IOSCO'. Available at http://www.iosco.org/library/pubdocs/pdf/IOSCOPD290.pdf (accessed January 19, 2011).

Jabko, N. (2006) *Playing the market: A political strategy for uniting Europe, 1985–2005*, Ithaca, NY: Cornell University Press.

Jackson, G. and Deeg, R. (2006) 'How many varieties of capitalism? Comparing the comparative institutional analyses of capitalist diversity', MPIfG Discussion Paper 06/02, Cologne: Max Planck Institute for the Study of Societies.

Jacobsson, K. and Noaksson N. (2010) 'From deregulation to flexicurity? The makeover of the OECD jobs strategy', in K. Martens and A. Jakobi (eds.) *Mechanisms of OECD governance: International incentives for national policy making?*, Oxford: Oxford University Press.

Johnson, C. A. (1982) *MITI and the Japanese miracle: The growth of industrial policy, 1925–1975*, Stanford, CA: Stanford University Press.

—— (ed.) (1984) *Industrial policy debate*, San Francisco: ICS Press.

Johnson, S. and Kwak, K. (2010) *13 bankers*, New York: Pantheon Books.

Jones, B. F. and Olken, B. A. (2005) 'Do leaders matter? National leadership and growth since World War II', *Quarterly Journal of Economics*, 120, 3: 835–64.

Jones, C. I. and Romer P. M. (2010) 'The new Kaldor facts: Ideas, institutions, population, and human capital', *American Economic Journal: Macroeconomics*, 2, 1: 224–45.

Jones, E. (2003) 'Liberalized capital markets, state autonomy, and European Monetary Union', *European Journal of Political Research*, 42, 2: 197–222.

—— (2010) 'Merkel's folly', *Survival*, 52, 3: 21–38.

Jones, L. (2009) 'Current issues affecting the OTC derivatives market and its importance to London', report, London: City of London.

Jones, L. and Il, S. (1980) *Government, business, and entrepreneurship in economic development: The Korean case*, Cambridge, MA: Harvard University Press.

Jordan, R., Maliniak, D., Oakes, A., Peterson, S., and Tierney, M. J. (2009) *One discipline or many? TRIP survey of international relations faculty in ten countries*, Williamsburg, VA: Program on the Theory, Research and Practice of International Relations, College of William and Mary.

Kakuchi, S. (2001) 'Japan: Turns to deft diplomacy on global warming', Third World Network. Available at http://www.twnside.org.sg/title/deft.htm (accessed January 25, 2011).

Kalotay, K. (2004) 'The European flying geese: New FDI patterns for an old continent?', *Research in International Business and Finance*, 18, 1: 27–49

—— (2006) 'The impact of EU enlargement on FDI flows', *International Finance Review*, 6: 473–99.

Kaplinsky, R. and Messner, D. (2008) 'Introduction: The impact of Asian drivers on the developing world', *World Development*, 36, 2: 197–209.

Katada, S. (2004) 'Japan's counterweight strategy: U.S.–Japan cooperation and competition in international finance', in E. S. Krauss and T. J. Pempel (eds.) *Beyond bilateralism: U.S.–Japan relations in the new East Asia*, Palo Alto, CA: Stanford University Press.

Katzenstein, P. J. (ed.) (1978) *Between power and plenty: Foreign economic policies of advanced industrial states*, Madison: University of Wisconsin Press.

—— (1985) *Small states in world markets: Industrial policies in Europe*, Ithaca, NY: Cornell University Press.

Katzenstein, P. J., Keohane, R. O., and Krasner, S. D. (1998) 'International organization and the study of world politics', *International Organization*, 52, 4: 645–85.

—— (eds.) (1999) *Exploration and contestation in the study of world politics*, Cambridge, MA: MIT Press.

Keohane, R. O. (1984) *After hegemony: Cooperation and discord in the world political economy*, Princeton, NJ: Princeton University Press.

—— (1986) 'Theory of world politics: Structural realism and beyond', in R. O. Keohane (ed.) *Neorealism and its critics*, New York: Columbia University Press.

—— (1989) *International institutions and state power: Essays in international relations theory*, Boulder, CO: Westview Press.

—— (1993) 'Institutional theory and the realist challenge after the Cold War', in D. A. Baldwin (ed.) *Neorealism and neoliberalism: The contemporary debate*, New York: Columbia University Press.

—— (2002). *Power and governance in a partially globalized world*, London: Routledge.

—— (2009) 'The old IPE and the new', *Review of International Political Economy*, 16, 1: 34–46.

Keohane, R. O. and Nye, J. S. (1972) *Transnational relations and world politics*, Cambridge, MA: Harvard University Press.

—— (1974) 'Transgovernmental relations and international organizations', *World Politics*, 27, 1: 39–62.

—— (1977) *Power and interdependence: World politics in transition*, Boston: Little, Brown.

Keohane, R. O. and Milner, H. (1996) *Internationalization and domestic politics*, Cambridge, UK: Cambridge University Press.

Keohane, R. O. and Victor, D. G. (2011) 'The regime complex for climate change', *Perspectives on Politics*, 9, 1.

Keynes, J. M. (1997) *The general theory of employment, interest and money*, Amherst, NY: Prometheus Books.

KIET (2009) *Key indications of major industries*, Seoul: KIET.

Killick, T., Gunatilaka, R., and Mar, A. (1998) *Aid and the political economy of policy change*, London: Routledge.

Kim, H. (2005) *Park Chung-hee ui Yannal ui Suntak: Yushin kwa Chungwhahak Konup* [*Korea's development under Park Chung Hee: Rapid industrialization, 1961–79*], Seoul: Iljogak.

Kim, K. and Leipziger D. M. (1993) 'Korea: A case of government-led development', World Bank Discussion Paper, Washington, DC: World Bank.

Kim, S. S. (ed.) (2000) *Korea's globalization*, Cambridge, UK: Cambridge University Press.

Kim, W., Koo, J., and Song, E. (2008) *Tooja Gwanrun Choseijiwon Juncheck Bikyo Bunsuck* [*Comparative Analysis of Tax Relief Policy*], Seoul: Korea Institute of Public Finance.

Kindleberger, C. P. (1973) *The world in depression 1929–1939*, Berkeley, CA: University of California Press.

—— (1986) *The world in depression 1929–1939*, 2nd edn, Berkeley, CA: University of California Press.

—— (1989) *Manias, panics, and crashes: A history of financial crises*, London: Macmillan.

Kindleberger, C. P. and Laffargue, J.-P. (eds.) (1982) *Financial crises: Theory, history, and policy*, New York: Cambridge University Press.

King, R. G. and Levine, R. (1993) 'Finance and growth: Schumpeter might be right', *Quarterly Journal of Economics*, 108, 3: 717–37.

KISTEP (Korea Institute of S&T Evaluation and Planning) (2007) *Survey of research and development in Korea 2007*, Seoul: KISTEP.

—— (2009) *Survey of research and development in Korea 2009*, Seoul: KISTEP.

Klare, M. T. (2004) *Blood and oil: The dangers and consequences of America's growing dependency on imported petroleum*, New York: Metropolitan Books.

Klein, N. (2007) *The shock doctrine: The rise of disaster capitalism*, New York: Metropolitan Books.

Klenow, P. J. and Rodriguez-Clare, A. (1997) 'The neo-classical revival in growth economics: Has it gone to far?', in B. S. Bernanke and J. J. Rotemberg (eds.) *NBER macroeconomics annual 1997*, Cambridge, MA: MIT Press.

Knack, S. and Keefer, P. (1995) 'Institutions and economic performance: Cross-country tests using alternative institutional measures', *Economics and Politics*, 7, 3: 207–27.

Knutsen, C. H. (2006) 'Political regime types and economic growth: Are democracies better at increasing prosperity?', Master's thesis, Department of Political Science, University of Oslo.

—— (2007) 'Democracy and property rights', Master's thesis, Department of Economics, University of Oslo.

—— (2011) 'Democracy, dictatorship and protection of property rights', *Journal of Development Studies* 47, 1: 164–82.

—— (forthcoming) 'The economic effects of democracy and dictatorship', PhD thesis, Department of Political Science, University of Oslo.

Knutsen, C. H., Rygh, A., and Hveem, H. (forthcoming) 'Does state ownership matter? Institutions' effect on foreign direct investment revisited', *Business and Politics*.

Kohl, W. L. (2010) 'Consumer countries energy cooperation: The International Energy Agency and the global energy order', in A. Goldthau and J. M. Witte (eds.) *Global energy governance: The new rules of the game*, Washington, DC: Brookings Institution Press.

Kohli, A. (2004) *State-directed development: Political power and industrialization in the global periphery*, Cambridge, UK: Cambridge University Press.

Kokko, A. and Kravtsova, V. (2007) 'The determinants of innovative capability building: A case of four transition economies', Stockholm School of Economics Working Paper 224, Stockholm: Stockholm School of Economics.

Kong, Bo (2010) *China's international petroleum policy*, Santa Barbara, CA: ABC-CLIO.

Konings, J. (2001) 'The effects of foreign direct investment on domestic firms: Evidence from firm-level panel data in emerging economies', *Economics of Transition*, 9, 3: 619–34.

Kosaka, M. (1968) *Saishô Yoshida Shigeru* [*Prime Minister Yoshida Shigeru*], Tokyo: Chûô Kôronsha.

Kose, M. A., Eswar Prasad, E., Rogoff, K., and Wei, S.-J. (2006) 'Financial globalization: A reappraisal', IMF Working Paper No. 06/189, Washington, DC: International Monetary Fund.

Krasner, S. D. (1982) 'Structural causes and regime consequences: Regimes as intervening variables', *International Organization*, 36, 2: 185–205.

—— (1985) *Structural conflict: The Third World against global liberalism*, Berkeley, CA: University of California Press.

—— (1999) *Sovereignty: Organized hypocrisy*, Princeton, NJ: Princeton University Press.

Krauss, E. S. (2004) 'The United States and Japan in APEC's EVSL negotiations: Regional multilateralism and trade', in E. S Krauss and T. J. Pempel (eds.) *Beyond bilateralism: U.S.–Japan relations in the new Asia-Pacific*, Stanford, CA: Stanford University Press.

Krauss, E. S. and Pempel, T. J. (eds.) (2004) *Beyond bilateralism: The U.S.–Japan relationship in the new Asia-Pacific*, Stanford, CA: Stanford University Press.

Kremer, M. (1993) 'The O-ring theory of economic development', *Quarterly Journal of Economics*, 108, 3: 551–75.

Kretzmer, D. (2010) 'The UN Human Rights Committee and human rights monitoring', paper presented in the International Legal Theory Colloquium, New York University Law School, March 10, 2010.

Krueger, A. (1990) 'Government failure in development', *Journal of Economic Perspectives*, 4, 3: 9–23.

Krugman, P. (1995) 'Dutch tulips and emerging markets', *Foreign Affairs*, 78, 4: 28–44.

Labaton, S. and Calmes, J. (2009) 'Obama proposes first overhaul of finance rules', *The New York Times*, May 13. Available at http://community.nytimes.com/comments/www.nytimes.com/2009/05/14/business/14regs.html (accessed January 19, 2011).

Lacher, H. (2006) *Beyond globalization: Capitalism, territoriality and the international relations of modernity*, London: Routledge.

Lake, D. A. (2009a) 'Trips across the Atlantic: Theory and epistemology in IPE', *Review of International Political Economy*, 16, 1: 47–57.

—— (2009b) *Hierarchy in international relations*, Ithaca, NY: Cornell University Press.

Lake, D. A. and Baum, M. A. (2001) 'The invisible hand of democracy', *Comparative Political Studies*, 34, 6: 587–621.

Lall, S. (1996) *Learning from the Asian tigers*, Basingstoke: Macmillan.

—— (1997a) 'Policies for industrial competitiveness in developing countries: Learning from Asia', report prepared for the Commonwealth Secretariat, Oxford.

—— (1997b) 'East Asia', in J. H. Dunning (ed.) *Governments, globalisation and international business*, Oxford: Oxford University Press.

—— (2003) 'Foreign direct investment, technology development and competitiveness: Issues and evidence', in S. Lall and S. Urata (eds.) *Competitiveness, FDI and technological activity in East Asia*, Cheltenham: Edward Elgar.

—— (2004) 'Reinventing industrial strategy: The role of government policy in building industrial competitiveness', Working Papers QEHWPS111, Oxford: Queen Elizabeth House, University of Oxford.

Lall, S. and Pietrobelli, C. (2002) *Failing to compete: Technology development and technology systems in Africa*, Edward Elgar: Cheltenham.

Lall, S. and Narula, R. (2006) 'FDI and its role in economic development: Do we need a new agenda?', in R. Narula and S. Lall (eds.) *Understanding FDI-assisted development*, London: Routledge.

Landmine Monitor Report (1999) 'ASIA-PACIFIC: States Parties, 355–366'. Available at at http://www.the-monitor.org/index.php/publications/display?url=lm/1999/report.html (accessed January 19, 2011).

Lankes, H. P. and Venables, A. J. (1996) 'Foreign direct investment in economic transition: The changing pattern of investments', *Economics of Transition*, 4, 2: 331–47.

Lasswell, H. D. (1935) *Politics: Who gets what, when, how*, New York: McGraw Hill.

Leacock, S. (1910) 'My financial career', in S. Leacock, *Literary lapses*, Montreal: Gazette Printing.

Leander, A. (2010) 'Practices (re)producing orders: Understanding the role of business in global security governance', in M. Ougaard and A. Leander (eds.) *Business and global governance*, London: Routledge.

Leblang, D. A. (1997) 'Political democracy and economic growth: Pooled cross-sectional and times-series evidence', *British Journal of Political Science*, 27, 3: 453–66.

Lee, Y. S. and Jung, Y. (2000) *Financial crisis and industrial policy in Korea*, Seoul: Institute for Global Economics.

Leftwich, A. (2000) *States of development: On the primacy of politics in development*, Cambridge, UK: Polity Press.

Leheny, D. (2006) *Think global, fear local: Sex, violence, and anxiety in contemporary Japan*, Ithaca, NY: Cornell University Press.

Leipziger, D. M. and Thomas, V. (1993) *The lessons of East Asia: An overview of country experience*, Washington, DC: World Bank.

Lemarchand, R. (2003) 'The Democratic Republic of the Congo: From failure to potential reconstruction', in R. I. Rotberg (ed.) *State failure and state weakness in a time of terror*, Cambridge, MA: World Peace Foundation/Brookings Institution Press.

Lesage, D., Van de Graaf, T., and Westphal, K. (2010) *Global energy governance in a multipolar world*, Farnham: Ashgate.

Li, Q. (2009) 'Democracy, autocracy, and expropriation of foreign direct investment', *Comparative Political Studies*, 42, 8: 1098–1127.

Likosky, M. (2009) 'Contracting and regulatory issues in the oil and gas and metallic minerals industries', *Transnational Corporations*, 18, 1: 1–40.

Lin, J. Y. (2009) 'New structural economics: A framework for rethinking development'. Available at http://econpapers.repec.org/scripts/redir.pf?u=http%3A%2F%2Fwww-wds.worldbank.org%2Fservlet%2FWDSContentServer%2FWDSP%2FIB%2F2011%2F01%2F18%2F000158349_20110118093922%2FRendered%2FPDF%2FWPS5197SPANISH.pdf;h=repec:wbk:wbrwps:5197 (accessed June 10, 2010).

Lindberg, S. I. (2006) *Democracy and elections in Africa*, Baltimore: Johns Hopkins University Press.

Lindblom, C. and Cohen, D. (1979) *Usable knowledge: Social science and social problem solving*, New Haven, CT: Yale University Press.

Lindert, P. H. (2005) *Growing public: Social spending and economic growth since the eighteenth century, vol. 1*, Cambridge, UK: Cambridge University Press.

Lipschutz, R. D. with Mayer, J. (1996) *Global civil society & global environmental governance*, Albany: State University of New York Press.

Lipson, C. (1985) *Standing guard: Protecting foreign capital in the nineteenth and twentieth centuries*, Berkeley, CA: University of California Press.

LiPuma, E. and Lee, B. (2004) *Financial derivatives and the globalization of risk*, Durham, NC: Duke University Press.

List, F. (1966 [1885]) *The national system of political economy*, New York: Kelley.

Lu, J. and Wang, Z. W. (2005) 'China's attitude toward the ICC', *Journal of International Criminal Justice*, 3, 3: 608–20.

Lucas, R. E. (1988) 'On the mechanisms of economic development', *Journal of Monetary Economics*, 22, 1: 3–42.

—— (1990) 'Why doesn't capital flow from rich to poor countries?', *American Economic Review*, 80, 2: 92–6.

Mackenzie, M., Bullock, N., and Tett, G. (2009) 'Big Bang arrives for credit default swaps industry', *Financial Times*, April 8. Available at http://www.ft.com/cms/s/0/4 b581dd0-23d4-11de-996a-00144feabdc0.html>#axzz1BUgF99RC (accessed January 19, 2011).

Maclachlan, P. L. (2006) 'Global trends vs. local traditions: Genetically modified foods and contemporary consumerism in the United States, Japan, and Britain', in S. Garon and P. L. Maclachlan (eds.) *The ambivalent consumer: Questioning consumption in East Asia and the West*, Ithaca, NY: Cornell University Press.

Maddison, A. (1991) *Dynamic forces in capitalist development*, Oxford: Oxford University Press.

—— (2006) *The world economy*, Paris: OECD.

—— (2007) *Contours of the world economy, 1–2030 AD*, Oxford: Oxford University Press.

Magaziner, I. C. and Hout, T. (1980) *Japanese industrial policy*, London: Policy Studies Institute.

Maliniak, D., Oakes, A., Peterson, S., and Tierney, M. J. (2007) *The view from the ivory tower: TRIP survey of international relations faculty in the United States and Canada*, Williamsburg, VA: Program on the Theory, Research and Practice of International Relations, College of William and Mary.

Mankiw, G. N., Romer, D., and Weil, D. N. (1992) 'A contribution to the empirics of economic growth', *Quarterly Journal of Economics*, 107, 2: 407–37.

Manuel, T. (2003) 'Africa and the Washington Consensus: Finding the right path', *Finance and Development*, September: 18–20.

Marcel, V. (2006) *Oil titans: National oil companies in the Middle East*, London: Royal Institute of International Affairs.

Marshall, M. G. and Jaggers, K. (2002) 'Polity IV Project: Dataset users', manual, College Park: Program Center for International Development and Conflict Management, University of Maryland.

Martens, K. and Jakobi, A. (2010) 'Conclusion: Findings, implications and outlook of OECD governance', in K. Martens and A. Jakobi (eds.) *Mechanisms of OECD governance: International incentives for national policy making?*, Oxford: Oxford University Press.

Maslovski, M. (1996) 'Max Weber's concept of patrimonialism and the Soviet system', *Sociological Review*, 44, 2: 294–308.

Mastanduno, M. (2008) 'System maker and privilege taker: U.S. power and the international political economy', *World Politics*, 61, 1: 121–54.

Mattli, W. and Woods, N. (2009) *The politics of global regulation*, Princeton, NJ: Princeton University Press.

Maxfield, S. (1998) 'Understanding the political implications of financial internationalisation in emerging market countries', *World Development*, 26, 7: 1201–19.

May, C. (2006) *Global corporate power*, Boulder, CO: Rienner.

McDonald, L. (2009) *A colossal failure of common sense: The incredible inside story of the collapse of Lehman Brothers*, New York: Random House.

McGrew, A. (2007) 'The logics of economic globalization', in J. Ravenhill (ed.) *Global political economy*, Oxford: Oxford University Press.

McKean, M. (1977) 'Pollution and policymaking', in T. J. Pempel (ed.) *Policymaking in contemporary Japan*, Ithaca, NY: Cornell University Press.

—— (1981) *Environmental protest and citizen politics in Japan*, Berkeley, CA: University of California Press.

Mearsheimer, J. J. (1994) 'The false promise of international institutions', *International Security*, 19, 3: 5–49.

—— (2001) *The tragedy of great power politics*, New York, NY: W. W. Norton.

Médard, J.-F. (1979) 'L'État sous-développé au Cameroun', in CEAN (ed.) *Année africaine 1977*, Paris: Pedone/CEAN.

—— (1991) 'L'État néo-patrimonial en Afrique noire', in J.-F. Médard (ed) *États d'Afrique noire: Formation, mécanismes et crise*, Paris: Karthala.

Meltzer, A. H. and Richards, S. F. (1981) 'A rational theory of the size of the government', *Journal of Political Economy*, 89, 5: 914–27.

Mencinger, J. (2003) 'Does foreign direct investment always enhance economic growth?', *Kyklos*, 56, 4: 493–510.

Meredith, M. (2005) *The state of Africa: A history of fifty years of independence*, London: Free Press.

Meyer, K. and Jensen, C. (2003) 'Foreign investor strategies in view of EU enlargement', in H.-J. Stuting, W. Dorow, F. Classes, and S. Blazejewski (eds.) *Change management in transformation economies: Integrating strategy, structure and culture*, London: Palgrave.

Meyer, K. E. and Peng, M. W. (2005) 'Probing theoretically into Central and Eastern Europe: Transactions, resources, and institutions', *Journal of International Business Studies*, 36, 6: 600–21.

Mihm, S. (2008) 'Dr. Doom', *The New York Times*, August 15. Available at http://www.nytimes.com/2008/08/17/magazine/17pessimist-t.html?_r=1 (accessed January 19, 2011).

Mill, J. S. (1974) *On liberty*, London: Penguin.

Ministry of Knowledge Economy (2010) 'National R&D development evaluation report'. Available at http://www.mke.go.kr (accessed January 25, 2011).

Minsky, H. (1975) *John Maynard Keynes*, New York: Columbia University Press.

—— (1982) 'The financial-instability hypothesis: Capitalist processes and the behaviour of the economy', in C. Kindleberger and J.-P. Laffargue (eds.) *Financial crises: Theory, history, and policy*, New York: Cambridge University Press.

Mitchell, J. V. (2007) 'Energy and Norwegian foreign policy', in A. Holm and H. Thune (eds.) *Energipolitiske interesser og utfordringer*, Oslo: Norwegian Ministry of Foreign Affairs.

MNC Hearings (1974) 'Multinational corporations and the United States' foreign policy', hearings before the Subcommittee on Multinational Corporations of the Committee on Foreign Relations, United States Senate, ninety-third Congress, Washington, DC: Government Printing House.

Mo, J. and C. Moon (eds.) (1998) *Democracy and the Korean economy*, Stanford, CA: Hoover Institution Press.

Moene, K. O. and Wallerstein, M. (2001) 'Targeting and the political support for welfare spending', *Economics of Governance*, 2, 2: 3–24, reprinted in A. Glazer and K. Konrad (eds.) (2003) *Conflict and governance*, Heidelberg: Springer.

—— (2003) 'Earnings inequality and welfare spending: A disaggregated analysis', *World Politics*, 55, 4: 485–516.

Mokyr, J. (1990) *The lever of riches: Technological creativity and economic progress*, New York: Oxford University Press.

Money Today (2010) Available at http://www.mt.co.kr (accessed May 18, 2010).

Moon, C. (1991) 'The political economy of defense industrialization in South Korea: Constraints, opportunities and prospects', *Journal of East Asian Affairs*, 5, 2: 438–65.

—— (1994) 'Changing patterns of business–government relations in South Korea', in A. MacIntyre (ed.) *Business and government in industrializing Asia*, Ithaca, NY: Cornell University Press.

—— (1995) 'Globalization: Challenges and strategies' *Korea Focus*, 3, 3: 62–77.

Moon, C. and Prasad, R. (1994) 'Beyond the developmental state: Networks, politics and institutions', *Governance*, 7, 4: 360–86.

Moon, C. and Mo, J. (1999) 'Globalization under the Kim Young Sam Government', in C. Moon and J. Mo (eds.) *Democratization and globalization in Korea: Assessment and prospects*, Seoul: Yonsei University Press.

—— (2000) *Economic crisis and structural reforms: Assessments and implications*, Washington, DC: Economic Strategy Institute.

Moon, C. and Lim, S. (2001) 'The politics of economic rise and decline in South Korea', in C. Moon and S. Kil (eds.) *Understanding Korean politics*, Albany: State University of New York Press.

Moon, C. and Rhyu, S. (2002) 'Dismantling the developmental state', in Y. R. Kim, H. Lee, and I. Mah (eds.), *Redefining Korean politics*, Seoul: Orum Press.

Moran, M. (1984) *The politics of banking*, London: Macmillan.

—— (1991) *The politics of the financial services revolution*, Houndmills: Macmillan.

Moravcsik, A. (2003) 'Theory synthesis in international relations: Real not metaphysical', *International Studies Review*, 5, 1: 131–6.

—— (2008) 'The new liberalism', in C. Reus-Smit and D. Snidal (eds.) *The Oxford handbook of international relations*, New York: Oxford University Press.

Morgenthau, H. J. (1948) *Politics among nations: The struggle for power and peace*, New York: Knopf.

Morris, C. (2008) *The trillion dollar meltdown*, New York: Public Affairs.

Morrison, W. M. and Labonte, M. (2009) *China's holdings of U.S. securities: Implications for the U.S. economy*, Washington, DC: Congressional Research Service.

Morse, R. M. (1964) 'The heritage of Latin America', in L. Hartz (ed.) *The founding of new societies: Studies in the history of the United States, Latin America, South Africa, Canada, and Australia*, New York: Harcourt, Brace & World.

Mügge, D. (2006) 'Private–public puzzles: Interfirm competition and transnational "private" regulation', *New Political Economy*, 11, 2: 177–200.

NABO (National Assembly Budget Office) (2010) 'Assessment of the future growth engine R&D project', Seoul: National Assembly Budget Office.

Narula, R. (1993) 'An examination of the evolution and interdependence of foreign direct investment and economic structure: The case of industrialized countries', PhD thesis, Newark, Rutgers University.

—— (2003) *Globalisation and technology*, Cambridge, UK: Polity Press.

Narula, R. and Lall, S. (2006) *Understanding FDI-assisted development*, London: Routledge.

Narula, R. and Jormanainen, I. (2008) 'When a good science base is not enough to create competitive industries: Lock-in and inertia in Russian systems of innovation', MERIT-UNU Working Papers 2008–059, Maastricht: United Nations University, Maastricht Economic and Social Research and Training Centre on Innovation and Technology.

Narula, R. and Dunning, J. H. (2010) 'Multinational enterprises, development and globalisation: Some clarifications and a research agenda', *Oxford Development Studies*, 38, 3: 263–87.

Newell, P. and MacKenzie, R. (2000) 'The 2000 Cartegena Protocol on Biosafety: Legal and political dimensions', *Global Environmental Change*, 10: 313–317. Available at http://www.jiwlp.com/contents/Newell.pdf (accessed January 19, 2011).

Nicolini, M. and Resmini, L. (2006) 'The impact Of MNEs on domestic firms in CEECs: A micro-econometric approach', ERSA Conference Papers, No. 411, Vienna: ERSA.

Noland, M. and Pack, H. (2003) *Industrial policy in an era of globalization: Lessons from Asia*, Washington, DC: International Economic Institute.

Nölke, A. (2004) 'Transnationale Politiknetzwerke: Eine Analyse grenzüberschreitender politischer Entscheidungsprozesse jenseits des regierungszentrischen Modells', Habilitationsschrift, Universität Leipzig.

—— (2009) 'The politics of accounting regulation: Responses to the subprime crisis', in S. Helleiner, S. Pagliari, and H. Zimmermann (eds.) *Global finance in crisis: The politics of international regulatory change*, London: Routledge.

—— (2011) 'Die BRIC-Variante des Kapitalismus und soziale Ungleichheit: Das Beispiel Brasilien', in I. Wehr and H.-J. Burchardt (eds.) *Soziale Ungleichheiten in Lateinamerika: Neue Perspektiven auf Wirtschaft, Politik und Umwelt*, Baden-Baden: Nomos.

Nölke, A. and Perry, J. (2007) 'The power of transnational private govvernance: Financialization and the IASB', *Business and Politics*, 9, 3: 1–25.

Nölke, A. and Taylor, H. (2010) 'Non-triad multinationals and global governance: Still a North–South conflict?', in M. Ougaard and A. Leander (eds.) *Business and global governance*, London: Routledge.

Nölke, A., Overbeek, H., and van Apeldoorn, B. (2007) 'Marketization, transnationalization, commodification, and the shifts in corporate governance regulation: A conclusion', in H. Overbeek, A. Nölke, and B. van Apeldoorn (eds.) *The transnational politics of corporate governance regulation*, London: Routledge.

Norman, V. D. and Venables, A. J. (1995) 'International trade, factor mobility and trade costs', *Economic Journal*, 105, 433: 1488–1504.

North, D. C. (1990) *Institutions, institutional change and economic performance*, New York: Cambridge University Press.

Nye, J. S. (1988), 'Neorealism and neoliberalism', *World Politics*, 15, 2: 235–51.

—— (1990) *Bound to lead: The changing nature of American power*, New York: Basic Books.

—— (2004) *Soft power: The means to success in world politics*, New York: Public Affairs.

—— (2009) 'Scholars on the sidelines', *The Washington Post*, April 13, p. A15.

Oatley, T. (2009) *International political economy: Interests and institutions in the global economy*, 4th edn, New York: Pearson Longman.

Oatley, T. and Nabors, R. (1998) 'Redistributive cooperation: Market failure, wealth transfers, and the Basel Accord', *International Organization*, 52, 1: 35–54.

Oberheim, E. (2006) *Feyerabend's philosophy*, Berlin: W. de Gruyter.

Obstfeld, M. (1998) 'The global capital market: Benefactor or menace', *Journal of Economic Perspectives*, 12, 4: 9–30.

Ocampo, J. A. (2009) 'Die globale Wirtschaftskrise: Auswirkungen und Folgen für Lateinamerika', *Nueva Sociedad*, Special Issue: 4–21

Odell, P. R. (1986) *Oil and world power*, Middlesex: Penguin Books.

—— (1996) 'Book review of M. A. Adelman's *The Genie out of the Bottle: World Oil since 1970* (1995, Cambridge, MA: MIT Press)', *Journal of Energy Literature*, 2, 1: 38.

OECD (n.d.) 'On-line guide to intergovernmental activity'. Available at http://webnet3.oecd.org/OECDgroups/ (accessed October 15, 2010).

—— (1960) 'Convention on the Organisation for Economic Co-operation and Development', Paris, December 14, 1960.

—— (1996) *The knowledge-based economy*, Paris: OECD.

—— (2004) 'A strategy for enlargement and outreach', report by the Chair of the Heads of Delegation Working Group on the Enlargement Strategy and Outreach, Ambassador Seiichiro Noboru, Paris: OECD.

—— (2007a) 'OECD Council Resolution on enlargement and enhanced engagement', adopted by the Council at Ministerial Level on 16 May 2007. Available at http://www.oecd.org/document/7/0,3746,en_2649_201185_38604487_1_1_1_1,00.html (accessed January 15, 2011).

—— (2007b) 'Official visit of the Secretary-General to India (8–9 October 2007)'. Available at http://www.oecd.org/document/6/0,3343,en_33873108_39418537_39416070_1_1_1_1,00.html (accessed January 15, 2011).

—— (2009a) 'Official visit of the Secretary-General to India (New Delhi, 3 December–4 December 2009)'. Available at http://www.oecd.org/document/26/0,3343,en_21571361_44315115_44250778_1_1_1_1,00.html (accessed January 15, 2011).

—— (2009b) 'OECD investment policy reviews: India 2009', Paris: OECD.

—— (2009c) 'Policy roundtables on competition policy, industrial policy, and national champions'. Available at http://www.oecd.org/competition (accessed June 20, 2010).

—— (2010a) 'Declaration on Propriety, Integrity and Transparency in the Conduct of International Business and Finance, 28 May 2010', C/MIN(2010)3/FINAL, Paris: OECD.

—— (2010b) 'Country surveys/reviews/guides'. Available on the respective country pages at http://www.oecd.org/publicationsanddocumentbycategory/ (accessed July 2010).

—— (2010c) 'The OECD Global Relations Programme 2009–2010, 2010 update', Paris: OECD.

OECD CCNM (Centre for Co-operation with Non-Members) (2009) *The OECD's partnership with India*, Paris: OECD.

OECD Council (2009) 'Declaration on Green Growth (adopted at the Council Meeting at Ministerial Level on 25 June 2009)', C/MIN(2009)5/ADD1/FINAL, Paris: OECD.

OECD Legal Directorate (1996) 'OECD decisions, recommendations and other instruments in force, vols 1–3', Paris: OECD.

OECD Secretary-General (2010) 'Secretary-General's Report to Ministers 2010', Paris: OECD.

OECD South Africa (2008) 'Joint statement by the South African Minister of Finance, Trevor A. Manuel, MP and the Secretary-General of the OECD, Angel Gurria, regarding enhanced engagement between South Africa and the OECD, 15 July 2008'. Available at http://www.oecd.org/dataoecd/30/1/41088594.pdf (accessed July 15, 2010).

Ohta, H. (2007) 'Saving the Kyoto Protocol: Japan–EU leadership with Canadian support', unpublished paper presented at Conference on Minervian Power, Vancounver, Canada.

Oldani, C. (2008) *Governing global derivatives*, Aldershot: Ashgate.

Olivier de Sardan, J.-P. (1999) 'A moral economy of corruption in Africa?', *Journal of Modern African Studies*, 37, 1: 25–52.

Olson, M. (1982) *The rise and decline of nations: Economic growth, stagflation and social rigidities*, New Haven, CT: Yale University Press.

—— (2003) 'Dictatorship, democracy and development', in S. Knack (ed.) *Democracy, governance and growth*, Ann Arbor: University of Michigan Press.

Oszlak, O. (1986) 'Public policy and political regimes in Latin America', *International Social Science Journal*, 38, 2: 219–36.

Ougaard, M. (2004) *Political globalization: State, power, and social forces*, Houndmills: Palgrave Macmillan.

—— (2008) 'Private institutions and business power in global governance', *Global Governance*, 14, 3: 387–403.

—— (2010) 'The OECD's global role: Agenda setting and policy diffusion', in K. Martens and A. Jakobi (eds.) *Mechanisms of OECD governance: International incentives for national policy making?*, Oxford: Oxford University Press.

—— (2011) 'Civil society and patterns of accountability in the OECD', in J. A. Scholte (ed.) *Building global democracy? Civil society and accountable global governance*, Cambridge, UK: Cambridge University Press.

Ougaard, M. and Leander A. (eds.) (2010) *Business and global governance*, London: Routledge.

Overbeek, H., Nölke, A., and Van Apeldoorn, B. (eds.) (2007) *The transnational politics of corporate governance regulation*, London: Routledge.

Padoan, P. C. (1994) 'The changing European political economy', in R. Stubbs and G. R. D. Underhill (eds.) *Political economy and the changing global order*, 1st edn, New York: St. Martin's Press.

Padro-i-Miquel, G. (2007) 'The control of politicians in divided societies: The politics of fear', *Review of Economic Studies*, 74, 4: 1259–74.

Pattberg, P. H. (2007) *Private institutions and global governance: The new politics of environmental sustainability*, Cheltenham: Edward Elgar.

Paulson, H. (2009) *On the brink*, New York: Business Press.

Pauly, L. W. (1988) *Opening financial markets: Banking politics on the Pacific Rim*, Ithaca, NY: Cornell University Press.

—— (1997) *Who elected the bankers?* Ithaca, NY: Cornell University Press.

—— (2002) 'Global finance, political authority, and the problem of legitimation', in R. Hall and T. Biersteker (eds.) *The emergence of private authority in global governance*, Cambridge, UK: Cambridge University Press.

—— (2005) 'The political economy of international financial crises', in J. Ravenhill (ed.) *Global political economy*, Oxford: Oxford University Press.

Pempel, T. J. (1998) *Regime shift: Comparative dynamics of the Japanese political economy*, Ithaca, NY: Cornell University Press.

—— (ed.) (1999a) *The politics of the Asian economic crisis*, Ithaca, NY: Cornell University Press.

—— (1999b) 'The developmental regime in a changing world economy', in M. Woo-Cumings (ed.) *The developmental state in historical perspective*, Ithaca, NY: Cornell University Press.

—— (ed.) (2004) *Remapping East Asia: The construction of a region*, Ithaca, NY: Cornell University Press.

—— (2007) 'Japanese policy under Koizumi', in G. Rozman (ed.) *Strategic thinking in Japan*, London: Routledge.

—— (2008) 'How Bush bungled Asia: Militarism, economic indifference and unilateralism have weakened the United States across Asia', *The Pacific Review*, 21, 5: 547–81.

Pempel, T. J. and Urata, S. (2005) 'Japan: A new move toward bilateral free trade agreements', in K. Vinod and S. Aggarwal (eds.) *Bilateral trade arrangements in the Asia-Pacific: Origins, evolution, and implications*, London: Routledge.

Perry, J. and Nölke, A. (2006) 'International accounting standards and transnational private authority', *Review of International Political Economy*, 13, 4: 559–86.

Persaud, A. (2000) 'Sending the herd off the cliff edge', *Journal of Risk Finance*, 2, 1: 59 –65.

Persson, T. and Tabellini, G. (2000) *Political economics: Explaining economic policy*, Cambridge, MA: MIT Press.

Pfaffermayr, M., Breuss, F., and Egger, P. (2001) 'The impact of Agenda 2000's structural policy reform on FDI in the EU', *Journal of Policy Modeling*, 23, 7: 811–24.

Phillips, N. (2004a) 'International political economy, comparative political economy and the study of contemporary development', IPEG Papers in Global Political Economy 8, paper presented at the Annual Convention of the International Studies Association, Montreal, March 17–20.

—— (2004b) *The Southern cone model: The political economy of regional capitalist development in Latin America*, London: Routledge.

Pirog, R. (2007) 'The role of national oil companies in the international oil market', Report RL-34137, Washington: Congressional Research Service.

Pitcher, A., Moran, M. H., and Johnston, M. (2009) 'Rethinking patrimonialism and neopatrimonialism in Africa', *African Studies Review*, 52, 1: 125–56.

Planning Committee on New Growth Engine (2008) *Shinsungjandongruck Visionkwa Baljunjuckrack* [*Vision for new growth engine and development strategy*]. Seoul. NGEPC.

Polanyi, K. (1957) *The great transformation*, London: Beacon Press.

Porter, T. (1999) 'The transnational agenda for financial regulation in developing countries', in L. E. Armijo (ed.) *Financial globalisation and democracy in emerging markets*, London: Macmillan.

—— (2005) *Globalization and finance*, Cambridge, UK: Polity Press.

Portes, R. (1998) 'An analysis of financial crisis: Lessons for the international financial system', paper presented at FRB Chicago/IMF Conference, Chicago, October 8–10, 1998.

Poulantzas, N. (1973) *Political power and social classes*, London: New Left Books.

Prasad, E., Rajan, T., and Subramanian, A. (2007) 'The paradox of capital', *Finance and Development*, 44, 1: 16–19.

Pronk, J. P. (2004) *Catalyzing development? A debate on aid*, Malden, MA: Blackwell.

Przeworski, A. and Limongi, F. (1993) 'Political regimes and economic growth', *Journal of Economic Perspectives*, 7, 3: 51–69.

Przeworski A., Alvarez, M. E., Cheibub, J. A., and Limongi, F. (2000) *Democracy and development: Political institutions and well-being in the world, 1950–1990*, New York: Cambridge University Press.

Putnam, H. (1981) *Reason, truth and history*, New York: Cambridge University Press.

Putnam, R. D. (1988) 'Diplomacy and domestic politics: The logic of two-level games', *International Organization*, 42, 3: 427–60.

Pyle, K. B. (1992) *The Japanese question: Power and purpose in a new era*, Washington, DC: AEI Press.

—— (2007) *Japan rising: The resurgence of Japanese power and purpose*, New York: Century Foundation.

Quilés, P. and Guillet, M. J.-J. (2006) 'Energie et politique: Rapport d'information par la commission des affaires étrangères, Assemblée Nationale de la France', Paris: Assemblée Nationale.

Radosevic, S. (1999) 'Transformation of S&T systems into systems of innovation in central and eastern Europe: The emerging patterns of recombination, path-dependency and change', *Structural Change and Economic Dynamics*, 10, 3–4: 277–320.

Ramo, J. C. (2004) *The Beijing consensus*, London: Foreign Policy Centre.

Ramos, J. (2000) 'Policy directions for the new economic model in Latin America', *World Development*, 28, 9: 1703–17.

Raustiala, K. and Victor, D. G. (2004) 'The regime complex for plant genetic resources', *International Organization*, 58, 2: 277–310.

Ravallion, M. and Datt, G. (1995) 'Is targeting through a work requirement efficient?', in D. van de Walle and K. Nead (eds.) *Public spending and the poor: Theory and evidence*, Baltimore: Johns Hopkins University Press.

Ravenhill, J. (2000) 'APEC adrift: Implications for economic regionalism in Asia and the Pacific', *Pacific Review*, 13, 2: 319–33.

—— (2008) 'In search of the missing middle', *Review of International Political Economy*, 15, 1: 18–29.

—— (ed.) (2010) *Global political economy*, 3rd edn, Oxford: Oxford University Press.

Reich, R. B. (1982) 'Why the U.S. needs industrial policy', *Harvard Business Review*, 60, 1: 74–81.

Reno, W. (1995) *Corruption and state politics in Sierra Leone*, Cambridge, UK: Cambridge University Press.

—— (1998) *Warlord politics and African states*, Boulder, CO: Lynne Rienner.

Review of International Political Economy (2009) 'Not so quiet on the Western front: The American school of IPE', Special Issue, Volume 16, Issue 1.

Riddell, R. C. (2007) *Does foreign aid really work?*, Oxford: Oxford University Press.

Riley, N. E. (2004) 'China's population: New trends and challenges', *Population Bulletin*, 59, 2: 1–36.

Robinson, J. A. (1998) 'Theories of bad policy', *Journal of Policy Reform*, 2, 1: 1–46.

Robinson, W. I. (2002) 'Capitalist globalization and the transnationalization of the state', in M. Rupert and H. Smith (eds.) *Historical materialism and globalization*, London: Routledge.

Rock, M. (2009) 'Corruption and democracy', *Journal of Development Studies*, 45, 1: 55–75.

Rodrik, D. (1996) 'Understanding economic policy reform', *Journal of Economic Literature*, 34: 9–41.

—— (1997) 'Trade, social insurance, and the limits to globalization', NBER Working Paper No. 5905, Cambridge, MA: National Bureau of Economic Research.

—— (1998a) 'Who needs capital-account convertibility?', Essays in International Finance, 207, Princeton, NJ: Princeton University.

—— (1998b) 'Democracies pay higher wages', paper, Cambridge, MA: John F. Kennedy School of Government, Harvard University.

—— (1999) *The new global economy and developing countries: Making openness work*, Baltimore: Johns Hopkins University Press.

—— (2000) 'Institutions for high-quality growth: What they are and how to acquire them', NBER Working Paper No. 7540, Cambridge, MA: National Bureau of Economic Research.

—— (2004) 'Industrial policies for the twenty-first century', CEPR Discussion Paper No. 4767, Cambridge, MA: John F. Kennedy School of Government, Harvard University.

—— (2006) 'Goodbye Washington Consensus, hello Washington Confusion?', *Journal of Economic Literature*, 44: 973–987.

—— (2007a) *One economics, many recipes: Globalization, institutions and economic growth*, Princeton, NJ: Princeton University Press.

—— (2007b) 'How to save globalization from its cheerleaders', *Journal of International Trade and Diplomacy*, 1, 2: 1–31.

—— (2010) 'Return of industrial policy', *Korea Times*, April 14. Available at http://www.koreatimes.co.kr/www/news/opinon/2011/01/160_64167.html (accessed January 19, 2011).

Rodrik, D., Subramanian, A., and Trebbi, F. (2004) 'Institutions rule: The primacy of institutions over geography and integration in economic development', *Journal of Economic Growth*, 9: 131–65.

Roett, R. (1984) *Brazil: Politics in a patrimonial society*, 3rd edn, New York: Praeger.

Rogowski, R. (1987) 'Trade and the variety of democratic institutions', *International Organization*, 41, 2: 203–23.

—— (1989) *Commerce and coalitions*, Princeton, NJ: Princeton University Press.

Rokkan, S. (1966) 'Norway: Numerical democracy and corporate pluralism', in R. A. Dahl (ed.) *Political oppositions in Western democracies*, New Haven, CT: Yale University Press.

Romer, P. (1990) 'Endogenous technological change', *Journal of Political Economy*, 98, 5: 71–102.

Roncaglia, A. (1985) *The international oil market*, Basingstoke: Macmillan.

Rosenbluth, F. M. (1989) *Financial politics in contemporary Japan*, Ithaca, NY: Cornelll University Press.

Rothstein, R. L. (1984) 'Regime-creation by a coalition of the weak: Lessons from the NIEO and the Integrated Program for Commodities', *International Studies Quarterly*, 28, 3: 307–28.

Ruggie, J. G. (1982) 'International regimes, transactions, and change: Embedded liberalism in the postwar economic order', *International Organization*, 36, 2: 379–415.

—— (1986) 'Continuity and transformation in the world polity: Toward a neorealist synthesis', in R. Keohane (ed.) *Neorealism and its critics*, New York: Columbia University Press.

Ruigrok, W. and van Tulder, R. (1995) *The logic of international restructuring*, London: Routledge.

Salzman, J. and Terracino, J. B. (2006) 'Labor rights, globalization and institutions: The role and influence of the Organisation for Economic Co-operation and Development', in V. A. Leary and D. Warner (eds.) *Social issues, globalisation and international institutions: Labour rights and the EU, ILO, OECD and WTO*, Leiden: Martinus Nijhoff.

Sampson, A. (1975) *The Seven Sisters: The great oil companies and the world they made*, London: Hodder and Stoughton.

Samuelson, P. A. (1988) *Economics*, New York: McGraw Hill.

Sandbrook, R. (1985) *The politics of Africa's economic stagnation*, Cambridge, UK: Cambridge University Press.

—— (2000) *Closing the circle: Democratization and development in Africa*, Toronto: Between the Lines.

Sandmo, A. (1991) 'Economists and the welfare state', *European Economic Review*, 35, 2–3: 213–39.

Scharpf, F. W. (1998) *Governing in Europe: Legitimate and effective?* Oxford: Oxford University Press.

Schimmelfennig, F. (2003) *The EU, NATO and integration of Europe: Rules and rhetoric*, Cambridge, UK: Cambridge University Press.

Schneider, S. A. (1983) *The oil price revolution*, Baltimore: Johns Hopkins University Press.

Scholte, J. A. (2005) *Globalization. A critical introduction*, 2nd edn. Basingstoke: Palgrave Macmillan.

Scholz, I. (2008) 'Climate change: China and India as contributors to problems and solutions', in H. Schmitz and D. Messner (eds.) *Poor and powerful: The rise of China and India and the implications for Europe*, Bonn: German Development Institute.

Schram, S. (2005) 'A return to politics: Perestroika, phronesis, and post-paradigmatic political science', in K. R. Mornroe (ed.) *Perestroika: The raucous rebellion in political science*, New Haven, CT: Yale University Press.

Schreurs, M. A. (2002) *Environmental politics in Japan, Germany, and the United States*, Cambridge, UK: Cambridge University Press.

Schultz, M., Hatch, M., and Larsen, M. (eds.) (2000) *The expressive organization: Linking identity, reputation and the corporate brand*, Oxford: Oxford University Press.

Schumpeter, J. A. (1954) 'The crisis of the tax state', *International Economic Papers*, 6: 5–38.

Schwartman, S. (1977) 'Back to Weber: Corporatism and patrimonialism in the seventies', in J. M. Malloy (ed.) *Authoritarianism and corporatism in Latin America*, Pittsburgh, PA: University of Pittsburgh Press.

Schwartz, H. (2000) *States versus markets: The emergence of a global economy*, 2nd edn, Basingstoke: Palgrave Macmillan.

Schwartz, H. (2009) *Subprime Nation: American power, global capital, and the housing bubble*, Ithaca, NY: Cornell University Press.

Schwartz, H. (2010) *States versus markets: The emergence of a global economy*, 3rd edn, London: Palgrave Macmillan.

Searle, P. (1999) *The riddle of Malaysian capitalism: Rent-seekers or real capitalists?*, Honolulu: Asian Studies Association of Australia.

Sechuwi (1995) *Segehwa Baksuh* [*White book on globalization*], Seoul: Sechuwi (Committee on Globalization).

—— (1996) *Segehwa Baksuh* [*White book on globalization*], Seoul: Sechuwi (Committee on Globalization).

—— (1998) *Segehwa Baksuh* [*White book on globalization*], Seoul: Sechuwi (Committee on Globalization).

Sell, S. (1998) *Power and ideas: North–South politics of intellectual property and antitrust*, Albany: State University of New York Press.

—— (2003) *Private power, public law: The globalization of intellectual property rights*, Cambridge, UK: Cambridge University Press.

Selvik, K. and Stenslie, S. (2011) *Stability and change in the modern Middle East*, London: I. B. Tauris.

Sen, A. (1999) *Development as freedom*, Oxford: Oxford University Press.

Sender, H. (2009a) 'Shake-up of GM complicated by prospect of credit insurance deals', *Financial Times*, May 12. Available at http://www.ft.com/cms/52bb328a-0ab9-11d e-95ed-0000779fd2ac.html (accessed January 19, 2011).

—— (2009b) 'AIG saga shows how dangerous credit default swaps can be', *Financial Times*, March 7. Available at http://www.ft.com/cms/4eff016e-3e8d-11de-9a6 c-00144feabdc0.html (accessed January 19, 2011).

Shanks, C., Jacobson, H. K., and Kaplan, J. H. (1996) 'Inertia and change in the constellation of international governmental organizations, 1981–1992', *International Organization*, 50, 4: 593–627.

Shapiro, I. (2005) *The flight from reality in the human sciences*, Princeton, NJ: Princeton University Press.

Sharma, A. (2006) 'Flexibility, employment and labour market reforms in India', *Economic and Political Weekly*, 41, 21: 2078–85.

Sikkink, K. (forthcoming) *The justice cascade.*

Sil, R. and Katzenstein, P. J. (2010) *Beyond paradigms: Analytic eclecticism in the study of world politics*, Basingstoke: Palgrave Macmillan.

Singer, D. (2008) *Regulating capital*, Ithaca, NY: Cornell University Press.

Sinn, H.-W. (1995) 'A theory of the welfare state', *Scandinavian Journal of Economics*, 97, 4: 495–526.

Sirowy, L. and Inkeles, A. (1990) 'The effects of democracy on economic growth and inequality: A review', *Studies in Comparative International Development*, 25, 1: 126–57.

Slaughter, A.-M. (2004) *A new world order*, Princeton, NJ: Princeton University Press.

Smith, A. (1937 [1776]) *An enquiry into the nature and causes of the wealth of nations*, E. Cannan (ed.), New York: Modern Library.

Smith, A. et al. (1986) 'Re-shuffling the decks of domestic reserves: Are zealous acquirers picking clean bones?', paper presented at the Eighth Annual American IAEE Conference, November.

Sørensen, G. (1998) *Democracy and democratization: Processes and prospects in a changing world*, 2nd edn, Boulder, CO: Westview Press.

—— (2006) 'Liberalism of restraint and liberalism of imposition: Liberal values and world order in the new millennium', *International Relations*, 20, 3: 251–72.

Sorkin, A. (2009) *Too big to fail*, New York: Viking.

Soros, G. (2005) *George Soros on globalization*, New York: Public Affairs.

—— (2008) *The new paradigm for financial markets*, New York: Public Affairs.

—— (2009) 'The game changer', *Financial Times*, January 29. Available at http://www.ft.com/cms/09b68a14-eda7-11dd-bd60-0000779fd2ac.html (accessed January 19, 2011).

Spero, J. E. and Hart, J. A. (1997) *The politics of international economic relations*, 5th edn, New York: St. Martin's Press.

Stasavage, D. (2005) 'Democracy and education spending in Africa', *American Journal of Political Science*, 49, 2: 343–58.

Steil, B. (ed.) (1994) *International financial market regulation*, Chichester: John Wiley.

Steil, B. (2010) 'China, the dollar, and the return of the Triffin dilemma'. Available at http://whatmatters.mckinseydigital.com/currencies/china-the-dollar-and-the-return-of-the-triffin-dilemma (accessed September 23, 2010).

Steinberg, R. H. (2002) 'In the shadow of law or power? Consensus-based bargaining and outcomes in the GATT/WTO', *International Organization*, 56, 2: 339–74.

STEPI (2005) *A content analysis on the S&T comprehensive plans in Korea: Focusing on five-year plans*, Seoul: STEPI (Science and Technology Policy Institute).

—— (2009) *Survey of R&D in Korea*, Seoul: STEPI (Science and Technology Policy Institute).

Stiglitz, J. E. (2000) 'Capital market liberalization, economic growth, and instability', *World Development*, 28, 6: 1075–86.

—— (2001) 'Whither reform? Ten years of transition', in H.-J. Chang (ed.) *The rebel within: Joseph Stiglitz and the World Bank*, London: Anthem.

—— (2002) *Globalization and its discontents*, New York: W.W. Norton.

—— (2006) *Making globalization work*, New York: W.W. Norton.

Stone, R. (2002) *Lending credibility: The International Monetary Fund and the post-communist transition*, Princeton, NJ: Princeton University Press.

—— (2011) *Controlling institutions: International organizations and the global economy*, Cambridge, UK: Cambridge University Press.

Stopford, J. and Strange, S. (1991) *Rival states, rival firms: Competition for world market shares*, Cambridge, UK: Cambridge University Press.

Strange, S. (1976) 'International monetary relations', in A. Shonfield (ed.) *International economic relations of the Western World 1959–1971, vol. 2*, Oxford: Oxford University Press.

—— (1986) *Casino capitalism*, Oxford: Blackwell.

—— (1988) *States and markets*, London: Frances Pinter.

—— (1996) *The retreat of the state: The diffusion of power in the world economy*, Cambridge, UK: Cambridge University Press.

—— (1998) *Mad money*, Manchester: Manchester University Press.

Sung-hoon, L. (2010) 'Five new industries that will feed Korea in the future', *Chosun Ilbo*, October 28. Available at http://event.chosun.com/index.php?no=366813 (accessed January 25, 2011).

Swenson, P. A. (2002) *Capitalists against markets: The making of labor markets and welfare states in the United States and Sweden*, Oxford: Oxford University Press.

Tait, N. (2009a) 'Tougher capital provisions for banks on risky products', *Financial Times*, May 7. Available at http://www.ft.com/cms/4f3b427c-3aa1-11de-8a2d-00144feabdc0.html (accessed January 19, 2011).

—— (2009b) 'Europe on the same wavelength as U.S., but moving more slowly', *Financial Times*, May 15. Available at http://www.ft.com/cms/70d90162-40e6-11de-8f18-00144feabdc0.html (accessed January 19, 2011).

—— (2009c) 'New move on CDS clearer for Europe', *Financial Times*, February 14. Available at http://www.ft.com/cms/e1a77770-f96f-11dd-90c1-000077b07658.html (accessed January 19, 2011).

Tavares, J. and Wacziarg, R. (2001) 'How democracy affects growth', *European Economic Review*, 45, 8: 1341–78.

Taylor, H. and Nölke, A. (2010) 'Global players from India: A political economy perspective', in K. Sauvant, G. McAllister, and W. Maschek (eds.) *Foreign direct investment from emerging markets: The challenges ahead*, New York: Palgrave.

Taylor, L. (1997) 'The revival of the liberal creed: The IMF and the World Bank in a globalized economy', *World Development*, 25, 2: 145–52.

Tetlock, P. (2005) *Expert political judgment: How good is it? How can we know?* Princeton, NJ: Princeton University Press.

Tett, G. (2009) 'Tale from the land of Borat is a lesson to the world at large', *Financial Times*, May 1. Available at http://www.ft.com/cms/3b1ee130-35e8-11de-a99 7-00144feabdc0.html (accessed January 19, 2011).

Tett, G. and Davies, P. (2008) 'Derivatives chiefs meet at crucial time for industry', *Financial Times*, April 16. Available at http://www.ft.com/cms/c666329c-0b4c-11dd-8cc f-0000779fd2ac.html (accessed January 19, 2011).

Tett, G., van Duyn, A., and Grant, J. (2009) 'Let the battle commence', *Financial Times*, May 20. Available at http://www.ft.com/cms/d4a7adfc-44a5-11de-82d6-00144feabdc0. html (accessed January 19, 2011).

Thaler, R. and Sunstein C. (2009) *Nudge: Improving decisions about health, wealth, and happiness*, New York: Penguin.

Therkildsen, O. (2005) 'Understanding public management through neopatrimonialism: A paradigm for all African seasons?', in U. Engel and G. R. Olsen (eds.) *The African exception*, Aldershot: Ashgate.

Tirole, J. (2002) *Financial crises, liquidity, and the international monetary system*, Princeton, NJ: Princeton University Press.

Toye, J. (ed.) (2003) *Trade and development*, Cheltenham: Edward Elgar.

Triffin, R. (1960) *Gold and the dollar crisis*, New Haven, CT: Yale University Press.

Tsebelis, G. (2002) *Veto players: How political institutions work*, Princeton, NJ: Princeton University Press.

Tsingou, E. (2006) 'The governance of OTC derivatives markets', in P. Mooslechner, H. Schuberth, and B. Weber (eds.) *The political economy of financial market regulation*, Cheltenham: Edward Elgar.

Turits, R. (2003) *Foundations of despotism: Peasants, the Trujillo regime, and modernity in Dominican history*, Stanford, CA: Stanford University Press.

UNCTAD (2005) *World investment report 2005*, New York: United Nations.

—— (2007) *World investment report 2007*, New York: United Nations.

—— (2009) *World investment report 2009*, New York: United Nations.

—— (2010) *World investment report 2010*, New York: United Nations.

Underdal, A. (1987) 'International cooperation: Transforming "needs" into "deeds"', *Journal of Peace Research*, 24, 2: 167–83.

—— (2010) 'Complexity and challenges of long-term environmental governance', *Global Environmental Change*, 20, 3: 386–93.

Underdal, A. and Young, O. R. (eds.) (2004) *Regime consequences: Methodological challenges and research strategies*, Dordrecht: Kluwer Academic Publishers.

Underhill, G. R. D. (1993) 'Negotiating financial openness: The Uruguay Round and trade in financial services', in P. G. Cerny (ed.) *Finance and world politics: Markets, regimes, and states in the post-hegemonic era*, Cheltenham: Edward Elgar.

—— (1995) 'Keeping governments out of politics: Transnational securities markets, regulatory co-operation, and political legitimacy', *Review of International Studies*, 21, 3: 251–78.

—— (1996) 'Financial market integration, global capital mobility, and the ERM crisis 1992–1995', Working Paper No. 12, Global Economic Institutions Research Programme, Swindon: Economic and Social Research Council.

—— (1997) 'Private markets and public responsibility in a global system', in G. R. D. Underhill (ed.) *The new world order in international finance*, New York: St. Martin's Press.

—— (1999) 'Transnational financial markets and national economic development models: Global structures versus domestic imperatives', *Economies et Sociétés, série 'Monnaie'*, ME, No. 1–2, September–October.

—— (2000) 'State, market, and global political economy: genealogy of an (inter-?) discipline', *International Affairs*, 76, 4: 805–24.

—— (2002) 'Global integration, EMU, and monetary governance in the European Union: The political economy of the "stability culture"', in K. Dyson (ed.) *European states and the euro*, Oxford: Oxford University Press.

—— (2006) 'Introduction: Global issues in historical perspective', in R. Stubbs and G. R. D. Underhill (eds.) *Political economy and the changing global order*, Oxford: Oxford University Press.

Underhill, G. R. D. and Zhang, X. (2003) 'Global structures and political imperatives: In search of normative underpinnings for international financial order', in G. R. D. Underhill and X. Zhang (eds.) *International financial governance under stress*, Cambridge, UK: Cambridge University Press.

Underhill, G. R. D., Blom, J., and Mügge, D. (eds.) (2010) *Global financial integration thirty years on: From reform to crisis*, Cambridge, UK: Cambridge University Press.

UNIDO (2005) 'Industrial development report 2005', Vienna: UNIDO.

—— (2009) 'Industrial development report 2009', Vienna: UNIDO.

United Nations (2000) 'United Nations Millennium Declaration', Resolution 55/2 adopted by the General Assembly, New York: UN.

Uricoechea, F. (1980) *The patrimonial foundations of the Brazilian bureaucratic state*, Berkeley: University of California Press.

U.S. Government (1999) 'Report of the US President's Working Group on Financial Markets: Over-the-counter derivatives markets and the Commodity Exchange Act', Washington: U.S. Government.

U.S. Government, Department of the Treasury (2009) 'Regulatory reform over-the-counter (OTC) derivatives', May 13. Available at http://www.ustreas.gov/press/releases/tg129.htm (accessed January 19, 2011).

U.S. Government, President's Working Group on Financial Markets (2008) 'Policy objectives for the OTC derivatives market', November 14. Available at http://www.ustr.gov/2010-trade-policy-agenda (accessed January 19, 2011).

USTR (2010) 'The 2010 report on national trade estimates on foreign trade barriers'. Available at http://www.ustr.gov/sites/default/files/uploads/reports/2010/NTE/NTE_COMPLETE_WITH_APPENDnonameack.pdf (accessed November 25, 2010).

van de Walle, D. (1998) 'Assessing the welfare impacts of public spending', *World Development*, 26, 3, 365–79.

van der Wusten, H. (2004) 'The distribution of political centrality in the European state system', *Political Geography*, 23, 6: 677–700.

van Duyn, A. (2008a) 'Investors fear another bank collapse', *Financial Times*, August 12. Available at http://www.ft.com/cms/0acb8ea4-6805-11dd-8d3b-0000779fd18c.html (accessed January 19, 2011).

—— (2008b) 'Regulatory moves raise profit fears', *Financial Times*, December 30. Available at http://www.ft.com/cms/10205616-d612-11dd-a9cc-000077b07658.html (accessed January 19, 2011).

—— (2009) 'US Democrats draft plan to curb CDS trade', *Financial Times*, January 31. Available at http://www.ft.com/cms/59bd8a98-ee70-11dd-b791-0000779fd2ac.html (accessed January 19, 2011).

van Duyn, A. and Bullock, N. (2008) 'Compression a logical progression', *Financial Times*, August 7. Available at http://www.ft.com/cms/0eeea192-6418-11dd-844 f-0000779fd18c.html (accessed January 19, 2011).

van Duyn, A. and Chung, J. (2008) 'NY watchdog delays credit derivatives plan', *Financial Times*, November 21. Available at http://www.ft.com/cms/6f652ae2-b76e-11dd-8e0 1-000079fd18c.html (accessed February 17, 2011).

van Duyn, A. and Davies, P. (2008) 'Regulators' moves insure more nerves for dealers in CDS', *Financial Times*, September 24. Available at http://www.ft.com/cms/s/0/ d3eee692-8997-11dd-8371-0000779fd18c.html#axzz1C2dLQI00 (accessed January 19, 2011).

van Duyn, A. and Gangahar, A. (2009) 'Exchanges sense bonanza in OTC overhaul', *Financial Times*, May 14. http://www.ft.com/cms/s/0/38fe6322-40b9-11de-8f18-00 144feabdc0.html#axzz1C2dLQI00 (accessed January 19, 2011).

van Tulder, R. (2010) 'Transnational corporations and poverty reduction: Strategic and regional variations', in P. Utting and J. Carlos (eds.) *Corporate social responsibilty and regulatory governance*, Geneva: Palgrave Macmillan.

van Tulder, R. with Van der Zwart, A. (2006) *International business-society management: Linking corporate responsibility and globalisation*, London: Routledge.

van Tulder, R. and Fortanier, F. (2009) 'Business and sustainable development: From passive involvement to active partnerships', in M. Kremer, P. van Lieshout, and R. Went (eds.) *Doing good or doing better: Development policies in a globalizing world*, Amsterdam: Amsterdam University Press.

van Tulder, R., van Wijk, J., and Kolk, A. (2009) 'From chain liability to chain responsibility: MNE approaches to implement safety and health codes in international supply chains', *Journal of Business Ethics*, 85: 399–412.

van Zon, H. (2001) 'Neo-patrimonialism as an impediment to economic development: The case of Ukraine', *Journal of Communist Studies and Transition Politics*, 17, 3: 71–95.

Vernon, R. (1968) 'Economic sovereignty at bay', *Foreign Affairs*, 47: 110–122.

—— (1971) *Sovereignty at bay*, New York: Basic Books.

Verspagen, B. (2005) 'Innovation and economic growth', in J. Fagerberg, D. C. Mowery, and R. R. Nelson (eds.) *The Oxford handbook of innovation*, Oxford: Oxford University Press.

Vivoda, V. (2008) *The return of the obsolescing bargain and the decline of big oil: A study of bargaining in the contemporary oil industry*, Saarbrücken: VDM Verlag Dr Müller.

Vogel, D. (2006) *The market for virtue: The potential and limits of corporate social responsibility*, Washington, DC: Brookings Institution Press.

Wade, R. H. (1990) *Governing the market: Economic theory and the role of government in East Asian industrialization*, Princeton, NJ: Princeton University Press.

—— (1998a) 'The Asian crisis', *New Left Review*, 228: 3–23.

—— (1998b) 'The Asian debt-and-development crisis of 1997–?: Causes and consequences', *World Development*, 26, 8: 1535–53.

—— (2003) 'What strategies are available for developing countries today? The World Trade Organization and the shrinking of "development space"', *Review of International Political Economy*, 10, 4: 621–44.

—— (2008) 'Globalization, growth, poverty, inequality, resentment and imperialism', in J. Ravenhill (ed.) *Global political economy*, Oxford: Oxford University Press.

—— (2010) 'After the crisis: Industrial policy and the developmental state in low income countries', *Global Policy*, 1, 2: 150–61.

Waever, O. (1996) 'The rise and fall of the inter-paradigm debate', in S. Smith, K. Booth, and M. Zalewski (eds.) *International theory: Positivism and beyond*, Cambridge, UK: Cambridge University Press.

Wallace, W. (1996) 'Truth and power, monks and technocrats: Theory and practice in international relations', *Review of International Studies*, 22: 301–21.

Walt, S. M. (2005) *Taming American power: The global response to U.S. primacy*, New York: W.W. Norton.

Waltz, K. N. (1979) *Theory of international politics*, Reading: Addison-Wesley.

Weaver, C. (2009) 'Reflections on the American school: An IPE of our own making', *Review of International Political Economy*, 16, 1: 1–5.

Webber, D. (2001) 'Two funerals and a wedding? The ups and downs of regionalism in East Asia and Asia-Pacific after the Asian crisis', *Pacific Review*, 14, 3: 339–72.

Weiss, L. (2005) 'Global governance, national strategies: How industrialized states make room to move under the WTO', *Review of International Political Economy*, 12, 5: 723–49.

Weiss, L. and Thurbon, E. (2006) 'The business of buying American: Public procurement as trade strategy in the USA', *Review of International Political Economy*, 13, 5: 701–24.

Whalen, C. (2009) 'What is to be done with credit default swaps?', comments to the American Enterprise Institute, February 23. Available at http://www.rcwhalen.com/pdf/cds_aei.pdf (accessed January 19, 2011).

Whipp, L. (2009) 'Japanese clearers seek CDS slots', *Financial Times*, April 22. Available at http://www.ft.com/cms/752c23ec-2ed6-11de-b7d3-00144feabdc0.html (accessed January 19, 2011).

White, N. J. (2004) 'The beginnings of crony capitalism: Business, politics and economic development in Malaysia, c. 1955–70', *Modern Asian Studies*, 38, 2: 389–90.

Wilkins, M. (2001) 'The history of multinational enterprise', in A. M. Rugman and T. L. Brewer (eds.) *The Oxford handbook of international business*, Oxford: Oxford University Press.

Williamson, J. (1990) 'What Washington means by policy reform', in J. Williamson (ed.) *Latin American adjustment: How much has happened?*, Washington, DC: Institute for International Economics.

—— (2002) 'Did the Washington Consensus fail?', outline of speech. Available at http://www.iie.com/publications/papers/paper.cfm?ResearchID=488 (accessed December 18, 2008).

Williamson, O. E. (1985) *The economic institutions of capitalism*, New York: Free Press.

Williamson, P. and Hu, Q. (1994) *Managing the global frontier*, London: Pitman.

Wilson, E. O. (1998) *Consilience: The unity of knowledge*, New York: Alfred Knopf.

Wintrobe, R. (1998) *The political economy of dictatorship*, Cambridge, UK: Cambridge University Press.

—— (2009) 'Wholesale market brokers association rebuffs the statement made by the Federation of European Stock Exchanges on the OTC markets', press release, WMBA, February 19. Available at http://www.wmba.org.uk/news_full.php?uid=20 (accessed January 19, 2011).

Wogart, J. P. (2006) 'Multiple interfaces of big pharma and the chances of global health governance in the face of HIV/AIDS', German Institute of Global Areas (GIGA) Working Paper Series 24, Hamburg: German Institute of Global and Area Studies.

Wogart, J. P., Calcagnotto, G., Hein, W., and von Soest, C. (2008) 'AIDS, access to medicines, and the different roles of the Brazilian and South African governments', Global Health Governance, German Institute of Global Areas (GIGA) Working Paper Series 86, Hamburg: German Institute of Global and Area Studies.

Wolf, M. (2009) 'Why Britain has to curb finance', *Financial Times*, May 22. Available at http://www.ft.com/cms/24bfcb30-4636-11de-803f-00144feabdc0.html (accessed January 19, 2011).

Woll, C. (2005) 'Learning to act on world trade: Preference formation of large firms in the United States and the European Union', MPIfG Discussion Paper 05/1, Cologne: Max Planck Institute for the Study of Societies.

—— (2008) *Firm interests: How governments shape business lobbying on global trade*, Ithaca, NY: Cornell University Press.

Wood, D. (2005) *Governing global banking: The Basel Committee and the politics of financial globalisation*, Aldershot: Ashgate.

Wood, E. M. (2002) 'Global capital, national states', in M. Rupert and H. Smith (eds.) *Historical materialism and globalization*, London: Routledge.

Woodruff, D. (1999) *Money unmade: Barter and the fate of Russian capitalism*, Ithaca, NY: Cornell University Press.

Woods, N. (2006) *The globalizers: The IMF, the World Bank, and their borrowers*, Ithaca, NY: Cornell University Press.

Woodward, R. (2010) *The Organization for Economic Co-operation and Development (OECD)*, Oxon: Routledge.

World Bank (1987) *World development report 1987*, New York: Oxford University Press.

—— (1993) 'The East Asian miracle: Economic growth and public policy', Policy Research Report, Washington, DC: World Bank.

—— (1996) *World development report 1996*, New York: Oxford University Press.

—— (2000) *Entering the 21st century: World development report 1999/2000*, New York: Oxford University Press.

—— (2005) *Economic growth in the 1990s: Learning from a decade of reform*, Washington, DC: World Bank.

—— (2006) *Global development finance 2006*, Washington, DC: World Bank.

—— (2007) *World development indicators*, New York: World Bank.

Yergin, D. (1991) *The prize: The epic quest for oil, money and power*, London: Simon & Schuster.

Yong Hyo, J. (2009) 'Liberalization of the Korea Investment Bank and systems crisis'. *E-Daily*, November 18. Available at http://www.edaily.co.kr/news/NewsRead.edy?SCD=DA21&newsid=01620326589887032&DCD=A00104&OutLnkChk=Y (accessed January 25, 2011).

Yoshihara, K. (1988) *The rise of ersatz capitalism in South-East Asia*, New York: Oxford University Press.

Young, C. and Turner, T. (1985) *The rise and decline of the Zairian state*, Madison: University of Wisconsin Press.

Zabludovsky, Z. (1989) 'The reception and utility of Max Weber's concept of patrimonialism in Latin America', *International Sociology*, 4, 1: 51–66.

Zürn, M. (2002) 'From interdependence to globalization', in W. Carlsnaes, T. Risse, and B. A. Simmons (eds.) *Handbook of international relations*, London: Sage.

INDEX